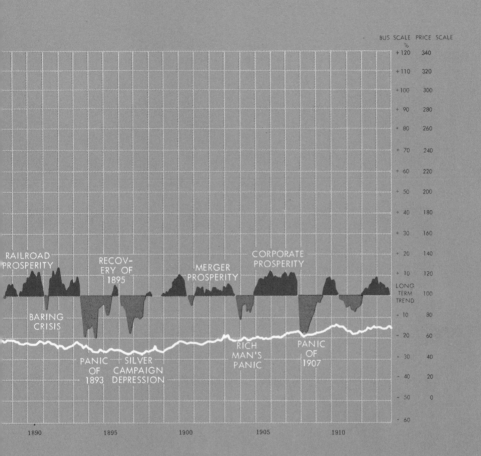

RAILROAD PROSPERITY

RECOV- ERY OF 1895

MERGER PROSPERITY

CORPORATE PROSPERITY

BARING CRISIS

PANIC OF 1893

SILVER CAMPAIGN DEPRESSION

RICH MAN'S PANIC

PANIC OF 1907

1890   1895   1900   1905   1910

This chart from 1860 through 1913 shows fluctuations above and below the long-term trend for wholesale commodity prices and industrial production.   The solid line represents the changes in wholesale commodity prices with 1926 having been selected as the base year of 100. The solid portion of the chart indicates the index of industrial production with percentage changes from the trend reduced to a per capita basis.

Source: The Cleveland Trust Company, Cleveland, Ohio.

 RICHARD D. IRWIN, INC. Homewood, Illinois 60430

Irwin-Dorsey Limited
Georgetown, Ontario
L7G 4B3

An introduction to the
**American business
enterprise**

Jerry B. Poe
College of Business Administration
Arizona State University

☆☆☆☆☆☆☆☆☆☆☆☆☆☆☆☆☆☆☆☆☆☆☆☆☆☆☆☆☆☆☆☆☆☆☆☆
☆☆☆☆☆☆☆☆☆☆☆☆☆☆☆☆☆☆☆☆☆☆☆☆☆☆☆☆☆☆☆☆☆☆☆☆

An introduction to the
American business
enterprise

Third Edition   1976

Third Edition

First Printing, February 1976
Second Printing, January 1977
Third Printing, June 1977

ISBN 0-256-01822-7
Library of Congress Catalog Card No. 75–28944

Printed in the United States of America

Preface

This third edition of *An Introduction to the American Business Enterprise* presents a balanced approach to the important role of business in our society. Changes occurring in business today are reflected in this edition, including the increasing influence on business of government, business's social responsibilities, equal opportunities for women and minorities, consumer interests, international business, the energy and pollution crises, and career opportunities.

Each chapter opens with an introductory statement of the general nature of the material covered, along with questions to direct your reading. A system of major and minor subheadings provides a guide for outlining each chapter. An end-of-chapter summary reviews the major topics discussed.

The end-of-chapter Terms for Review list some of the key concepts and terminology. Because of the importance in an introductory course of learning the language of business, an extensive glossary containing approximately 600 words and terms used in the book is included.

The end-of-chapter questions draw on an understanding of specific concepts discussed in the text or require outside research or original thinking based on background information from the chapter.

The Business Briefs at the end of each chapter provide a basis for understanding the dynamic nature of today's business world. Each business brief has been taken from public news reports of current interest. However, the basic issues in the business briefs reflect future problem areas as well as matters of topical interest.

The Cases contain discussion material which will help develop your capabilities of problem identification, analysis of alternatives, and recommendations for action. The cases also present an opportunity for specific application of your understanding of the concepts raised in the chapters. Questions at the end of each business brief and case provide a starting point for your analysis. In analyzing a case the following approach is recommended:

1. Identify and state the issues or problems in the case. Indicate the most important or central problem facing management.
2. List the alternative solutions to the problems.
3. State your recommended course of action.
4. Indicate the reasons for your decision. Why is your recommendation better than other alternatives? What will be the probable consequences of accepting your recommendation?

My sincere thanks go to all the faculty members and students across the country who made constructive suggestions for this third edition. Rachel Anderson of the University of Northern Colorado and Alexander Langfelder of Middlesex County College provided helpful reviews of the entire manuscript. Lohnie J. Boggs and Albert A. Evans made useful suggestions for the text and collaborated with James A. Carson on the *Review Guide and Workbook* to accompany this book. Wilber C. Bothwell of Drury College made available his labor arbitration files for case materials and his writing on the motivations of workers in joining labor unions. Thomas R. Lloyd wrote three cases in the marketing and business ethics areas. "Employment Outlook" material throughout the text was taken from the *Occupational Outlook Handbook* published by the U.S. Department of Labor.

I also appreciate the cooperation of the many business people who provided case materials, examples, and pictures including Joanne Ralston & Associates, Inc. of Phoenix, public relations counselors, for making available a number of the pictures for this edition.

Every attempt has been made to avoid errors; any of which remain are my responsibility.

Special thanks go to my wife, Carol, for her editorial assistance and encouragement in this and past editions.

January 1976   JERRY B. POE

Contents

5   Management   119

The nature of management. A systems approach to management of the business enterprise. Traditional functions of management. Planning requisite for successful operations: *Objectives. Policies. Procedures. Good planning is essential.* Organizing the business enterprise: *Departmentalization. Staffing and management succession. Authority-responsibility relationships. Span of control. Line and staff relationships.*

6   Control   147

The process of control. The elements of a control system: *Establishing standards. Measuring performance. Analysis and correction of deviations.* Requirements for effective control: *Controls should be diagnostic. Controls should be therapeutic. Controls should be accurate and timely. Controls should be understandable. Controls should be economical.* The budget—a key management device: *The operations budget. Simplified example of an operations budget. Cash budgets. Example of a cash budget. Capital budgets.* Cost accounting for control.

Appendix—Break-even analysis, 161

section three
Human elements of administration

7   Human relations and direction   177

The individual and the business enterprise: *Individual needs versus enterprise goals. Motivation of the individual.* Direction—dealing with people at work: *Skills required of the manager. Different types of leadership. The importance of good communication.* Organizational aspects of human relations: *The formal organization. The informal organization.* The importance of status: *Kinds of status. Prestige and esteem. Status symbols.* Developing a healthy work climate.

8 Personnel management 207

The personnel management function. Responsibilities of the personnel department: *Hiring and placement of employees. Employee induction. Employee training. Job analysis. Performance rating. Promotion. Employee transfer. Downgrading and layoffs. Discipline of employees. Safety and health.* Relationship between personnel management and labor relations. The personnel department: *Personnel manager. Employee services. Housekeeping duties. Advisory role.*

9 Labor relations 237

Legislation affecting labor relations: *The Wagner Act. The Taft-Hartley Act. The Landrum-Griffin Act.* Growth in union membership. Why workers join unions: *Economic motives for union membership. Noneconomic motives for union membership. Union membership required for employment.* The structure and organization of the labor union: *Craft and industrial unions. Local unions. National union organization.* The union contract: *The bargaining unit. Union security. Grievance procedure and arbitration. Wages and hours. Pay or work guarantees. Holidays and vacations. Employee benefits. Discipline and discharge. Management and union rights. Seniority provisions. Strikes and lockouts. Working conditions and safety.* The grievance process and arbitration: *The grievance process. Benefits of the grievance process.*

section four
The provision of goods and services

The importance of marketing. The marketing concept of business. Translating consumer needs to wants. The consumer: *Ultimate consumers. Individual consumer behavior.* The consumer of the 1970s: *Higher consumer income. Factors contributing to higher family income. More discretionary income. Demographic changes.* Consumerism and consumer protection agencies: *Consumerism. Government protective agencies. The FTC and advertising. The Consumer Product Safety Commission. Other legislation. Private groups aiding consumers. Business aid to consumers.*

The marketing mix. Product: *Product defined. Classification of consumer products. Importance of new products. Developing the product.* Promotion: *Personal selling. Advertising. Sales promotion. Total promotion mix.* Price: *Practical pricing considerations. Consumer demand. Importance of nonprice competition. Costs. Pricing strategies. Government controls.* Place: *Channels of distribution. Functions performed in channels. Institutions of distribution—wholesalers. Institutions of distribution—retailers. Physical distribution.* Organization of the marketing department.

The location of production facilities: *The importance of factory location.* The production system: *Research and product design. Process design.* Production control and scheduling: *Orders and authorization of production. Production scheduling.* Purchasing industrial goods: *Steps in the purchasing process. Price and quality considerations. Selecting sources of supply.* Make-or-buy decision. Inventory control. Purchase of capital equipment. Other elements of the production system: *Motion and time analysis. Quality con-*

trol. Maintenance. Automation. Organization of the production department: *Manufacturing management. The factory foreman.*

Business briefs
Float the glass, 359
Metrication mayhem, 360

Cases
The Drivewell Corporation, 361
The Sunflower Dairy, 363

section five
Accounting and finance

The use of accounting information: *Management uses of accounting. Outsiders' use of accounting information.* The basic accounting statements: *The balance sheet. The income statement. Statement of changes in financial position.* The financial analysis of accounting statements: *Measures of liquidity. Measures of profitability. Measures of solvency.*

Business brief
Fight or switch? 384

Cases
The Chocolate Heart Candy Store, Inc., 386
Bradley Cafeterias, Inc., 388

Our system of financial institutions. Role of the U.S. Treasury. The Federal Reserve System: *Functions of the Federal Reserve System.* Specific financial institutions: *Commercial banks. Savings and loan associations. Life insurance companies. Mutual savings banks.* Other financial institutions: *Finance companies. Credit unions. Personal trust departments. Pension funds. Fire and casualty insurance companies. Investment companies.* Functions of the investment banker: *Primary and secondary securities markets. Underwriting. Best-efforts offering. Private placements. Brokerage function.*

Appendix—The stock market and investing in securities, 414

Business briefs
Supermarket savings and loans, 424
More conservative lending? 424
How much to reveal? 425

Case
Family financial planning, 426

15 **Financial management** 431

The finance function. Responsibilities of the finance department: *Size of
the business enterprise. Specific asset management. Financing of assets.
The dilemma of liquidity versus profitability.* Financial responsibilities of
top management: *Planning for profits. Determination of dividend policy.
Determining capital structure. Consolidation and merger proposals.* Organization of the finance department.

Business briefs
The burden of debt, 448
Plow them back, 449
Public financing—private use, 450

Cases
Pine Tree Wood Products Company, 451
Zero Duplicator Corporation, 454

section six
Business in a changing world

16 **Computers** 459

Uses of computers in business: *Record keeping. Information retrieval. Computer systems. Complex computation and business simulation.* Components
of the computer: *Input of data. Memory unit. Control and arithmetic/logic
units. Output unit.* Programming. Communicating with computers. Considerations when installing a computer: *Equipment choice. Equipment
leasing or time sharing. Employee attitudes.*

Business brief
Massed minicomputers, 477

Cases
Middletown National Bank, 478
A computer decision reviewed, 481

17 **International business** 487

The importance of international trade to the United States: *Reasons for
the export of goods. Reasons for the import of goods.* Direct investment
abroad: *Multinational business corporations.* International monetary balances: *Balance of trade. Balance of payments. National currencies in international business. The role of gold.* Tariffs and other trade barriers: *Tariffs.
Quotas. Embargoes. Aid to domestic enterprises. Customs administration
and technical regulations. Private barriers to trade.* International trade
cooperation: *The General Agreement on Tariffs and Trade (GATT). The
Trade Expansion Act of 1962 (TEA). Foreign trade zones. Federal and
international financing agencies.* Differences between management in Amer-

ica and abroad: *Government relations. Financing international commercial transactions. Language and cultural barriers. Relations with the home office. Importance of good management.* Training for overseas assignment. Building the work team abroad: *Organization for foreign operations.*

18 Pollution and energy 519

Definition of pollution. Increasing public awareness of pollution. Systems approach to flow of matter. Types of pollution: *Air pollution. Water pollution. Solid waste pollution. Noise pollution. Damages from pollution and costs of its control.* Actions to control pollution: *Government actions. Actions by business. Problems for business. Who will pay for pollution control?* The energy crisis. Causes of our energy problems: *Increased use of energy. Energy costs increase.* Approaches to the energy situation: *Better technology needed. Conservation—slower growth of energy use. Development of economical energy sources. Realizing both energy and environmental goals.* What can be done? *What government can do. What business can do. What consumers can do.*

section one

The economic,
political, and
social environment
of business

*Today jet air
transportation links
economic centers.*

1

The economic basis of business

As we move into our third century as a nation the study of business provides students many insights into the challenges facing society. Over the years the provision of goods and services has been the main focus of business activity. However, the production and distribution of those goods and services have changed dramatically. The issues facing us in business today are more complex. New products and problems, unheard of only a few years ago, are becoming increasingly important.

Each of you is affected by business. Many of you are already working for business enterprises or are preparing for careers in business. The majority of Americans spend their adult lives as part of the business system producing goods and services. All of us are consumers of the products of business enterprises. We all make vital decisions as to how our incomes will be spent. How well our total economic system operates influences your individual standard of living.

This chapter focuses on the economic environment within which business functions. The following issues are discussed:

What is the nature of economic activity?

How are societies organized to answer the three basic economic questions?

What are the major characteristics of the private enterprise system?

How do business enterprises create utility for consumers?

Why is the corporation such an important legal form of business organization?

3

THE NATURE OF ECONOMIC ACTIVITY

What is the most recent purchase you made? Was it for breakfast this morning or to buy gasoline if you drove to school or for a Coke between classes? Have you ever bought a stereo set or a camera or a radio? Have you ever been faced with the decision of whether to spend or save money that you earned or were given? Even though you may have been unaware of it, in all these actions you were involved in economic activity.

Economics defined

The word "economics" has its derivation in Latin and Greek. Originally economics referred to the management of a family household and was gradually extended to include not only the management of households but the management of businesses, communities, and governments. Therefore, *economics* may be defined as the study of how we manage the human and material resources available to society. There are several aspects of the management of business enterprises which are discussed in later chapters. However, the distinguishing feature of management is that it involves decision making. Business managers are required to make choices from among alternative courses of action.

The economic problem of scarcity

Economics may also be defined as the study of how scarce resources are allocated in a society of unlimited wants. Every society has an economic system which provides food, clothing, shelter, and other material goods and services for the basic and acquired needs of its people. Because these goods and services are available in limited quantities, with many people wanting them, they have value. Scarcity is a basic fact which underlies all economic activity. If there were a complete abundance of goods and services then society would not have to be concerned with the issue of allocating scarce resources.

There are limits imposed upon us by nature and economic circumstances. There is only so much land we can till. Natural resources such as oil and minerals are definitely limited. At any particular time we have only so many factories equipped with machinery. There are only so many workers with the necessary knowledge and skills to produce goods and services which we consume. Our knowledge about how to produce more goods, although constantly expanding, is finite. In short, we live in a world where material goods are limited.

Although the resources of our world are limited, our wants are not. Indeed, one of the important assumptions of economics is that total human wants can never be fully satisfied. No matter how much we have, we seem to want more. As people's incomes increase so does their desire for more and better goods and services. How many times have you said, "If I could just have this particular item I would be completely satisfied." But when you obtained the good, perhaps an automobile, did it satisfy your material wants? It did not, if you are a typical person. When some material wants are satisfied others take their place. This means that the economic system can never produce enough to satisfy everyone completely. Thus arises the need for a system of efficient allocation of the scarce goods of society among peoples who have unlimited wants.

The economic resources

Scarce economic resources consist of all the natural, man-made, and human factors that go into the production of goods and services. These resources can be classified broadly as property resources and human resources.

Property resources consist of land and capital. *Land* refers to all natural resources which are used in the production process including timber, oil and mineral deposits, and water, as well as land itself. *Capital* refers to all machinery, tools, equipment, and buildings required to produce goods and distribute them to consumers. The use of capital goods enables workers to produce more with the same amount of physical effort. Consider the relative productivity of a service station attendant hand-polishing automobile finishes all day compared with another worker doing the same job with an electric buffing machine. The addition of a piece of capital equipment greatly improves the worker's productivity.

Human resources consist of labor and entrepreneurial ability. *Labor* refers to all physical and mental talents that individuals expend in producing goods and services with the exception of entrepreneurial talent, which is classified separately. Labor includes the manual labor of the trash hauler and the knowledge and skill of the brain surgeon. *Entrepreneur* was originally a French word which means enterpriser. The entrepreneur provides the managerial ability to bring together land, capital, and labor to produce goods and services. The entrepreneur assumes the risks associated with the organization and operation of a business enterprise and in return hopes to make a profit.

In traditional economic theory the compensation or return for labor is called *wages.* The return for the use of land is *rent;* and the return for capital resources is *interest.* The return to the entrepreneur is the profit from business operations, although if the business enterprise is not well managed the profits may turn into losses.

One measure of the returns to the various factors of production is national income as determined by the U.S. Department of Commerce. *National income* is defined as the total earnings of labor and property

TABLE 1–1
Components of U.S. national income, 1964 and 1974

	Billions of dollars		Percent change
	1964	1974	
National Income			
Compensation of employees............	$366	$856	+134%
Rental income.........................	18	27	50
Interest...............................	16	62	288
Proprietors' income....................	52	93	79
Corporate profits......................	38	85	124
Total	$490	$1,123	129

Source: U.S. Department of Commerce, *Business Statistics, 1973,* and *Survey of Current Business,* March 1975.

which result from the production of goods and services in our economy. National income is the sum of compensation of employees, rental income, interest, proprietors' income, and corporate profits. The components of national income for 1964 and 1974 are compared in Table 1–1 along with the percentages of change over this ten-year period.

Technology

Another important part of our economic society is technology. *Technology* is the accumulated fund of knowledge which promotes the efficient organization for the production of goods and services. Economic efficiency depends in large part on the technical state of knowledge of production and distribution processes. The state of technology in a particular business area is the practical application of science which has been accumulated from previous generations to the present.

Employment outlook

Economists

Economics is concerned with how to utilize scarce resources to provide goods and services for society. Economists study the problems that arise in the use of such resources as land, raw materials, and manpower.

Economists who work for business firms provide management with information to make decisions on marketing and pricing of company products; the effect of government policies on business or international trade; or the advisability of adding new lines of merchandise, opening new branch operations, or otherwise expanding the company's business.

Business enterprises will continue to provide the largest number of employment opportunities for economists because of increased reliance on scientific methods of analyzing business trends, forecasting sales, and planning purchases and production operations. Economists will also find employment opportunities in colleges and universities, and in state, local, and federal government agencies.

The number of persons who will graduate with degrees in economics through the mid-1980s is likely to exceed available positions that will arise from the expected moderate growth of the occupation and the need to replace economists who will retire or die during this period. As a result well-trained economists having a doctorate or master's degree are expected to face keen competition for choice academic positions. Persons who have bachelor's degrees in economics may find some employment in business or government as trainees or management interns, but competition may be keen.

TYPES OF ECONOMIC SYSTEMS

Whenever a society faces choices between alternative uses of scarce resources an economic system must be organized. All economic systems must provide means of answering three basic questions:

1. What goods will be produced from the scarce resources that are available?
2. How will these goods be produced?
3. How will these goods be distributed; that is, who will consume the goods?

How these questions are answered depends upon the nature of the economic system of the society being studied. There are two theoretical ways by which economic systems in industrialized countries may be organized—capitalism and socialism. Under *capitalism* the means of production and distribution of goods are privately owned and controlled. Under the economic system of *socialism* the means of production and distribution are owned and controlled by the government.

In practice the economic systems functioning in the world today have elements of both private and governmental ownership and control. However, there is quite a difference among the economic systems of major industrial nations ranging from the United States at one end of the spectrum to the Soviet Union at the other end. In between are the economies of countries such as Great Britain.

In describing the economic systems existing today it is also important to consider the political environment within which the economic activity takes place. Political systems may be organized on a democratic or totalitarian basis. Essential to the functioning of a *democracy* is the choice of governmental leaders by the people through free elections with freedom of speech, the press, and assembly. A *totalitarian* governmental system is one in which one party or group has absolute control. The people are not free to change their leadership through elections since candidates for office are chosen by the one party that is in power. Freedom of speech, the press, and assembly are restricted.

The following examples illustrate some of the basic differences in the organization of existing political-economic systems.

Great Britain

In Great Britain the political-economic system might be characterized as democratic socialism. Although there is still much private business ownership, basic industries, including gas, electric power, communications, transportation, steel, mining, and central banking, are owned and operated by the government. There is some degree of central planning. In the nationalized industries private profit is not a goal or a measure of the efficiency by which the economy's needs are met.

In a democratic-socialist country the people have free elections to choose political leaders who will legislate and govern their country. Strong opposition parties exist which compete for the votes and confidence of the people.

The Soviet Union

In the Union of Soviet Socialist Republics the political-economic system might be characterized as totalitarian socialism. The means of production and distribution are owned and controlled by the state. The concept of private profit is lacking in economic planning and motivation. There is a high degree of central planning for the economy. Generally the economic objectives are set by state planning agencies. They emphasize the production of industrial and military goods rather than consumer goods.

In the Soviet Union there is no freedom to organize opposing political parties. Dissent from the established order is discouraged both in politics and in economics.

CAPITALISM AND THE PRIVATE ENTERPRISE SYSTEM

In the United States the political-economic system might be characterized as democratic capitalism. In general the means of production and distribution are owned and controlled privately. Private profit is an incentive to business to supply the goods and services desired by individual, industrial, and governmental customers.

In our political system individuals are free to organize or join political parties. Differences of view are often very much in the open.

The form that capitalism has taken in the United States is the *private enterprise system*. It is sometimes called the free enterprise system, the market economy, or the profit system. Our economic system has developed in a pragmatic fashion. Americans have been willing to experiment to solve economic problems. The result has been an economic system which, although predominantly capitalistic, has a positive role for government. Because of this willingness to use various means to achieve economic ends, we have a mixed economic system. The emphasis is on private ownership and the profit motive, but government also has a role in many aspects of the economy. There are five important characteristics of American capitalism:

1. Private property.
2. The profit motive.
3. The market system and competition.
4. The nature of the relationship between business and government.
5. Freedom of choice by consumers.

Private property

Private property is a basic element in a capitalistic society. Without it there could be no private ownership and use of capital. Private property means individuals can own things of value and control their use. Especially important is the freedom of individuals to acquire, utilize, and dispose of the factors of production. An extension of this right is the legal contract which specifies the conditions under which anything that is owned may be used by others.

Private property serves two important functions in capitalism. First, it places in the hands of individuals power over the use of productive resources. Economic activity cannot occur unless someone makes decisions about which goods are to be produced and when and how they are to be produced. The more complex the method of production the more crucial is the decision-making process. The owners of resources may delegate part of their powers to others, but for there to be capitalism the owners must have the final say as to how resources are used. Second, private property serves as an incentive for the accumulation of wealth. This incentive is necessary if the stock of capital in the economy is to grow. The right of property owners to benefit from the use of their property in the productive process encourages them to save and invest in capital goods.

In the United States the capital owned by individuals is used by them to make a profit through investing in the production process. In the Soviet Union individuals are permitted to own property for their own use but with few exceptions are not permitted to own property for the production or distribution of goods and services. One exception in the U.S.S.R. is the small truck farming plots where the individual family has about one-half acre of its own to cultivate, with the produce being sold in markets operated by the collective farm.

The profit motive

The profit motive is another important characteristic of capitalism. *Profit* is defined as the money difference between what it costs to produce and sell a product and the revenue from its sale. The term *profit motive* refers to the desire to engage in economic activity in order to earn profit.

In every economic system someone must decide how to combine the scarce resources of capital and labor to produce goods. In the American economy private enterprise management determines the most efficient balance between the factors of production, depending on their availability, quality, and price. The profit motive acts as the central controlling mechanism. Business managers are motivated by profits to expand the output of goods for which consumer demand is great and to cut back the production of less sought-after goods. Without the lure of profit the owners of business enterprises would not be willing to bear the risks inherent in the production process. To the extent that business owners activate the entire economic system and that their decisions are based on profit calculations, the profit motive is the key institution of the capitalistic economy.

In the U.S.S.R., except for the concept of planned profit used by government officials in setting industry goals, profit does not play an important role in the production process. Government planners can choose to subsidize industries in which the sales of goods do not cover the cost of labor and materials if it is to the state's advantage to do so. For example, in international trade it may be politically desirable to sell goods below cost. In a totalitarian planned economy the whole concept of "costs" is different from that in a free market economy. In the planned economy the government arbitrarily allocates the various kinds of costs to meet its objectives, rather than allowing the costs of labor and materials to be determined in the marketplace.

The market system and competition

In the private enterprise system the economy is organized as a system of markets in which buyers and sellers exchange money for goods and services. The market price which results from these exchanges reflects the behavior of the buyers and sellers. The market functions to match the supply and demand for each type of product. As a consumer you strongly influence what will be produced by exerting economic power in purchasing a product or passing it over for a competing product.

Producers attempt to influence you by introducing new products, improving existing products, and using various types of promotional activities.

An essential characteristic of the marketplace in the American economy is that it is not formally regulated as to type, quantity, and price of goods that are produced and sold. It is our national policy to encourage competition by business enterprises for the consumers' dollars. There are many ways to determine prices, but free and competitive market pricing is the one most consistent with the private enterprise system. It is this open market which is responsible for the creation and preservation of fair prices and economic efficiency. The degree to which the market system is permitted to function without excessive controls is a measure of the extent of democratic capitalism in the economy.

In socialistic economies there is an absence of competition and the free marketplace. In totalitarian socialism what will be produced and in what quantity is based on production quotas set by government planning bureaus. Prices are set to control consumption of different types of products based on "costs" that have been set by government.

The relationship between business and government

Capitalism, particularly democratic capitalism, has always stressed the importance of individual freedom in economic affairs. In the 18th and 19th centuries the economic doctrine of laissez faire was associated with capitalism. Laissez faire is a French term meaning "leave us alone." This was the cry of businessmen in those days against the regulation by the state of their private economic activities. In its most extreme form laissez faire capitalism limited the government's participation in economic activity merely to the provision of such vital public services as police and fire protection.

Today it is generally accepted that the role of government in our complex industrial society is different from what it was in the days of the laissez faire capitalists. As a result of the depression of the 1930s, the American people expect our government to manage taxation, government spending, and the money supply so as to encourage the full employment of labor and other resources in the economy. A number of governmental agencies, such as the Federal Trade Commission, the Securities and Exchange Commission, and the Food and Drug Administration, show that we have recognized the need to be protected from harmful or deceptive business practices.

Despite the increased role which government has assumed in economic affairs in the United States over the past 40 years, our economic system remains predominantly capitalistic. We still depend upon individual consumers and business enterprises to make the vast proportion of economic decisions. About 80 percent of all the goods and services produced in the economy are purchased by individuals and private business enterprises with the remainder being purchased by various levels of government.

Freedom of choice by consumers

One of the strengths of our form of democratic capitalism is the fact that as consumers we have much freedom to choose what goods and services we will buy and have many products to choose from. The freedom in the American economic system tends to encourage innovation and change, both for new products and improved methods of producing and distributing them. Generally goods are distributed among consumers on the basis of their ability and willingness to pay the going market price. Since we cannot consume all the goods and services we want, the existing stock of goods is allocated on the basis of the purchasing power of the many consumers.

In totalitarian economies one of the major criticisms by the people is the lack of quantity and quality of consumer goods since government planners have generally emphasized production of industrial and military goods at the expense of consumer goods. Although in these countries people are relatively free to spend their incomes, the lack of consumer goods or their poor quality limits that freedom.

By American standards the marketing system of the Soviet Union is inefficient. Frequently people have to stand in one line to determine whether a product is available, then move to another line to pay for merchandise, and finally stand in a third line to receive their goods. In the Soviet Union more attention is beginning to be given to consumers, but the emphasis continues to be on industrial products.

CLASSIFICATION OF BUSINESS ENTERPRISES

From your point of view as a consumer, the end result of business activity is the goods you consume. *Goods* are anything useful in satisfying human wants. Goods may be either tangible, such as automobiles and stereo sets; or they may be intangible, such as legal advice or school teaching. Intangible goods are usually called *services*. Goods also may be classified as consumer or producer goods. *Consumer goods* satisfy individual needs directly and include nondurable items such as food and clothing and durable items such as automobiles, furniture, and appliances. *Producer goods* are the tools, machines, and equipment used to make consumer goods, and thus they satisfy individual needs indirectly.

Utilities possessed by goods

Utility is the power to satisfy human wants. For something to be a tangible good it must have four different types of utility:

1. *Form utility.* Goods must possess the proper physical characteristics. A motorist wants an automobile, not steel, rubber, glass, and paint.
2. *Place utility.* Goods must be where the consumer has access to them. The new automobile in Detroit is of no use to the prospective purchaser until it has been transported to the local dealer.
3. *Time utility.* Goods must be available when they are wanted. When you purchase a new car, you want delivery as soon as possible.
4. *Possession utility.* Goods must be owned or controlled by the people who consume them. Through credit arrangements you are able to possess an automobile even though you do not have enough money to pay for it immediately.

Types of business enterprises

A *business enterprise* is a privately owned and operated organization that brings together the factors of production to provide goods or services which are sold with the expectation of earning a profit. Business enterprises may be classified according to the four types of activities performed to provide goods with utility.

1. *Processing enterprises* transform the natural resources that come from the mines, forests, farms, and oceans into the raw materials used to manufacture goods.
2. *Manufacturing enterprises* fabricate consumer and producer goods out of raw materials.

3. *Marketing enterprises* distribute the finished goods to ultimate consumers.
4. *Facilitating enterprises* perform necessary auxiliary functions in such fields as finance, insurance, transportation, construction, and services.

Those business enterprises which engage in the same type of economic activity constitute an *industry*. For example, the manufacturers of passenger cars make up the automobile industry. However, this is a somewhat vague concept because many business enterprises produce more than one type of good or service. They really are a part of the much broader industry sector called manufacturing. Figure 1–1 indicates the broad industrial sectors which make up the economy and shows the percentage of national income which each sector supplied in 1974.

Figure 1–1 reveals the key role of manufacturing enterprises in our economy. This sector of business not only accounts for more than one

FIGURE 1–1
Percentage of 1974 national income generated by different industries

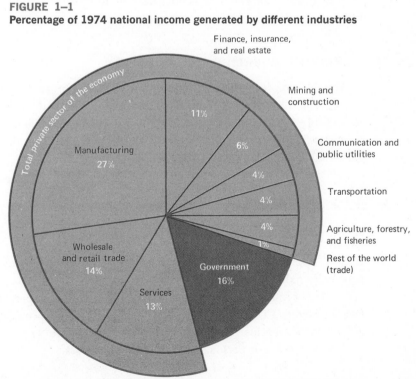

Source: U.S. Department of Commerce, *Survey of Current Business*, March 1975.

fourth of national income, but also greatly influences economic activity in such fields as transportation, trade, and finance.

Franchising. The *franchise* is an agreement by a manufacturer or operating company to give another enterprise or individual exclusive rights to the use of a product and trade name. In exchange the distributor agrees to purchase and promote the manufacturer's products. This type of business has expanded rapidly in recent years. Well-known franchises include Coca-Cola bottlers, Kentucky Fried Chicken, H & R Block income tax service, Holiday Inns, and McDonald's drive-ins.

The U.S. Department of Commerce estimates that franchising operations accounted for 30 percent of total retail sales in 1974.[1] The major part of these sales were by auto and truck dealers and gasoline stations although convenience and fast foods enterprises accounted for $13 billion in sales.

Benefits to franchisees include company advertising, standardized operating methods, centralized purchasing, location analysis, loan assistance, and management training. Problems which some franchisees may face are a lack of funds to invest in the business, difficulty in borrowing, and lack of business experience.

LEGAL FORMS OF BUSINESS ORGANIZATION

The three most important legal forms of business organization in the United States are the proprietorship, the partnership, and the corporation. Table 1–2 shows a summary of the more than 12 million business enterprises in the United States according to their legal form of organization and the major type of economic activity performed.

The proprietorship

The proprietorship is the most simple legal form of business organization. The proprietor is the sole owner of the business enterprise and is able to exercise complete control over its operation. The owner is personally liable for the debts and other legal obligations of the enterprise. The profits of the proprietorship are considered part of the owner's income. Therefore, there is no separate federal income tax on the business's profits. However, the owner does have to report the enterprise's profits as personal income for tax purposes.

---

[1] *Franchising in the Economy, 1972–74,* U.S. Department of Commerce.

TABLE 1–2
Number of enterprises operating in principal industries in the United States, period ending June 30, 1972

Industry	*Proprietor-ships*	*Active partner-ships*	*Active corpo-rations*
		Number of firms (in thousands)	
Agriculture, forestry, and fisheries.............................	3,126	121	40
Mining..........................	59	13	13
Construction...........................	736	53	143
Manufacturing..........................	186	27	201
Transportation, communication, and public utilities..................	300	15	71
Trade...............................	2,115	195	539
Wholesale............................	319	29	168
Retail..............................	1,765	166	371
Finance, insurance, and real estate.............................	588	353	418
Service................................	2,593	172	288
All industries......................	9,745	959	1,733

Note: Because of multiple industry listings, totals are less than the sum of individual items.
Source: Department of the Treasury, Internal Revenue Service, *Statistics of Income 1971, Business Income Tax Returns,* April 1975.

The proprietorship is by far the most common legal form of business in the United States as Table 1–2 indicates. Proprietorships are most numerous in farming and fishing and the retail trades. Generally they are small enterprises. Frequently proprietorships are not very profitable because of their size, problems of obtaining efficient management, and intensive competition. However, this form of legal organization continues to be popular because of the number of persons who want to have their own business and because of the ease in starting a proprietorship.

The partnership

A partnership is formed when two or more persons agree to start a business enterprise as co-owners. Each partner customarily contributes some economic assets to the business enterprise in the form of money, property, skill, or labor. Partners share in the profits or losses of the business according to an agreed upon ratio. However, all partners are liable for legal obligations, such as losses or court judgments against the partnership, to the full extent of their personal fortunes. This tends to limit the size of partnerships. Another limiting factor is that customarily when one of the partners dies a new partnership must be formed.

The control and management of the partnership is vested in the hands of the partners equally. Any one of the partners has the power to make decisions. Therefore, a serious mistake by one partner can affect all the partners.

The partnership is relatively easy to form. Although a written partnership agreement is desirable, there need not be a written statement between the partners for them to join together in business activity. However, if a disagreement occurs and there is no written partnership agreement it may be necessary for the courts to determine if a partnership was really formed.

The profits of the partnership are considered to be part of the owners' incomes. Therefore, there is no separate federal income tax on the partnership's profits, but the partners do have to report their portion of the enterprise's profits as part of their respective personal incomes for tax purposes.

The corporation

A corporation is a legal entity, separate and distinct from the persons who are its owners. It comes into being when a charter is obtained from the state. The corporation has only those powers which are given by the state and expressed or implied in its charter. The owners exchange money or other assets for shares of stock in the corporation.

There is a legal distinction between the corporation and its stockholders. This permits the corporation to buy, own, and sell property; enter into contracts; sue and be sued; and carry out business activities as a legal entity separate from its owners. This separate entity concept also means that the income of the corporation is taxed by government. Any cash dividends which are paid to the stockholders are taxed as personal income of the individual stockholders.

The stockholders of the corporation elect a board of directors to exercise control of the corporation. Usually each share of stock is entitled to one vote. Shareholders either vote in person at stockholders' meetings or by *proxy,* which is a written authorization for someone else to cast a stockholder's votes. The board of directors solicits proxies from stockholders which are then voted to support the incumbent board of directors. If a group of stockholders becomes dissatisfied with the board of directors they may solicit proxies in an attempt to gain control of the corporation. Such proxy fights are relatively rare and may be expensive to conduct when there are thousands of stockholders.

In the corporate form of legal organization there is a separation of roles. The stockholders are the owners. The president and other executives manage the corporation, and the board of directors exercises control. The board of directors is responsible for seeing that the corporation functions in the best long-run interests of the stockholders. Specific duties of the board include the election of the officers including the chief executive officer or president. Other board responsibilities include the formulation of major policies, approval of important operating decisions, and the general exercise of control. Directors are usually elected annually by the stockholders.

Board members who are fulltime employees active in the day-to-day management of the corporation are called *inside directors*. Such directors may include the corporation's president and various vice presidents. Directors who serve only on the board and are not full-time management employees of the corporation are called *outside directors*. Outside directors normally do not have as close an understanding of the detailed operation of the corporation as insiders. However, outside directors should be able to take a more independent view of corporate activities since they do not have to work under the president.

There are considerably fewer corporations than proprietorships, as Table 1–2 indicates. However, Table 1–3 shows that the corporation has by far the greatest economic impact upon society in terms of business receipts (sales) and net profits.

There are a number of advantages to the corporation form of legal organization over the proprietorship and the partnership:

1. The liability of the owners of the corporation for the corporation's obligations is limited to the amount of their investment in the corporation. Therefore, stockholders' entire personal fortunes are not placed in possible jeopardy as with the proprietorship and the partnership.

2. Depending upon the terms of its charter, the corporation may have perpetual life. Its existence does not depend upon any particular group of owners.

3. There is relative ease of transfer of ownership of the corporation.

TABLE 1-3

Business receipts and net profits of U.S. enterprises in principal industries, period ending June 30, 1972 (in billions of dollars)

Industry	Business receipts			Net profit (less loss)		
	Sole proprietorships	Active partnerships	Active corporations	Sole proprietorships	Active partnerships	Active corporations
Agriculture, forestry, and fisheries	43.8	7.6	14	2.9	.5	.2
Mining	1.6	1.3	18	*	*	2.2
Construction	23.3	8.3	95	3.5	.9	1.9
Manufacturing	6.9	5.3	751	.7	.3	38.8
Transporation, communication, and public utilities	7.1	1.4	145	1.0	.1	7.9
Trade	120.1	35.3	564	8.0	2.2	11.4
Wholesale	23.9	11.0	255	2.0	.5	4.8
Retail	94.3	24.3	306	6.0	1.7	6.5
Finance, insurance, and real estate	9.5	17.1	105	3.0	*	16.0
Services	42.4	19.6	70	15.2	6.4	1.5
All industries	255.2	96.3	1,764	34.5	9.1	79.7

* Net loss exceeds net profit.
Note: Because of multiple industry listings, totals are less than the sum of individual items.
Source: Department of the Treasury, Internal Revenue Service, Statistics of Income 1971, Business Income Tax Returns, April 1975.

TABLE 1–4
Comparison of factors relating to corporations, partnerships, and proprietorships

Factors	*Corporations*	*Partnerships*	*Proprietorships*
Ease of formation	Most complicated. Must be chartered by state or federal government. May need city license.	Medium complexity. Partnership agreement needed. May require city or state license.	Least complicated. Individual starts business. May need city or state license.
Length of Life	Life limited only by success of operations and charter.	Limited by life of each partner and partners' agreement.	Limited by life of proprietor or proprietor's sale of the business.
Transfer of ownership	Partial or complete ownership easily changed through sale of corporation's stock.	By mutual agreement of partners.	By sale or inheritance of assets of business.
Liability of owners	Limited to amount invested in corporation's stock.	At least one partner must have unlimited liability.	Unlimited liability for personal assets.
Ease of raising funds	Relatively easy to sell stock to many parties. Borrowing based on corporation's credit capacity.	Limited to partners' resources and ability to borrow.	Limited to owner's personal resources and ability to borrow.
Activities and flexibility	Limited by corporate charter which may be amended.	Limited to partnership agreement and partners' wishes.	Unlimited except by personal wishes of proprietor.
Taxation	Income taxes on corporate profits. Stockholders taxed individually on cash dividends.	Business income taxed as part of partners' personal incomes. Inheritance taxes.	Income taxed as proprietor's personal income. Inheritance tax liability at owner's death.
Information on operations and profits	Provided to stockholders. Large, widely owned corporations make much financial information public.	Provided to partners. Generally not known to public.	Known by proprietor. Generally not known by public.
Ownership, management, and control	Generally separated.	Exercised by partners. May have separate managers.	Generally exercised by proprietor.

Stockholders can simply sell their shares of stock to someone else without directly affecting the functioning of the corporation or the other stockholders.

4. Because of the advantages of the corporate form, it is generally easier to attract the large amounts of capital necessary for many types of business operations than with other legal forms of organization.

5. Because of the relative ease of assembling large amounts of economic resources, the corporation frequently is able to obtain managerial talent and specialized skills easier than when other legal forms of organization are used.

The owners of the small corporation may not always be able to realize all the advantages listed above. For example, a bank may require the principal owners to personally endorse a loan which the bank makes to a small corporation. Such an endorsement negates the advantage of limited liability for those stockholders since if the corporation is unable to repay the loan the bank has a legal claim against the personal assets of the endorsers of the loan. However, such an arrangement is not usual with the large corporation which has numerous stockholders.

SUMMARY

Economics is the management of the human and material resources of society. Economics can also be defined as the allocation of scarce resources in a society of unlimited wants.

Economic resources consist of all the natural, man-made, and human factors that go into the production of goods and services. Property resources are land and capital. Human resources are labor and entrepreneurial ability.

The three basic economic questions which must be answered in every economic system are:

1. What goods will be produced?
2. How will these goods be produced?
3. Who will consume (or control) these goods?

Economic systems functioning today have elements of capitalism and socialism. The U.S. economic system is a modified form of capitalism called the private enterprise system. Private property, the profit motive, the market system, a particular relationship between business and government, and freedom of choice by consumers are important characteristics of the private enterprise system.

Goods, which may be either tangible or intangible, are useful in satisfying human wants. Intangible goods are called services. Goods may also be classified as consumer goods or producer goods.

In order for goods to have economic value they must have some type of utility. Utility is the power to satisfy human wants. Tangible goods have form, place, time, and possession utility.

Business enterprises may be classified by activity as enterprises for processing, manufacturing, marketing, or facilitating. Businesses may also be grouped by industry classification.

The three most commonly used legal forms of business organization are proprietorships, partnerships, and corporations. Corporations are the dominant legal form of organization in their impact on the economy.

Appendix
The systems approach to business

The systems approach to business has received much attention in recent years because of the breadth and complexity of the issues facing management. These issues include the changes brought on by exploding technological advances, vastly improved communications throughout the world, and a questioning of the traditional priorities and values of society. The relationship between business and other institutions and the impact of economic, political, and social problems has made it necessary for managers to reexamine their approach to the functioning of the business enterprise.

The emphasis of the systems approach is upon the wholeness of the functioning of the business enterprise in society with an examination of business relationships to the total environment and to its component parts. The systems approach to business is useful because it emphasizes an understanding of the comprehensive nature of business activities and the structure and process through which these activities are carried out.

A *system* is defined as a set of elements which have a relationship to each other. The elements within a system are referred to as *subsystems*. Thus each system is composed of subsystems which in combination have a meaningful unity or wholeness. The elements within the system are interrelated and interdependent and constitute the internal environment of the system. If the economy as a whole is considered as a system, then individual enterprises would be viewed as subsystems. If, for purposes of study, a single business enterprise is considered as a system, then the various departments and functions performed are the subsystems which interact with each other.

Business functions as an open system which is continually influenced by factors in the external environment. As a result of information received, which is called *feedback,* business is constantly changing both to adapt to its environment and to influence the external systems with which it comes into contact.

When business is studied in the framework of the whole economic system, the total flow of economic activity by business and consumers is examined. This is referred to as *macroeconomic* analysis. The "macro" approach to business deals with the institution of business in its relationship with other systems in society.

Figure 1–2 shows the functioning of a simple model of the economic system which is influenced by a number of other systems in its external environment. This broad macroeconomic approach to business illustrates how business functions in the economic system and how it is influenced by other systems. Throughout this book several topics are discussed which relate the whole institution of business to its external environment. These topics are covered in such chapters as those dealing with government relationships, social responsibility, labor unions, consumers, financial institutions, pollution, and energy.

Notice in Figure 1–2 how business enterprises use the inputs of labor, capital, land, and management in order to produce the outputs of goods and services which are demanded by individual and institutional consumers. This activity takes place within the internal environment of the economic system.

The economic system is affected by other institutions in society and in turn influences them. The legal system is important to business because our economic system is based upon the concept of private property rights. Business operations depend upon contractual agreements which may be enforced through the courts of law. Business is involved in the political system because of the effect of political decisions on business operations and because of business influence on the governing process.

Since people are important in the functioning of the economic system there is a system of social relationships which influences business. Business is influenced by cultural and religious institutions because of the interrelated nature of people's values and business activities.

Another way to study business is from the point of view of the functioning of the individual business enterprise. This approach is called *microeconomic* analysis. "Micro" analysis is concerned with the in-

FIGURE 1–2
The economic system in American society

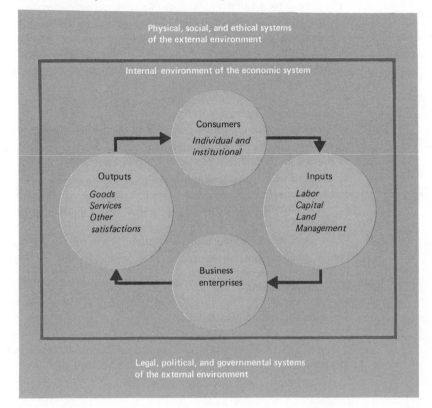

ternal functioning of the subsystems of the enterprise and with the total management of the firm as it relates to its environment. Several chapters, including those on management, control, marketing, personnel, production, and finance, are devoted essentially to the study of the functioning of the individual business enterprise.

TERMS FOR REVIEW

economics

economic resources

national income

technology

capitalism

socialism

private enterprise system

profit motive

utility

franchise

proprietorship

partnership

corporation

QUESTIONS

1. Why is scarcity a fundamental part of the economic system?
2. *a.* What changes have occurred in the components of national income from 1964 to 1974?
   b. Determine what recent changes have occurred in national income by checking the *Survey of Current Business, Economic Indicators,* or other government publications in the library.
3. *a.* What are the three basic economic questions which must be answered in every society?
   b. How are these questions answered in the United States today?
4. In what ways does the functioning of the U.S. economy differ from that of the Soviet Union? In what ways are they similar?
5. *a.* Should some governmental body have the power to control prices and wages?
   b. What would be possible positive and negative consequences of such controls?
6. What kinds of economic utility are there? Give an example of each.
7. Under what circumstances would it be most advisable to organize a business enterprise as:
   a. a proprietorship?
   b. a partnership?
   c. a corporation?
8. Using Tables 1–2 and 1–3, analyze the relative importance of proprietorships, partnerships, and corporations in the various broad industrial categories. How do you account for these relationships?

Business briefs

A new generation enters business

College graduates going into business management in the 1970s are quite different from those who entered business in the 1950s and 1960s. In the 1950s the young manager was typified as being an organization man who was willing to accept management's goals and values. In the 1960s the junior executive was more skilled at problem solving; he was pragmatic and confident of his role, without too much questioning of corporate goals. In the 1950s and 1960s junior executives had a strong commitment to the established business system.

According to *Fortune* magazine, today's young people are going into business as junior managers "not as comfortable successors to power but as rebels and reformers who will carry out important changes in both the substance and the style of managing corporations."[1]

These young persons are interested in the improvement of society and its environment and feel that business enterprises should actively pursue these goals. The current generation has been characterized as being competent and self-confident with an interest in human values, change, and individuality. They are impatient because they feel there has been an inadequate response by the business community to what they define as relevant problems and inequities in the economic system. Many are idealistic, anxious to help others, and willing to work hard for the objectives they consider worthwhile. These young executives are interested in personal projects which they consider socially important, such as advising minority owners of small businesses, doing ecological research, and organizing cleanup campaigns.

Many young managers are critical of their bosses for being overly concerned about profits. While most do not criticize the concept of profit or its necessity, many young managers do question the way in which profit is utilized.

This new breed of junior managers wants the responsibility for making important decisions and is eager for rapid advancement. Although materialism is not a stated objective, beginning pay levels between $10,000 and $15,000 are expected as a matter of fact, but the junior managers do not emphasize fringe benefits.

1. Summarize the values held by young people going into business management positions today.
2. What problems do older management personnel face with this new type of junior manager?
3. What values are important to you as a person going into business?

Directing directors

Following the 1970 bankruptcy of the Penn Central railroad, the Securities and Exchange Commission charged that some former outside directors of the corporation failed to live up to their responsibilities. The SEC charges included the complaint that these outside directors aided and abetted alleged frauds because they had special knowledge in financial matters. Penn Central officials were charged with improper

---

[1] Judson Gooding, "The Accelerated Generation Moves into Management," *Fortune* (March 1971), p. 101.

accounting and failure to disclose pertinent information to investors. The SEC claimed that directors attended meetings at which some allegedly fraudulent activities were discussed or approved.

Others have questioned the role and effectiveness of outside corporate directors. These include former Supreme Court Justice Arthur Goldberg who resigned as a director of Trans World Airlines because he did not believe he could get the information needed to meet his responsibilities as a director. Professor Myles Mace of the Harvard Business School suggests that boards of directors be made up of outsiders (rather than insiders who are members of operating management), have written agreements with management on their responsibilities, and review their chief executive officers' performance annually. Other experts have suggested that more information is needed by directors about corporate activities, and that audit boards should report directly to a directors' committee rather than to management.

More corporations are providing outside directors with written reports in advance of directors' meetings. Members of management who are not directors are being called in more frequently to report directly to the board.

More than ever directors are being sued personally for liability for corporate decisions and actions. Many corporations now provide liability insurance for directors. Occasionally directors are found guilty of improper activities and face fines or jail sentences as well as civil penalties.

1. What should be the role of the corporation's board of directors?
2. From the point of view of stockholders and the public what advantages are there to having a board composed primarily of outside directors?
3. How are outside directors at a disadvantage when making important decisions affecting the corporation?
4. What can be done to improve the functioning of corporations' boards of directors?

Courtesy Motorola Inc.

*Private enterprise
provides many of the
goods used by
government.*

*T*oday in our complex economic society, the impact of government on business is increasingly important. Indeed, over the past 200 years government has had an influence on business. Government has the basic responsibility of providing society with a system of equity, order, and protection. This is necessary if our economic institutions are to function efficiently. The Constitution specifically states that the federal government should regulate interstate and foreign commerce and provide a monetary system.

The courts system, headed by the Supreme Court, affects business by deciding whether laws passed by the legislative branch of government are constitutional. In addition, disputes between business enterprises are settled in the courts and legal contracts enforced. Besides its traditional functions of regulation and taxation, government purchases billions of dollars of goods and services from business enterprises.

You can study the evolving role of government's influence on business by examining the following questions discussed in this chapter:

What taxes does business pay to support government?

What services are provided by government?

How is business regulated by government?

In what ways does government subsidize business?

What enterprises are government-owned and -operated in the United States?

2

Business and government

TAXATION OF BUSINESS

The activities of government are paid for either with tax collections, receipts from users of government services or goods, or borrowed money. When government borrows money, interest is paid for the use of these funds. Ultimately the borrowing must be repaid through the collection of taxes or by additional borrowing.

In addition to raising revenue, taxes may be used for the regulation of business. An example of this is the taxation of narcotics under the Federal Narcotics Act which restricts dealing in narcotics to scientific and medical purposes. The taxes on these narcotics are relatively low and little revenue is produced. However, the regulations require record keeping which emphasizes the criminal nature of unauthorized traffic in drugs. Therefore, the primary purpose of the tax on narcotics is not to raise revenue but to regulate the flow of drugs.

The principal revenue-producing taxes levied by the federal government include individual and corporation income taxes, social insurance taxes, and excise taxes on specified manufacturers' and retailers' sales transactions. State and local governments' main tax sources include sales taxes, individual and corporation income taxes, property taxes, and various types of license fees. Figure 2–1 illustrates the relative importance of these various types of tax revenues to federal, state, and local governments.

Types of taxes

Income taxes. Income taxes are levied upon both personal and corporation income by the federal government and by many state and local governments. Corporate income is taxed after the deduction of business expenses. The income of business enterprises organized as proprietorships and partnerships is taxed after deduction of business expenses as part of the personal incomes of the owners of these enterprises.

The income tax is viewed by many authorities on taxation as a desirable type of tax. It is relatively easy to collect, falls upon those who have the ability to pay, and produces substantial revenue. Critics claim that high income tax rates reduce profits, which lessens the incentive of individuals and business enterprises to take risks by investing funds. However, to some extent business may be able to pass on the effect of income taxes to its customers through higher prices. Despite

FIGURE 2–1
Sources of federal and state and local government tax dollars, 1974

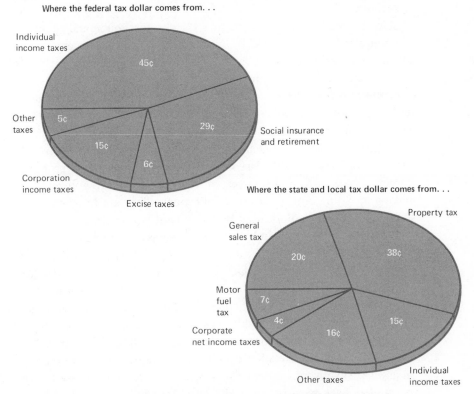

Where the federal tax dollar comes from. . .

Individual income taxes 45¢

Other taxes 5¢

Corporation income taxes 15¢

Excise taxes 6¢

Social insurance and retirement 29¢

Where the state and local tax dollar comes from. . .

General sales tax 20¢

Property tax 38¢

Motor fuel tax 7¢

Corporate net income taxes 4¢

Other taxes 16¢

Individual income taxes 15¢

Source: *The Budget of the U.S. Government Fiscal Year 1976,* and *Bureau of the Census.*

complaints about the income tax, it continues to be a very important source of governmental revenue. Approximately 55 percent of the total tax revenues collected in the United States are from the individual and corporate income taxes levied by federal, state, and local governments.

In 1975 corporate profits were taxed by the federal government at a rate of 20 percent on the first $25,000 of taxable income; 22 percent on income between $25,000 and $50,000; and 48 percent on corporate income above $50,000. In addition, many states have corporate income taxes, although their rates are considerably lower than those of the federal income tax.

Sales taxes. Sales taxes are levied on the sale of goods to consumers and sometimes on consumer services. Sales taxes provide the largest single source of tax revenue for state governments. Sales taxes may be *general* if they apply to all, or nearly all, retail sales, or they may be *selective* in applying to some specific product such as cigarettes, liquor, or gasoline.

Selective sales taxes are used in all states for liquor and gasoline. General sales taxes are used by most states. The business enterprises collect the sales taxes when retail sales are made and turn the funds over to state revenue departments.

Property taxes. Property taxes are levied on the assessed value of real estate and on tangible and intangible property. For the business enterprise this means that taxes are levied on the assessed value of its land and buildings, equipment, and inventories. Property taxes are determined on annual rates based on the appraised value of property. Property taxes are vital sources of revenue for local governments, making up 80 percent of local tax collections. They are insignificant to state governments and not used by the federal government.

Other taxes. A tax paid by business but passed on to the consumer is the excise tax. This is either a *manufacturers excise tax* or a *retailers excise tax* depending upon which type of enterprise collects the tax. Manufacturers federal excise taxes are levied on such items as tires, liquor, tobacco, motor fuel, firearms, fishing equipment, and sugar. These taxes take the form of added costs which you as a consumer pay—usually without knowing that they have been collected by the manufacturer of the goods. Retailers excise taxes have been levied in the past on jewelry, silverware, and other luxury items. Most federal excise taxes on retailers have been repealed although these taxes are still collected on motor fuels, liquor, and tobacco products. Federal excise taxes are collected on such services as air transportation and telephone service.

Employment taxes are paid by employers and employees who come under the Federal Insurance Contributions Act (FICA). These taxes provide for old-age, survivors', and disability insurance benefits and for government health insurance. Self-employed individuals are also subject to this tax. In 1975 business and employees were each taxed 5.85 percent on the first $14,100 of each employee's annual wages. These taxes pay the Social Security benefits which are received by millions of retired, disabled, and dependent Americans.

Business also pays *unemployment insurance taxes* and *workmen's compensation taxes* under a national system administered by the states. States use unemployment insurance taxes to finance payments for a stipulated number of weeks to workers who are out of work and searching for employment. Workmen's compensation insurance covers employee payments for job-related injuries. Some states have state coverage, and some states permit employers to purchase private insurance protection against accidents. Costs depend upon the employer's accident record and the type of work in which the employees are engaged.

Customs duties are taxes collected on goods imported into the United States from other countries. These serve both as a revenue measure and to protect American producers from competing lower priced imports.

A variety of other taxes are levied upon business at different levels of government including licenses, incorporating fees, and utilities taxes. The importance of these taxes to business depends upon the nature of the enterprise's operations and the particular location of the business enterprise.

PROVISION OF PUBLIC SERVICES

In return for the taxes paid by business enterprises and individuals, a wide variety of services are provided by government ranging from national defense to police and fire protection and social services.

Federal government services

The wide variety of federal programs is illustrated by the federal government's budget expenditures for 1974. Figure 2–2 shows the major categories of these expenditures.

FIGURE 2–2
Federal government spending programs, 1974

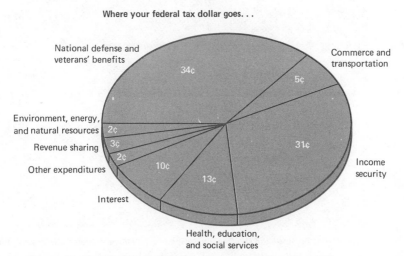

Where your federal tax dollar goes. . .

National defense and veterans' benefits — 34¢

Commerce and transportation — 5¢

Environment, energy, and natural resources — 2¢

Revenue sharing — 3¢

Other expenditures — 2¢

Interest — 10¢

Health, education, and social services — 13¢

Income security — 31¢

Source: *The Budget of the United States Governmental Fiscal Year 1976.*

National defense and veterans' benefits accounted for about 34 cents of each dollar spent. A close second in federal spending was 31 cents of each tax dollar spent on income security which includes payments to individuals for Social Security retirement, disability, and dependents' benefits. In addition to a variety of other programs, about 10 percent of the federal government spending went for interest on money borrowed to finance past governmental operations. A number of the federal government's programs were carried out in cooperation with state and local governmental units.

State and local government services

Many of the functions of government which directly affect the business enterprise and individual citizens are performed by state and local governments. Figure 2–3 shows the spending of state and local governments based on the nature of the service provided.

FIGURE 2–3
State and local government general expenditures by function

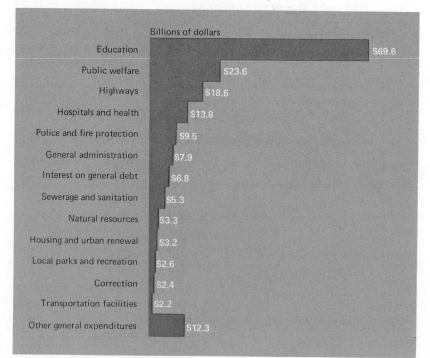

Function	Billions of dollars
Education	$69.6
Public welfare	$23.6
Highways	$18.6
Hospitals and health	$13.8
Police and fire protection	$9.5
General administration	$7.9
Interest on general debt	$6.8
Sewerage and sanitation	$5.3
Natural resources	$3.3
Housing and urban renewal	$3.2
Local parks and recreation	$2.6
Correction	$2.4
Transportation facilities	$2.2
Other general expenditures	$12.3

Source: U.S. Bureau of the Census, *Governmental Finances in 1972–73*, October 1974.

Government's impact on the economy

The relationship between tax receipts and governmental expenditures has an effect on the overall economy. When government's spending exceeds its tax receipts the effect is expansionary on the economy. This deficit spending is accomplished by government borrowing. When the economy is functioning with less than full employment of people and productive facilities, the general effect of government deficit spending is to stimulate economic activity and increase the flow of goods and services. When the economy is already operating at or near capacity the result of deficit spending is a further stimulation of the economy which contributes to inflationary price increases.

When government collects more taxes than it spends a budget surplus occurs. The general effect is to reduce the level of economic activity (an opposite effect of deficit spending).

The roles of the U.S. Treasury and the Federal Reserve System in managing the federal government debt and influencing the money supply are discussed in Chapter 14.

REGULATION OF BUSINESS

The major purpose of regulation of business by government is to promote the public welfare and to benefit the economy as a whole. At times special interest groups may take advantage of government regulation for their own gain. However, government's general approach to economic matters in this country has been to protect the public interest and promote employment, production, and purchasing power. Government influences business through legislation, judicial review, and actions by the executive branch.

Legislation affecting business

The laws passed by the Congress which affect business are wide-ranging and complex. In addition, each of the states and municipalities in which a business enterprise operates has laws regulating the conduct of business. Much of the significant national legislation and the role of several important government agencies are discussed in other chapters. In Chapter 9 the labor-management laws and the National Labor Relations Board are discussed. Legislation relating to environmental pollution is discussed in Chapter 18. Government protection of the consumer is discussed in Chapter 10. This chapter's discussion covers the impact of government's influence on business through the antitrust laws, including those on competition and monopoly, price discrimination, and resale price maintenance.

The background of antitrust legislation

The economic development of the United States during the period following the Civil War was characterized by the construction of a network of railroads which extended to the West Coast. America was industrialized with the corporation becoming the dominant form of business organization. The corporation facilitated the growth of enterprises and fostered increasing concentration in many industries. The economic fluctuations following the Civil War caused business to seek relief from cut-throat competition. This was done by combining operations, dividing markets, controlling industry practices through trusts, and by other actions which were characteristic of monopolies. A monopoly results when one producer or distributor has such control over the supply of a product that the price can be determined independently. By the 1880s, such major industries as petroleum, cottonseed oil, linseed oil, whiskey, sugar, and lead were essentially monopolies in the United States.

These monopolies functioned through a form of organization called a *trust*. A trust was created when the owners of the controlling shares of stock in competing corporations transferred control of their shares to a group of trustees. In exchange for their controlling shares, the former corporate shareholders received trust certificates and were entitled to a share in the profits of the combined corporations. The trustees voted the stock certificates in all the participating corporations thereby electing corporate directors and controlling corporation policies. The result was that several corporations were run as a single business enterprise. The laws passed dealing with these trusts came to be known as *antitrust laws*. This phrase is now broadly applied to any legislation which deals with restrictions on trade and business organization.

With the development of the trusts in the latter part of the 19th century many different groups in the community were adversely affected. Farmers, laborers, producers of raw materials, and small businesses were all forced to conform to the policies laid down by these industry giants. Farmers experienced a decline in farm prices combined with high costs of materials, credit, and freight rates. Laborers were faced with increased competition for jobs, severe working conditions, and poor living conditions in the cities. Raw materials producers were forced to sell to a single manufacturer. Owners of small companies were driven out of business in some instances when they refused to cooperate with the trusts. The powerful economic action of the trusts resulted in a political reaction from those groups which felt oppressed. As a result, in 1889 a number of states passed antitrust laws and the way was opened for national legislation in 1890.

Antitrust laws

The important antitrust legislation passed by the U.S. Congress started with the Sherman Act and includes the Clayton Act, the Federal Trade Commission Act, the Robinson-Patman Act, and the Antimerger Act of 1950.

The Sherman Act (1890). The Sherman Act passed in 1890 contained two major provisions:

> Section 1. Every contract, combination in the form of a trust or otherwise, or conspiracy, in restraint of trade or commerce among the several states, or with foreign nations, is hereby declared to be illegal. Every person who shall make any such contract or engage in any such combination or conspiracy, shall be deemed guilty of a misdemeanor. . . .
> Section 2. Every person who shall monopolize, or attempt to monopolize, or combine or conspire with any other person or persons, to monopolize any part of the trade or commerce among the several states, or with foreign nations, shall be deemed guilty of a misdemeanor. . . .

Restraint of trade and monopolization were made federal offenses with the U.S. Justice Department administering the law. United States attorneys under the Attorney General could institute both civil and criminal proceedings against those who allegedly violated the law. Criminal penalties included both fines and prison sentences. Those persons who were injured by illegal restraint of trade or monopolies were entitled to sue for triple damages.

Administration of the Sherman Act, 1890–1912. The Sherman Act was the only significant antitrust legislation for nearly a quarter century. Its enforcement was variable from one presidential administration to another.

Shortly after the turn of the century there were several spectacular prosecutions during Theodore Roosevelt's administration, including one in which the American Sugar Refining Company was found guilty of tampering with its scales to avoid duties on sugar imports. The federal government recovered more than $4 million from this action. Under Roosevelt, proceedings were begun to dissolve the American Tobacco and Standard Oil trusts. However, Roosevelt felt that not all trusts were bad and those which had developed as a result of natural business growth should not be bothered as long as they operated within the law. Regulation, not destruction, became Theodore Roosevelt's answer to the trust problem. He stated, "We do not wish to destroy corporations, but we do wish to make them subserve the public good."

In 1912 Democrat Woodrow Wilson was elected president. Wilson felt that the answer was to restore competition and, unlike Roosevelt, contended that excessive size of corporations was in itself bad. He wanted a strengthening of the antitrust laws, tariff reduction, and a reform of the national banking system.

The Clayton and Federal Trade Commission Acts (1914). In 1913, with Wilson as president, the new Congress passed laws establishing the Federal Reserve System, reducing tariffs, and instituting the federal income tax. In 1914 the problem of monopoly received detailed congressional attention. Extensive hearings preceded passage of the Clayton Act, which outlawed price discrimination, exclusive and tying contracts, intercorporate stockholdings, and interlocking directorates.

The principal provisions of the Clayton Act included:

> Section 2, which forbade sellers to discriminate in price between different purchasers of commodities unless there were differences in the grade, quality, or quantity of the commodity sold, where the lower prices made only due allowance for differences in the cost of selling or transportation and where they were offered in good faith to meet competition.
>
> Section 3, which prohibited sellers from leasing or making a sale or contract for the sale of commodities on the condition that the lessee or purchaser shall not deal in the commodity of a competitor.
>
> Section 7, which prohibited any corporation engaged in commerce from acquiring the shares of a competing corporation or from purchasing the stocks of two or more corporations that were competitors.
>
> Section 8, which prohibited interlocking boards of directors between business corporations where one of them had capital accounts of more than $1 million and where the elimination of competition between them would constitute a violation of any of the provisions of the antitrust laws.

Provisions of Sections 2, 3, and 7 were not absolute prohibitions and were forbidden only where their effect would be to substantially lessen competition or tend to create a monopoly.

In the Federal Trade Commission Act unfair methods of competition in commerce were declared unlawful. The Federal Trade Commission was set up to police the antitrust laws. This act also allowed the federal government to file suits against those possibly engaged in illegal monopoly practices without waiting for suits from private individuals or business enterprises. The general provisions of the Sherman Act were made more explicit by the Clayton Act. The Federal Trade Commission dealt with prevention as well as punishment for practices which reduced competition.

The Robinson-Patman Act (1936). With the growth of large chain stores, smaller business enterprises began to demand increased protective legislation. They charged chain stores and other mass merchandisers with obtaining price concessions which were greater than the saving in costs allowed under the Clayton Act. In 1936 the Robinson-Patman Act revised the Clayton Act to give increased protection to smaller retailers, including grocers and druggists, from large competitors. The Robinson-Patman Act outlawed:

1. Discounts on volume purchases which cannot be justified by the lower cost of selling and delivery of large quantities.
2. Payments of a broker's commission (in effect a reduction in price) when an independent broker is not employed.
3. Allowances for advertising and promotion on purchases made by volume buyers which were not available on proportionally equal terms to smaller competing buyers.
4. Discounts which varied for the same quality of merchandise in the same quantities to different purchasers.
5. Sale of goods at unreasonably low prices where the practice was for the purpose of destroying competition or eliminating a competitor.

The Miller-Tydings Act (1937). Owners of small businesses had also been active in securing protective legislation at the state level. By 1937 most of the states, following California's lead, had passed fair trade legislation. This permitted manufacturers or distributors of branded merchandise to establish the minimum retail price for which the product would be sold to the consumer. However, these laws passed by states on fair trade practices were applicable only in intrastate commerce. In interstate commerce, where manufacturers and retailers or wholesalers were in different states, the resale price maintenance contracts violated the antitrust laws. Because the majority of branded goods moved across state borders the effectiveness of state laws was limited. The Miller-Tydings Act was passed by Congress in 1937 as an amendment to the Sherman Act. It exempted resale price maintenance contracts from antitrust laws provided they were permitted by state laws. By 1941, only Missouri, Texas, Vermont, and the District of Columbia did not have state fair trade laws.

The McGuire Act (1952). The Congress passed the McGuire Act in 1952 which permitted states to include nonsigner clauses in their resale price maintenance laws. The nonsigner clause required that all retailers in a state were bound by resale price agreements as long as one retailer in the state signed such an agreement.

The Consumer Goods Pricing Act (1975). Fair trade pricing was not popular with consumers. A number of states repealed their resale price maintenance laws. In December 1975 Congress passed the Consumer Goods Pricing Act. This repealed the exemption from federal antitrust laws for the fair trade laws still in effect in 21 states. The Miller-Tydings and McGuire Acts were nullified. This eliminated fair trade pricing which had been practiced in some states for almost 40 years.

The Antimerger Act (1950). The Congress passed the Antimerger Act of 1950, which strengthened the Clayton Act. This legislation provided that not only was the purchase of stock of a competing corporation a violation of the antitrust laws, but it was now illegal to acquire the assets of a competing firm. Thus all types of mergers were prohibited provided the Federal Trade Commission could demonstrate that the result might be a substantial lessening of competition. This would include horizontal, vertical, and conglomerate mergers.

A *horizontal merger* occurs when two or more companies which manufacture or distribute the same product join together. For example, in 1974 the Standard Oil Company of Indiana proposed a merger with Occidental Petroleum which would have been a horizontal merger. A *vertical merger* occurs when enterprises involved in successive stages of production or distribution of a product are joined. For example, in the automobile industry the acquisition of a glass manufacturer or a steel producer by an automobile maker would be a vertical merger. A *conglomerate merger* exists when enterprises producing or distributing unrelated product lines are joined. An example is Litton Industries, which has acquired companies with product lines ranging from book publishing to electric typewriters and missile guidance systems.

TABLE 2–1
A review of federal antitrust laws

Year enacted	Legislation	Goal
1890	The Sherman Act	To eliminate monopoly power of big business by making restraint of trade and monopolization federal offenses with prosecution by the U.S. Justice Department.
1914	The Clayton Act	To make more explicit the antimonopoly provisions of the Sherman Act by outlawing: Price discrimination. Exclusive and tying contracts. Intercorporate stockholdings. Interlocking boards of directors.
1914	The Federal Trade Commission Act	To deal with prevention as well as punishment for monopolistic business practices and to establish the Federal Trade Commission to police the antitrust laws along with the Justice Department.
1936	The Robinson-Patman Act	To protect small retailers by outlawing: Volume purchase discounts without cost justification. Payment of broker's commission if no broker is used. Advertising and promotion allowances only to large purchasers. Discriminatory discounts to different purchasers. Sale of goods at unreasonably low prices to reduce competition.
1937	The Miller-Tydings Act	To aid small business by permitting the establishment of minimum retail prices (fair trade prices) if allowed by state law.
1952	The McGuire Act	To strengthen state fair trade laws by legalizing state nonsigner clauses where all retailers in a state were bound by one retailer's signing of a resale price agreement with a manufacturer.
1975	The Consumer Goods Pricing Act	To repeal the Miller-Tydings and McGuire Acts, thereby nullifying the exemption of state fair trade laws from federal antitrust laws.
1950	The Antimerger Act	To outlaw all types of mergers where the result might be substantial lessening of competition whether by merger of stock or assets of competing enterprises.

GENERAL IMPACT OF THE COURTS UPON BUSINESS

Our judicial system has an impact upon the conduct of business just as do the laws passed by state and national legislative bodies. The courts function to adjudicate disputes which arise between business enterprises or between business and its customers. The courts provide a mechanism for the interpretation and enforcement of contracts. The legal system constitutes a framework for the orderly transfer of property among parties. Court rulings along with laws provide a set of ground rules for the basic conduct of business. The courts also interpret questions regarding legislation and actions taken by other government agencies. In this sense, the interpretation process of the U.S. courts is that of remaking or clarifying legislation passed by Congress. The Supreme Court acts as the interpreter of the U.S. Constitution in economic matters as well as in social and political areas.

The interpretations of the courts are not completely rigid. Constitutional interpretations reflect in part the needs of the economy in a given era. With changes in the nature and structure of the economy there have been changed legal interpretations. The same interpretations and laws which were relevant for the relatively rural economy of the past century often hinder the solution of the complex problems of today's urban, manufacturing economy. Within the past 40 years interpretations of how business activities are affected by the public interest and interstate commerce have changed drastically from views prevailing at the turn of the century. The rights for women and minorities provided by the Civil Rights Act of 1964 probably would have been viewed differently by the courts in an earlier era of American social and economic development.

INFLUENCE UPON BUSINESS BY THE EXECUTIVE BRANCH OF GOVERNMENT AND ADMINISTRATIVE AGENCIES

Along with the various legislative bodies of government and the courts system, the executive branch of government and administrative agencies have an influence on the conduct of business.

Influence of the president on business

The president of the United States exercises influence over business in a number of ways. The president may recommend legislation to the Congress to deal with economic problems either of a national character or those which may arise in a given industry or region of the country. Although the Congress is not necessarily obliged to follow these recommendations, presidential influence with the legislative branch of government is substantial.

The president appoints top officials of various administrative agencies which directly influence and in some instances control the conduct of business. These appointments range from the president's cabinet to the commissioners of various administrative agencies. The president has direct control over cabinet officers. However, the president has only indirect control over the administrative agencies. Once commissioners in these agencies are appointed, customarily they are independent of the president's direct control during their term of office.

The president is able to influence public opinion toward business and other groups in society through speeches broadcast over nationwide television and radio and in press conferences. The influence of the president may be felt in bringing industry and union leaders together to press for a solution to labor disputes which threaten the nation's economy.

The president may appeal personally to business leaders to influence business decisions. Such personal appeals can be effective because business owners are reluctant to refuse a request from such a high public official. They also are aware of the considerable powers the president has. These powers include administrative leeway under laws passed by Congress in matters affecting business. The government's important purchasing agencies in the Department of Defense and the General Services Administration have a profound influence in their negotiations for goods and services. The Office of the President has stand-by powers in import and export controls, stockpiling of strategic materials, and credit controls. The threat of investigations from governmental agencies concerning alleged antitrust activities, tax return irregularities, or other violations of the law is another power of government over business. These investigations, whether or not the executive is ultimately found guilty, are difficult because of the time and expense required in answering the government's charges.

An example of how the president can influence business was President Kennedy's public denunciation in 1962 of some major steel producers who attempted to raise prices. In view of the economic situation, the president said that the higher steel prices would be inflationary and therefore contrary to the public interest. At the same time the Department of Defense indicated it would buy industrial products made of steel only from those producers who did not raise prices, and the Justice Department talked of initiating antitrust studies of the steel industry. Following these actions by the Office of the President the increases in steel prices were revoked.

The Council of Economic Advisers

The president is assisted in economic matters by a Council of Economic Advisers. It consists of three members appointed by the president and approved by the Senate. These three council members are professional economists who analyze and interpret economic developments and recommend national economic policy to the president. The council was created by the Congress with the passage of the Employment Act of 1946. The purpose of the Employment Act was to state as a matter of national policy the responsibility of the federal government in assisting the private sector of the American economy to promote maximum employment, production, and purchasing power. The Employment Act also requires that early in each regular session the president must give to Congress an economic report. This report covers the state of employment, production, and purchasing power in the United States along with current trends in the economy. In this report the president also reviews federal government programs and may recommend legislative action to improve the state of our economy. The act also established a Joint Committee on the Economic Report composed of members of the House of Representatives and the Senate to guide legislative thinking on economic matters.

The administrative agencies

The federal administrative agencies are important in determining government's relationship to business. There is no single type of administrative agency. Usually a commission consisting of a given number of officials is established by law and appointed by the president with the consent of the Senate.

The administrative agencies act to regulate various sectors of the economy. By law they are given certain policy formulating powers such as the Federal Reserve System's power over the nation's money supply and the general level of interest rates. Some of the agencies exercise judicial functions such as the National Labor Relations Board which determines whether certain actions by businesses and labor unions are unfair labor practices.

The investigative function of these federal agencies is important. Without the ability to do fact finding, the effectiveness and purpose for which these agencies were created would be severely hampered. Therefore, sufficient staffs and budgets are required if administrative agencies are to be effective. Indeed, one of the prime means of control which the Congress has over most federal administrative agencies is through the budgetary appropriations, which are made on an annual basis.

The federal administrative agencies are becoming increasingly important in the complex pattern of business-government, labor-government, and individual-government relationships. Examples of these administrative agencies discussed in other chapters include the National Labor Relations Board, which deals with labor-management disputes; the Securities and Exchange Commission, which deals with financial markets and protection of investors; the Board of Governors of the Federal Reserve System, which deals with national monetary and banking policy; and the Federal Trade Commission, which polices the antitrust laws. Other federal agencies include the Federal Deposit Insurance Corporation, which insures the deposits of all federal banks and state banks which want to participate up to a maximum of $40,000 for each account; the Export-Import Bank, which aids in financing trade between the United States and other nations; the Civil Aeronautics Board; the Federal Power Commission; the Small Business Administration; and the Interstate Commerce Commission, which regulates carriers engaged in interstate commerce. This list is by no means exhaustive of the administrative agencies in the federal government. However, it does illustrate the scope and importance of these bodies.

GOVERNMENT AS A CONSUMER

Even though the private sector of the economy consumes the vast majority of goods and services produced in America, government also constitutes an important consumer. The magnitude of government's importance as a purchaser of goods and services over the years is illustrated in Table 2–2. This shows government expenditures for goods and services in relation to the Gross National Product, the total value of goods and services produced in the nation.

Table 2–2 is shown in constant 1958 dollars, which means dollar

TABLE 2–2
Government purchases of goods and services in relation to Gross National Product in constant dollars (billions of 1958 dollars)

| | | Government purchases of goods and services | | | |
| | | | | | |
Year	GNP	Total	Federal	State and local	Percent of GNP
1940........	$227.2	$ 36.4	$ 15.0	$21.4	16%
1945........	355.2	156.4	139.7	16.7	44
1950........	355.3	52.8	25.3	27.5	15
1955........	438.0	85.2	50.7	34.4	19
1960........	487.7	94.9	51.4	43.5	19
1965........	617.8	114.7	57.9	56.8	19
1970........	722.5	139.3	64.3	75.0	19
1974........	821.2	146.0	56.5	89.5	18

Source: U.S. Department of Commerce, *Business Statistics, 1973,* and *Survey of Current Business,* March 1975.

amounts for each year are stated in terms of the 1958 price level. This adjustment of GNP and government purchases for price changes makes dollar amounts from one year to another comparable in terms of real goods and services.

Government purchases of goods and services amounted to 18 percent of GNP in 1974. This does not include $140 billion in current dollars of government transfer payments to individuals. The recipients of transfer payments rather than government make decisions on how these funds will be spent. *Transfer payments* consist of income paid to persons from whom no services are currently received. Transfer payments include payments under social security, state unemployment insurance, veterans' benefits, and direct relief.

As was indicated earlier, the largest portion of federal spending is for national defense. In areas such as armaments and the aerospace industry the federal government is virtually the sole purchaser of goods produced by private business enterprises. Such large corporations as McDonnell-Douglas Corporation, General Dynamics, and North American Aviation are greatly dependent upon government contracts. Corporations such as General Electric, RCA, and General Motors supply significant amounts of goods to governmental agencies. Medium-size and small business enterprises share in government spending directly and as subcontractors to prime contractors. The Apollo program, involved in putting American astronauts on the moon, used some 20,000 different business enterprises employing an estimated 300,000 workers in nearly every state in the nation.

The fact that government purchases account directly for 18 percent of GNP expenditures shows the importance of government as a consumer. This represents a huge amount spent by a single class of consumer and is very influential in the overall functioning of the economy.

SUBSIDIES TO BUSINESS

Government has acted to promote business through subsidies beginning with protective tariffs against imported goods in the early 1800s. Business has received substantial direct subsidies over the years along with government assistance to other groups in the economy.

The economic growth of this country was assisted by government in the development of transportation systems. This assistance included early government programs to encourage the building of roads and canals and the development of rivers and harbors. In the middle of the 19th century the government provided subsidies to the railroads to encourage the development of the rail system. These subsidies consisted of large land grants, guaranteed loans, and other forms of assistance.

Subsidies have been authorized to the ocean shipping industry for the difference in the higher cost of construction of ships in American shipyards over the cost in foreign shipyards. Certain preferences for government-financed cargoes in U.S. flagships, mail payments, and tariff benefits have all aided the ocean shipping industry.

In recent years the U.S. airline industry has benefited by subsidization beginning with mail subsidies in the 1920s, which have continued to the present. Airlines also receive government help in the form of aids to navigation and aeronautical research and development expenditures.

The trucking industry along with the general public has received the benefit of the highway system which has been built with state and federal funds provided by gasoline excise taxes.

Another form of subsidy to business has been the lower postal rates given to mail other than first-class mail. Newspapers and magazine publishers have benefited from these lower rates as well as businesses which send their merchandise or advertising through the mails. In general the cost of carrying other than first-class mail has not been fully covered by the postal charges on second-, third-, and fourth-class mail.

Several general government aids and subsidies to business exist, in-

Employment outlook

Federal civilian government workers

The federal government is the nation's largest employer. It employs over two and a half million civilian workers. Training in business administration can be useful for many different government jobs.

Entrants into administrative positions usually are not required to have knowledge of a specialized field. They must show potential for future development by graduation from a four-year college or by responsible job experience. The entrant usually begins at a trainee level. Typical jobs in this group are budget analyst, claims examiner, purchasing officer, administrative assistant, and personnel officer. There are professional positions for economists, accountants, and individuals in the computer field throughout the government.

Federal employment is expected to grow slowly through the mid-1980s. However, population expansion will create more jobs for social security claims examiners, accounting and budget workers, and business and industry specialists.

About 9 out of 10 jobs in the federal government are under the merit system. The Civil Service Act, administered by the U.S. Civil Service Commission, covers 61 percent of all federal jobs. This act was passed by Congress to insure that federal employees are hired on the basis of individual merit and fitness. It provides for competitive examinations and the selection of new employees from among those who make the highest scores. The Commission through its network of 65 Civil Service area offices examines and rates applicants.

Applicants are notified as to whether they have achieved eligible or ineligible ratings. The names of eligible applicants are entered on a list in the order of their test scores. When a federal agency requests names of eligible applicants for a job vacancy, the area office sends the agency the names at the top of the appropriate list. The agency can select any one of the top three. Names of those not selected are restored to the list for consideration for other job openings.

cluding the monopoly protection given to invention and written creativity under the patent and copyright laws. The federal government is also important in the financing of research and development by industry. As mentioned earlier, the Small Business Administration has a program for assisting small business enterprises in obtaining loans and other assistance.

Reductions in federal income taxes are available to business through investment tax credits and accelerated depreciation allowances on new factories and equipment. The tax laws have also provided special depletion allowances of benefit to the oil and mining industries. These allowances have had the effect of reducing the income taxes paid by companies in these industries.

Over the years the federal government has stockpiled strategic materials, including mineral products, which has provided price supports for these products.

A number of subsidy and assistance programs have been available to agriculture in the United States. These include commodity price support programs, programs to remove surplus production from the marketplace, programs to restrict production of farm goods, and programs to assist in conservation, farm credit, technical assistance, and research.

GOVERNMENT OWNERSHIP OF BUSINESS

It has been the general practice of government in the United States to purchase goods and services from private industry. However, in a number of instances government owns and operates businesses. This is true at the federal, state, and local levels.

Federal business operations

The ownership of businesses by the federal government ranges from the production and sale of electric power to retail enterprises located on military reservations. In service areas such as finance and insurance the government has active agencies which directly serve private business and individual consumers.

The federal government is deeply involved in the production and sale of electric power. The Tennessee Valley Authority came into being in the 1930s and is one of the largest government hydroelectric power operations in the world. Its purpose is overall promotion of the economic and social welfare of the Tennessee River basin. In addition to the production and distribution of electricity, TVA controls floods and shipping, creates recreational areas, and encourages industrial expansion of the area. Other important hydroelectric power facilities owned and operated by the federal government include the Hoover Dam and projects on the Colorado, Columbia, St. Lawrence, and Missouri rivers. Some of these projects are carried out in cooperation with private utility companies and local governments.

The Department of Defense operates a variety of business activities on military bases which are directly or indirectly in competition with private business. These include retail operations such as restaurants and bakeries, laundries, motion picture houses, and merchandise sold in military post exchanges and commissaries. The military manufactures products which help make the military establishment self-sufficient and independent of civilian sources of supply. It also manufactures products which are not produced in sufficient quantity by the private sector of the economy. However, where feasible the Department of Defense has generally chosen to purchase goods and services from private commercial producers.

The financial and insurance agencies of the federal government include the Social Security System, the Federal Deposit Insurance Corporation, and the Federal Savings and Loan Insurance Corporation. The Federal Home Loan banks and other agencies act to encourage the construction of residential housing. The Rural Electrification Administration and other agencies assist in improving the economic condition of the farmer.

There are other important government-sponsored business operations. The U.S. Government Printing Office is the largest publishing house in the world. In 1971 the National Railroad Passenger Corporation (Amtrak) began the operation of railway passenger service in the United States. Also in 1971 the U.S. Postal Service, organized as an independent government agency, took over the mail service formerly provided by the Post Office Department.

State and local government business operations

Business operations are not limited to the federal government. State and local governments also own a variety of businesses, sometimes in competition with private business.

Municipalities frequently operate their own electric, water, and gas utility distribution systems. City ownership and operation of airports, harbors, and local transportation facilities are common in the United States.

A number of states operate liquor stores for the purpose of controlling the liquor traffic and for the substantial source of revenue which is collected for state treasuries. In some areas where state liquor stores exist, private businesses may be licensed to sell beer and wine or to sell liquor by the drink with package sales of hard liquor limited to state-owned monopoly.

SUMMARY

Government has an impact on business through taxation, provision of public services, regulation, subsidization, and as a consumer of goods and services produced by business.

Income taxes are the greatest source of revenue for the federal government. Sales taxes and property taxes provide the majority of tax revenues for state and local governments.

Important antitrust laws which affect business include the Sherman Act, the Clayton Act, the Federal Trade Commission Act, the Robinson-Patman Act, and the Antimerger Act of 1950. The Justice Department and the courts have been influential in determining how the antitrust laws are administered and interpreted.

The president of the United States exercises influence over business by public statements and personal prestige, by the legislation recommended to the Congress, and by the appointments made to the cabinet and the administrative agencies.

The Employment Act of 1946 placed responsibility with the federal government to assist the private sector of the economy to promote maximum employment, production, and purchasing power. The act created the Council of Economic Advisers to assist the president in economic matters.

The various administrative agencies of government are becoming increasingly important in government's relations with business, labor organizations, and the public.

Government is an important purchaser of goods and services from private business enterprises. Governmental units have generally chosen to purchase goods from private business rather than to establish government production facilities. In some instances, such as in electric power production and military retailing operations, the government has gone into the production and distribution of goods or services directly or indirectly in competition with private business.

Government has acted to promote business through subsidies to transportation, agriculture, publishing, mining and petroleum, and other industries.

TERMS FOR REVIEW

income tax	*trust*
sales tax	*antitrust laws*
property tax	*merger*
excise tax	*Council of Economic Advisers*
FICA taxes	*Employment Act of 1946*
deficit spending	*Gross National Product*
monopoly	

QUESTIONS

1. What types of taxes are most important at the federal and state and local levels of government?
2. *a.* What types of taxes are paid by business enterprises?
   b. Which taxes does a business enterprise have to pay whether or not it makes a profit?
3. Give at least five examples of business enterprises which would receive direct benefits from government spending even though for most enterprises these spending programs would provide only general benefits as part of society.
4. *a.* Why is business regulated?
   b. Why were the Sherman, Clayton, and Federal Trade Commission acts passed?
5. *a.* What is the difference between horizontal, vertical, and conglomerate mergers?
   b. In what ways might these different types of mergers be contrary to the public interest?
   c. How might these different types of mergers serve the public interest?
6. How do the courts have an impact on business?
7. How can the president of the United States influence business?
8. *a.* What advantages might there be for a business enterprise if a substantial portion of its sales were made to a unit of government?
   b. What problems might be created for such a business enterprise?

9. *a.* List several arguments that might be made to justify government subsidies to business.
    b. What are some negative aspects of government subsidies?
10. How can the ownership of business operations by government be justified in the United States? What advantages and disadvantages come with government ownership?

Business brief

Federal charters for all corporations?

Traditionally businesses organized as corporations have been chartered by the states. Some competition has existed among the states to be chosen as the state of incorporation for major business enterprises. In modern times the State of Delaware has been a popular state for incorporation. Generally Delaware's law permits the most flexibility in corporation charters. About one third of the nation's largest businesses are chartered in Delaware. Incorporation fees provide an estimated 15 percent of the state's annual budget.

Critics of present corporation chartering by states include followers of Ralph Nader and some members of Congress. These critics point out that stockholders' rights are not adequately protected by state incorporation laws. Stockholder voting procedures tend to keep current managements in office. Also, the emphasis on management flexibility by some state charters fails to emphasize management responsibility to groups in society such as employees, customers, creditors, and the general public.

Those persons generally opposed to federal charters for business enterprises indicate that the 1934 Securities and Exchange Act already provides protection for stockholders against management fraud and negligence. More and more information is being made public about corporations' operations and activities without federal chartering. Opponents of federal charters are concerned that such a practice could lead to political control of corporations. In Great Britain a number of key industries have been nationalized. In Germany corporate laws provide for employee and public representatives on boards and there is partial state ownership.

In the United States there is already federal chartering for banks and savings and loan associations. However, there is also a system of state charters for these financial institutions. Therefore, a bank or savings and loan association may operate under a charter from either the federal government or a state government.

1. What is the purpose of the corporate form of business organization?
2. How should corporations be governed in the 1970s and 1980s?
3. What advantages and disadvantages for the public would there be in a federal chartering system for business corporations?

*Equal employment
opportunity is an
important business
responsibility to society.*

Courtesy Valley National Bank of Arizona

*T*he vast social changes in recent years in the United States and around the world emphasize the total environment within which business functions. The great human and material resources available to business provide an opportunity for business enterprises to contribute to the solution of the social problems we face. This chapter discusses business's responsibilities to society and what business is doing to meet these challenges.

It is appropriate for you to consider the present and future role of business in our society. You and other students will be the decision makers in decades to come not only in business but in the many other groups which make up society.

The following issues are considered:
What does society expect business ethics to be?
Does business have a responsibility to support philanthropic projects?
How can public relations aid in improving business's relationships with others in society?
What can business do to improve the economic condition of women and minorities?
How can minority-owned enterprises be increased?
What response can business make to the continued urbanization of America?

3

The social responsibility of business

BUSINESS AND SOCIETY

Business enterprises have an important role in providing goods and services for consumers which can be sold at a profit. The private enterprise system has provided the vast majority of the American people with an increasingly higher standard of living over the years. Table 3–1 indicates there was an increase of 23 percent in median family income[1] over the recent ten-year period. The dollar amounts are shown in constant 1974 dollars which means they have been adjusted to account for higher prices caused by inflation and are stated in 1974 buying power.

TABLE 3–1
Median family income in the United States (in constant dollars—1974 base)

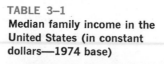

1974	$12,836
1964	10,444
Increase	$ 2,392

Source: U.S. Bureau of the Census, *Current Population Reports*, Series P-60, no. 99, July 1975.

Despite the importance of profits, there are other vital factors to be considered in the successful long-run conduct of business. Business has a responsibility to produce and distribute goods and services at a price consistent with their quality and purpose. These goods should be fairly advertised and merchandised. Employees should have fair wages and satisfactory working conditions. Enterprises and business managers should contribute a portion of their resources to improving the community. Business needs to increase the opportunities available to women and members of minority groups. American business does not function in a social vacuum. To fulfill its role in a responsible manner, business must relate positively to the society of which it is a part.

---

[1] The term *median income* means that half of the families had incomes higher than the stated figure and half had lower incomes. Thus the *median* represents the midway point in a series of data which divides the number of units in half.

ETHICS IN BUSINESS

We expect persons in business to conduct their activities in an ethical manner. *Ethics* is a code of conduct and values that is accepted by society as being right and proper. In general, business managers support a concept of business ethics based on honesty, fairness, and adherence to the law. However, there is always a possibility of a divergence between what is considered to be ethical and what is actually practiced. From time to time incidents such as expense account padding, rigging of bids, and price fixing come to light that contradict the consensus of what are ethical business practices.

There are several influences shaping the ethics which are practiced by persons in business. These include the individual's personal code, the behavior of the individual's colleagues, attitudes and actions of superiors in the enterprise, financial circumstances, the enterprise's policy on specific ethical questions, and the ethical practices of the industry of which the firm is a part. From this lengthy list it is apparent that no single factor determines completely the manager's actions when faced with a hard decision. However, of all the factors influencing ethical decisions in business, a case could be made that the individual's own

FIGURE 3–1
Factors influencing an ethical decision in business

personal code and views expressed by his boss are especially important. This places great responsibilities on the superior in a business situation to set the proper ethical climate. As will be discussed in Chapter 7, the top management in a business has the responsibility for setting the basic tone of the enterprise.

In every industry there is a generally accepted way of doing business. These industry practices also have an important influence upon the ethics which exist in a given enterprise. When industry practices leave something to be desired, the responsibility for improving them clearly lies with top management. An industry which continues to ignore the basic codes of conduct considered to be right by the public can expect that eventually the public will demand changes. In the past these changes have come through government legislation and increased regulation of business. Enlightened self-regulation is one of the best ways to avoid more government control of business conduct.

CONTRIBUTIONS TO EDUCATIONAL, HEALTH, AND CHARITABLE INSTITUTIONS

A wide range of views may be found regarding business philanthropy. At one extreme are those who maintain that the corporation should not practice philanthropic giving, leaving the support of nonprofit institutions to individual shareholders and employees. The proponents of this negative attitude toward corporate giving indicate the sole function of business is to provide goods and services which can be sold at a profit. Persons with this viewpoint say that corporate giving is an indirect tax which results in shareholders receiving lower dividends, employees receiving lower wages, and customers paying more for goods and services.

At the other extreme are those who call for a much greater share of corporate wealth to be devoted to socially desirable projects. Advocates of substantially higher contributions by business enterprises point to increasing profits which they say demonstrate the ability of business to support such gifts. These advocates suggest that private business ought to meet recognized social needs which otherwise would not be met, or would be handled by government less effectively.

Most business managements follow a practice between these extremes. Corporate contributions amounted to $1.17 billion in 1974 according to the American Association of Fund-Raising Counsel. Most managements attempt to be prudent in their corporate giving. They consider a variety of factors—ranging from a desire not to antagonize shareholders or employees by excessive gifts, to the extent to which contributions can be counted as federal income tax deductions. Under present federal law, a corporation may deduct charitable contributions which do not exceed 5 percent of the corporation's taxable income. For the nation as a whole, total corporate giving in the past years has amounted to about 1 percent of corporate income before income taxes.

While corporate giving is frequently thought of in strictly financial terms, the time and effort devoted by managers and other enterprise employees to philanthropic projects should not be overlooked. Civic projects, committees, and organizations occupy a considerable amount of the time of many persons engaged in business. With the approval of top management, much of this time is given during office or factory hours. In a very real sense this represents corporate giving to a wide range of socially approved projects.

PUBLIC RELATIONS IN BUSINESS

Public relations at its best has provided a means of relating the business enterprise to the different groups constituting the public. Identifiable groups with which the enterprise needs to communicate include shareholders, customers, employees, suppliers, and governmental agencies. There are four basic ways in which public relations can aid in improving the relationship of the business enterprise to others in the society.

First, the public relations department or outside counsel can assist management in clearly defining the company's broad economic and social objectives. Second, the public relations department can help translate these goals into imaginative programs which can be achieved. Third, this department provides advice as to how the image of the socially responsible business enterprise may be effectively communicated to the groups which have an interest in the firm's activities.

Fourth, the public relations department should be sensitive to misunderstandings that might arise between the enterprise and its public. After a diagnosis of these problems, recommendations can be made to management for their correction. In some instances the difficulties may be due to an inaccurate and unjustified image in the public's mind stemming from ignorance, misinformation, or distortion. However, sometimes the problems can be traced to unsound policies or actions on the part of the enterprise. When this is the case, the public relations function is to assist in improving the enterprise's policies and actions.

This broad definition of public relations makes its function much

Employment outlook

Public relations

Public relations workers help an employer build and maintain a beneficial public image. To accomplish this, they must understand changing attitudes and opinions of customers, employees, and other groups. Public relations workers gather and provide information to make the public aware of their employer's projects and accomplishments.

Employment of public relations workers is expected to increase moderately through the mid-1980s. The demand for public relations workers will grow as population increases and the general level of business activity rises. In recent years, public relations spending has increased, and many organizations have developed new public relations departments. This trend should continue in the years ahead.

A person choosing public relations work as a career needs an outgoing personality, self-confidence, and an understanding of human psychology. Courses in business administration, journalism, psychology, and public speaking help in preparing for a public relations position. Extracurricular activities, such as writing for a school publication, give valuable experience. Part-time or summer jobs in selling or public relations provide training that can help overcome competition for entry positions.

Some companies—particularly those with large public relations staffs—have formal training programs for new workers. In other firms, new employees learn by working under the guidance of experienced staff members.

more than merely gaining publicity for the enterprise through the press, radio, or television; or resorting to manipulation and subterfuge to present a picture of the enterprise which is not wholly accurate. In the long run the public relations program of the business enterprise should focus attention on clarifying the needs of society and should suggest ways in which the enterprise can help meet those needs.

BUSINESS AND THE POLITICAL PROCESS

What do you think is a proper role for business in the political arena? According to law no business corporation may engage directly in political activity nor may a business corporation provide direct financial support to political candidates. This legislation is rooted in the history of America when business interests frequently dominated political decisions. In the 1970s some corporate managements broke these laws prohibiting political contributions. The corporations were subjected to fines, and in some cases their officials were given jail sentences.

However, the fact that the business corporation is prohibited from having an active political voice does not preclude business owners and managers as individuals from being politically active. Each business manager should accept a responsibility for taking part in the political process. For some this may mean a relatively modest role, such as becoming an informed voter and communicating with elected officials on public issues. For others in business this political involvement may include actively supporting political parties or running for office. There are many examples of businessmen who have turned to politics. Senator Charles Percy of Illinois was president of Bell & Howell before running for political office. Senator Barry Goldwater of Arizona was active in the management of department stores before being elected to Congress.

Business's views are considered when deciding political issues affecting the economy. The views of business groups on national political issues are publicized by trade associations, business study groups, and in statements by corporate executives. The U.S. Chamber of Commerce and the National Association of Manufacturers express the collective views of their members.

BUSINESS AND SOCIAL PROBLEMS

As one of the significant groups in society, business can have an important role in taking actions to help mankind deal constructively with the socio-economic problems we face. It is difficult for us to forecast the future. However, an examination of our present society reveals certain socio-economic problems requiring long-run solutions. Socially responsible business enterprises are needed to help solve problems arising from discrimination in employment and income, minority business ownership, and increasing urbanization.

EQUAL EMPLOYMENT OPPORTUNITY

A socio-economic problem receiving major attention by business is the discrimination in employment and income that women and members of minority groups have traditionally faced. To examine this problem we need to look at the economic status of women and minorities, government civil rights actions, and what business is doing to promote equal employment opportunities.

Women in business

A dramatic change in the American economy in recent decades has been the increase in the proportion of women in the labor force. Sixteen million women have entered the civilian labor force since 1950, compared with only seven million men. By 1974 there were 35 million women workers who made up 39 percent of the civilian labor force.

A number of factors have contributed to the increase in women working outside the home. Attitudes in society toward the role of women are changing. An increased number of households are headed by women. There are more labor-saving devices in the home. There is a trend toward fewer children in families. Women are receiving more education leading to better-paying jobs. Government actions prohibiting employment discrimination based on sex have contributed to increased job opportunities for women.

Women's earnings. When median earnings of year-round full-time workers are compared, women earn less than 60 percent of men's wages. In 1973 the median earnings for women were $6,335 and for men $11,186. This earnings differential reflects a variety of factors. They include differences in the training or education a worker has received, in the number of hours worked per week, and in the length of work experience.

Occupational status of women. One of the significant causes of the difference between the earnings of women and men has been the concentration of women in certain lower-paying occupations. As can be seen from Figure 3–2, the occupational distribution of women differs

FIGURE 3–2
Occupational distribution for women and men in U.S. labor force, 1973

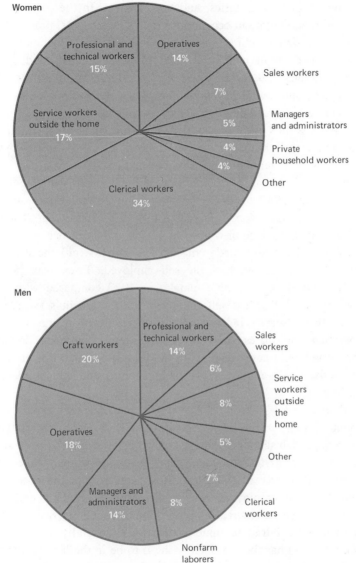

Women

Professional and technical workers 15%

Operatives 14%

Sales workers 7%

Managers and administrators 5%

Private household workers 4%

Other 4%

Service workers outside the home 17%

Clerical workers 34%

Men

Craft workers 20%

Professional and technical workers 14%

Sales workers 6%

Service workers outside the home 8%

Other 5%

Clerical workers 7%

Operatives 18%

Managers and administrators 14%

Nonfarm laborers 8%

Source: "Women Workers Today," U.S. Department of Labor, 1974.

greatly from that of men. Two thirds of employed women work in three occupational groups. In clerical occupations women are mainly stenographers, typists, secretaries, and bookkeepers. In the service category women predominate in occupations such as waitresses, practical nurses, dental assistants, and beauticians. In the professional-technical category more women than men are employed as elementary and secondary teachers, registered nurses, social workers, librarians, dietitians, physical therapists, and dental hygienists.

Society has traditionally assigned certain roles to men. Higher-paid occupations such as physician, dentist, airline pilot, architect, and certified public accountant are male-dominated. However, more women are beginning to enter male-intensive occupations. For example, in 1940 only 1 physician out of 20 was a woman compared with 1 out of 8 in 1973. From 1940 to 1973 the proportion of real estate agents and brokers who were women increased from 9 to 36 percent. There is an increasing acceptance of women in a wide variety of occupations.

Women have also made considerable inroads into the traditionally male-intensive category of the self-employed. Twenty-six percent of self-employed persons were females in 1973 compared with only 17 percent in 1940. Most self-employed women are in service or retail fields. In the service industry over 60 percent are in personal services operating enterprises such as beauty shops, laundries, dressmaking shops, and child-care facilities. In the professional services area women are actively self-employed in nursing homes and educational service facilities.

Changing job interests. A young woman can now expect to spend about 20 years in the labor force. Typically a woman enters the labor force after high school or college and works a few years before she marries or has her first child. Only a small portion of women leave the labor force permanently at this time. Most women who marry experience some breaks in employment during their child-bearing and child-rearing years. However, an increasing proportion of young married women with and without children continue in their jobs. Generally the more education a woman has the more likely she is to be in the labor force.

Because women are spending a significant portion of their adult lives working outside the home, they are becoming more career minded while attending school and in choosing an occupation. As women begin to view paid employment not just as an interlude between completion of their formal education and marriage but as a long-range commitment, the choice of an occupation and the satisfactions of a particular job become more important. These changes in women's attitudes toward jobs have important implications for employers in their hiring, training, and promotion of women.

Minority employment

Today the largest minority group in American society is Negroes who constitute about 11 percent of the population. The second largest minority group is Spanish-speaking Americans who make up about 5 percent of the population. Most Spanish-speaking persons are Mexican-

FIGURE 3–3
Employed men by occupation and race, 1963 and 1973 (percent distribution)

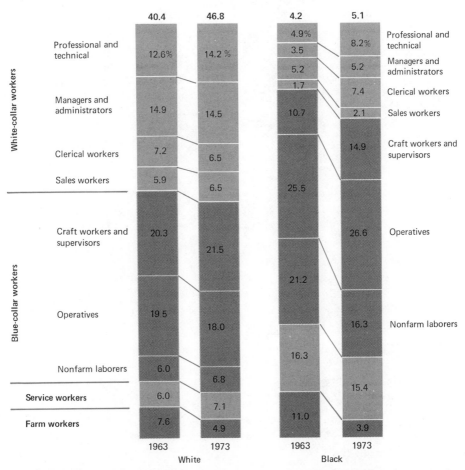

Millions of workers

	White		Black	
	40.4	46.8	4.2	5.1
Professional and technical	12.6%	14.2%	4.9%	8.2%
Managers and administrators	14.9	14.5	3.5 / 5.2	5.2
Clerical workers	7.2	6.5	1.7	7.4
Sales workers	5.9	6.5	10.7	2.1
Craft workers and supervisors	20.3	21.5	25.5	14.9
Operatives	19.5	18.0	21.2	26.6
Nonfarm laborers	6.0	6.8	16.3	16.3
Service workers	6.0	7.1	11.0	15.4
Farm workers	7.6	4.9	11.0	3.9

1963 1973 1963 1973
White Black

Note: Department of Labor statistics include other minority races with Negroes, although blacks account for more than 90 percent of the data.
Source: U.S. Bureau of the Census, *Current Population Reports,* Series P-23, no. 48, July 1974.

Americans with Puerto Ricans and Cubans making up the greatest proportion of the rest. Asian Americans are less than one percent of the population. Less than one-half of one percent are American Indians.

Occupational status of minorities. As is the case with women, members of minority groups are generally concentrated in occupations and industries where earning potential is the lowest. Figure 3–3 shows the occupational distribution of employed men by race for 1963 and 1973. Figure 3–4 shows the occupational distribution of employed women by race over the same ten-year period.

You can see by comparing the occupational distributions for 1963

FIGURE 3–4
Employed women by occupation and race, 1963 and 1973 (percent distribution)

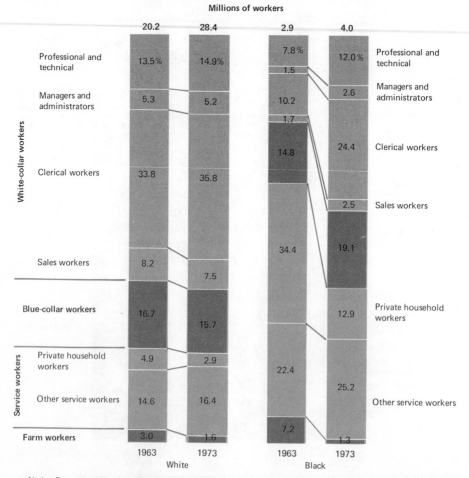

Millions of workers

Note: Department of Labor statistics include other minority races with Negroes, although blacks account for more than 90 percent of the data.
Source: U.S. Bureau of the Census, *Current Population Reports,* Series P-23, no. 48, July 1974.

and 1973 that there has been improvement in the occupational status of blacks and other minorities. There have been significant increases in the percentage of male minority workers who hold white-collar jobs, especially as professional and technical workers. Improvement is shown in blue-collar jobs in the skilled craft positions. Among farm workers their percentage has greatly declined from 1963 to 1973.

The change in the percentage of women minority workers in different occupations has been even more dramatic in this period. The percent of minority women employed as white-collar workers has almost doubled. Sizable gains were made in the professional and technical category and in that of clerical workers. There has been a large decline in the percentage of minority women employed as service workers because of the drop in private household workers. Farm workers also showed a sizable percentage decline in the female minority work force.

Minority earnings. In spite of the shift in minority employment into more highly paid occupations, the level of wages for blacks, America's largest minority group, is still considerably below that of whites. Figure 3–5 compares median income levels for year-round full-time black and

FIGURE 3–5
Comparison of earnings for full-time workers by race and sex, 1967 and 1973

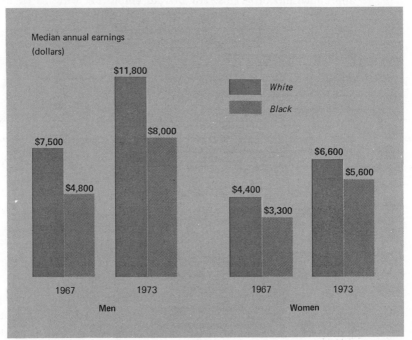

Source: U.S. Bureau of the Census, *Current Population Reports,* Series P-60, no. 97, January 1975.

white workers by sex. These data show there has been improvement in nonwhite income relative to white income since 1967 especially for black females. However, wages for blacks are still below those of whites. Also, the absolute difference in dollar wages increased over the 1967–1973 period for white male workers compared to black males.

Government equal-opportunity actions

Government action to improve the employment status of women and minorities has come through legislation, court decisions, and executive orders.

The Civil Rights Act of 1964. At the federal government level the Civil Rights Act of 1964 is the most important antidiscrimination legislation of modern times. The act has a number of titles including those outlawing discrimination in voting, public accommodations and schools, federal assistance programs, and employment. Title VII, which was amended by the Equal Employment Opportunity Act of 1972, deals with employment.

Title VII bans discrimination in employment by business, educational institutions, government, labor unions, employment services, and apprenticeship programs. All private employers with 15 or more employees are covered. Under Title VII the hiring, promotion, and discharge of persons is to be based on ability and qualifications without regard to race, color, religion, sex, or national origin.

The Equal Employment Opportunity Commission (EEOC) was set up to receive and investigate charges of job discrimination. When the EEOC finds reasonable cause that the charges are justified, it attempts through voluntary agreements to eliminate the discriminatory practices. If this approach fails, the 1972 amendments gave EEOC power to go directly to court to enforce the law. This has resulted in a significant increase in EEOC legal actions against employers which practice job discrimination. Claims of racial discrimination have accounted for the largest number of complaints to the EEOC. Charges of sex discrimination now make up about one fifth of all the charges filed with the EEOC.

The Equal Pay Act of 1963. This law, which was amended in 1972, requires employers to pay men and women in an enterprise equally for work of the same skill and responsibility. In the ten-year period ending in 1973 the Department of Labor found more than 150,000 employees, nearly all women, were underpaid by more than $75 million under the Equal Pay Act. Small wage differentials often added up to large amounts. This is illustrated by the $200,000 paid to 197 women nursing aides in Kentucky who were receiving 30 cents an hour less than male orderlies for the same work.

The Age Discrimination in Employment Act of 1967 prohibits employers of 25 or more persons from discriminating in the employment of persons between the ages of 40 and 65 because of age.

State and local legislation. Fair employment practice (FEP) legislation outlawing various kinds of discrimination has been passed in over half the states and in many cities. FEP laws generally establish a commission which can investigate complaints of discrimination, conduct public hearings, and attempt to resolve complaints through conciliation.

Many states have laws which were passed in earlier years to protect women from work that was dangerous or required heavy physical demands. With improved safety conditions and extensive use of machinery to replace physical labor, these laws have excluded women as a group from many good-paying jobs that some might have the capacity, ability, and preference to perform. EEOC guidelines and court decisions have held that the equal employment requirements of Title VII replace these state protective laws. Now the employer must consider women as individuals in determining their capacity to do particular jobs.

Court decisions

Women and minorities have turned increasingly to the courts to overcome discrimination by employers and unions. When discrimination is determined to exist the courts have ordered employers to establish Affirmative Action Plans. An Affirmative Action Plan begins with an analysis by the enterprise of its present work force to identify jobs and departments where few females or members of minority groups are employed. Then specific hiring and promotion goals are set up to compensate for the effects of past discrimination. The goal of affirmative action is the measurable, yearly improvement in hiring, training, and promotion of minorities and women throughout the business enterprise.

The federal courts have held that a small number of women or minorities in any job classification in relation to their number in the population or workforce constitutes strong evidence of discrimination. When such statistics are found the burden of proof is on the employer to show that the situation is not the result of discrimination.

Some examples of practices found to be discriminatory by federal courts include:

Black workers of an electric utility company were paid $250,000 as compensation for wages they would have earned if they had not been kept from promotion by a discriminatory system. Affirmative hiring was ordered, with at least 25 percent of new union hires to be nonwhites until their level of employment in union jobs reached 21.5 percent.

White-collar female employees in a large financial corporation were paid more than $125,000 because they were allegedly denied promotion because of their sex. The corporation agreed to hire more females for branch representative openings and to provide training to help them qualify for better jobs.

Executive orders

Another means of enforcing equal access to job opportunities is by an executive order issued by the president of the United States. A number of these directives have been issued since 1941 to prevent discriminatory employment practices.

One of the most important directives is Executive Order 11246 (as amended by Executive Order 11375) which covers all employers who have federal government contracts. Approximately one third of the labor force is employed by business enterprises having government contracts. This order forbids discrimination based on race, creed, color, sex, or national origin. Also, it requires employers to have Affirmative Action Plans and to state in all job advertisements that they are equal employment opportunity employers. Subcontractors and labor unions are included in the order's provisions. The Office of Federal Contract Compliance (OFCC) was set up in the U.S. Department of Labor to administer these orders.

Business actions in equal employment

Management can develop its own nondiscriminatory employment system. This involves a commitment throughout the enterprise to provide opportunity for equal employment. The present work force should be analyzed to determine where minorities and women are underutilized. Specific hiring and promotion goals for minorities and women need to be set with target dates for attaining these goals. All employees as well as supervisors and top management should be committed to the enterprise's affirmative action program if the program is to be successful. An insensitive receptionist or security guard at the factory entrance can make a woman or minority applicant feel unwelcome.

Some job descriptions may need to be revised if they specify higher qualifications than are actually necessary to perform the job. For example, requiring a high school education as a condition of employment or promotion tends to disqualify minorities at a higher rate than others. For some blue-collar jobs there is no evidence that a high school education is necessary for satisfactory job performance.

In help-wanted advertising care can be taken to insure that the ad does not indicate any race, sex, or age preference. If the job opening has traditionally been typed as "male" or "female" the ad can emphasize interest in recruiting both sexes.

Discrimination is most likely to occur in the process of selecting the employee for the job. Care needs to be taken that any tests used are valid predictors of success for the job in question. Instead of traditional tests, a work-sample technique may be used. For example, an applicant for a production job could be asked to assemble nuts and bolts or electrical components in a certain sequence. This would test the applicant's manual dexterity, ability to follow directions, and tolerance for repetitive routines.

The person who conducts the job interview should be free of stereotyped images about minorities' or females' abilities for particular jobs. One commonly held stereotype is that women are more prone to absenteeism or job turnover than men. However, studies show there is little difference in absentee rates of men and women. Job turnover is more related to the type of job and the level of pay than to sex. The applicant's previous work record is usually the most valid evidence of employee stability.

Management and unions can adopt company-wide promotion plans and publicize job promotion opportunities to all workers. Apprenticeships, on-the-job training, and management development programs should also be open to all employees.

Many business enterprises are now making special efforts to do more for women and minorities. For example, Union Carbide has assembled a list of promotable women and is providing them with special job counseling. Avon has been recruiting at women's colleges and has instituted an upward mobility and job opportunity program for women. Norton Simon Corporation is now grading its supervisors on how well they train women employees.

An example of what business is doing to provide job training and opportunities for the hard-core unemployed is the National Alliance of Businessmen. This organization was formed after the Detroit riots of 1967 to expand employment opportunities, especially for persons who had been considered unemployable because of a lack of job skills. Many large corporations are participating in this program along with thousands of smaller business enterprises which make up the voluntary alliance.

Some of these programs have had notable successes. Levi Strauss & Co., makers of the popular denim "Levis," has been one of the leaders in the NAB. It has had a long experience of hiring employees from minority groups. In the early 1960s Strauss moved to integrate its plants in the South beyond the level of tokenism and before it was required to do so by law. This company has also opened its management ranks to qualified persons from minority groups in significant numbers. Western Electric Company, manufacturing and supply company for the Bell Telephone systems, has developed creative programs for hiring and training disadvantaged Americans. Both Western Electric and Strauss have encouraged the development of minority suppliers.

Despite the success stories, problems have been encountered and not all cases have worked out satisfactorily. An automobile corporation executive reporting on that company's experience said many of the hard-core unemployed were unable to fill out a simple job application. Some of the applicants who signed up for job training failed to appear. Others who did report were consistently late. Many had never been counted in a census, had no social security number, had never registered to vote, and had no community ties. Some employees had trouble getting to work because of their inability to read the route markings on the city buses. As the result of these problems many of the trainees have been given basic courses in reading, writing, and arithmetic.

MINORITY BUSINESS OWNERSHIP

Most students of American society feel that better opportunities for job training, employment, and promotion are vital to improve the economic status of minorities. However, the following quotation of the late Whitney M. Young, Jr., when he was executive director of the National Urban League, points up the importance of minority business ownership as well as job opportunities:

> Important as jobs in the larger society are—and creation of such jobs must be the main thrust of economic efforts toward equality—there is a pride and dignity in ownership that must be satisfied within the black community, as it is within the white.

Although blacks, Spanish-speaking Americans, Asians, and Indians make up about 16 percent of the U.S. population, less than 5 percent of the nation's business enterprises are owned by members of these minority groups. Minority-owned enterprises are usually small and account for less than 1 percent of the economy's business receipts and assets.

Obstacles to minority enterprise

Minority entrepreneurs are confronted by many obstacles. Those business enterprises located in the ghettos are faced with a hostile environment subject to frequent crimes ranging from pilferage and robbery to vandalism. Some businesses, both black and white, have been closed after numerous holdups. When minority enterprises are located in high crime-rate areas the cost of insurance, if available, is more. If the enterprise is to be profitable such added costs mean higher prices for goods and services or lower quality merchandise if regular prices are charged. This problem results in frustration among ghetto residents who complain that they are being overcharged by businesses in their neighborhoods.

Another major obstacle for the minority business has been difficulty in securing the necessary capital funds. Any new business enterprise entails considerable risk. Over the years it has been estimated that 50 percent of new businesses change ownership or cease operations in their first 18 months. Commercial banks recognize this high risk for any new business and have either been reluctant to make loans to minority enterprises or would do so only at higher interest rates.

One result is that minority business owners who were unable to get necessary loans elsewhere have turned to the loan sharks. They have had to obtain short-term loans for long-term needs such as for the purchase of necessary equipment. Funds are often insufficient to permit the purchase of adequate inventories. Loan sharks have been able to exact as much as 20 percent interest per month for the money they lend to hard-pressed black businesses.

Some potential owners of minority enterprises may lack skills in key business functions such as purchasing, personnel hiring and training, sales and promotion, and accounting and finance. Although minority owners may have knowledge of the goods or services they sell, they may need management training in marketing, finance, and accounting if they are to operate profitably.

Aids to minority-owned business

There are numerous ways that majority businesses can aid in the further development of minority business enterprises. A number of the more than 85 federal government programs to aid minority business ownership require participation from private enterprise.

One of the federal agencies which assists the minority-owned enterprise is the Office of Minority Business Enterprise (OMBE) in the Department of Commerce. One of OMBE's roles is to coordinate the different federal assistance programs to encourage minority citizens to take advantage of these opportunities. The Small Business Administration (SBA) provides management and financial assistance to small enterprises which have difficulty securing financing from private sources on reasonable terms. The General Services Administration has committed millions of dollars to purchase goods from minority suppliers.

Private financial help has come through Minority Enterprise Small Business Investment Companies (MESBIC) which are private investment companies licensed by the SBA. MESBICs specialize in providing long-term capital funds and management assistance to minority business enterprises. Local Development Companies (LDC) are organized to help in the economic growth of a community. The LDC may help in acquiring land, buildings, or equipment for minority enterprises sometimes in cooperation with the SBA, insurance companies, or banks. Some banks have also expanded their minority loan programs.

Less than one half of one percent of the banks in the United States are minority owned. Since most are small their capacity to provide loans to other minority enterprises is limited. Large enterprises can place deposits in minority-owned banks. This not only strengthens the minority bank but also provides more funds to be loaned in the minority community.

Another way business can help is by purchasing goods and services from minority suppliers engaged in manufacturing, processing, packaging, and other services. Lists are available to aid purchasing agents in locating these new suppliers.

Sometimes the managements of a majority and a minority business enterprise will work together by contracts or in partnership on a joint project. The minority business manager often has specialized skills and knowledge in dealing with the $30 billion minority market. By working together the majority enterprise can gain entry into a specialized market while the minority firm can obtain the management skills and capital resources needed to succeed profitably.

Franchising can be a valuable technique in developing minority enterprises. The well-known name of a successful franchise will tend to attract customers who recognize that they will be getting a quality product or service. Also, the national franchisor provides much assistance in the form of management training, marketing techniques, and accounting and financial systems. All of these factors help reduce the risks of failure for the minority enterprise. Although minority groups are participating more in franchising, they only own about 1.3 percent of the total number of franchised businesses.

The four major U.S. automobile manufacturers have agreed to co-operate by increasing the opportunities for minority-owned auto dealerships. This is taking place through the creation of new dealerships and by transfer of existing dealerships to minority owners when the opportunity arises. The first black auto dealership was established in 1967 in Chicago through General Motors. By the end of 1974, some 39 Ford dealerships were owned in whole or in part by members of minority groups. Also, 77 Ford dealerships were owned in whole or in part by women active in the day-to-day operations of the business.

INCREASING POPULATION AND ITS CONCENTRATION

The increasing population and its concentration in metropolitan areas is another of our socio-economic problems. Figure 3–6 shows the Standard Metropolitan Statistical Areas designated by the U.S. Bureau of the Census as urban areas having at least one city with a population of 50,000 or more. The 261 SMSAs contain about two thirds of the country's population. Major problems facing many of these cities include increased costs of government; high property taxes; traffic congestion; robberies, assaults, and other crime; need for improved housing and recreational areas; and racial tensions.

A fight or flight response has developed on the part of some businessmen to these urban problems. Some managements are relocating home offices and other facilities outside the heart of the central city metropolitan areas. Several major corporations have moved their headquarters from New York City to the suburbs or to other less populated areas of the country. Such moves by industry tend to aggravate the problems of the central cities by decreasing the property tax base and reducing the number of jobs available to inhabitants of the inner city.

Other business managements have chosen to stay in the cities and become more involved in community action. For example, in St. Louis, businessmen helped in developing and carrying out programs to clean up the Mississippi River waterfront. In Los Angeles and Chicago, businessmen joined in supporting improved law enforcement. In numerous cities

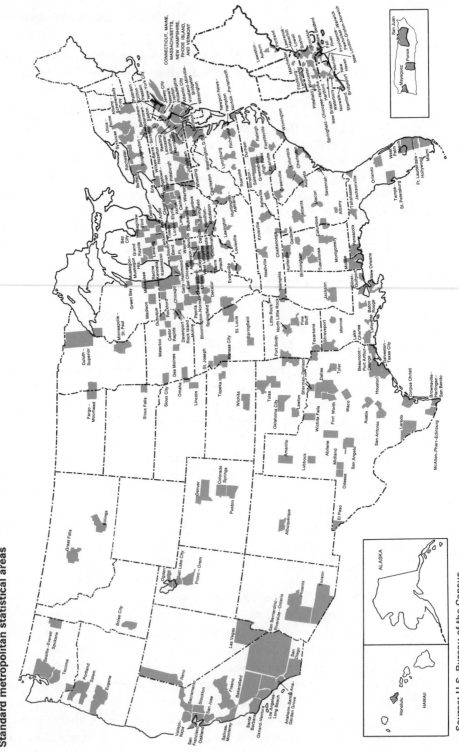

FIGURE 3–6
Standard metropolitan statistical areas

Source: U.S. Bureau of the Census.

other examples can be found where businessmen have helped in improving slum housing, providing municipal recreational areas and downtown parking, and supporting public education needs.

THE ROLE OF PRIVATE ECONOMIC POWER

The issue of how business is to relate to society as a whole may be summed up in the question "What is the proper role of private economic power in the last quarter of the 20th century?" This basic question includes many other social issues in addition to those discussed in this chapter. American business also can work with government to solve the problems of inflation and unemployment as well as assist other nations in their economic development. The role of private economic power in the United States will have to be worked out in all these issues.

In summary, when we consider the proper role of private economic power it should be emphasized that economic power is not an end in itself. Indeed, even the goods and services produced by business in the hands of industrial and individual consumers are not the ultimate objectives of our economic society. The end purpose of the way in which we organize our economy is to provide a fuller measure of freedom for our citizens. The wealth of the American economy should be used in such a way as to further individual dignity and meaningful living.

Because of the concentration of private economic power at the command of business managers there is a great burden of responsibility on their shoulders for good stewardship of these resources. The words of Robert G. Menzies, former Prime Minister of Australia, which were applied to America as a nation, are also appropriate for today's business leaders: "Great power can breed great selfishness unless it is wedded to great responsibility."[2]

SUMMARY

Society expects business to fulfill its role in a responsible manner. Persons engaged in business should be ethical in the conduct of their activities.

Business enterprises contribute to a wide range of philanthropic projects both in money and in employees' time.

The public relations department can help the business enterprise relate its purposes and programs to the various groups in society.

---

[2] From an address delivered at Drury College, October 15, 1966.

Business's responsibility to society goes beyond providing goods and services. Business cannot solve all our social problems. However, socially responsible business actions are needed to help solve such problems as employment discrimination against women and minorities, minority business development, and increasing population and urbanization.

Changes are occurring in our economic society. An important question is: What is the proper role of private economic power in the last quarter of the 20th century?

The provision of goods and services by business is important. However, our economy should function so as to provide a fuller measure of freedom for all citizens. American private enterprise can help promote this objective.

TERMS FOR REVIEW

ethics
philanthropy
public relations
occupational distribution
median income
Civil Rights Act of 1964
Equal Employment Opportunity Commission

Equal Pay Act of 1963
Affirmative Action Plan
Executive Order 11246
National Alliance of Businessmen
Standard Metropolitan Statistical Area

QUESTIONS

1. What factors determine the ethics practiced by a business manager at a given time?

2. *a.* Develop an argument to support the following statement: "As a stockholder in American corporations, I resent their philanthropic gifts to charitable, educational, and community projects. I wish corporate boards of directors would declare higher cash dividends for the stockholders and let the individual stockholders give to the philanthropic projects of their choice."

   b. Develop an argument to refute the above statement.

3. *a.* What does a positive program of public relations do for an enterprise and its public?

   b. Comment on the statement: "Public relations is simply a gimmick to whitewash the practices of business and to dodge the real issues."

4. Why is it so important that business managers have socially responsible attitudes and practices?
5. How has discrimination affected the economic position of women workers in the United States?
6. *a.* How has the economic status of blacks improved in the past 10 years?
    b. In what ways has the economic position of blacks either declined or improved only slightly over the past six to 10 years?
7. *a.* How have legislation, including Title VII of the Civil Rights Act of 1964, and executive orders of the president improved economic opportunities for minority persons and women?
    b. What further steps need to be taken if minority persons and women are to achieve greater economic opportunities?
8. *a.* Comment on the merits of giving blacks and women preferential treatment in hiring, training, and promotion to improve their economic status.
    b. What problems would be faced by the management of a business enterprise which carried out such a policy of preferential treatment?
9. Through a study of current publications, select examples of practices or projects that businesses have undertaken which demonstrate an awareness of the critical economic, political, and social issues facing the country today. What can be learned from these examples that would be helpful to other business enterprises?
10. Based on your study in this course and your outside reading, write a 300-word summary of the most important issues that will be relevant for business enterprises in the next five years.

Business briefs

Burger King

Burger King is a chain of franchised fast-service restaurants owned by the Pillsbury Company. It competes with other fast-food restaurants such as McDonald's, Burger Chef, and A & W. Burger King has been involved in cooperative programs with the federal Office of Minority Business Enterprise since 1972 when it established the Burger King MESBIC.

In late 1973 a program was announced for the construction of at least 30 Burger King self-service restaurants in the Chicago area involving $38 million. The construction is being performed by minority-owned enterprises in the building trades. Other minority business firms are providing a variety of services including real estate, security, extermination, advertising, and uniform supply. The construction program involves $18 million and extends over a five-year period. Ownership opportunities of the new Burger King restaurants are being offered to interested minority groups and individuals.

Corporate activities in the Chicago area include deposits estimated at $16 million over ten years in a black-owned bank. In addition, Burger King announced that three $1,000 scholarships will be awarded annually to a deserving Burger King employee from Chicago's West, South, and Near North Side communities.

In 1975 the first minority-owned Burger King restaurant located in the state of North Carolina was opened. This franchised restaurant is located in Winston-Salem and was financed by an SBA-guaranteed bank loan along with a loan from a local MESBIC. Additional financing was provided by the black owner and by the franchisor, Burger King, Inc.

1. Why do you think the management of Burger King is engaged in these minority-related activities?
2. What benefits could occur as the result of these actions for:
   a. The minority owners of these new units?
   b. The communities where such units are located?
   c. Burger King, Inc.?
3. What possible problems could arise from these actions?
4. What should Burger King's management be prepared to do in addition to providing some financing for these projects?

Pillsbury Company and Vietnamese refugees

Following the collapse of the U.S.-supported government in South Vietnam in the spring of 1975, the American government encouraged business enterprises and private individuals to help relocate 130,000 Vietnamese refugees who fled to the United States.

The Pillsbury Company offered a four-month supply of 14 Pillsbury products to the first 600 American families sponsoring Vietnamese refugees after May 1, 1975. This offer totaled $170,000. Pillsbury also announced an award of $1,000 to any employee who sponsored a refugee.

The Burger King subsidiary of Pillsbury volunteered to train and provide jobs for 150 refugees in company-owned restaurants. Burger King had done this some years earlier with Cuban refugees.

1. How can the Pillsbury management justify to stockholders spending company funds to help Vietnamese refugees?
2. If you were a company official, what response would you make to the question, "How can you 'make jobs' for Vietnamese at a time when the unemployment rate of Americans exceeds 9 percent?"

Cases

The image scrimmage

Bob Cramer closed his notebook and rose to his feet, "I believe I have all the background information I need at this point, Mr. Chase. We will conduct our investigation into those problem areas we have discussed and submit a report detailing our findings and recommendations."

As Cramer left the office he reflected on his conversation with Craig Chase, president of American Wood Products, Inc. This was his third meeting with the president, who had contacted the firm of Bayer, Bassick, and Botlich a week ago. Bayer, Bassick, and Botlich (B,B,&B) was a medium-sized public relations agency. Chase was considering the possibility of contracting for their services as public relations consultants. Bob Cramer, a senior account executive with B,B,&B, was chosen to develop the account.

In their first meeting Chase had told Cramer, "Public relations is something we have always taken for granted. Consequently, we do not have an adequate understanding of what is involved or of how the function should be managed within our organization. I hope that our experience with the problems we are now facing will generate a better understanding and appreciation for public relations so that we can eventually manage this function ourselves."

In his conversations with Bob, Chase had outlined those problem areas where he thought better public relations might be a help. First, American Wood was not in very good standing in the various communities in which it operated plants. The company had trouble securing the cooperation needed from many different groups. For example, some of American's timber holdings were not readily accessible from public roads. As a result, the forest management division depended heavily on the cooperation of farmers and landowners in leasing temporary access across their property so that timber crops could be harvested. These persons had been very reluctant to provide this cooperation. The resulting delays and the need to use indirect access routes had proved very costly for the division.

Another problem of increasing concern was the pressure in the state legislature and in Congress to set aside certain of American's timber holdings as parklands or as state-controlled conservation preserves. The pressure came from various interest groups concerned with wildlife conservation and the preservation of natural timberlands. Governmental agencies, such as the National Park Service and the state fish and game division, had provided little support for American's position in these matters. Even legislative representatives from the district in which American's home office is located had not taken a strong position in the company's behalf.

Still another major problem area was that of recruiting new personnel for the company. Personnel officers reported that, despite competitive wage scales, American was finding increasing difficulty in competing with other employers for top quality recruits.

Problems were also being experienced in the sale of the company's products. Most of their products were distributed through retail and wholesale lumber dealers who supplied a variety of contractors, decorators, and individual consumers. While sales in the industry had been rising, American was not maintaining its share of the market. In some cases dealers had dropped the American line altogether and the company had been unable to gain the support of another qualified dealer in that area.

In the weeks that followed, Bob Cramer and the other B,B,&B personnel who helped him on the American account conducted numerous interviews, in person and by questionnaire, in an effort to shed more light on the problems which company president Craig Chase had outlined. In every case, the objective was to determine what image American had and how this image had been gained.

In conversations with landowners, state fish and game officials, and other persons interested in conservation, American was portrayed as an inconsiderate neighbor which used the area's natural resources without regard to the consequences for those whom their actions affected. Landowners who had denied access across their property felt that this privilege if it were granted would be abused by the company. They told of previous incidents in which heavy logging equipment had torn up roads with no attempt by the company to restore these roads. Gates had been carelessly left open. Logging crews had violated property lines.

State conservation officials generally regarded the company as "either inconsiderate or ignorant" of the importance of managing timberlands with regard for the fish and game resources which can be affected. In some cases entire valleys had been denuded by logging crews. The resulting land erosion had made the area unfit for replanting, and the silting of the river had taken a substantial toll in the fish population.

In talking with local officials and community leaders, it was apparent that American was viewed as a "mediocre" or "apathetic" citizen of the various communities in which it operated. It did not become actively involved in community projects, either as an organization or through the participation of its management personnel as individuals. One official stated that "the company seldom does more than what is necessary in cooperating with community interests. In controlling their contamination of local streams, for example, American meets the standards imposed by current pollution control legislation. But that's as far as they go. There is no effort to go further than that just for the sake of being a good citizen."

Conversations with state employment security officials and the personnel officers of other companies provided some insight into American's recruiting problems. The company apparently had developed a bad image as an employer. Such problems as poor first-line supervision, an inadequate grievance procedure, and poorly devised promotion and layoff policies had contributed to rather serious incidents. These gained a considerable amount of attention in the communities in which they occurred. In recent years the company had made progress in dealing with these problems and the present situation was much improved. "But apparently this fact has not been communicated to the community and to potential recruits," noted one observer. "The negative image seems to have lingered on."

A survey of dealers and customers for wood products revealed something of the image American projected in the trade. Dealers did not consider the company to be reliable or cooperative as a supplier. They cited failure to meet delivery schedules, inadequate sales and service calls, and unwillingness to cooperate or make special arrangements when problems arose. Contractors and other users were familiar with the American brand, "Timberline," which was associated with paneling, wallboard, insulation, and other construction materials produced by the company. However, they did not associate either the brand or the company with the idea of a "progressive or innovative supplier, a front runner in new product development." In contrast, American's competitors seemed to have the reputation of being more progressive. This "nonprogressive" image was surprising since American, at least in recent years, had been more active in new product development and research than any of its competitors.

Customers also felt that American had an image of unreliable product quality. This was apparently a carry-over from the introduction three years earlier of a new type of wall paneling. The product had not been adequately developed before being placed on the market and a number of serious defects, including warping and discoloration, had occurred. The product was quickly withdrawn from the market but not before considerable damage had been done to the company's image.

In reporting his findings to the president of American, Bob Cramer realized that he would have to submit detailed recommendations for action to remedy the various problems facing the company. These recommendations should define the various publics with whom American should be concerned and should suggest the kind of image which should be projected to each public. In each instance specific measures should be suggested to develop the desired image.

1. Identify the various publics with which this company should be concerned.
2. What is the image of the company which each of these publics has?
3. What can American Wood Products management do to improve its public image?

Personal decisions in business

I

"See you in the morning, Norma."

"Good night, Mr. Keating."

Norma Spalding looked up from her typewriter and watched as her boss stopped at the supplies cabinet before leaving the office. It was a common practice for executives of the company to take note pads, pens, and other items for use at home. Although these were, in part, used for company work, they were often used for other purposes in the home. Norma had never before given much thought to this practice. It seemed to be accepted by employees and executives of the company. Now, however, as she turned back to her work, she wondered if it was "right" to take company supplies for one's personal use.

II

"It's silly to go out and buy this stuff," Sam said as he reached into a carton marked 'rejects.' "Here, take one of these." Tom reached out and caught the can of car polish which Sam had tossed to him.

Tom Farber was finishing the second week of his summer warehouse job. He had been assigned to work with Sam Bartels, lift truck operator and senior man on the warehouse crew. Sam was a good-natured, easy-going, middle-aged worker who knew his job well. Tom had already learned a good deal from Sam, not only about the warehouse, but about people. In his relationship with his peers and superiors Sam demonstrated an understanding of human nature which had quickly won Tom's confidence and admiration.

Turning the can of car polish in his hands, Tom found the reason it had been "rejected": A small dent in the side of the can. Although such rejects were not given to employees, it was not uncommon for warehouse personnel to "help themselves" when they had a need for some item. "After all," they reasoned, "these rejects are to be destroyed, so it's no loss to the company."

III

Larry Peters looked over his travel expense form. He had just returned from his first sales trip with the Sun-Ripe Food Company. During his training period, Larry had been associated with several of the other salesmen of his district. From his conversations with these men Larry understood that it was common practice for the salesmen to report travel expenses equal to the amount allowed by the company, whether they spent that amount or not. For example, if a salesman spent only $25 of the allotted $40 per day, he reported the full $40 and kept the difference. They justified this practice in the following manner: "If the company is willing to have one spend $8 on a steak dinner, but I would just as soon have a hamburger, why shouldn't I keep what I save?"

IV

Herb Schelling studied his shipping records carefully. There seemed to be no question about it—one of the tank cars which had been shipped that morning was contaminated.

Herb was the shipping coordinator for the Ace Chemical Corporation. Most of the company's products were shipped in railroad tank cars to a wide variety of industrial customers. Since a variety of products were shipped, a tank car had to be flushed out if its shipment was different from the chemical which it had previously carried. Herb's subordinates had told him that no cars had been flushed that morning because they had all previously contained the same chemical that was being shipped that morning. Herb's records, however, clearly showed that this had not been the case. One car had carried a different chemical and therefore should have been flushed.

Herb considered the possible consequences of letting this shipment continue. He knew that the contaminating chemical would not react with the shipment. Furthermore, there seemed to be little chance that the customer would encounter difficulties in processing the chemical. This, however, would depend upon the use to which the chemical was put. For some uses it is possible that the "batch" in which the chemical was used would be ruined. The customer in question was a small plant which ordered only about five cars each year from Ace. Schelling knew that he would risk losing this customer if they should encounter problems with the shipment. However, he felt confident that the chances of such problems arising were quite slim.

On the other hand, the cost of correcting the error would undoubtedly be very high. The shipment would have to be called back and another sent in its place. The contents of the shipment would have to be reprocessed, or possibly disposed of. Herb estimated that the cost of such an effort would be between five and ten thousand dollars. In addition, the customer had placed a "rush" on this order and would not appreciate a delay.

1. What factors will likely influence individual actions in each of these situations?
2. Under what circumstances, if any, should an ethical position be compromised?
3. What could an enterprise do to help employees attain a higher standard of ethics in dealing with these situations?

section two

Management of the business enterprise

*Investment in new
construction projects is
undertaken because of
the expectation of profits.*

You need to understand the profit motive. It is one of the essential characteristics of the private enterprise system. The profit motive has been attacked by some groups in recent years as being not quite legitimate in today's modern and complex society. In fact, some business executives are apologetic about the profit motive. They turn discussions on profits to other aspects of business such as the provision of goods and services, providing jobs, or supporting community betterment programs. Many attacks on the profit motive and apologies for profits may be traced to a lack of understanding of the role of profits in our economic system.

In this chapter the following questions which deal with profit and the profit motive are discussed:

What is the profit motive?
How are profits defined?
How do risks relate to profits?
What are the functions of the profit motive?
How profitable are American corporations?

DEFINITION OF THE PROFIT MOTIVE

Both words in the phrase "profit motive" are important. *Profit* is what is left after all appropriate costs have been deducted from business revenues. A *motive* is a drive, impulse, or desire that moves one to action. Thus the *profit motive* refers to the financial difference between revenues and costs as an incentive to action. The profit motive is in operation when individuals, partnerships, or corporations undertake economic ac-

4

The role of profits

tivity because the prospects are that sales revenue will exceed expenses. An important aspect of the profit motive is that we are motivated to take economic action because of prospects for *future* profits. Business managers are influenced by past profits (or losses) only as the events of the past may provide information about probable happenings in the future.

The profit motive implies that people are stimulated to undertake economic activity because of the expectation of profit. However, in a private enterprise society there is no guarantee that profits will result from business activity. When costs exceed revenues, the company operates at a loss. An enterprise may be able to operate at a loss for a time before being forced out of business. However, over the long run the private business enterprise must generate some profits in order to survive. Thus, while the profit motive may stimulate economic activity by business, the possibility of loss also exists. Because of this risk of loss the private enterprise system is sometimes referred to as a *profit and loss system*.

CALCULATION OF BUSINESS PROFIT

Business profit is calculated by subtracting the appropriate portion of fixed and variable costs from the total receipts from the sale of a product. *Fixed costs* are those costs which continue whether or not the enterprise is producing goods. Fixed costs include such expenses as rent, property taxes, and the interest on borrowed money. *Variable costs* are directly influenced by the number of units produced. Variable costs include such expenses as materials used in the production of goods and the wages of production workers. In general the costs provide for returns to all factors of production except for the owners of the business enterprise. What is left after the deduction of all "outsiders" costs represents *business profit* and accrues to the owners of the business enterprise. The calculation of business profit is discussed in more detail in Chapter 13 on accounting. The business profit figure is on the bottom line of the accounting report called the Income Statement. It is labeled as net income or net profit if the figure is positive. If total costs exceed income, the figure is negative and represents a business loss.

BUSINESS RISKS

The profit motive causes an owner of business to assume the risks inherent in the production and distribution of goods and services in a

FIGURE 4–1
Types of risks faced by business enterprises

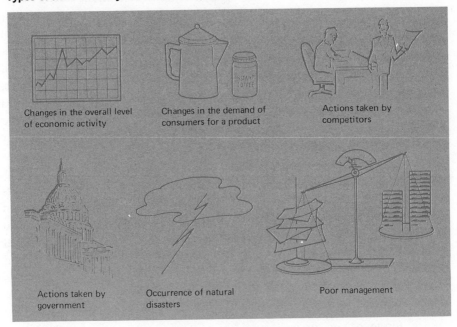

Changes in the overall level
of economic activity

Changes in the demand of
consumers for a product

Actions taken by
competitors

Actions taken by
government

Occurrence of natural
disasters

Poor management

private enterprise economy. Among the many risks involved in the
operation of a business enterprise are the six illustrated in Figure 4–1.

Risk due to changes in overall economic activity

In our country there are fluctuations in the level of economic activity
which are characteristic of industrialized economies. The fluctuations
in business activity affect both individuals and organizations in our economy. Business fluctuations are of concern to government because of their
impact on orderly economic growth. Business managers are interested
in business fluctuations because of their influence on operations and
their impact on profitability.

Economists have identified three types of fluctuations in economic
activity. These are the trend, seasonal changes, and business cycles.

The trend. The *trend* is the underlying long-run tendency which
persists despite shorter term changes. In the United States the trend
in overall economic activity has been upward at a rate of about 3 percent per year in real growth of goods and services. This upward trend

is due to many factors including the development of a new continent, natural resources, increases in population, increases in the stock of capital goods, improved productivity of labor, better management, and continuing technological development.

Seasonal changes. *Seasonal changes* are due to the changing seasons of the year, to holidays, or to the calendar. Certain agricultural products are available for processing only at particular times of the year. Both manufacturing and retailing enterprises are affected by sales demand stemming from the Christmas holiday period and the Easter season. Extra shopping days in a month due to variations in our calendar and the timing of paydays by business enterprises also contribute to seasonal changes in economic activity.

Business cycles. The trend and seasonal fluctuations are overshadowed in the short run by the recurring expansion and contraction of the level of business activity. These recurring variations are called *business cycles.* Starting from a low in cyclical business activity called a *trough* in the business cycle, the generation of demand for goods and services from a relatively low level causes business to expand production. Numerous factors may account for expansion of production including increased government or consumer spending to increase demand for goods and services.

As production expands, earning power improves, and the economy moves into a period of "recovery" or "expansion." Some industries show improved business conditions. This spreads to other industries, and the expansion continues until a *peak* in business activity is reached. The peak is followed by a decline in business activity called a "recession" or "contraction." The factors which contribute to the decline include reduced spending by business for capital equipment, excessive inventories built up during expansion which when cut back reduce production, and changing patterns of consumption. Recessions have also occurred in the adjustment of the economy following some of the wars in which the United States fought. Should a recession become pronounced and prolonged it is called a depression. Figure 4–2 illustrates the overall growth of the Gross National Product, the total goods and services produced in the economy. The trend line shows a 3.1 percent growth rate. Periods of recession in business activity are indicated in white on the chart.

Business cycles have been the subject of extensive study. A number of explanations have been advanced as to the cause of business cycles. These reasons include the cost and amount of credit available;

FIGURE 4–2
Gross National Product in constant dollars and average growth rate

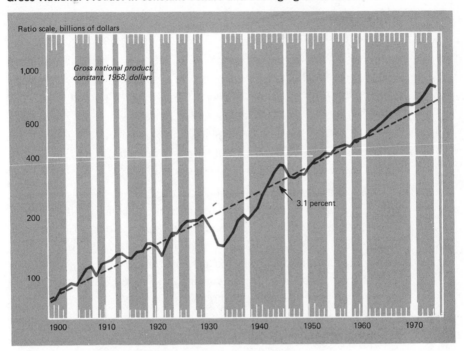

Source: Federal Reserve System, *Historical Chart Book*, 1975

changes in consumption, saving, and investment patterns; whether there are innovations, such as the invention of the automobile or the discovery of plastic which create opportunities for further investment; and the prevailing psychological climate—whether business or consumers tend to be generally optimistic or pessimistic about the future. Many economists believe business cycles are caused by a number of factors with no single explanation being sufficient for this problem.

The National Bureau of Economic Research, a private nonprofit research organization,. has identified economic indicators which normally tend to either lead, lag, or coincide with the general level of economic activity. Examples of the leading series are:

Average hours worked per week by employees in manufacturing.
New orders for durable goods industries.
New building permits for private housing.
Corporate profits after taxes.
Changes in business inventories.

Examples of the economic indicators which tend to coincide with the business cycle are:

Employment in nonagricultural enterprises.
Index of industrial production.
Level of Gross National Product.
Sales of retail stores.

Examples of the economic indicators which tend to lag or follow the business cycle are:

Business expenditures for new plants and equipment.
Wage and salary cost per unit of output in manufacturing.
Bank interest rates on short-term business loans.

Despite the complexity of business cycles and of forecasting them, business managers should attempt to anticipate fluctuations in the overall level of economic activity and make applications to their own industries and enterprises. Help is available from private sources such as trade associations and from federal government agencies which employ economists to measure the current state of the economy and attempt to forecast its direction of movement.

Risk due to changes in consumer demand

A business manager must also be concerned with the market demand for the enterprise's product. Even though the product is as good or better than the competitor's product, there is no guarantee that a profit will be made. There may be a shift in consumer demand away from the entire industry. Look what the development of the automobile did to the sale of buggy whips!

Actions taken by competitors

The business manager also must be aware of what competitors are doing. Profits are threatened whenever new products are brought onto the market by competitors or whenever they take actions such as lowering the price of goods or lengthening the credit terms extended to customers.

Actions taken by government

Actions taken by governmental bodies may substantially affect the profit of business enterprise. Such activities range from restriction by a city council on a manufacturer's dumping of waste products to a U.S. Justice Department suit to block a merger between two firms which might reduce competition.

Natural disasters

The impact on business profits of some natural disasters, such as fire, hail, and wind damage, can be minimized by taking out insurance, but it is not possible to eliminate all such risks. The business enterprise which has its main plants located along a large river that periodically floods may find the cost of flood insurance will be extremely expensive if it is available. Also, it is difficult to measure the impact on business profits of a natural disaster in terms of the opportunity to operate normally had the event not occurred.

Poor management

Last, but not least in importance of the risks faced by business, is the possibility of financial loss because of poor management. Big business is not immune to poor management, but the small business enterprise is especially vulnerable to this risk. Problems of morale, organization, and communication are often found in the small business. A common problem of small businesses is that they are too small to obtain the management skills they need. The top jobs in small and medium-size business enterprises may require as much ability and greater versatility than similar positions in big business. The small business is faced with a lack of financial resources to hire competent management. Generally there are fewer managers available in the small firm for specialized decisions. Sometimes the business is family-owned, and the best jobs go to family members regardless of their qualifications. This tends to discourage good people from accepting employment in the small business enterprise. Too often small business managers are not willing to subject their decisions to outside advice, a common practice for the top management of a large-scale business enterprise.

Willingness of businessmen to bear risks

With this long list of risks that could result in losses, you may wonder why people are willing to invest money in business enterprises. However, Americans show a surprising willingness to bear risk. The degree of risk investors are willing to assume depends on profit expectations. Normally, additional risks will be assumed only if there is a chance to earn profits high enough to justify the risk.

Some industries have traditionally been more stable with less risk than those which are speculative in nature. An industry which has been relatively stable has been that of electric utilities. The well-defined growth of demand for electric power and the monopoly nature of electric utilities with government regulation of rates has generally assured profitable operations. However, even in the utilities industry the higher interest rates on borrowed money and the increased operating costs have demonstrated that no industry is without some risk. In 1974 Consolidated Edison, which supplies electric power to New York City, briefly eliminated cash dividends to common stockholders because of financial difficulties.

On the other hand, a much greater degree of risk is assumed by the "wildcat" oil drilling operator where there are wide ranges of profit potential. The possibilities for the oil driller range from a dry hole with a complete loss of money invested to the gusher which will return substantial profits.

Why do some persons invest in utilities while others invest their last dollars in a drilling company which may bring either fortune or bitter disappointment? The difference is in the subjective values each places upon risk bearing. The former wants security, and the latter's slogan is "nothing ventured, nothing gained." Neither investor is right or wrong in his willingness to accept risk. They merely express different preferences, and both are needed to provide the wide variety of investments required in our complex private enterprise system. What is your attitude toward investment risk?

Business failures

Although profit is an important goal and motivating force behind business activities, not all enterprises succeed in making a profit. If a business does not earn a profit for a period of time it is likely to go bankrupt. How long this will take depends upon the financial strength of the enterprise, the amount of losses, the availability of credit, and the expectations for improved conditions.

The rate of business failures is shown in Figure 4–3. Failures declined from a high in 1939 of 70 per year for each 10,000 enterprises to a low in 1945 of 4. In 1974 the failure rate was 38.4.

FIGURE 4–3
Business failure rates, 1939–1974

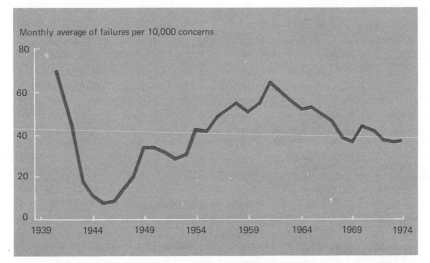

Source: U.S. Department of Commerce, *Business Statistics.* 1973 ed., and *Survey of Current Business,* March 1975.

Characteristics of failing enterprises. Typically about three fourths of the business enterprises that fail owe less than $100,000 at the time of failure. This indicates that a high proportion of failures are in small enterprises. Many of these failures are in new companies. The majority of business failures occur in enterprises no more than five years old. Dun & Bradstreet, which specializes in the analysis and rating of business credit, reports that failure rates in 1973 were highest in retail stores selling men's and women's clothing, infants' and children's wear, gifts, books, furniture, and sporting goods. Failure rates in manufacturing were relatively high in the leather and shoe industry, transportation equipment, and apparel manufacturing.[1]

Dun & Bradstreet indicates that over 90 percent of the causes of business failure could be classified under the general heading of poor management. The underlying causes of these failures are lack of experience in the industry, lack of managerial experience, and general incompetence. These resulted in an inability to compete, inadequate sales, heavy operating expenses, poor credit management, and improper inventory management. This evidence emphasizes the im-

---

[1] *The Business Failure Record 1973* (New York: Dun & Bradstreet, Inc., 1974), p. 3.

portance of effective management of the business enterprise, especially in its early years.

Use of economic resources. In the private enterprise system it is important that businesses have the freedom to make a profit, but it is also necessary that inefficient enterprises fail. The business enterprise that fails does so because it is not as efficient in meeting the needs of consumers as someone else is. The economic resources which were used by enterprises that fail flow to the successful enterprises to be employed so as to make a profit. The profit motive gives an incentive to produce goods and services at a competitive price and quality. Thus, the profit motive results in the efficient utilization of resources to provide those goods and services which you as a consumer desire to purchase.

FUNCTIONS OF THE PROFIT MOTIVE

There are three important functions which the profit motive fulfills in the private enterprise system. These are the allocation of economic resources to the goods and services most desired by consumers, stimulation of our economy to greater levels of production and consumption, and the provision of a means for choosing among various investment opportunities.

The profit motive and allocation of resources

In any society the supply of goods and services is limited in the short run. This means all our material wants cannot be satisfied. At any given time there is just so much capacity for producing steel, assembling automobiles, processing food, or generating electric power.

How are resources allocated among various alternative uses in the economy? How do business managers determine whether to produce automobiles, or tractors, or motorcycles? In the private enterprise system in the United States the allocation of the economy's resources is accomplished in large measure by the expectation of profits on the part of those who control productive goods. A manufacturer produces ten-speed bicycles because of the belief they can be sold at a profit. If the manufacturer has correctly assessed our wants, there will be a demand for such bicycles. Basically, goods and services are provided by enterprises in response to consumer demand, although at times consumer demand can be influenced or stimulated through sales promotion programs.

The result of each producer attempting to market goods and services with the expectation of profit will theoretically be the allocation of resources to those goods which are most desired by our society. The statement that the profit motive results in allocation of goods to fulfill most desired needs is based on several assumptions: that producers are able to move freely into and out of markets, that competition exists among sellers, and that buyers have full knowledge of competing products. However, in the reality of our complex society these conditions are seldom, if ever, met. Because of large investment and the need for skilled workers and technological know-how, it is not possible to start or stop many business operations easily. A steel mill with its large investment in plant and equipment, skilled work force, and research laboratories is a good example of a business enterprise which cannot be established quickly even though the stimulant of profit prospects exists. Once an entrepreneur, along with many others, has made a large investment in a steel mill it is difficult to quit the steel business, sell its assets, and move the funds to some other type of business.

There are still some enterprises, such as the dry-cleaning business, which offer greater ease of entry and exit. Unlike the steel mill, dry cleaning does not require as much capital, as many skilled workers, or such a diversity of technological know-how. Furthermore, manufacturers of dry-cleaning equipment are generally willing to finance the necessary machinery, provide managerial assistance, and aid in determining a good shop location. If the business does not develop into a profitable operation, a market exists for the used equipment. Thus the entrepreneur may be able to withdraw from the dry-cleaning business with a minimum loss of capital. The larger and more complex the business enterprise, the greater the difficulty of entry and exit. Service enterprises and small retailing establishments provide the greatest ease of entry into and exit from the marketplace.

There are other limits to the statement that the profit motive results in the allocation of economic resources as desired by consumers. An enterprise may gain control of the production of some good. This control over the supply side of the market by one producer is called a *monopoly*. With monopoly control the producer may set prices higher than might be the case if there were many suppliers competing to sell that particular product. The higher profit which results from this control over supply is called *monopoly profit*. You will recall from Chapter 2 that Congress has enacted laws to control the growth and actions of monopolists to protect the public. The general intent of Congress has been to prohibit restraint of trade, unregulated monopolies, unjustified price competition, unfair competition, and generally to protect the public's interest in the marketplace.

In addition to the possibility of monopoly, there are other factors which influence the allocation of resources in our economy. These include government controls, especially in time of national emergency; geographic limits on both producers and consumers; and traditional preferences toward goods, such as consumer allegiance to brand names.

Despite these limiting factors, when profits occur this is a good sign that our society wants a particular industry to expand. When an industry or a firm does not make a profit and suffers losses, this is often a signal that consumers are not anxious to have more resources devoted to this purpose. The absence of profits for a year or so is not necessarily proof that the resources should be changed to some other type of operation since profits or losses are dependent on many factors. However, when a business enterprise suffers losses, this is a sign for the management to investigate the cause of the loss with the possibility of allocating future capital spending to fields where the expectation of profits is greater.

The profit motive and increased production of goods and services

Because of the expectation of profits, the entrepreneur is stimulated to invest resources in a business enterprise. This sets off a chain reaction throughout the economy whereby demands for other goods and services are stimulated by utilizing the human and material resources of our economy more fully. As the goods or services produced by business are purchased by consumers, consumption needs are being met. The production of these goods provides employment for more workers and a higher level of personal income. As the result of increased income, individuals are able to consume more goods and services which in turn stimulates the demand for additional production. Buildings are purchased or rented and these rents can be spent by landlords. Machinery is purchased from other manufacturers who employ workers and capital resources. All of this activity stemming from the enterprise's investment based on the expectation of profits tends to stimulate the economy.

Profits may result from the entrepreneur providing a new product or significant improvement or greater variety of an old product. When this happens profit is a reward for venturing out and providing a new good or improving existing products. The entrepreneur's ventures do not succeed in every case. Frequently a new business enterprise will lose money instead of making a profit, but the profit motive encourages men and women to make other innovations to meet our basic and ever-changing acquired needs.

The profit motive and choice of investment alternatives

The profit motive provides a criterion for management in determining which investment projects to select from a variety of alternatives. The rate of profit expected on a project in relation to risk may be the key factor in deciding which piece of machinery to purchase, whether to build a new factory, or how to market a new product. It is unlikely that enough funds will be available for all investment possibilities. Some screening device must be adopted to establish project priorities. The rate of expected profit on each project is an excellent criterion for investment suitability.

The simplest way of measuring profitability is to calculate the percent of profit in relation to the asset value of the investment. Thus if profits on a piece of machinery were anticipated at a level of $3,000 annually and the machine cost $15,000 including installation, the expected return on this investment would be 20 percent.

PROFITABILITY OF AMERICAN CORPORATIONS

Critics of the American private enterprise system often say that profits earned by corporations are too high. Let us examine some of the data which are available to determine the magnitude of corporate profits.

Table 4–1 shows the ratio of profits to sales for all manufacturing corporations in the United States and for selected industries for 1966, 1970, and 1974. Corporate profits in 1966 were $50 billion after taxes, which was a historic high at the time and the highest as a percentage of sales since 1950. The year 1970 was a year of recession with a drop in profits to $39 billion. Corporate profits rose to $85 billion in 1974.

Table 4–1 indicates that the profit percentage on sales for all manu-facturing corporations in 1974 was 5.5 percent after taxes and 4.0 per-

TABLE 4–1

Manufacturing corporations' profits as a percentage of sales, 1966, 1970, and 1974, after federal income taxes

	1966	1970	1974
All manufacturing corporations.....................	5.6	4.0	5.5
Petroleum..	11.2	9.3	12.7
Drugs..	10.8	9.4	12.2
Instruments......................................	9.5	7.3	9.3
Chemicals..	8.0	5.0	8.2
Motor vehicles and equipment....................	6.2	2.4	2.7
Tobacco manufactures............................	5.9	5.8	9.1
Iron and steel...................................	5.8	2.5	6.3
Electrical equipment.............................	4.8	3.3	3.9
Aircraft and parts...............................	3.0	2.0	3.0
Food and kindred products.......................	2.7	2.5	2.8
Textile products.................................	2.4	1.9	2.5

Source: Federal Trade Commission and Securities and Exchange Commission.

cent after taxes in 1970. The highest return on sales was in the petroleum, drugs, and instruments industries. Several industries earned 3 percent or less on sales after taxes in all three years.

Another way of measuring profits is the ratio of profits to the owners' equity. This is the measure of profitability on the invested capital of corporation stockholders. Table 4–2 shows the ratio of profits to owners'

TABLE 4–2

Manufacturing corporations' profits as a percentage of owners' equity, 1966, 1970, and 1974, after federal income taxes

	1966	1970	1974
All manufacturing corporations.....................	13.4	9.3	14.9
Instruments......................................	20.9	14.2	16.1
Drugs..	20.3	17.6	18.8
Motor vehicles and equipment....................	15.9	6.1	6.9
Electrical equipment.............................	14.8	9.1	11.1
Aircraft and parts...............................	14.4	6.8	10.6
Tobacco manufacturers...........................	14.1	15.7	15.6
Chemicals..	14.0	8.5	17.5
Textile products.................................	13.3	9.3	8.2
Petroleum..	12.4	11.0	21.0
Food and kindred products.......................	11.2	10.8	14.0
Iron and steel...................................	10.2	4.3	16.8

Source: Federal Trade Commission and Securities and Exchange Commission.

FIGURE 4-4

Corporate profits, taxes, and dividends, 1929–1974

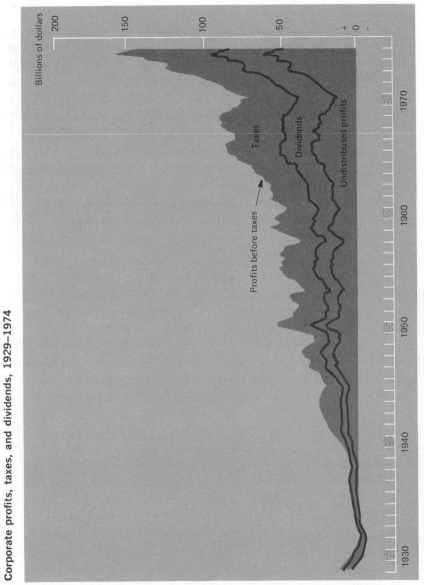

Source: Federal Reserve System, *Historical Chart Book*, 1975.

equity for all manufacturing corporations in the United States and for selected industries in 1966, 1970, and 1974.

In periods of recession, business profits are reduced as Tables 4–1 and 4–2 indicate. Pressures from competing business enterprises, labor unions, and government tax policies also tend to reduce unusually high profits. Historically, business profits have been unstable although trending upward. This is illustrated by Figure 4–4, which shows corporate profits before taxes, taxes, dividends (profits paid to stockholders), and undistributed profits (profits retained by the business enterprise) from 1929 through 1974.

Any statement about the level of profits being good or bad represents a value judgment on the part of the person making the statement. Would you be willing to go into business, assume the risks of investing your own money, and then have a return on your investment of no more than that shown? It may be that the critics of the profit (and loss) system are focusing on individual cases of excesses or abuses and not on the overall level of profits.

What about profit maximization?

Business enterprises seldom attempt to maximize profits at the expense of everything else. Producing a product of shoddy quality to be sold at a premium quality price may succeed until consumers become aware of the inconsistency. However, this enterprise's share of the market is likely to decline when the product's shortcomings are discovered. This will result in lower sales and perhaps substantial losses to the manufacturer. The best managed enterprises take a long-run view of profit potential.

It is questionable whether a realistic objective of today's business enterprise is to *maximize* profits, especially over a short period of time. Also, there is the further question of whether the business manager is able to determine at just what point profits are being maximized. Although economists can describe the theoretical conditions when profits will be maximized, it is very difficult for management to determine this in an actual business situation.

Even though business managers may not be able to determine the point at which their operations return maximum profits, this has not reduced the importance of the profit motive to business. Executives of large corporations proclaim the importance of business's social responsibility to the community and the increased financial support by business for charitable, educational, and welfare projects. However, such support comes from business enterprises which are operating profitably and where the rate of return on the owner's investment is satisfactory considering the degree of risk involved. A satisfactory level of profits may be defined as profits which are high enough to attract sufficient capital investment to provide the level of goods and services desired by the consuming public.

Profit is an essential element of the private enterprise system where capital is privately owned and controlled. Just as individuals do not always act only as economic beings, so business enterprises which are managed by humans do not always operate strictly on a dollar profit basis. However, the expectation of profit represents the carrot of incentive to stimulate individuals and enterprises to invest money to produce goods and services which we consumers want.

SUMMARY

One of the essential characteristics of the private enterprise system is the profit motive which moves individuals and business enterprises to undertake economic activity because of the prospects of receipts which are greater than the expenses necessary to generate the receipts.

Business profits are calculated by subtracting appropriate fixed and variable costs from the total sales receipts of an enterprise. The difference between the revenues and attendant costs is the profit.

Although business managers seek a profit from enterprise operations, there are a variety of risks which may result in losses. Business risks include changes in the overall level of economic activity, changes in consumer demand, actions taken by competitors, actions taken by government, natural disasters, and poor management.

A business enterprise can be expected to fail if it does not earn a profit over a long period of time. When an enterprise fails, the capital resources which were used by it flow to enterprises which appear to have better prospects for profitable utilization.

Thus, the profit motive serves to allocate economic resources to those goods and services which are most desired by consumers. It stimulates the economy to greater levels of production and consumption and provides an important criterion for choosing among various investment opportunities.

Two ways of calculating profits are to determine the ratio of profit after taxes to sales and the ratio of profit after taxes to owners' equity.

Most enterprises do not attempt to maximize profits in the short run because it is difficult to determine the operational point at which profit is being maximized and because businesses may have other goals which tend to negate the sole pursuit of profit. Most owners and managers do seek a satisfactory level of profits, which may be defined as profits high enough to attract capital investment in sufficient quantity to provide the level of goods and services desired by the consuming public.

Appendix
Economic profit: An alternative definition of profit

DEFINITION OF ECONOMIC PROFIT

Business managers and economists view profit somewhat differently. The distinction between business profits and economic profits depends upon the definition of the costs which are considered in the calculation of each. The concept of *economic profit* requires the subtraction of opportunity costs from business profits. *Opportunity cost* is an important economic concept and represents the cost assumed when persons or business enterprises forgo the alternative of making some other use of their economic assets. There are various ways in which economic assets may be employed. When persons elect to invest their money in a particular business enterprise they give up the opportunity of investing those funds in any other way, at least for the time being. The opportunity cost for those funds would be what they could earn employed in some other manner and would be subtracted from business profits to obtain an economic profit figure.

Opportunity cost can also be applied by individuals to the value of their labor as they consider how much their work efforts might be worth in another enterprise. In a proprietorship the opportunity cost of the owner's labor would be deducted from business profit to determine economic profit.

EXAMPLE OF CALCULATION OF ECONOMIC PROFIT IN A PROPRIETORSHIP

As an example of how the concept of economic profit might apply to an individual, consider a man who owns and works in his small retail store. The shop is organized as a proprietorship, and in 1975 a business profit of $15,000 was calculated for the year. In the proprietorship form of legal organization the owner's work efforts are not considered a business cost, so the owner does not receive a salary for working in the store. Any money the owner takes out of the enterprise is simply a withdrawal of part of the investment made as the proprietor of the store.

The owner has had an offer to work for a large discount store for an annual salary of $10,000 and is considering whether it would be better to continue as a business owner or to take the job at the discount store. The $25,000 presently invested in the retail store could be invested in some other way if the store were sold. Using the concept of economic profit to help make a decision, the store owner would make the following calculations:

Business profit for 1975.................................		$15,000
(Total receipts from the sale of goods less appropriate portion of fixed and variable costs.)		
Less opportunity costs:		
Alternative salary cost.................................	$10,000	
Imputed interest cost.................................	1,250	
(Amount that could be earned from $25,000 derived from sale of store and invested at 5% in a bank savings account.)		
Total opportunity costs..........................		11,250
Economic profit...		$ 3,750

The proprietor, using this analysis, would see that in 1975 the economic profit was $3,750. What should then be considered are the advantages and disadvantages of owning one's own store compared with being an employee of the discount store. Some factors to be weighed are the independence of being one's own boss plus the additional $3,750 against the extra responsibility, longer hours, and greater uncertainties an owner faces.

APPLICATION AND LIMITATIONS OF THE CONCEPT OF ECONOMIC PROFIT

Consideration of the concept of economic profit may be valuable to a person in business in the selection of projects for the investment of economic resources. A careful appraisal should be made of the full range of investment alternatives open before committing time or money to a particular project. The question, "Is this the best opportunity available to me for the investment of money and effort?" can be a valuable check before a project is undertaken to see if profit prospects are consistent with the amount of risk the individual is willing to assume.

However, you should realize that there are some significant problems involved in the determination of opportunity costs. Should the value of labor be calculated by its worth in another enterprise? A person might have an offer for employment in another business, but this would be the situation only in a limited number of cases. To change one's place of employment might mean severe personal adjustments which could be more costly than the money benefits to be gained. Generally it is difficult for a person to determine what alternative value should be placed on his own work efforts.

Problems also arise when the concept of opportunity costs is applied to the money a proprietor has invested in a business enterprise. Should the alternative calculation be on an investment in the same risk class as the present business operation? Or should the calculation be made on a lower-risk investment such as government bonds or an insured savings account? The savings account may earn less than the present investment, but also would have less business risk.

An awareness of the concept of economic profit with its consideration of opportunity costs, even though such costs are difficult to calculate, may provide useful insights in business decision making. However, the concept of business profit is used in this book since business profit provides the basis for our system of financial and investment analysis, taxation, and industry comparisons. You will recall that business profit is calculated by subtracting the appropriate fixed and variable costs from the receipts for the sale of a product.

TERMS FOR REVIEW

profit	*business cycle*
profit motive	*economic indicators*
business profit	*monopoly profit*
trend	*ratio of profits to sales*
seasonal changes	*ratio of profits to owners' equity*

QUESTIONS

1. What is business profit? How is it determined?
2. Are all types of business enterprises equally subject to the various kinds of business risks? Give specific examples to explain your answer.
3. By checking publications such as *Business Conditions Digest* (published by the Commerce Department), *Survey of Current Business,* or the *Federal Reserve Bulletin,* determine the status of the economic indi-

cators outlined in this chapter and the present state of the business cycle.

4. *a.* Why do business enterprises fail?

   b. Do you agree with the statement "It is necessary that inefficient enterprises fail"? State the reasons for your answer.

5. How may the profit motive serve the public interest?

6. *a.* What explanations might there be for the wide variation in profit percentages among different manufacturing industries (see Tables 4–1 and 4–2)?

   b. Explain the variation in profit percentages in the same industry from one year to another.

Business briefs

Offshore oil drilling

Oil drilling rights to a large underwater area in the northern Gulf of Mexico off the coasts of Mississippi, Alabama, and Florida were sold by the federal government in December 1973. Oil companies paid $1.5 billion for drilling rights on 485,000 acres offshore.

The U.S. Geological Survey had estimated that the tracts contained between 2 and 4 billion barrels of oil. Other experts estimated the region might have more oil than the western Gulf of Mexico where about 8 billion barrels of oil have been found.

A dozen drilling tracts south of Mobile, Alabama, sold for $230 million. In 1974 Mobil and California Standard both drilled dry holes in the area. In another area a group of oil companies composed of Champlin Petroleum, Exxon, and Mobil spent over $600 million for six tracts. This group sunk two dry holes. One was in a tract which cost over $200 million.

The oil companies have not given up on their $1.5 billion investment. More wildcat wells will be drilled. Executives recalled that dozens of dry holes were drilled before the big oil strikes were found in the North Sea fields. However, as of late 1974 the only oil discovery in the northern Gulf area was on a tract adjacent to a producing oil field off Louisiana.

1. Why would oil companies pay hundreds of millions of dollars for offshore drilling rights in unproven oil fields?

2. As a director of one of these oil companies, would you approve

additional millions of dollars for further wildcat drilling operations
in the area?

3. In view of America's need for more oil reserves, should further
incentives be provided by government for wildcat drilling operations
(drilling in unproven fields)?

The cost of crimes against business

The cost of crimes against business increased to $20 billion in 1974
from $18 billion in 1973 and $15 billion in 1971 according to estimates
by the U.S. Department of Commerce. This amounted to $89 for each
man, woman, and child in the country and equaled about 17 percent of
total corporation profits for 1974.

These losses by business were from "ordinary" crimes such as
burglary, robbery, vandalism, arson, bad checks, credit card fraud, and
employee theft. The Commerce Department figures generally did not
include losses from embezzlement, airplane hijacking, or organized
crime.

Crime losses by retailers reached almost $6 billion in 1974, an in-
crease of 20 percent over 1971. Losses by wholesalers exceeded $2
billion, up a whopping 50 percent from 1971.

1. What can be done to reduce the incidence of crimes against business?
2. What can business do to reduce the impact of these crimes on profits?
3. How is the public affected by crimes against business?

Case

Jack Anderson

Jack Anderson graduated ten years ago from a large school of business administration located near his home town in the southwest. While
in college Jack had studied management under Professor Montgomery,
who had taken a personal interest in him and had followed his career
since graduation. When he was visiting in his home town, Jack would
drive over to the university to chat with Professor Montgomery about
his work and economic conditions in general. The following conversation took place during Jack's most recent visit.

"Dr. Montgomery, I'm facing a real crossroads in my life," said Jack

Anderson. "As you know, after I graduated I joined a large New York department store in their merchandising training program. While the starting salary wasn't as good as some of the other job offers I had, the opportunities developed very nicely for me. I was made an assistant buyer and then promoted to the job of buyer of women's coats. Two years ago I joined a New York firm which provides smaller merchandisers across the country with assistance and buying power in the major clothing markets. I have been pleased with this move. It has broadened my experience and I have made many contacts in the industry.

"Last year I had an offer to take a buying job with a major chain store organization which would have meant a move to Chicago. After my wife and I talked it over we decided against the change. It would have narrowed my contacts in the industry and the money wasn't that much more than I was already making.

"Now we're faced with another major decision. Two weeks ago I was contacted by the owner of a clothing store in Orlando, Florida. He wants to sell out and retire because of a heart condition which his doctor has just diagnosed. He contacted me as I had helped him on a number of sales promotions which gave us the chance to become acquainted over the past two years.

"The business apparently is considered to be one of the better clothing stores in the community. While the store does most of its business in men's clothing, there is a women's clothing department which has been remodeled and has shown a good increase in sales recently. This department specializes in women's sportswear.

"My wife and I would have to invest essentially all of our savings in the down payment for this store. The present owner would be willing to finance the rest of the purchase price by a loan which would have to be paid over the next ten years. There is a bank in the community which has been providing short-term loans to finance the purchase of merchandise for the principal selling seasons. I suppose they would continue these credit arrangements if I were to purchase the business.

"We've enjoyed living in New York City these past years. I guess it would take some adjustment to a smaller city although both of us grew up in small communities in the southwest. Of course my wife is concerned about schools right now since our boy will be six years old his next birthday.

"I doubt that I would be able to draw as large a salary out of the business as I'm presently making in New York. But, if the area looks like a good prospect for retail sales growth, I should be able to do very well after a year or two.

"I don't feel like I absolutely have to make a move at this time. I'm doing well where I am. Also, I think there will be other opportunities in the future if I want to get out of the 'rat race' in New York. However, the idea of owning my own business is one I've toyed around with for some time. This is an attractive situation and the price would probably work out to be a fair one.

"I suppose the reason I came by today, Dr. Montgomery, is that I want you to react to these ramblings of mine. What do you think of this situation?"

1. Assume that this conversation occurred in the context of the present economic conditions. How would you respond to Jack Anderson's conversation if you were in the professor's position?
2. What factors should Anderson take into account in arriving at a decision?
3. How could Jack Anderson obtain answers to the questions which would be raised in Question 2?
4. If you were in Jack Anderson's position what would you do next? Why?

Planning is an important part of the management process.

*B*usiness management has been called the oldest of the arts and the youngest of the professions. From the time people began to specialize their labors, problems of coordination have arisen which have required managerial attention. Earlier studies of management have come from schools of public administration where techniques for the administration of governmental bodies were developed. Today the practice of management has benefited from the findings of the behavioral sciences of psychology, anthropology, and sociology. The systems concept adapted from the natural sciences and the use of electronic computers also aid management. Many of the generalizations regarding management are applicable to any institution or group which has common objectives. However, our discussion will center on the business enterprise as the focal point of managerial activities.

The following issues are discussed regarding management of the business enterprise:

What is the nature of management?
How does the systems approach relate to management of the business enterprise?
Why is planning necessary for successful operations?
What factors are considered in developing the organizational structure of the business system?
How do authority-responsibility relationships apply to management?
What is the relationship between line and staff functions in the business system?

5

Management

THE NATURE OF MANAGEMENT

Management may be defined as achieving results by coordinating the activities of other people. This means that the manager provides leadership which results in the achievement of the objectives of the organization. There are many dimensions to managerial activity. A supervisor in a factory acts as a manager when scheduling production runs and making work assignments for employees. The vice president for marketing acts as a manager when confering with district sales supervisors to work out the marketing program for the coming season. In turn the district sales supervisors act as managers when they organize and direct their sales people to contact customers and sell the enterprise's products. In all these examples the function of the manager is to provide an environment for others to perform the actual work involved in the production and distribution of the enterprise's products.

An individual who is designated as a member of management may on occasion also do some specific work in producing or selling the enterprise's product. Sometimes even the president will act as a sales person in entertaining important customers or in working out an important contract. However, when a person has the label of "manager" this implies that the individual's main responsibility lies in indirect achievement rather than in the actual production of goods or services.

Management has also been called the art of decision making. It is true that managers are required to make decisions in the process of problem solving. Some of the outstanding managers in this country have been able under difficult conditions to make decisions which have been proven to be sound by the events that followed. The types of managerial decisions vary from those made by the board of directors and president of an enterprise as to whether to produce a new product to a supervisor's responsibility for assigning workers to particular jobs.

A SYSTEMS APPROACH TO MANAGEMENT OF THE BUSINESS ENTERPRISE

In the appendix to Chapter 1 the systems approach to business was introduced. The systems concept can be applied to the management functions of an individual business enterprise. Although the external environment is important, in this chapter the internal system of the individual enterprise is emphasized. This is done to focus attention on the internal functions of management. The basic system of the enterprise is illustrated in Figure 5–1.

FIGURE 5–1
General model of the system of a business enterprise

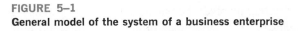
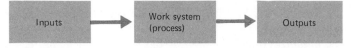

Figure 5–1 shows how the inputs flow into the work system where they are processed and become outputs. The inputs consist of material and human resources. The outputs are goods and services and other forms of satisfactions of human needs.

As a business enterprise increases in size and complexity, further division of labor is required for efficient functioning of the work system. Specialized workers and capital equipment are used to make the work system more productive. To achieve an orderly flow of work in an increasingly specialized organization, coordination and direction by management is necessary. The work system may be thought of as being composed of technical, organizational, and human subsystems. The addition of these subsystems to the model of the business enterprise is illustrated in Figure 5–2.

The *technical subsystem* consists of the equipment, layout, and technology required to produce and distribute a particular product. The nature of the technical subsystem depends upon the requirements of the product and varies widely from one industry to another. For example, a research laboratory of a chemical manufacturer requires a technical subsystem which is quite different from that of a magazine publisher. The requirements for a technical subsystem relate closely to the human and material inputs needed to make the subsystem function effectively. Chapter 12 on production deals extensively with the functioning of the technical subsystem of the business enterprise.

The *human subsystem* exists in all business enterprises and consists of the values, motivations, and interactions of the persons in the enter-

FIGURE 5–2
Model of a business enterprise depicting the technical-organizational-human subsystems

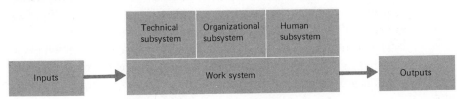

prise. This subsystem involves the management in the practice of human relations. Because of the importance of developing a good human relations climate in the business enterprise, Chapter 7 is devoted to a discussion of this subject.

The *organizational subsystem* is the way in which the technical and human subsystems are organized, directed, coordinated, and controlled by management. In the traditional view of management this involves issues such as planning, departmentalization, staffing, and authority relationships. The organizational subsystem could be considered as the formal means by which the technical and human subsystems are related to each other.

There are numerous interactions among the technical, organizational, and human subsystems. Changes occurring in the technical subsystem can profoundly affect the human subsystem and may necessitate changes in the organizational subsystem. For example, the installation of automated equipment may reduce the need for some production employees or require workers with different skills than those presently on the job. Such a technical change will have an impact on the morale of the work force and will create a problem requiring the attention of management. It also may require a structural change in the departmental arrangements of the production system. As an example of a different type of change, the development of a new product will cause changes in the human and organizational subsystems. New production facilities and the marketing program for the new product expand the requirements for personnel and an organization to direct their activities.

In any business system the various subsystems are constantly in a state of adjustment to changes caused by internal and external forces. The job of management is to deal with these change agents in such a manner that the total system of the enterprise will function efficiently in producing outputs desired by society.

TRADITIONAL FUNCTIONS OF MANAGEMENT

The activities of management can be incorporated into the model of the business enterprise in the organizational subsystem. In the traditional view of management its functions are planning, organizing, direction, and control. These functions are systematized in Figure 5–3.

The relative importance of each of these management activities at a particular time depends upon the stage of the enterprise's development, its growth rate, competition, and other factors in the environment.

FIGURE 5–3
The functions of management

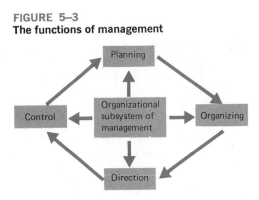

Planning and organizing are discussed in this chapter. Direction is discussed in Chapter 7 along with human relations, and control is discussed in the next chapter.

PLANNING—REQUISITE FOR SUCCESSFUL OPERATIONS

Planning is a primary function of management. In the new enterprise planning precedes the other functions of management. In the established enterprise system planning is a continuing part of the total management process. Without adequate planning the manager's decisions are frequently made to deal only with immediate problems without considering future expected needs. The management that does not plan will function on a random, day-to-day basis. The executives in such an enterprise never seem to have time to anticipate the problems which may arise tomorrow. They do not create conditions within the enterprise to reduce future emergencies. Thus, *planning* may be called the process of rational decision making done sufficiently in advance to promote the more effective functioning of the enterprise's total system. This involves formulation of objectives, policies, and procedures, and the determination of the organizational structure which will provide a framework to achieve the enterprise's broad goals.

Objectives

The first step in the planning process is formulating objectives. *Objectives* embody the broad goals toward which the group activity of the business enterprise is directed. The following statement is the published objective of the Ideal Cement Company of Denver, Colorado:

> To manufacture and sell cement of the types and qualities, in such quantities, at such times and places, and to do such things in connection therewith, as will result in increasing the returns to the Company to the greatest extent with due regard for the rights and proper interest of customers, stockholders, employees, and all others affected by the activities of the Company.

This type of statement is an overall enterprise objective. To be effective it should be supplemented with objectives of a more specific nature throughout the subsystems of the organization. Meaningful subgoals are needed for each division and department of the enterprise. A subgoal of one of the manufacturing departments might be to produce the necessary quantity of cement of a particular specification at the lowest possible cost. The traffic division might have a subgoal of maintaining shipping dates.

The formulation of enterprise objectives is a necessary first step in the planning process since objectives establish the basis for enterprise operations.

Management by objectives. One approach for appraising the performance of an enterprise's managers is by measuring their achievements toward a specified set of goals or objectives. This concept of *management by objectives* emphasizes evaluation based on measurable results rather than on subjective, personal judgments of higher management. Planned objectives are agreed upon by both the manager and boss. Then the manager is evaluated on how well the objectives are fulfilled. The broadest application of the management-by-objectives concept integrates the enterprise's planning process and also its control system with the shared objectives of managers. A number of business enterprises including General Electric have emphasized management by objectives.

Policies

A *policy* is a framework for decision making that is consistent with the objectives of the enterprise. Good policy statements are very important as guidelines for supervisors to use in dealing with issues which arise. Without policies each situation might have to be rethought completely by management before action could be taken. Examples of areas in which business enterprises typically have policies include new product development (does the company lead in research and new product development or follow other enterprises product leads?), production (does the enterprise produce only for specific orders or are long-production runs emphasized with a build-up of inventory?), and finance (are funds for expansion provided by owners or by borrowing or by some combination of sources?).

Policies may be broadly stated so as to give considerable discretion to executives in their decisions or they may be quite specific as to how the policy is to be carried out. The amount of discretion allowed by a policy statement is usually greater the higher up in management one goes. At the top management level, consisting of the board of directors and the chief executive officer, policy statements provide for consider-

FIGURE 5–4

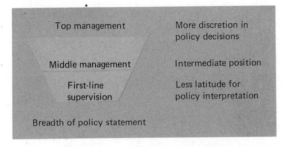

able freedom of thought and action. At the first-line supervisor's level, policies are usually more specific and less flexible. For example, a fairly specific statement regarding enterprise policy on absenteeism is most helpful to a supervisor who oversees many persons where production schedules are important. At the top management level work schedules are less rigid and responsibilities much broader. Therefore, a less specific policy about hours of work and presence in the factory or office is appropriate. Figure 5–4 illustrates the concept of freedom of policy interpretation discussed above.

Despite less latitude for policy interpretation by first-line managers, some flexibility of policy interpretation is important here too. It is almost impossible to write a statement which will be applicable in every set of circumstances. Therefore, a certain amount of policy flexibility is usually desirable at the level of the first-line supervisor to provide for varying circumstances.

Although flexibility in policy administration is desirable, it does come into conflict with the concept of consistency of policy application. Policy flexibility tends to lead to variations in application by individual supervisors. Wide inconsistencies in a particular policy's application can result in lower levels of employee morale. Even though a particular policy does not meet with the complete approval of employees, it is generally accepted if it is consistently applied. Management should be aware of the conflict between flexibility and consistency of policy application and should seek to achieve a balance between these two important elements of policy administration.

As a part of policy administration, executives should understand that there is often a difference between the formal stated policy on a particular issue and what the actual policy application may be in the enterprise. Where circumstances have made the formal policy obsolete and resulted in informal policy changes, management should be prompt to update written policies. Departments concerned with the problem should participate in the review and revision. Significant problems have arisen for those managements which have openly tolerated vast differences between stated policies and actual policy administration in areas of employee safety, welfare, operational efficiency, and customer relations.

For policies to be most effective they should be well understood throughout the business system. Policies should be clearly stated and written so that all employees will understand the basic framework within which decisions will be made. The old joke, "There's no good reason, it's company policy," has no place in today's business enterprise.

Procedures

Procedures constitute the third part of the planning process. A *procedure* is a series of steps carried out in a particular sequence to implement a given policy. Procedures provide little or no discretion on the part of the individual. They may be instituted to carry out certain policies where a chronological sequence of events or uniform applications are important. For example, procedures may relate to such matters as to how information shall be released to the public about the enterprise's profit picture or what steps must be taken to insure safe operation of machinery.

In setting up procedures for implementing company policies and in establishing the guidelines for employee conduct, management should make clear whether a particular statement is a rule or a guide. *Rules* are statements which must be obeyed. *Guides* represent recommendations for action which are not necessarily mandatory. A rule usually is stated in a negative manner such as "No Smoking in This Area" or

"No Admittance Without Safety Glasses." Even if the rules are stated in a more positive manner such as "Safety Glasses Must Be Worn Here," the negative connotation is still present. Rules should be applied only when necessary to govern employee conduct. There should be a reason for the rule if it is to be understood and well accepted.

Good planning is essential

The planning process culminates in the development of programs which represent a mixture of policies and procedures to achieve the enterprise's objectives. These programs include the necessary financial budgets to support the projects.

Planning is a continuous process to meet changing conditions and new needs of the business system. Once the new enterprise is established, planning becomes integrated with the rest of the functions of management. Planning reduces unproductive work. It provides a necessary basis for controlling operations by setting a standard against which results may be measured.

In today's dynamic environment the process of planning can be utilized to accomplish changes in the system of the enterprise. Planning can be used throughout the enterprise to improve awareness of the total system and to promote creative change. Without planning changes can cause more problems in the human and technical subsystems than might otherwise be the case.

No business enterprise should spend more money on planning than the value of the anticipated benefits. The measurement of dollar benefits of planning are difficult. The amount of money that could be spent on evaluation of alternative courses of action, forecasting of probable results, and alternative actions by competitors could be unlimited. Each management must determine how much it wishes to spend to get the information necessary for good planning. Time and executive talent available are also limiting factors in the planning process. However, good planning reduces the chances that executives will be forced to make snap decisions without adequate information on critical issues. Careful planning provides a sound basis for the further managerial functions of organizing, directing, and controlling.

ORGANIZING THE BUSINESS ENTERPRISE

Organization of the business enterprise is the second important management function. The various activities must be systematically arranged and assigned for efficient use of time and energy. There are a number of factors which should be considered in developing the organizational structure of any business system. These factors include departmentalization, staffing, authority-responsibility relationships, span of control, and line and staff relationships.

Departmentalization

The many different activities of the business enterprise must be assigned so that the employees will clearly understand who is responsible for which activity. Can you imagine going into a large store that sells many different kinds of merchandise and does not have any departments? Suppose that each morning all the employees were assigned to their work places for that day on a random basis without any relationship to what they had done the day before, and that supervisors could do whatever they wanted without any division of the work load. The result of this unorganized situation would be chaos! It would be only through chance and a good deal of luck if the store were able to provide goods and services to the public and operate profitably.

Departmentalization provides the basis for organizing the work to be done in the business enterprise. When the business enterprise is thought of as a system, departments can be viewed as subsystems. The value of considering the departments of the enterprise as subsystems is that this emphasizes the interrelatedness of each department in achieving both its own objectives and those of the enterprise. Such an approach stimulates individuals in the various departmental subsystems to expand their view beyond a single narrow functional activity.

The usual ways of organizing an enterprise into departments are by function, by product line, or by geography. Other methods of departmentalization include those based on the type of customer served or by individual projects.

Functional departmentalization. When an enterprise is departmentalized on a functional basis the activities of a similar nature are grouped together. Thus, the activities of production and marketing are placed in separate departments and function as different subsystems. Other functional departments customarily include personnel, finance, and accounting. Figure 5–5 illustrates the typical manufacturing enterprise's top management structure when it is departmentalized by function. The five major departments illustrated in Figure 5–5 perform such an important role in the operation of the business enterprise that

separate chapters are devoted to an analysis of the functions of each
of these subsystems.

Product line departmentalization. A business enterprise may be
organized according to the various types of products which it manufactures and sells. This is *product line departmentalization* and results in
each product being handled almost as a separate system. An example
of an industry where product line departmentalization is used is the
automobile industry. The major automobile manufacturers have separate divisions for the production and distribution of each line. This
concentrates management attention on the problems peculiar to each
segment of the market.

FIGURE 5–5
**Simplified organization chart of a typical manufacturing corporation
on a functional basis**

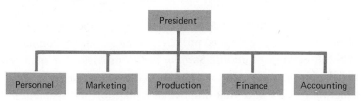

Departmentalization by geography. *Geographical departmentalization* is logical when activities are carried on over a wide territorial
range. Geography provides a good means for organizing subsystems
when different markets and conditions exist across the country. Selling
of the product is frequently departmentalized on a geographical basis
to have local control of sales activities and to keep in touch with
changes in local market conditions.

Other means of departmentalization. Sometimes an enterprise may
find it profitable to departmentalize on the basis of the *type of customer
served*. This is done many times by enterprises producing both civilian
and governmental products. Those enterprises which sell products to
the Department of Defense often have a separate division for defense
contracts. This helps the enterprise maintain close control on standards
and keep up to date on the complex requirements for dealing with the
federal government. These same enterprises may use separate departments to produce and sell products for civilian use. Sometimes commercial banks and other financial institutions organize departments on a
type-of-customer-served basis, such as departments for loans to retail
stores, to consumers, or to farmers.

In engineering and construction industries the *single-project type of departmentalization* is useful where large one-time projects are undertaken which will extend over a period of months or years. Highway construction contracts serve as a logical basis for single-project departments. Sometimes these subsystems are referred to as task forces where personnel and materials are marshalled for one special effort. Once the project is completed the personnel and equipment are reassigned to other activities.

There is no single best way to departmentalize a business enterprise. A careful analysis of the circumstances of the particular business enterprise should be undertaken before deciding upon the departmental structure.

Staffing and management succession

Once the organization structure has been planned and the subsystems identified, the next step is providing managerial personnel to fill the decision-making positions. *Staffing* is the provision of qualified managerial personnel for the enterprise. A key element in a good staffing program is to be sure that an adequate plan for management succession is developed and put into practice. No matter how competent a particular manager or team of executives is, these persons will not always be with the enterprise. Therefore, management should have a training program to provide qualified managerial personnel as replacements.

Providing for management succession is critical for the small and medium-sized enterprise since most likely there will be proportionately fewer competent managers in smaller firms than in the large enterprise. In the enterprise where one executive acts as the principal decision maker and where no program to train future managers is undertaken, the existence of the enterprise depends upon the health and capacity of a single person.

Sources of executive talent. There are two ways of obtaining executives. The first is to promote from within employees either in lower management echelons or in nonmanagerial work. The second is to bring in executive personnel from the outside. Generally executive morale is higher if promotion comes from within the company ranks. However, if inside promotion is practiced this means that executive training programs should be in operation to assure that personnel will be prepared when vacancies occur. Also, there is a danger that inbreeding may tend to stifle new ideas.

Hiring executives from outside the enterprise can also have merit. Besides bringing new ideas into an organization, hiring an outside executive generally means there is a person who should be immediately ready to assume the responsibility for a given position. The lead time required for training of personnel may be cut down by hiring experienced executives from other business enterprises. This is a good practice especially where no training programs have been undertaken and no capable managers have been brought along within an organization.

Management training. When management is faced with a shortage of trained personnel within an enterprise this may reflect a weakness in the management training program. There are four ways that personnel can acquire managerial training to qualify them for promotion. These are through job rotation, special assignments, formal training programs, and by staff assignments.

Job rotation involves the transfer of employees through a series of different types of positions to acquaint them with the different elements of the enterprise's operations. This is especially helpful with the young person who is new to the enterprise and serves to provide a basis for a more permanent assignment later.

Special assignments may be given somewhat more experienced personnel where they will have responsibility for a project that will show what abilities they have for organizing and carrying out a program. Special assignments provide one measure of a person's ability to deal with new and varied situations.

Formal training programs can be conducted within the enterprise and include lectures, special training courses, and discussions. Or the executive may go to some institution of higher learning for professional management training. Such a program tends to broaden the scope of the executive's knowledge outside a special field such as marketing or accounting.

By placing an individual in a *staff position,* such as an assistant to a member of top management, a real insight into the operation of the enterprise from the top down is provided. The assistant's role may be varied, but when used as a training device it should include work at various levels in the organization. As a staff official the individual acts to provide assistance or information but does not have to bear the final responsibility for decision making. Such assignments give young managers a better understanding of the complexities of the decisions made by top executives and improve their grasp of the total managerial job.

Executive development and management succession is an area that should not be the sole responsibility of the personnel administrator or lower-level management. This is a responsibility of top management. Without an adequate program of managerial training the long-run success of the enterprise is endangered.

Authority-responsibility relationships

In organizing the business enterprise management must determine the nature of the authority-responsibility relationships. *Authority* as applied to the business enterprise is the delegated power to make decisions. Sometimes authority is defined as the right to direct the actions of others. This definition appears to de-emphasize greatly the importance of human relationships in the business enterprise. In its most extreme position, this latter view makes authority a divine right of business owners to exercise complete domination over employees. To counter this "right to direct" concept of authority, the concept has been developed that authority flows upward from the subordinate to the superior. This means that no authority can be exercised in the business enterprise without the permission of the employee. This "permissive" view of authority emphasizes the human relations aspect of enterprise management.

For the executive faced with the many problems of running a firm, both points of view may provide helpful insights into better management of the business enterprise. The authority to manage an enterprise does stem from its owners, who bring together the assets to begin operations. The concept of private property is a basic value in our society. In this respect, the "right to direct" or more traditional view of authority is relevant. On the other hand, in a free society an employer is neither able to command enthusiastic cooperation of employees nor to make them obey commands they do not understand. Therefore, good communications, respect for the individual worker, and reasonable work standards are critical in the exercise of authority in the modern industrial enterprise. The definition of authority as the delegated power to make decisions seems to be a logical middle ground which takes into account both the traditional and permissive views of authority.

Responsibility. Those with decision-making power are held accountable for their decisions. The concept of responsibility is closely tied to accountability. Supervisors at all levels of business are well aware of the nature of responsibility. They know that responsibility rests on their shoulders for the results of employees and materials put under their direction. However, one of the most frequently voiced complaints by supervisory personnel is that they do not have authority in decision making which is commensurate with their responsibility. A concept of good management is that with every responsibility should go sufficient authority to carry out the assigned mission. Responsibility for results should never be separated from the power to make the decisions necessary to achieve those results. This means that authority should be placed at the subsystem level where needed so that decisions can be made as close as possible to where the activities are being undertaken.

Delegation of authority. Another aspect of authority-responsibility relationships is the importance of proper delegation of authority to subordinates. A particular responsibility, as such, cannot be delegated to a subordinate. However, you can delegate authority to make decisions to a subordinate and then create a new responsibility relationship from the subordinate to the superior. This does not relieve the superior of being responsible to higher management, but such a delegation does make possible the disposition of work assignments.

Consider the example of the office manager who is responsible for the work of many clerks and other office employees. These responsibilities are not removed from the office manager when the office workers are divided into four sections with a supervisor appointed for each section. The office manager is still responsible for the smooth functioning of the office. However, new responsibility relationships have been created from the section supervisors to the office manager.

In this example, the office manager should make clear to the section supervisors what their responsibilities are and what authority is delegated to them to meet these responsibilities. Without a clear understanding among supervisors and employees as to authority and responsibility, morale will deteriorate. Employees will be unable to have their questions answered by supervisors. Employees may bypass section supervisors and go to the office manager with their problems. This not only creates misunderstanding but negates the purpose of the section supervisor: that of performing many administrative details in the office to enable the office manager to concentrate on broader matters of more long-run importance.

Degree of decentralization of decision making. In recent years many large enterprises such as General Electric Company have become much interested in the concept of decentralization of decision making in their organizations. As a matter of fact, the concept of complete centralization of decision making is not appropriate to the large business operation. The really relevant question is not whether there is to be decentralization but to what extent shall decision making be decentralized. Even in medium-size and small-size business enterprises, where problems of great geographic distances and multiplant operations are not present, subsystems are being more effectively utilized through some decentralization of decision making.

In view of the interest in decentralization, the answers provided by management to each of the following five questions will give some guidelines for the extent of decentralization in a particular business enterprise.

1. What is the significance of the decision? In those instances where the decision is relatively minor it ought to be made by operating personnel on the spot. The cost of having the problem passed up through the organization may exceed the value of the decision itself. When the decision is critical to the overall success of the enterprise it probably should be made by more senior executives.

2. Who in the organization has the information necessary to make an informed decision? Most decisions should be made at the level in the organization where the needed information is readily available. With more complex decisions the necessity of drawing information from several areas of the enterprise means that clear channels of communication will be required.

3. At what level in the organization do personnel have the capacity to make the decisions? Authority should normally be delegated as far down in the organization as employees have the experience and knowledge necessary to render a sound decision. There are times when personnel at the operating level of management are better equipped to make a decision than higher management because their close association with the problem gives them a good understanding of the ramifications of whatever decision is made.

4. How rapidly must the decision be made? Some authority must be placed on the point of impact of the decision making. There is no sense in requiring permission from the plant manager before taking a fire extinguisher and putting out a trash fire in a wastebasket! To delay the decision to act could be extremely costly as well as stupid. On the other hand, a major decision relating to expansion of plant capacity or extension of marketing areas can wait until sufficient evidence is gathered.

5. What will be the effect on employee morale of the degree of de-

centralization in the enterprise? Generally decentralization improves initiative and creates good morale among employees. People like to feel that they can influence events where they are employed.

Span of control

A concept closely related to the issue of decentralization of authority is that of executive span of control. *Span of control* refers to the number of subordinates a manager can effectively supervise. There are three main factors that tend to limit the number any single manager can supervise. These are the executive's time and energy available, mental capabilities and personal abilities for dealing with individuals, and the nature of the supervisory problems that will be encountered on the job.

The more face-to-face contacts that are necessary each day in the conduct of a department's affairs, the more time-consuming and demanding is the supervisor's role. Generally, the more complex the supervisory situation and the greater the variety of activities a person directs, the more limited will be the number of individuals who can be supervised. Consequently the span of control is more narrow. Some authorities indicate that at higher levels in the enterprise fewer persons can be effectively supervised. This leads to a more narrow span of control than at lower levels in the organization where problems are not of such great magnitude. However, in those enterprises where considerable decentralization of authority exists, a wider span of control at top management level can be very effective. In such cases the shorter lines of communication from the bottom to the top of the organization and the fewer levels of management personnel can improve the morale and effectiveness of subordinates. Figure 5–6 illustrates the difference in organization structure between a wide and narrow span of control.

Notice in Figure 5–6 that the number of production workers in each company is the same. However, the two organization structures are quite different. There are 18 production workers in each supervisory work unit in Company A and only 8 in Company B. In Company A there are only two levels of management between production workers and the president. In Company B four levels separate workers from the president. While it is rather unrealistic to assume that workers will have much direct contact with the president, communication is more direct when fewer levels of supervision exist. The dangers that communication will be impaired are greater where the span of control is narrow with many levels of supervision. In Company A more authority

FIGURE 5–6

Comparison of organization structures with wide and narrow spans of control

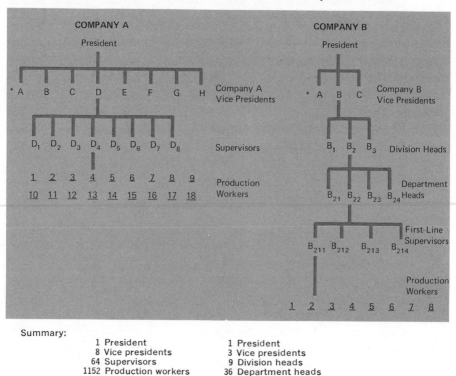

Summary:

1 President	1 President
8 Vice presidents	3 Vice presidents
64 Supervisors	9 Division heads
1152 Production workers	36 Department heads
1225 Total employees	144 First-line supervisors
	1152 Production workers
	1345 Total employees

* Each level below the departmental level has a similar structure of supervisors and production workers as does Department D in Company A and Department B in Company B.

and responsibility are placed with individual supervisors than in Company B where authority is likely to be more divided among the various levels of supervisors.

There are 120 more supervisory personnel in Company B than there are in Company A. While this does not mean that all executives in Company B are not performing satisfactorily, the question can be raised as to the added expense of these additional salaries. Top management should always attempt to determine whether additional levels of supervision with more executives can be economically justified. Although some supervisory personnel in Company A may be more highly paid in view of their greater responsibilities than in Company B, the total executive wage bill probably will be higher in Company B.

Despite the issues which have been raised concerning the organization structure of Company B, it would be wrong to assume that a wide span of control is always best. The optimum span of control or supervision for each level in the enterprise should be determined by the variety and importance of the activities being supervised, the stability of enterprise operations, the abilities of the executive, the abilities of subordinates, and the importance of executive salaries as an expense item in the enterprise. There are no easy answers to questions relating to organization structure. Earlier concepts generalizing about the specific number of subordinates who can be directed effectively are giving way to a situational analysis of the enterprise's system and the nature of the problems faced by a particular management.

Whether the span of control is wide or narrow, it is important that employees know the chain of command. The *chain of command* concept involves an understanding by all employees as to whom they are directly responsible. All persons should also understand the nature of their authority and how it is to be exercised.

Line and staff relationships

Problems arise in the organization of the business enterprise because of misunderstanding of line and staff functions. These justify a discussion of the nature of line and staff relationships.

The *line function* consists of those activities that directly result in the achievement of the goals of the enterprise. Thus, line activities in a manufacturing enterprise would be those relating to producing and selling the product. The *staff function* would include all other activities which assist the line in fulfilling the enterprise's objectives. Activities such as finance, personnel administration, and accounting are normally considered to be staff functions. This means line and staff functions may be defined in terms of the kinds of activities accomplished. Those which are part of the main stream of enterprise goals are line functions, and those which support line activities are staff functions. These are illustrated by Figure 5–7.

Line and staff functions may also be defined with regard to authority relationships. The concept of chain of command implies a direct line of authority running throughout the enterprise's system. In this sense, the line executive is one who has direct authority over another employee. Line authority consists of the power to make decisions and follow through to see that a mission is accomplished. The role of the staff

FIGURE 5–7

Partial organization chart for manufacturing corporation showing line and staff functions

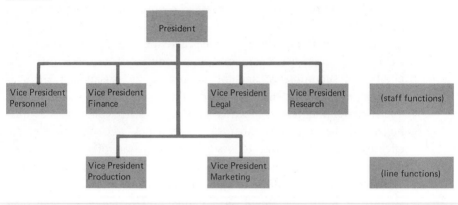

executive is that of advice and consultation, not of final decision making. In terms of authority relationships the staff function is not decision making or direction but provision of assistance to improve decisions made by persons with line authority.

Thus, the concept of line and staff may be defined either according to the kind of activity accomplished or in terms of authority relationships. A particular executive may be considered to perform both line and staff functions. For example, the personnel manager is head of the personnel department and exercises a line function with respect to his department. However, personnel administration is generally considered to be a staff function since it provides advice and assistance to other departments.

Dimensions of the staff function. Although any staff function represents an activity necessary to support the line, there are different dimensions to the staff function. Staff personnel include technical advisors, personal assistants, housekeeping staff, and specialized staff.

Technical advisors are personnel such as legal counselors, public relations personnel, and engineers who provide information of a highly specialized nature. The advice given by technical staff members is almost a directive. The line manager may ignore the advice, but is unlikely to be in a position to make a different decision which will be more sound technically.

Personal assistants are persons who provide busy executives with information or recommendations or who handle details that the manager may not have time for. This type of staff person is often titled as

"Assistant to . . ." and the exact nature of the responsibilities involved must be determined by the top executive.

Housekeeping staff means just what the name implies. This includes the large number of personnel who perform custodial and maintenance duties, record keeping, health services such as giving physical examinations and providing first aid, and routine personnel functions such as interviewing prospective employees and providing testing services.

Specialized staff includes a variety of staff personnel whose common denominator is understanding in a particular field of knowledge that can be of vital assistance to the line executive. The accounting function in the business enterprise is generally considered a specialized staff role as are elements of finance, purchasing, and engineering.

What constitutes a staff function in one business enterprise may be a line function in another. Purchasing for many manufacturers is considered a staff function, but in a large retailing enterprise the buying or purchasing function is a vital responsibility of the line coupled with successful selling or marketing. Whatever represents the main thrust of an enterprise's economic function may properly be called the line, and those elements that support and assist may be called the staff.

SUMMARY

Management consists of achieving results by coordinating the activities of other people.

The systems approach to management of a business enterprise focuses on the coordination of inputs of material and human resources into the work system where they are processed and become outputs of goods and services and other satisfactions of human needs. The work system is composed of technical, organizational, and human subsystems.

The traditional functions of management are planning, organizing, direction, and control.

Planning is the process of rational decision making done in advance to promote the enterprise's more efficient functioning. Planning includes the formulation of objectives, policies, and procedures.

Organizing enterprise activities is an important function of management. The organization process includes departmentalization, staffing and providing for management succession, and establishing authority-responsibility relationships. Persons in the enterprise need to understand the span of control and the nature of line and staff relationships.

Authority is the delegated power to make decisions. When decision-making power is delegated an authority-responsibility relationship is created. Decentralization of decision making is an important trend in management today.

The line function consists of those activities which directly result in the achievement of the enterprise's goals. The staff function includes all other activities which assist the line in fulfilling enterprise objectives.

TERMS FOR REVIEW

management	*staffing*
work system	*authority*
planning	*responsibility*
objectives	*span of control*
policy	*chain of command*
procedure	*line function*
departmentalization	*staff function*

QUESTIONS

1. How is the management of organizations such as government and educational institutions similar to the management of business enterprises? How does the management of business enterprises differ from other institutions?

2. Discuss the relationship between the technical, organizational, and human subsystems in a business enterprise. Give a specific example of how changes in one subsystem affect the other two subsystems.

3. An owner of a small business recently commented, "I can't afford to take the time to plan because of all the immediate problems I have to solve." What comments would you make to this businessman about the importance of planning and its benefits?

4. Why is consistency of policy administration important in managing the enterprise? Does consistency mean that there should never be variations in policy administration? Explain your answer.

5. Determine the nature of departmentalization in a business enterprise with which you are familiar or obtain a copy of a corporation's annual report from a stock brokerage firm or by writing to the secretary of the corporation. Draw up an organization chart of the enterprise showing its present form of organization. What other methods of organization could the enterprise have utilized? What possible advantages could be gained from a different form of organization?

6. *a.* When vacancies occur in key management positions in the business enterprise what are the advantages of filling these positions with persons presently employed by the enterprise?

   b. What are the advantages of filling key management vacancies with
       persons from outside the firm?
7. a. Contrast the traditional "right to direct" concept of authority with
       the "permissive," or human relations, concept of authority.
   b. What types of authority have you seen exercised in organizations
       of which you have been a part? Was the exercise of authority ef-
       fective? Explain your answer.
8. What problems can arise if supervisors do not understand their respon-
    sibilities and the authority delegated to them?
9. What are the strengths and weaknesses of:
    a. A narrow span of control?
    b. A wide span of control?

Business briefs

Don't discount management

   The wild and woolly field of discount chain stores is a study in
contrasts of profitability and management effectiveness. During the
1960s new discount chains multiplied like flowers in the spring. In the
1970s a shake-out has taken place. Kresge's K-Mart discount stores
are providing a standard of performance envied by many other dis-
counters. K-Mart's sales reach almost $100 per square foot of selling
space, with stock turning over six to eight times annually.
   S. S. Kresge Co. opened its first K-Mart store in 1962 when the
company was floundering as a 63-year-old variety chain. Kresge's
whole emphasis was shifted from variety stores to discounting. By 1975
there were more than 750 K-Marts in operation in 230 of the country's
261 Standard Metropolitan Statistical Areas. During this period Kresge
became the nation's third largest retailer behind Sears and J. C. Penney,
and the country's largest discounter.
   Kresge's total retail sales increased nine times and profits rose 15
times in the 12 years after K-Mart was started. In an industry which
traditionally has low profit margins, Kresge has raised its after-tax
profits from less than 2 percent of sales in 1962 to 3 percent in 1973.
   Kresge's K-Mart formula for success includes the following:

1. Emphasis on first-quality merchandise with 75 percent of K-Mart's
    items being nationally advertised brands.

2. Aggressive pricing—storewide discounting to match or beat competition.
3. A liberal refund policy.
4. Avoidance of high-cost shopping centers with careful analysis of every new store site for profitability.
5. Location of several store units in each major metropolitan area to spread the cost of advertising, distribution, and supervision.
6. A strong corporate staff of merchandise buyers for centralized purchasing power.
7. Authority for local store managers in selecting merchandise for their stores and in local advertising.
8. Intensive training and good pay for store managers.

In contrast to K-Mart's success, 70-year-old W. T. Grant Co. encountered serious difficulties in the mid-1970s. Unable to decide whether to go the K-Mart route of discounting or to try and be more like Sears, Grant's opted for a position between the two and found the public had no clear-cut image of its merchandising. Profits declined 78 percent in 1973, and in 1974 losses amounted to $175 million.

Sales per square foot were running about $38. Grant had indulged in an overly aggressive expansion program without adequate attention to store location. The expansion of the management organization lagged behind expansion of new stores. Inventories piled up and the retailer's failure to stock staple items led to an excess of slow-moving merchandise. Interest costs were high. Contrary to K-Mart's policy, Grant depended heavily on private-label merchandise for special promotions.

In 1975 W. T. Grant filed for protection from its creditors under the federal bankruptcy law.

1. Contrast the approach to retailing in the 1970s by S. S. Kresge and W. T. Grant.
2. Discuss management techniques of K-Mart to achieve both "value and volume" needed for successful discounting.
3. *a.* How does K-Mart management make use of both centralization and decentralization in decision making?
   b. What are the potential strengths and weaknesses of this approach?

Dropping Cs at Chrysler

Chrysler Corporation ceased production of its largest luxury car, the Imperial, with the 1976 model year in the fall of 1975. In the automobile industry the full-size cars are built on what are called C bodies. For years the Imperial had been Chrysler's competitive answer to the luxury models of GM's Cadillac and Ford's Continental Mark IV.

During 1975 Chrysler's C body cars in the Plymouth, Dodge, and Chrysler lines accounted for less than 20 percent of company sales. In 1973 more than one third of the enterprise's sales had been in big cars. The auto industry encountered a sharp drop in big-car sales beginning with the Arab oil embargo in the fall of 1973.

The four American auto manufacturers are committed to improving average fuel economy of their 1980 line by 40 percent over 1974. Some of these economies will be achieved through engineering improvements. However, there will likely be a higher proportion of smaller, more fuel-efficient cars produced.

Stories from Detroit have indicated that Chrysler executives plan to eliminate all full-size autos beginning with the 1978 model year. Then the number three U.S. auto manufacturer will not be able to match GM and Ford, model for model, across the board. If these reports prove to be correct, the largest Chrysler car will be its current intermediate-size vehicle.

In 1974 Chrysler Corporation lost $52 million following profits in 1973 of $255 million.

1. How does the decision to drop the Imperial affect Chrysler's major objectives and policies?
2. What factors likely influenced management to consider elimination of all C body car models?
3. Do you think Chrysler can compete effectively with GM and Ford without a full-size automobile? Why or why not?

Case

United Insurance Company

Sharon Findlay, office manager of the Aton district office of United Insurance Company, was faced with the question of what to do about the absenteeism of one of the most efficient typists in the office.

Sharon prided herself that she had been consistent in applying personnel policies since she had been promoted to office manager eight months ago. Under her supervision were five analysts, four typists, three filing clerks, and a mailroom clerk. Typing and clerical work were sent into the office from other departments of the Aton district. The analysts worked on specific policy problems which were reported by the agents and referred by the district sales manager for detailed study.

The written personnel policies issued by the company's home office were quite explicit regarding absenteeism. Employees were expected to be at work on time. Absenteeism was viewed as a serious matter except for genuine cases of personal hardship. District managers, who were in charge of all operations within their geographic areas, were directed to draw up specific procedures to be followed in dealing with absenteeism in their districts. The Aton district's written personnel policies stated that the procedure to be followed for unexcused absenteeism was:

First unexcused absence—oral warning by the supervisor.
Second unexcused absence—written warning by the supervisor.
Third unexcused absence—two days' suspension without pay.
Fourth unexcused absence—discharge of the employee.

Whether the absence was excused or not was left up to the supervisor. However, the district manager indicated that absences due to personal illness, family illness, or death of a relative would be considered excused, provided the supervisor was notified at the time. Other reasons by employees for being absent would have to be evaluated by the immediate supervisor. The United Insurance Company had a companywide policy allowing up to seven working days annually for such "excused" absences.

Shortly after she was named office manager, Sharon Findlay had fired one of the clerks for excessive absenteeism. The young woman had failed to come to work for reasons which Sharon had not considered "excused." She had been warned according to the established procedure. After the fourth absence Sharon Findlay dismissed her after briefly outlining the case to the district manager.

Now a similar situation had arisen with one of the best typists in the office. Jayne Jones had been absent three times in the past four months without what Sharon Findlay considered to be a satisfactory explanation. Following the third absence Sharon sent Jayne home for two days without pay. At the time she indicated that she had been having problems with her parents and really needed her job to enable her to pay some debts and then to move into an apartment she had been looking for. Jayne had been hired about six months ago and had proved to be an excellent worker except for the recent absences.

On Monday morning, two weeks following her third absence, Jayne called in sick. Late that afternoon an agent for the company returned to the office and remarked to Sharon Findlay as he passed her desk, "Say, I saw Jayne Jones this afternoon at the Crestview shopping center. I thought she worked in this office."

The agent's remark disturbed Sharon Findlay. She knew Jayne had a number of friends among the other girls in the office force and that the typing section functioned more smoothly when Jayne was there. Sharon was aware that some of the managers in the insurance company were more liberal than she in the interpretation of unexcused absences. On the other hand, she wanted to avoid potential future morale problems in the office which could occur if she "let Jayne get away with something." Sharon felt certain that her future promotion depended upon how well she managed the office and whether the work was accomplished efficiently. She wondered what she should do about Jayne.

1. What should Sharon Findlay do at this point? Discuss both the immediate and long-range actions to be taken.
2. Discuss the merits and limitations of consistency in policy administration.

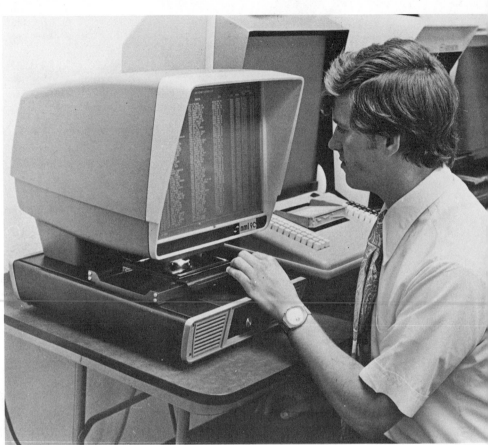

*Microfilm readers are
examples of modern
control devices used by
management.*

Control is sometimes thought of as the last step in the management process of planning, organizing, directing, and controlling. However, a good system of control will be built into the management of the business system from its beginning.

The control system provides a means of informing management whether the other systems are functioning according to plan. It also provides a basis for changes to correct problems which have already occurred. The following issues regarding control are discussed:

> *How does the process of control relate to management?*
> *What are the elements of a control system?*
> *What are the requirements for effective control systems?*
> *Why is the budgeting process a key management device?*

THE PROCESS OF CONTROL

Without a good system of control the technical, organizational, and human subsystems of the business enterprise may be ineffective. The control system provides a means for measuring the progress of the business toward its objectives. Control systems function in relation to the planning which is done throughout the business enterprise. Also, feedback from the control process points out the need for adjustments in plans.

Control enables management to coordinate different activities by measuring actual output against expected performance. Control systems usually focus on a limited number of measurements and may be limited to a single criterion. This

6

Control

means management should concentrate on control systems for those enterprise activities which are both controllable and important. In the established enterprise the standards which are set should relate to past performance as well as to absolute standards desired by management.

Today's business enterprises are complex systems requiring the services and knowledge of many persons. If the enterprise is to achieve its goals these persons must work together for the common good. You should recognize the need for cooperation and a certain amount of conformity on the part of employees. Control systems help maintain individual behavior within limits which are tolerable for the efficient functioning of the business enterprise. However, the need for a certain amount of conformity to attain common goals should not result in the stifling of creativity and individuality. Therefore, the control system must also be geared to accommodate creative changes, especially those which enable the business enterprise to serve our society better.

THE ELEMENTS OF A CONTROL SYSTEM

Whether it is control of production, product quality, personnel performance, or cash, there are three essential elements in a control system. These are the establishment of standards, the measurement of performance, and the analysis and correction of deviations from planned standards. Figure 6–1 illustrates the basic elements in a control system.

Establishing standards

Standards represent the goals which the business enterprise strives to attain. There are different types of standards which may be used as guidelines for control. These include monetary standards, physical standards, and intangible standards.

Monetary standards generally relate to the cost of operation, such as materials or labor cost per unit produced. Sometimes monetary standards are in terms of revenues, such as the average sales per person in a particular marketing area. Monetary standards are widely used in business as a means for control when quantitative measurement is possible.

Physical standards, like monetary standards, are frequently quantitative in nature, but they may also be qualitative. Physical standards are quantitative when used to measure such things as number of units produced per hour or amount of energy expended per unit of production. The qualitative aspect of physical standards includes such things as the consistency in a color or the tensile strength of metals or fabrics.

Intangible standards cannot be stated precisely in either monetary or physical terms and therefore tend to be difficult to determine. How do you judge the effectiveness of the enterprise's public relations program? Or establish loyalty standards for the president's secretary who has access to confidential data? There are problems in establishing intangible standards. But just because intangible standards are difficult to define and somewhat vague does not diminish their importance. Management must attempt to establish good intangible standards.

FIGURE 6–1
Elements of a control system

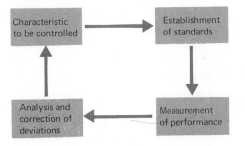

In setting up any standards the broad objectives of the business must always be kept in mind. It is easy for management to become overly impressed with specific quantitative standards which can be easily measured. At the same time management may miss the significance of broader issues which will have greater impact on operating results. For example, a sales manager may keep logs on the number of telephone calls in an attempt to eliminate unnecessary long-distance calls and thereby reduce telephone expenses. However, a telephone expense account may be overcontrolled to the extent that additional sales and significantly higher profits are being missed. Management needs to take a broader view to see whether greater use of the telephone might not increase sales and profits. Similar examples can be found in other areas of control.

Measuring performance

If a standard has been set properly, the measurement of performance should be a relatively simple matter. With routine production work the question may be simply, Do results meet the standard? On the other hand, measuring performance against a standard is not so easy in a shop where all work is custom orders and each order requires a different combination of patterns and materials. In such a job-lot shop the careful analyst may be able to work out standards that can be applied. However, more allowance for variations may be necessary than in the routine production line.

One of the most difficult areas for measuring performance is in the evaluation of managers. A production manager can often be evaluated by the performance of the production department, or a sales manager by the number of units sold. However, there may be conditions beyond the control of production or sales managers which will affect the results in their departments. Evaluation of the performance of a staff executive such as a personnel manager is even more difficult. The personnel manager as a staff executive may give excellent assistance and advice, but line managers may choose to ignore it.

Analysis and correction of deviations

A good control process includes as part of its system an analysis of the deviations from standards and suggests the nature of the correction needed to bring performance back within acceptable limits. Sometimes this requires examining all the steps in the management process to determine the best way of applying corrective action.

The analysis of deviations illustrates how controls should be built into the total management of the enterprise and not be added on after all plans are made, resources assembled, and action initiated. Management should have in mind the range of expected results at any particular time in the cycle of a product's development and should devise means for making corrections before the enterprise encounters serious problems.

Most control systems tend to emphasize the negative factors of performance. Management becomes concerned when productivity in a department fails to reach expectations or when sales of a product do not meet quotas. In these cases the control system seeks an explanation for the unexpected deviations and prods production or sales personnel to meet enterprise expectations. Not often enough does management become excited when something is correctly done or when an objective is exceeded by good performance. Management has a responsibility to see that the enterprise functions well with profitable operations. However, mobilizing employees to do their best is likely to be most effective when communication is not limited to criticism of an individual or a department for below-standard performance.

REQUIREMENTS FOR EFFECTIVE CONTROL

The controls needed in an enterprise will vary depending upon its size, the nature of the work performed, and the degree of accuracy and detail required. However, there are some characteristics which apply to any good control system. Controls should be diagnostic, therapeutic, accurate, timely, understandable, and economical.

Controls should be diagnostic

Controls should apply to significant processes or problems. Controls ought to point out errors, mistakes, deviations, and differences for management attention. Controls should be sensitive enough that deviations are reported in time so that operations are not permitted to sink into deep difficulty before any intelligent action is taken to remedy the situation.

Controls should be therapeutic

The effective control system will not only call attention to deviations but also will suggest a means of curing the difficulty. Today's automated processes have built-in corrections for variations from standards. These problems will be corrected automatically. Even in less automated situations the controls should present evidence to management in a form that suggests a solution to the problem. At times causes of deviations will be difficult to determine. A skilled manager may be required to solve the problem.

Controls should be accurate and timely

You may think it is obvious to point out that controls should be accurate and also timely in reporting deviations. However, when one desires both accuracy and timeliness in a control system a conflict situation may arise. In striving for a high degree of accuracy more time may be required to seek additional data to increase the certainty of one's conclusions.

An example of conflict between accuracy and timeliness can be seen in a typical problem of the market research director. To determine the success of a new product the market research director might require a carefully selected sample of sales reports, customers' reactions, and re-orders from retailers. After receiving this information and processing it to remove some of the sampling errors, the marketing executive would be prepared to report how nearly the demand for the new product is in line with expectations. However, consider the time and expense required for such a lengthy analysis. Often management cannot wait this long before setting production schedules and starting sales promotion pro-grams. More rapid analysis, based on less elaborate data, with more generalized conclusions may be necessary for immediate control. Later more detailed analysis can be used in a report on total campaign effectiveness.

When time and accuracy come into conflict in controlling operations then management must decide which is more critical. The answer will depend on the importance of the decision, the time pressure under which management is operating, and how much help the additional in-formation is likely to be in making a better decision.

Controls should be understandable

The most sophisticated control systems are likely to be worthless if they are not understood by those who use them or who make use of the information they provide. Technical and staff personnel have a special responsibility to explain control systems to line personnel who will be judged by these controls. Line management must be made aware of how these controls may improve operations and profitability. The line manager should then see that subordinates understand the controls appropriate to their areas.

Frequently, the most significant difficulties in initiating new control systems are not technical problems but involve human relations and communications. A new report form, thrust into the hands of a super-visor without an adequate explanation of how it may improve the functioning of that department, may not be filled out properly. You should not be surprised if the form, for which the supervisor sees no clear purpose, ends up at the bottom of a stack of desk work.

Controls should be economical

The cost of controls should be justified in terms of the profit objec-tives of the business system. Controls should not be so elaborate and restrictive that they become an end in themselves. The amount of money spent on controls should depend upon the importance of the process being controlled, the loss which might be incurred without controls, and the size of the enterprise's operations. The elaborate control systems with sophisticated computers used by McDonnell-Douglas Corporation and the National Aeronautics and Space Agency to track space explorations are obviously ridiculous for the small shop selling children's clothing. However, economy is a relative concept. Effective controls for a small enterprise are just as necessary for profitable management as are the extensive control systems used in a giant industrial firm. Under any circumstances, the cost of controls should not exceed the savings to be gained from them.

THE BUDGET—A KEY MANAGEMENT DEVICE

The budget is a key device for management in planning, coordination, and control of operations. It is a document outlining in quantitative terms the planned operations of the enterprise for a specified period of time. The budgeting process begins with planning by top management of the needs the enterprise hopes to satisfy. Data are gathered from marketing and production and translated into budgets which will become a financial plan of expected expenditures and receipts with an estimate of the profits. Thus, budgeting translates the goals of the enterprise into quantitative terms and also sets a basis for control. The budget provides a guideline for informing different departments of their part in the overall plans of the enterprise.

Though budgeting practice varies among business enterprises, there are three types of budgets used in business. These are operations budgets, cash budgets, and capital budgets.

The operations budget

The *operations budget,* sometimes called the revenue and expense budget, consists of a forecast of expected sales along with an estimate of the costs necessary to achieve the sales goal. Usually this budget will be made up in detail for the year ahead, though sometimes estimates for two or three years are also made. However, the most important part of the operations budget is the estimate of revenues and expenses for the coming year.

The revenues portion of the operations budget comes from a forecast of sales. Since the sale of goods or services is the main source of operating revenues for business enterprises, the sales forecast is a key variable in operations budgeting. The information for developing the sales forecast comes from both external and internal sources.

External sources of sales estimates are economic data developed by public and private agencies. The federal government is the most important source of national economic data. The U.S. Department of Commerce issues the monthly *Survey of Current Business* which contains information useful for all business enterprises. Both the *Federal Reserve Bulletin* published monthly by the Board of Governors in Washington, D.C., and the *Economic Indicators* issued by the staff of the Joint Congressional Committee on the Economic Report contain timely economic data. The U.S. Bureau of the Census can provide useful information to business on a national or regional basis.

Private sources of business news include the daily *Wall Street Journal*, weekly *Business Week* and a number of monthly magazines such as *Fortune* and *Dun's Review*. These publications provide information on general business trends and an analysis of economic developments. A wide variety of trade publications are also available that serve the needs of particular industries and areas. Trade journals not only interpret the broad economic view but through the cooperation of member firms collect and present data for their own industries.

General economic data obtained externally must be analyzed by the particular enterprise and integrated with other material. Sampling techniques are available whereby the enterprise can conduct its own surveys to obtain information about consumer attitudes or reactions to its products. This market research is valuable when the sample is properly prepared and the survey is well done.

The enterprise must also use internal data in preparing the sales forecast. These data come from reports of sales personnel, marketing managers, and top executives, and from an analysis of past sales. Despite the availability of mathematical models and statistical analysis, the art of sales forecasting still requires the judgment of managerial personnel.

After the sales forecast, a sales budget is drawn up. This sales budget translates plans into quantitative terms not only for anticipated revenues but also for the expenditures necessary to generate those revenues. This means that anticipated costs for product development, advertising, and sales promotion are part of the operations budget.

In order to check how closely actual results are conforming to expectations, the sales budget is broken down by products and months.

Without this detailed breakdown a comparison of actual results with expectations would be relatively useless for good direction and control. Ultimately all sales persons should have their own budgets so they can check their own performance as well as being subject to management's evaluation.

Budget review and flexibility.   A means of review and revision is necessary if the operations budget is to be useful as a control device. The prompt reporting of actual sales results and comparison with the budget provides the basis for control. There is no point in setting up a budget and blindly pursuing it without regard to later developments. Marketing executives should be able to make immediate adjustments to new opportunities or difficulties.

This does not mean that the basic operations budget is changed every time actual results vary from projected sales or every time circumstances change. The basic budget should serve as a frame of reference with an explanation being made for variations which are bound to occur. This should not prevent revisions during the year as circumstances dictate to make the budget more meaningful for coordination of the activities of the enterprise.

Sometimes two operations budgets representing the extremes of business optimism and pessimism will be drawn up for a year. One will be based on the assumption of excellent economic conditions with the highest level of sales projected. This will be compared with a budget projecting the lowest level of operations assuming less positive economic circumstances and less effective results from management programs. Then the most likely forecast, which normally comes somewhere between the extremes, will be outlined. This most probable expectation is adopted as the budget for the coming period with spending programs and expected sales being based on this. However, contingency budgets are prepared to be put into effect if results improve beyond expectations or if they do not measure up to budgeted figures.

Simplified example of an operations budget

Figure 6–2 is an example of an operations budget for a small retail enterprise showing operating results for 1974 and the operations budget for 1975. The management is projecting an increase in sales of 20 percent based on its analysis that 1974 was not a good year for retail sales in the area because of a high level of unemployment. Also, the owner plans to increase advertising spending by 50 percent in 1975, which

FIGURE 6–2
Tot-Teen Shop operations budget—1975

	Actual 1974		Budget 1975	
Sales..		$70,000		$84,000
Cost of merchandise sold.....................		42,000		50,000
Gross profit on sales.........................		$28,000		$34,000
Operating expenses				
Selling expenses				
Sales salaries............................	$10,200		$10,400	
Advertising..............................	2,400		3,600	
Miscellaneous selling expenses...........	400		500	
Total selling expenses....................	$13,000		$14,500	
General expenses				
General salaries.........................	$ 4,800		$ 5,200	
Rent.....................................	2,400		2,400	
Utilities.................................	900		1,000	
Miscellaneous taxes......................	700		900	
Insurance...............................	300		300	
Miscellaneous general expenses...........	1,200		1,600	
Total general expenses...................	$10,300		$11,400	
Total operating expenses.....................		23,300		25,900
Profit from operations.......................		$ 4,700		$ 8,100
Income taxes...............................		1,200		2,100
Net profit.................................		$ 3,500		$ 6,000

should stimulate sales. This budget was prepared during the latter part of 1974 and finalized as the 1975 budget period was beginning.

The operations budget provides a means of systematic planning for the future and is a basis for control. Actual results can be compared with budgeted plans to determine whether operations are conforming to expectations. In actual practice the owner of the Tot-Teen Shop would prepare more detailed budgets for each department or for major items in the budget. This would aid remedial action if results were below expectations. Also, the annual budget would customarily be broken into quarterly or monthly budgets to improve its timeliness and usefulness.

Cash budgets

The cash budget is an estimate of the business enterprise's cash receipts and cash disbursements over a specified period of time. This budget is used to forecast requirements for cash during future periods. It is a helpful means of justifying a request for a short-term loan from a bank to finance a seasonal increase in business operations.

The cash budget usually extends over the year ahead with cash receipts and disbursements being estimated on a monthly basis. When closer control is justified the inflows and outflows of cash will be estimated on a semimonthly, weekly, or daily basis. The cash budget can be adapted to any time period which will help management do a better job of estimating cash needs, planning for short-term loans, or investing surplus cash. The complexity of the cash budget will depend upon the needs of the enterprise, the nature of cash inflows and outflows, and the degree of their predictability.

Example of a cash budget

Figure 6–3 illustrates a cash budget prepared for the Tot-Teen Shop, a small retail enterprise, over a 9-month period. There is a sales peak in the spring and again in the late summer.

An analysis of the cash budget for Tot-Teen Shop reveals that additional cash will be required for the months of February, March, and August. With this information the management can request a short-term loan from its banker. In March it is estimated that $1,350 could be repaid on the loan from March's cash surplus so that necessary bank credit at the end of March is projected at only $4,500. In April the monthly net cash inflow from operations is forecast at $6,300. This will be enough to repay completely the $4,500 bank loan and leave a cash surplus of $1,800 by the end of April. No further bank credit will be necessary until the month of August when payment for large purchases, probably for the Christmas selling season, necessitates borrowing an estimated $2,250. This can be repaid during the month of September leaving a cash surplus of $400 if cash flow projections are reasonably accurate.

The preparation of a cash budget requires the management to consider carefully the nature of future operations. The Tot-Teen Shop is a relatively simple business. Cash receipts and disbursements are made regularly throughout the month. The most significant variations in disbursements are for purchases which normally are made about three months ahead of the retail selling season. Advertising and sales promotion expenses also vary depending on seasonal factors. This management has found that in off-season months additional money spent on advertising generates very few additional sales.

FIGURE 6-3
Tot-Teen Shop cash budget forecast for January through September, 1975

	Jan.	Feb.	Mar.	April	May	June	July	Aug.	Sept.
Cash receipts:									
Cash sales..............	$3,000	$2,000	$4,000	$6,000	$3,000	$2,000	$2,000	$3,000	$5,000
Credit collections..........	6,000	4,000	2,000	4,000	6,000	3,000	2,000	2,000	4,000
Total monthly receipts.................	$9,000	$6,000	$6,000	$10,000	$9,000	$5,000	$4,000	$5,000	$9,000
Disbursements:									
Purchases..............	7,000	11,000	2,000	2,000	7,000	4,000	2,500	7,000	4,000
Wages................	800	800	1,000	1,000	800	800	800	800	1,000
Rent.................	200	200	200	200	200	200	200	200	200
Utilities and miscellaneous.	150	150	150	100	100	100	150	150	150
Advertising.............	350	200	100	400	300	200	150	200	400
Taxes................			1,200			1,200			600
Total disbursements...	$8,500	$12,350	$4,650	$ 3,700	$8,400	$6,500	$3,800	$8,350	$6,350
Monthly cash change, inflow or outflow..........	+500	−6,350	+1,350	+6,300	+ 600	−1,500	+ 200	−3,350	+2,650
Cumulative inflow or outflow of cash..........	+500	−5,850	−4,500	+1,800	+2,400	+ 900	+1,100	−2,250	+ 400
Beginning cash...........	1,500								
Minimum cash desired.......	1,500								
Excess cash or cash shortage at the end of month............	+500	−5,850	−4,500	+1,800	+2,400	+ 900	+1,100	−2,250	+ 400
Monthly needs— Bank borrowings..........		5,850	4,500					2,250	

Credit collections normally will be the month following credit sales. The Tot-Teen Shop makes about half its sales to 30-day credit customers. Management carefully screens requests for credit. There is a very small proportion of overdue accounts which become bad debts.

As you can see from this illustration, the cash budget can be useful as a planning tool since it requires management to review the entire operation. Besides planning normal cash receipts and disbursements for operations, the cash budget can be used to plan future capital spending for equipment or building improvements.

Capital budgets

The capital budget consists of investment plans for assets which will last longer than a year. Such capital budgeting items include machinery, buildings, land, and improvements to facilities. As with the operations budget, the capital budget is usually prepared for the year immediately ahead. However, capital budgets are also prepared for a longer period in the future to program large-scale investments and to coordinate finance, production, and marketing activities associated with major long-term expenditures.

The capital budget is a list of proposed investment projects and normally includes a justification for each item on the list. One important criterion for justification of a capital investment proposal is the rate of return which the project is expected to yield. However, not all projects requiring capital investment can be evaluated on the basis of their profit returns since not all generate profits or savings over older investments. Such capital expenditures as money spent on an employees' cafeteria, or on paving the parking lot, or on renovating the home office building cannot be measured by the percentage of return on the required investment. Instead, this type of expenditure is usually justified for improved morale, convenience, appearance, or safety.

Approval of the capital budget normally is done by the board of directors after budget committees have analyzed the capital budgets of the various departments of the business enterprise. In the multiproduct company, with divisions functioning almost as independent systems, an overall framework is worked out by the board within which each division develops its own capital budget. These are then submitted to top management for approval. Once a major capital expenditure has been approved in principle, the managers who have responsibility for the project present detailed plans for final authorization of actual cash expenditures.

The level of management which actually authorizes specific capital expenditures depends upon the amount of money involved and the policies adopted in each enterprise. An example of the type of authority required for capital expenditures might be something like this:

Departmental superintendents may authorize capital spending up to $500.

The factory manager may approve capital investments from $500 to $2,500.

The finance committee of the board of directors may approve projects from $2,500 to $20,000.

Full board of directors' approval is required on all capital investment projects of over $20,000.

Once approval has been granted for a capital investment project, control should be a continuing part of the procedure. Reports should be prepared to show how nearly actual expenditures are in line with planned spending. This check continues through the construction and installation phases. After the project begins operation, the anticipated rate of return on the investment or the expected savings are compared with the amounts projected when the proposal was approved. Postcompletion audits of capital budgeting projects are essential to check on profit progress and to improve future budget planning.

COST ACCOUNTING FOR CONTROL

The accounting system in the business enterprise provides a means for control. Cost accounting generates data which can be used to establish centers of managerial responsibility for judging performance. Responsibility centers can be established for a division, a department, or at the foreman's level wherever costs can be controlled. Cost accounting provides a basis for analyzing the controllable costs in a responsibility center.

When a responsibility center's activities generate measurable revenues it is possible to move one step further by designating a profit center where not only costs but also profits are analyzed. It is not feasible to designate all responsibility centers as profit centers since not all sub-systems have operations which directly produce revenues. A manufacturing department can usually be divided into profit centers. However, the engineering department which provides staff services is not judged on its profit contributions but on how well it assists other departments.

Another important aspect of cost accounting is assigning the proper costs to each unit of production. This helps determine product costs, pricing decisions, and profit planning. Cost accounting may also be used to provide information on the expected costs of taking various courses of action in the future. Cost accounting is a valuable planning and decision-making tool as well as being useful for control purposes.

The accounting statements discussed in Chapter 13 provide information which is the basis for other financial controls.

SUMMARY

Control is an important part of the management process. Control provides a means for measuring the progress which an enterprise is making toward its objectives. The three elements of control are the establishment of standards, measurement of performance, and analysis and correction of deviations from expectations.

Control systems will vary with the nature of the enterprise. However, any good control system should be diagnostic, therapeutic, accurate, timely, understandable, and economical.

The budget is a key control device. Budgets outline in quantitative terms the planned operations of the business system for a specified period of time. A variety of budgets are used, including operations budgets, cash budgets, and capital budgets.

Cost accounting generates data which can be used to establish centers of managerial responsibility for judging performance. Cost accounting can be used to assign costs for each unit of production for the determination of product costs, pricing decisions, or profit planning.

Appendix
Break-even analysis

The technique of break-even analysis can be a useful management planning and control device for understanding the relationship between costs and revenues at different levels of operations. The break-even chart, sometimes called the profitgraph, assumes a particular pattern of variable and fixed costs and provides management with an estimate of profits or losses that would occur at various levels of sales. In constructing a break-even chart, first the cost functions are analyzed and then the sales revenue function is added.

You will recall from Chapter 4 that *variable costs* are directly influenced by the number of units produced. Variable costs include such expenses as materials used in the production of goods and the wages of production workers. *Fixed costs* are those costs which continue whether or not the enterprise is producing goods. Fixed costs include such expenses as rent, property taxes, and the interest on borrowed money.

Figure 6–4 illustrates fixed and variable costs. At any given volume of operations the sum of fixed and variable costs equals total costs at that level of units. Variable costs in this example are estimated at $5 per unit. Therefore, the variable costs line, *AB,* increases at a rate of $5 for each additional unit produced to reflect the added costs of materials and labor for the extra units. Thus at the zero level of production there are no variable costs, while at the level of 200,000 units of production the total variable costs equal $1 million.

Fixed costs of $3 million remain constant regardless of the level of output for this particular business enterprise. Fixed costs are shown on Figure 6–4 as the vertical distance between the *AB* and *CD* lines on

FIGURE 6–4
Estimated cost structure

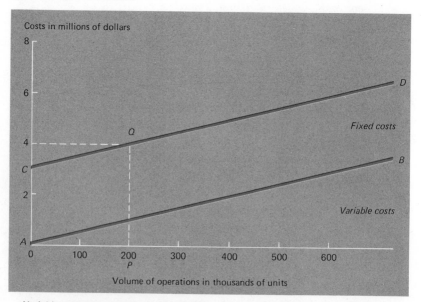

Variable costs are calculated at $5 per unit.
Fixed costs are at a level of $3 million for range of operations from 0 to 600,000 units annually.

the chart. At a level of zero units of production the fixed costs of $3 million are shown by the distance between points *A* and *C*. That fixed costs are constant at any level of output is illustrated by measuring the vertical distance between *AB* and *CD* at any level of production. Note that the distance between *AB* and *CD* remains a constant $3 million.

Total costs of operations for the enterprise are represented by the *CD* line which includes both the total variable costs and fixed costs at any particular volume level. Total costs can be verified for any level of production by multiplying the units produced by the $5 variable costs per unit and adding the $3 million fixed costs. For example, if the 200,000 units of production are multiplied by the $5 per unit variable cost, this equals $1 million. The $1 million variable cost figure added to the $3 million fixed cost figure means that the total cost of producing 200,000 units is $4 million, the distance from *P* to *Q*.

In the second stage, Figure 6–5 is the complete break-even chart. It has the same cost structure as Figure 6–4. However, now a sales revenue line, designated as *AE,* has been added to complete the revenue

FIGURE 6–5
Break-even chart

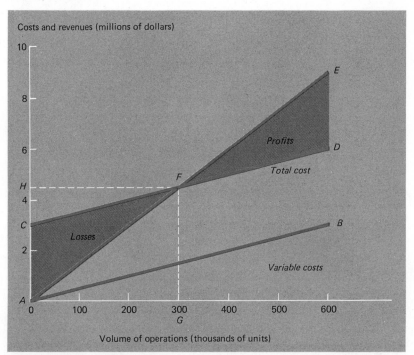

Variable costs calculated at $5 per unit. Fixed costs calculated at $3 million total. Sales revenue calculated at $15 per unit.

and cost relationship. Sales revenue increases at a rate of $15 per unit, the assumed price for which each unit of the enterprise's product could be sold. The rate of sales revenue increase is constant, which implies that each unit is sold at the same price regardless of the number of units sold.

Notice that the total revenue line, *AE*, crosses the total costs line, *CD*, at point *F*. Point *F* is called the break-even point and is where revenues equal costs. In this example this is at a level of sales of 300,000 units, marked by point *G,* and at a cost of $4,500,000, marked by point *H*. At the break-even point the enterprise is neither earning a profit nor incurring a loss. At sales levels higher than *G* the enterprise generates a profit from operations. Below the break-even point sales revenue is insufficient to cover total costs and the enterprise suffers a loss.

Since the break-even point is where sales revenue is equal to total costs of operation, the break-even point may be determined more precisely by using the following formula than by looking at the graph:

$$\text{Sales revenue} = \text{Total costs}$$

or

$$\begin{bmatrix} \text{No. of} \\ \text{units sold} \end{bmatrix} \begin{bmatrix} \text{Price per} \\ \text{unit} \end{bmatrix} = \begin{bmatrix} \text{Total fixed} \\ \text{cost} \end{bmatrix} + \begin{bmatrix} \text{No. of} \\ \text{units sold} \end{bmatrix} \begin{bmatrix} \text{Variable costs} \\ \text{per unit} \end{bmatrix}$$

To calculate the break-even point by formula from the information given in the example for Figure 6–3: Let *X* equal number of units sold at break-even point.

$$(X)\,(\$15) = \$3,000,000 + (X)\,(\$5)$$
$$10X = 3,000,000$$
$$X = 300,000 \text{ units}$$
$$15X = \text{Total sales revenue at break-even}$$
$$= \$4,500,000$$

These figures may also be read at points *G* and *H* on the break-even chart in Figure 6–5 as was shown, although graphic presentations are more difficult to read with accuracy to the last digits.

The break-even chart is useful in demonstrating the factors which affect profits and the way in which profits may be controlled. A study of the break-even chart shows that profits will vary for each level of volume of operations. Observe on Figure 6–5 that the level of profits increases as sales increase past the break-even point. There are four ways in which the profit of a business can be increased, each of which can be analyzed through break-even analysis:

Variable costs per unit can be decreased.

Fixed costs can be decreased.

Selling price per unit can be increased.

More units can be sold.

Note what effect varying any of the above could have on the profits as shown in the break-even chart Figure 6–5. It would be useful for you to work out a numerical example to demonstrate your understanding. Each factor should be worked through assuming the other three remain constant, even though in actual practice changes in one factor will likely have an influence on others. For example, an increase in the sales price per unit may well result in a lower volume of units sold.

In order to see the limitations in the use of break-even analysis you should keep in mind the assumptions on which the chart is based. It is assumed that variable costs increase at a constant rate; that is, materials and direct labor costs are the same for each additional unit of production. Fixed costs are the same throughout the given range of operations assuming no changes in the level of capital invested or changes in overhead which would alter these fixed costs. It is assumed there will be no changes in the market which may affect selling prices. The break-even chart assumes that production and sales move together with no significant change in inventories which might affect cost relationships. By depicting cost and revenue relationships simply as straight lines the estimates of losses at the low end of the scale and profits at the upper end of the scale may be of only limited value. However, normally the enterprise is not faced with a question of eliminating sales or cutting them back to a very small fraction of previous levels. Also, it is rare that management can increase sales as much as three times or more without significant additional capital investment. Therefore, the break-even chart can be used best by management in the analysis and control of business operations over a limited period of time and range of volume.

TERMS FOR REVIEW

control	*sales budget*
standards	*cash budget*
budget	*capital budget*
operations budget (*revenue and expense budget*)	*cost accounting*

QUESTIONS

1. What is the purpose of control in the business enterprise?
2. What recommendations would you make to the owner of a new manu-facturing enterprise for the development of a control system? What different types of controls would be needed?
3. Explain the requirements of an effective control system.
4. What is a budget? Why are budgets important?
5. Outline a step-by-step procedure for developing an operations budget for a manufacturer supplying replacement auto parts to wholesale sup-ply distributors on the West Coast. How would you develop the sales forecast for such an enterprise?
6. Assume the cash disbursements for purchases shown in Figure 6–3 for the Tot-Teen Shop were made during the first ten days of each month instead of throughout the month. Restate the cash budget for the Tot-Teen Shop assuming that all other disbursements are made regularly throughout the month and that cash receipts are received in an even flow throughout the month.
7. What is the relationship of the capital budget to the operations budget and the cash budget?
8. In what ways is cost accounting useful to management?

Business briefs

Planning change—changing plans

The rapid changes of the 1970s and their unpredictability have raised new problems for business budget makers. This has given rise to an increased importance for contingency planning and lowered the confidence of managements in a single annual budget.

During 1974 costs and prices were rising so fast that budgets made six months earlier were of little value. For example, one regional air-line's maintenance costs increased 40 percent in less than a year. Short-term interest rates for prime business borrowers skyrocketed from 6 percent to 10 percent in less than nine months during 1973. In 1974 bank interest rates rose to a historic high of 12 percent on these high quality business loans.

Inflation, materials shortages, the energy crisis, and political un-certainties were quickly followed in 1974 by recession, increasing in-ventories, lower production, and rising unemployment. Because of these rapid changes business planners are reviewing and changing budgets more frequently. Instead of updating long-range budgets yearly, many enterprise managements are updating plans quarterly, monthly, or weekly. Also, instead of relying on a single budget, more attention is being given to a range of contingency plans based on alternative assumptions.

For example, Xerox is developing long-range planning to 1990 but based on five sets of alternative assumptions instead of one. Ralston Purina Company reviews its corporate planning any time there is a one percent price change in one of its major commodities.

Computers are being used increasingly to provide analysis for assessment of the changing conditions affecting business. Many corporations constantly monitor a number of important economic conditions and run changes in these through computers programmed to show the effects on company budgets. These factors include interest rates, consumer spending, the price of basic raw materials, and inventory levels. Dow Chemical Company has a computer model of its operations which is revised weekly for more than 100 different cost factors including raw materials costs around the world. Hewlett-Packard, computer manufacturer, calculates as many as 50 different possible economic alternatives depending on a variety of conditions. Such calculations help planners not only with production and sales decisions but also assist in decisions relating to cash management and borrowing.

1. With the increased uncertainty of economic conditions is meaningful budgeting and business planning virtually impossible and therefore a waste of time and money?
2. If you were a budgeting officer in the following enterprises, which economic conditions would you consider important?
    a. American Airlines
    b. Kroger Stores
    c. Ford Motor Company
    d. Georgia-Pacific Corporation
3. What effect do changing conditions and resulting budget changes have for:
    a. Manufacturing supervisors?
    b. Marketing managers?
    c. Nonmanagement employees?

Belt tightening at Chrysler

Following a loss of $52 million in 1974, Chrysler Corporation was faced with a long-term debt repayment of $140 million early in 1975. To meet this financial bind Chrysler took a variety of actions to control a potentially critical situation. Chrysler's management negotiated a three-year $400 million revolving line of credit from 40 of the country's largest banks.

The nation's third largest auto maker reduced its payroll expenses by laying off indefinitely about half of its 80,000 hourly workers and half of its 40,000 white-collar employees. Payroll expenses normally run about $600 million a quarter. Chrysler suspended cost-of-living allowance payments to its nonunion employees to save about $5 million a quarter. Top executives reportedly took a one-month pay cut of 50 percent. The company also ended its employee stock purchase plan to which the company made matching contributions.

Car sales continued to be slow. Chrysler's inventory of new cars approached 50,000 units with an estimated worth of between $90 and $150 million. Chrysler announced $200 to $400 price rebates on certain 1975 models during the spring to boost sagging sales. While such rebates reduced profits on these cars, the company's funds flow was improved by turning cars into cash.

1. What circumstances brought about Chrysler's financial bind in early 1975?
2. What changes in Chrysler's operating budget had to be made as the result of sharply lower sales and profits?
3. *a.* Which cash expenses does Chrysler's management have control over in the short run?
   b. Which cash expenses are not subject to short-run control by management?
4. What will be the long-term solution to Chrysler's financial bind?

Cases

Jim Rader, proprietor

After a period of several years as foreman and chief estimator for McGill Cabinet Shop, Jim Rader quit his job to begin his own woodworking shop. Two of the best craftsmen at McGill quit to join Jim's operation. Some custom orders were received, and an initial order was obtained from a local lumber yard for preassembled door frames and windows which would keep the men occupied for a reasonable period of time.

Despite this good start for his new enterprise, Jim Rader was concerned as he recalled the nature of the control system used by his former employer. Jim felt that if his business were to prosper he would need controls on the costs and quality of his products. However, he was thoroughly dissatisfied with the control system under which he had been forced to work in the McGill Shop.

Jim called his friend Larry Thomas, who was a certified public accountant and a partner in a local accounting firm. He asked for an appointment to discuss the new business and the kinds of controls which he would need. On the day of the appointment Jim arrived at the accounting firm's suite of offices.

"Larry," began Jim, "I want to approach you for some help with my new business. We have been successful initially in generating business. and I am pleased with the quality of our work force. However, with all my experience at McGill I never did get a clear understanding of their control system. If what they had represents good controls I don't want any part of it. What I would like for you to do, Larry, is to analyze my business at this point and indicate what you think I need in the way of controls."

"I believe we are prepared to do a control analysis for you," responded the consultant. "Most of my time is spent now in providing management consulting services to our clients rather than the more traditional public accounting work.

"Why don't you start off by telling me something about the kinds of controls you didn't like at your former situation and then what your present operations are like. After this I can proceed with a preliminary written report for you. Then we can get together and talk it over before any elaborate system is designed. Among other things, you will need to control such items as the cost of consultants!"

"To begin with," Jim said, "it seemed like McGill's management was penny-wise and pound-foolish. One of the things that really bugged me was telephone usage in the shop. Part of my job consisted of contacting customers as a kind of technical advisor. It would have been a lot easier to call out-of-town customers than to write letters. But Bill McGill, the company president, put his foot down on the use of long-distance telephone calls and said that such calls would be held to an absolute minimum. Also, every time I made a long-distance call I had to fill out a chit for the bookkeeper so when the phone bill came in it could be checked to see that none of us were making long-distance personal calls which were billed to the company.

"Another thing that I didn't like was the way the bookkeeper kept pestering the foremen to get in their time sheets and materials-in-process reports. You would have thought that everything revolved around the bookkeeper's office in that shop. I guess Mr. McGill thought so too since he always was complaining to the office force about not having reports completed on time.

"We never knew how we stood with the company although I'll say that the Christmas bonuses paid out by the McGills were sure nice to have at that time of the year. However, very little was ever said on how things were going in the shop unless McGill came down to complain about something going wrong.

"I guess you wonder, Larry," continued Jim Rader, "why I stuck it out as long as I did at McGill's. Sometimes I wonder myself. The old-timers said that Mr. McGill had been like that ever since his son was killed in Vietnam in 1967, and they just put up with it. Also, the firm does have a good reputation for quality work. I learned a lot there and the money was good. When I quit, Mr. McGill seemed surprised. He said that he had me picked to be promoted to general manager of the shop when Sam Jones retired in a few years! That was sure news to me and by then I already had made up my mind to start my own business. However, this doesn't have anything to do with control systems.

"There was one good thing done in McGill's shop. That was the care which all the foremen were forced to use in keeping the jobs separate. As you may know, most of their business is big custom deals. Every stick of wood that went into a job was accounted for. They sure knew which jobs they came out on and which lost money. There weren't many jobs that they had any losses on!

"As I outlined over the telephone the other day, my business is a small one at present. We have two men working in the shop. I also employ a student part-time to handle miscellaneous jobs ranging from answering the telephone while I'm gone to cleaning up the shop and handling some paper work. However, most of the office work is done by my wife who comes in when she can. I do all the selling as well as ordering the raw materials. We think we have the beginning of something which could work out very nicely, but I don't want to foul it up by too many controls or not enough."

1. Appraise the control system in the McGill Cabinet Shop as described by Jim Rader. Discuss positive and negative elements of the system as it is understood by Rader.

2. What steps could the management of McGill Cabinet Shop have taken to improve the effectiveness of its control system?
3. Outline a preliminary report from the accountant's office suggesting the basic nature of controls needed by Jim Rader at this time. Does Jim Rader need to be concerned with a control system with such a small business? Why or why not?

Tot-Teen Shop

The Tot-Teen Shop was established early in 1971 by Mr. and Mrs. Lloyd Bethany in a town of 20,000 in upstate New York. Mrs. Bethany acted as general manager of the shop and did the buying. Mr. Bethany, who was a manufacturer's representative for several builders' supply companies, had little active part in the business except for general advice and assistance. The shop was stocked with a quality price line of merchandise for children from birth up to age 13. Although there were other stores in town selling children's clothing, the Tot-Teen Shop lines were of higher quality.

Tot-Teen quickly became known for the quality of its merchandise and personal service. Business was brisk. In addition to Mrs. Bethany who put in full time at the shop, one full-time woman sales clerk was employed. Part-time sales personnel were used during seasonal sales periods or when Mrs. Bethany was required to be out of town on buying trips or on vacation. A part-time bookkeeper handled the paper work of the business.

In December 1975, Mrs. Bethany was planning her sales program for next Easter, which was April 18, 1976. In past peak seasons the Tot-Teen Shop had borrowed funds from the First National Bank to cover inventory buildups. These seasonal borrowings had been promptly reduced after the selling season had ended. Mrs. Bethany assumed that funds would be available again from the bank.

To prepare her request for short-term credit Mrs. Bethany put down the information necessary to prepare a cash budget of cash receipts and disbursements for the first six months of 1976. Based on past years' results and her expectations for the current year ahead Mrs. Bethany estimated sales as given in Exhibit 1.

Approximately one half of the shop's sales are cash sales with the remainder being made on 30-day charge accounts. The Bethanys screen requests for credit carefully. For planning purposes it may be assumed that charged sales will be collected in the month following sale

EXHIBIT 1
Sales estimates for first 6 months of 1976

January..........................	$ 8,000
February.........................	5,000
March............................	9,000
April............................	13,000
May..............................	8,000
June.............................	6,000

of merchandise. Customers' accounts receivable on December 31, 1975, will be $7,000 according to estimates.

In late December 1975, the Tot-Teen Shop had a cash balance of approximately $1,500. The Bethanys considered this to be a satisfactory minimum level of cash so that funds would be available to take care of unforeseen needs which might arise.

The customary terms under which the Bethanys purchased merchandise for the shop provided for cash discounts for prompt payment. It had been the practice of the Tot-Teen Shop to take all cash discounts, which means that merchandise would be paid for in the month following its shipment. The cash discounts have already been deducted from the purchase figures in Exhibit 2. Therefore these amounts would be paid the month following purchase.

For planning purposes, it may be assumed that the payments for merchandise will be made on a regular basis throughout the month in which they were due, not falling in large volume on any specific date.

The preceding schedule (Exhibit 2) was prepared by the Bethanys for their purchases for December, 1975, and estimated purchases the first six months of 1976. The amounts shown are for estimated invoice dates although actual order placement would occur in some cases before the time indicated.

Wages to be paid during the first six months of the year were esti-

EXHIBIT 2
Estimated purchases of merchandise

December, 1975....................	$ 8,000
January, 1976.....................	10,000
February..........................	5,000
March.............................	2,000
April.............................	3,000
May...............................	5,000
June..............................	5,000

mated at $1,000 per month, except during March and April when an additional part-time salesperson would be employed; this would result in approximately $200 per month being added to wages expense. The $1,000 included Mrs. Bethany's drawings as proprietor of the shop.

Rent and utilities payments had averaged $500 per month for the past year. There was no indication that this could not be expected in 1976, since two years remained on the Bethanys' lease on the shop building. Advertising was paid for in the month following its use. The advertising schedule was as follows:

December, 1975	$500
January, 1976	200
February	100
March	300
April	200
May	100
June	100

In addition, Mrs. Bethany estimated tax payments of approximately $1,200 in each of the months of March and June. Although the estimates were rough, it was likely that $200 monthly would be spent on miscellaneous items ranging from charitable contributions to minor repairs and expenses associated with buying trips.

After collecting this information, Mrs. Bethany sat down to put together a cash budget forecast to present to the loan officer with her request for credit to the First National Bank.

1. Prepare in good order the cash budget forecast from the information assembled by Mrs. Bethany.
2. What is the maximum amount of bank credit required assuming that any cash shortage will have to come from bank loans since there is no excess cash presently in the enterprise's bank account?
3. When will the maximum need for funds arise?
4. When, if at all during the six-month period, will Tot-Teen Shop be able to get out of debt to the bank?
5. If you were a bank loan officer what information would you want in addition to the cash forecast prepared for this case? Would you extend credit to this enterprise?

A problem in profit analysis

The ABC Manufacturing Corporation had one main product line for which management believed rather accurate costs had been calculated.

Between production levels of 30,000 and 150,000 units it was estimated that variable costs were $10 per unit. At these levels of production the fixed costs were about $700,000. The current sales price of the product was $30 per unit in the quantities purchased by most customers.

Required:

1. Construct a break-even chart showing cost and revenue functions over the range of production indicated.
   a. What is the break-even sales volume in units and dollars?
   b. What is the amount of profit or loss at 30,000 units of production and sales? At 100,000 units? At 150,000 units?
2. In what ways could this analysis be helpful to the management of ABC Manufacturing Corporation?
3. What limitations are there to this analysis?

section three

Human
elements of
administration

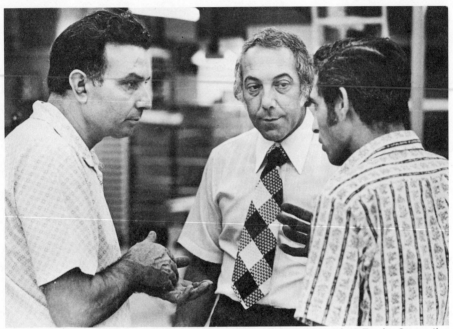

Positive human relations
encourages employees
to do their best work.

An understanding of human relations is essential for the effective manager in directing the activities of employees to achieve the objectives of the enterprise. This chapter discusses the nature of human relations and direction. The following issues concerning this function of management are introduced:

> *What are the individual needs of employees?*
> *What is the importance of direction in the management process?*
> *Why must both the formal and informal organization be considered in developing effective human relations?*
> *How do status and status symbols relate to the business enterprise?*
> *How can managers develop a healthy work climate?*

7

Human relations and direction

THE INDIVIDUAL AND THE BUSINESS ENTERPRISE

Sometimes managers, particularly those at the head of a business enterprise, assume that because they are completely devoted to their company's endeavors all employees will be similarly motivated. However, this simply is not true! The good manager will understand the difference between individuals' goals and enterprise goals, what motivates individual employees, and the importance of human relations in modern management.

Individual needs versus enterprise goals

The principal goal of the business enterprise is the provision of goods and services to consumers at a profit. To a certain extent all persons employed by a business share this goal, since without the enterprise they would not have their present jobs. However, individuals are also concerned about their own personal needs and objectives. These are distinctly separate from the principal goals of the organizations where they are employed. It is important to provide a climate in the business enterprise which will both satisfy the employees' needs and achieve the broad economic objectives of the enterprise.

Individuals have physical and material needs which are met largely through wages and fringe benefits. In today's expanding economy what will satisfy our material needs in the United States has changed greatly over the last 50 years. What was considered a luxury item only a few years ago may be considered a necessity today by a large proportion of the population. The level of wage payments is one factor affecting the morale of the work force. This topic is discussed in the next chapter on personnel administration.

However, human relations involve much more. Nonmaterial needs of employees must be considered in developing a good human relations climate. These nonmaterial needs are both psychological and social. Psychological needs pertain to the individual's own self-image. These include love, self-respect, and a feeling of accomplishment. Social needs include all those which arise from relations among individuals and groups. These include the needs for recognition, acceptance, and group activity.

Some of these psychological and social needs are met by the family and other groups. However, a large proportion of an individual's waking hours are spent on the job. People cannot shut off their social and psychological needs when they step into the factory or office. They cannot be expected not to have feelings about the situations and people encountered in the workplace. Employee morale can be greatly improved when management recognizes and meets these psychological and social needs insofar as possible.

Motivation of the individual

How does management deal with its employees so as to motivate them to do their work well? Early in Chapter 4 a motive was defined as a drive, impulse, or desire that moves one to action. Motivation begins with management recognition of the material, social, and psychological needs that individuals bring to the work situation. Workers act in order to satisfy their needs.

Individuals are motivated to work satisfactorily because of their desire for more goods and services. Once material needs are provided for, then other needs take on a greater importance. Psychologists suggest that in the United States social and psychological needs are becoming more important because we already have a high material standard of living.

The fact that material needs may be considered less important than social and psychological needs is shown by a study of nearly 1,000 managers who changed jobs. It was found that money ranked fifth among the reasons they gave for quitting. The four leading factors which ranked above money were: dissatisfaction with the present job; poor chance for advancement; conflicts at work, particularly with the boss; and altered duties or status because of corporate reorganization.

What seems to be the case for managerial personnel is also relevant for production employees. Workers bring to the job a variety of needs which motivate them. When management has a clear understanding of these needs, it has a firm basis for good human relations in the enterprise.

DIRECTION—DEALING WITH PEOPLE AT WORK

Direction is the process of aiding an enterprise's employees in carrying out their jobs. Direction is at the heart of management. Coordinating the activities of many different workers requires the major part of most managers' time. The process of direction occurs at all levels. This means that managers throughout the enterprise should be concerned with good direction of subordinates. What skills are required of a manager? What are the different types of leadership? How important is communications? As you read the following pages look for answers to these questions about the direction function of management.

Skills required of the manager

In today's business enterprise the manager's job is complex. Different types of skills are required depending upon the manager's level in the organization. These skills may be classified as technical, human, and conceptual.[1] The mix among these three skills is illustrated in Figure 7–1.

Technical skill consists of a manager's ability in and knowledge of

---

[1] Robert L. Katz, "Skills of an Effective Administrator," *Harvard Business Review,* September–October 1974, pp. 90–102.

a particular process or technique. Technical skill basically requires knowledge of things rather than people. Examples of technical skill are to be found in the activities of typists, accountants, and engineers. Technical skill is especially important at the first level of supervision. Here a close understanding of techniques is frequently necessary. The higher in the management hierarchy one moves, the less important technical skill becomes. Middle management relies more upon others for technical information and is increasingly involved in human and conceptual problems. By the time a person reaches top management

FIGURE 7–1
Skills required of the effective manager

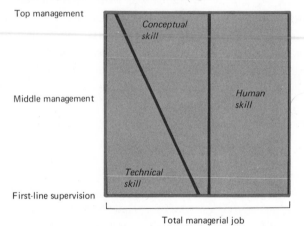

Total managerial job

little or no time is devoted to the exercise of technical skills. This may be one reason why top executives with well-developed human and conceptual skills can move easily from one industry to another in positions of high responsibility.

Human skill is the ability to work with people and to build effective work teams. Throughout the organization managers are required to work with people to further the enterprise's objectives. Human skills should be part of the new managers' orientation and should be developed throughout their careers.

Conceptual skill is the ability to diagnose a problem in relation to its total environment and to develop creative solutions. It is the ability to visualize the entire picture and use original thinking in problem solving. Conceptual skill is very important for top management in formulating long-range plans and making broad policy decisions. Conceptual skill deals primarily with ideas, human skill with persons, and technical skill with things.

Different types of leadership

Leadership is the element of direction which causes subordinates to follow. It results in accomplishment of the goals of the enterprise. Leadership can be classified as authoritarian or participative.

With *authoritarian leadership* there is centralized authority and autocratic decision making. Subordinates are given little or no discretion in carrying out work assignments. They merely follow orders! *Participative leadership* consists of decentralization of authority among subordinates. Decisions are made by those where action is required. Suggestions from subordinates are encouraged. This type of leadership emphasizes communication from the leader to all members of the group and from the group to the leader.

These two leadership styles, authoritarian and participative, are exercised by what one writer has called "Theory X" and "Theory Y" type managers.[2] Theory X (authoritarian) managers presumably view their employees as basically lazy, preferring to avoid responsibility, and requiring close supervision and control to achieve enterprise objectives. Theory Y (participative) managers presumably look upon their employees as work-oriented, anxious to assume responsibility, and willing to exercise initiative and self-control to achieve results. These two types of direction are theoretical extremes. In practice elements of both may be observed in most managers.

Authoritarian leadership is sometimes criticized. However, the competent manager who directs in an autocratic manner may be able to accomplish the work of the enterprise quite well, especially in the short run. Less time is required than with participative leadership. Employees do not have to exercise much independent judgment. Therefore, personnel who have fewer capabilities may be hired. Despite some advantages for authoritarian leadership, in the long run the failure to use the capabilities of all employees and the dependence upon one person weakens this type of leadership for the business enterprise.

Participative leadership is widely regarded as having the most long-run advantages for the successful business enterprise. Management

---

[2] Douglas McGregor, *The Human Side of Enterprise,* McGraw-Hill Book Company, 1960.

training programs tend to emphasize direction by this method because employee satisfactions and enterprise productivity tend to be maximized. Participative leadership recognizes the dignity of each employee. It attempts to draw upon not only managers but all employees for the smooth functioning of the enterprise.

Participative leadership should not be used unless the manager is genuinely concerned about the views of subordinates. Employees will quickly perceive when it is merely a pretense and its usefulness will be severely limited. Under such circumstances the manager might be better advised to use authoritarian leadership openly so employees will clearly understand what is expected from them.

Also, not all workers want to share the authority and assume the responsibility that goes with participative management. When employees have been managed autocratically by a previous manager, a new supervisor may encounter difficulties when he attempts to use participative methods. A gradual dispersion of authority throughout the enterprise or department concerned is advisable. Abrupt changes in leadership methods may result in uncertainty and lower morale for the work force. When a manager comes into a new supervisory situation, he or she is well advised to determine what has been the type of leadership before beginning to make changes.

The exercise of good leadership by the manager can result in increased efficiency among employees. With mediocre leadership subordinates will likely carry out their assigned tasks well enough to avoid reprimand or dismissal. However, good leadership can result in employees putting out extra effort above the minimum required.

The importance of good communication

Definition of communication. Good communication is essential in the process of direction. Without communication the most brilliant plans conceived by management cannot be carried out. Management cannot be informed by subordinates of the severe operating problems which arise from time to time in all enterprises. Just what is communication? *Communication* is the transmission of understanding. This requires both a sender and a receiver, each in tune with the other.

A supervisor who, preoccupied by a problem at home, comes into the shop or office one morning and fails to speak to the employees as usual may set the entire department to wondering what is wrong. This may actually reduce production for the day. Failure to greet the employees may be misinterpreted by them as displeasure with something they have done. The boss's comment to an employee, "Chuck, you're doing a hell of a job," may have either positive or negative interpretations depending upon the circumstances. Unless the intent of the boss's remark is crystal clear to the employee, a compliment may be interpreted as a criticism when it was not so intended by the boss.

Communication throughout the organization structure. There are three dimensions of communication within the organization structure of the business enterprise. Information can be transmitted down through the organization from superior to subordinates, frequently following the

FIGURE 7–2
Diagram of vertical and horizontal communication

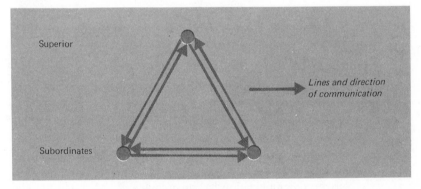

chain of command. Communication may occur as information being sent up from lower echelons to higher levels in the organization. Or there can be horizontal communication as between departments or among employees at about the same level in the organization. Figure 7–2 symbolizes these dimensions of communication.

Too often management personnel assume that the only communication going on is the orders and information they send down to subordinates. However, valuable information may be received from throughout the organization if managers are sensitive to communications feedback. The number of employee grievances and their source, attitudes reflected in absences or high scrap rates, and suggestions by subordinates may be useful information when communicated upward to management. Horizontal communication in the business enterprise can improve coordination between departments and individuals throughout the organization.

Written and spoken communications. Both written and spoken communications have important places in the business enterprise. Written communications are used for policy statements, procedures, rules, job descriptions, advertising, press releases, office memos, organization charts, letters, and legal documents. Regardless of its nature, a written communication should be stated clearly and concisely with the reader in mind. The advantage of written communications is that they may be retained for future reference. Also when a person writes something for someone else the chances are good that it will be better stated than if it were spoken. Many persons give greater consideration to the written word since they can be more easily held accountable for it.

Written communication has two disadvantages. First, the present volume of paper work in business and government is reaching staggering proportions. Many reports, contracts, memoranda, and other papers are saved long past their usefulness. Duplicated files are kept to justify decisions or recommendations to higher management should any questions ever be raised. These files frequently far outlive their necessity. The result is that valuable space and clerical help are required for their maintenance.

Second, the fact that information is written does not guarantee it will be carefully thought out or clearly stated. Furthermore, the written word may be costly by the time it is reproduced and sent to those for whom it is intended.

Spoken communication has advantages of speed and possible amplification. In face-to-face communication real meaning can be conveyed through tone and facial expression as well as through discussion. The telephone industry has greatly expanded because of the advantages of instant oral communication over great distances.

As with written communication, clarity and conciseness are important in spoken communication. A conference or meeting can involve the valuable time of many persons. Their time should not be wasted by excessive talk. A previously circulated written agenda, which is followed by the chairman, will be a help in making meetings worthwhile for all participants. The main weakness in spoken communication is that in the future it may be difficult to remember exactly what was said unless some type of recording is made of the conversation.

The importance of listening. For good communication to occur there must be a communicator who clearly transmits information. Equally important is the person to whom the message is directed. Unless the receiver of the information understands what is being said, communication cannot take place. Effective listening is as important to good communication as clear speaking.

The two elements to consider in effective listening are what the listener hears and what the speaker means. When the listener hears the meaning intended by the speaker then true oral communication has occurred.

The listener needs to understand the frame of reference of the speaker. Often we do not really understand what is being said to us because instead of just listening carefully we are busy evaluating the speaker's words from our own frame of reference. The question running through our minds when someone is speaking to us, especially when it is the boss, frequently is, "How is this going to affect me?" A more appropriate question would be, "What is this person trying to say?" There will be time later to evaluate the remarks from our own frame of reference. First, we should attempt to understand the speaker's meaning. The next time someone comes to you with a problem or question listen quietly to what is said without making any judgments. Listen with a view to perceiving the problem through the eyes of the speaker. By doing this you will have made an important step in improving the communication.

When people listen more effectively they will discover that many miscommunications occur because of the failure of speaker and listener to have a similar perception of what the problem is. One of the most important elements of communication, when persons attempt to discuss a situation which at least one of them views as a problem, is to establish the dimensions of the problem from the frame of reference of all parties. Then discussion can proceed on the merits of various solutions from the different points of view. Sometimes just a careful definition of the issue results in a conclusion that what was thought to be a problem is really not a problem after all. A lack of communication had resulted in misunderstanding, fear, or frustration.

ORGANIZATIONAL ASPECTS OF HUMAN RELATIONS

Human relations is usually thought of in terms of interpersonal relationships. However, there are also organizational aspects to human relations. The formal and informal organization of the business enterprise, the importance of status in organizations, and the labor union are three important organizational elements of human relations. The first two of these elements are discussed here while the role of unions is analyzed in detail in Chapter 9, which deals with labor relations.

The formal organization

The formal organization of the business enterprise has been discussed in some detail in Chapter 5. Recall that every business enterprise of any size is organized into departments. Each department must develop

FIGURE 7–3
Smith Brothers Corporation (partial organization chart)

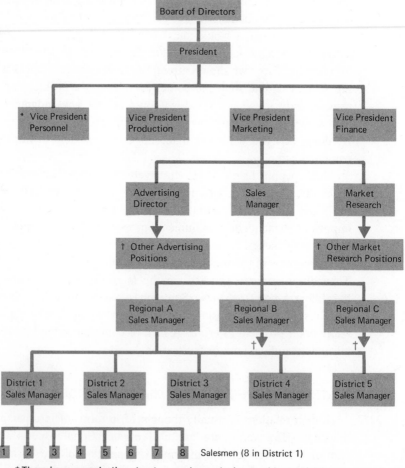

*There is an organization structure under each vice president which is not shown here except for the marketing department.
†Not detailed here for lack of space.

workable authority-responsibility relationships, select line and staff personnel, delegate decision making, and establish the width of the management span of control. A strong thread of human relations runs through all aspects of the formal organization because of the involvement of persons.

In the formal organization each person occupies a particular position or *status*. This can be diagrammed on an organization chart similar to Figure 7–3. Each status position carries with it an expected behavior pattern which is referred to as the *role*. Thus, individuals perform the activities of the roles associated with the statuses they occupy. These statuses and roles are formally organized into a functioning unit designed to promote the enterprise's objectives. The duties and responsibilities involved in these roles continue regardless of who performs them. This means that if the vice president for marketing retires, the status of head of the marketing department does not disappear. Someone else must be selected to fulfill this position in the business enterprise.

Figure 7–3 depicts part of a simple organization chart showing how the different status positions relate to each other in a hypothetical business enterprise. There are no persons named on this organization chart. Only the statuses to be filled are given. A job description outlining the duties of each position would accompany this chart. Notice how in the formal organization of the enterprise the lines of authority and responsibility from the board of directors and the president run throughout the organization. This represents the formal and more traditional concept of the authority exercised in the enterprise. It is important for subordinate managers and workers to understand top management roles in addition to their own. All employees must realize the authority associated with a particular status position if this authority is to be exercised effectively.

The informal organization

The formal organization in the business enterprise makes little allowance for the natural desire of the individual to associate with other persons. In every enterprise informal organizations develop spontaneously to meet this social need of people. An *informal organization* is a self-grouping of employees in the work situation that is not detailed on the formal organization chart. The informal organization depends upon the personalities of individuals for its being rather than upon abstract statuses and roles.

Functions of the informal organization. The informal organization provides for the social needs and control of its members and communication among employees. In providing an outlet for the social needs of employees the informal organization may benefit management. On the assembly lines and in large offices a single production worker or filing clerk may not have much recognition in the formal status hierarchy of the enterprise. However, as a member of an informal work group each is recognized, participates in exchanges of views and jokes, and has a circle of acquaintances with whom there are relationships. This can be a positive contribution to the work situation.

However, sometimes informal groups become a negative factor. They may exert strong pressure on individual employees to conform. Informal groups may withhold social recognition if the employee does not conform. The social control exercised by informal groups frequently includes setting production standards that fit the work group's concept of a "fair day's work." These work standards will not necessarily be the same as those of management or the labor union. Various means are available to the informal work group in enforcing its standards. These include refusing to communicate with the individual who does not accept their values. More extreme sanctions include property damage or physical injury.

Informal communication—the grapevine. The second function of the informal organization—communication—is customarily known as the *grapevine*. Managements have found the grapevine to be both a help and a hindrance in operating the business enterprise.

The grapevine can be an effective means of rapidly disseminating information. Management may also get informal reactions to an idea being considered by placing information judiciously with informal group leaders in the business enterprise. This provides management with a trial balloon to test out the idea on employees. Sometimes information may be gained through this means which will cause changes in management's plans.

The grapevine can be a hindrance to management when rumors are passed along its channels. In the business enterprise a *rumor* is characterized as incomplete, unconfirmed information which is frequently either incorrect or malicious in its intent. To avoid negative consequences of rumor, management should act to see that correct information is a part of the grapevine. This may include explaining or denying informally circulated information which is incomplete or incorrect and providing an accurate explanation of the situation. Rumors will be less of a problem in the enterprise when workers feel secure in their positions and know that management seeks to inform them on matters of importance.

Nature of the informal work group. There are three factors that determine the nature of the informal work groups which develop in a business enterprise:

1. *The type of work performed.* There is a tendency for people whose occupation is the same to group together. Thus informal work groups may be composed either of factory workers or of office workers. Only rarely will both types of workers be members of the same informal group. The difference in occupation leads to physical separation of the workplace as well as to different informal contacts based in part on the way different types of workers view their status and role as against those of others.

2. *Physical location of the workplace.* Generally people become members of the informal group that is located in their own work area. People naturally form associations with those individuals with whom they have frequent contact. The more frequent the contact between people the greater the likelihood that they will become members of the same informal work group.

3. *The values held by the individuals.* The values of members of an informal work group must be compatible if the group is to hold together. For this reason an informal group is not likely to include union and nonunion workers or production workers and supervisors.

Structure of an informal work group. The structure of an informal work group is depicted in Figure 7–4. Notice that there are three classes of individuals who make up the group: those in the inner circle, those in the fringe area, and those who are not members of the group (the out group). The inner group is the heart of the informal work group. It is composed of a closely knit group of people who perform the same general kind of work in the same location and hold the same values. The inner group sets the tone of the informal work group and determines the membership. Smith, Jones, Roper, Day, and Forbes make up the membership of the inner group. The dotted lines indicate relations between the members in frequent contact. Notice that Randolph and Mason are in the outer circle as fringe members of the informal group. They have not been fully accepted by the members of the inner group, or they are not yet willing to give full allegiance to the values of the informal social system. Eventually they will either move into the inner circle of membership or to the out-group status.

FIGURE 7–4
Structure of an informal work group

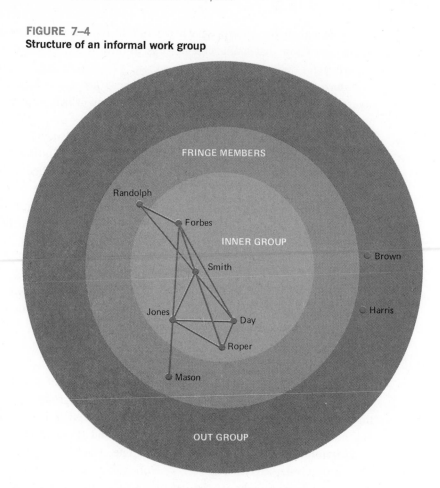

Brown and Harris are not members of the informal work group. They may work in the same department or have a formal status relationship with the informal group members. However, they have neither close informal ties with the group members nor with each other. In a word, they are "loners." Usually such individuals are members of the out group by choice. They do not want to surrender their independence to the group or their values are different in some significant way from those of the members of the group.

A group leader will emerge in the informal group situation. In Figure 7–4 Smith is the leader. He has frequent contact with five of the other six persons who compose the inner circle and the fringe membership in the system. Members of the inner group come to Smith with their problems and ideas. They listen to Smith's opinions and generally follow suggestions made by Smith. In short, Smith commands the voluntary respect of the members of the informal work group. In contrast, a supervisor is obeyed because of the status held in the formal organization of the business enterprise.

THE IMPORTANCE OF STATUS

Status has been defined as a relative position in the business organization. Articles, books, and comic strips have all contributed to the public's interest in business status. Many persons laugh about others' concern over status and the symbols attached to it. However, these same individuals may become quite agitated when some event occurs that seems to diminish their status in a business organization. Status is something which the business manager must understand to be effective in human relations.

Kinds of status

When an individual works to fulfill the requirements for a particular position and attains it, this is known as *achieved status*. Being a college graduate is achieved status since a person must earn a degree. Occupational status is achieved status since a person is not born as a business manager, a banker, a physician, or a bricklayer.

However, there are some status positions which are not achieved but instead are *ascribed*—that is, persons are assigned a status on the basis of some inherited characteristic such as sex, race, or the family into which they are born. Ascribed status can affect an individual's chance to achieve a position in a business enterprise based on ability. Although family background in business seems to be less important today than in recent decades, status may accrue to a person in business because of family ties. Higher status generally is afforded in industry to men than women despite legislation which outlaws employment discrimination by business on the basis of the sex or race of individuals.

The status of a racial or ethnic group of individuals in a work situation is influenced not only by achieved status positions they hold but also by the ascribed status of that particular group as viewed by the external community. In large metropolitan areas where ethnic and racial minorities live in relative isolation from the dominant society, patterns of status arise which the business manager should understand in developing a productive work force. Employees bring to the workplace their views of ascribed status which may not be wholly consistent with the formal status achieved by members of the minority in the enterprise. Despite management's interest in avoiding status based on race, cultural background, or sex, the informal organization in the enterprise is likely to take account of these factors for some time to come. For management this means a continuing program of promoting understanding among its workers as to the basis on which formal status, promotions, and job assignments are made along with management's recognition that problems may arise from time to time because of ascribed status.

Prestige and esteem

Associated with each status position is a certain amount of prestige. *Prestige* is the recognition and regard resulting from a person's status. Thus prestige accrues to an individual because of the status position occupied. A person with more formal education generally has a higher status and therefore more prestige than one with less education or training. Employees using mental skills usually have higher status and more prestige than those doing manual labor.

How persons perform the role associated with their status determines the amount of *esteem* in which they are held. An employee such as a custodian has a position of relatively low status and prestige in the organization. However, if he or she fulfills the role well by doing a good job of keeping the office clean, the person should be held in high esteem. A person of high status and prestige, such as vice president for sales, could be held in low esteem because of poor role behavior. This low esteem might result from lack of attention to the job, poor moral conduct, or general inefficiency. Nevertheless, the vice president would still occupy a status with much prestige. If over a period of time the people who occupy a certain prestigious status do not perform their role well, the status itself may come to have less prestige.

Two people can occupy similar status positions with one being held in high esteem and the other in low esteem. The person held in high esteem may show personal qualities of leadership and resourcefulness while the other tends to do a poor job. These individual differences do not show up on the formal organization chart of the business enterprise. However, they are of great importance to management in the operation of the business.

Factors determining the prestige of a status. Among the business factors determining the prestige of a status are the level in the organization structure the position occupies, the nature of the work, the salary, and the industry of which the business enterprise is a part.

The formal organization chart determines an individual's prestige level in the enterprise. A vice president has higher status and more prestige than a department head, who in turn has higher status and more prestige than a production worker. Likewise, the production worker has higher status than the production trainee. Interestingly enough, prestige may be generalized to include those who work closely with persons at the top of the organization structure. This means that the secretary to the president of the enterprise has higher status and more prestige than a vice president's secretary.

The type of work performed and the working conditions also determine the prestige of the status in the business enterprise. Clerical work has a greater prestige and higher status than production work.

Pay is also a determinant of the amount of prestige of a status. The level of wages is one recognition by higher management of the importance of the individual's contribution to the operation of the enterprise. The higher the pay, the higher the prestige of the status in the organization when other factors are approximately equal.

Status symbols

With all the factors which determine status in the business enterprise, the matter of status is complex indeed! These factors sometimes conflict with one another. The result is a complex pattern of status hierarchies for every business enterprise. Status in business is recognized by permitting certain symbols to be a part of the work environment. These status symbols are visible evidence of a person's rank in the business enterprise.

Examples of status symbols are wide-ranging. They vary from desk pen sets and telephones in offices to rugs and paintings in executive suites. A cardinal rule of status symbols is that the symbol has meaning only if it is relatively scarce. Or at least it must be limited to those persons having about the same status level in the organization. Status symbols lose their significance when they become widespread. In one organization the vice presidents' offices had carpeted floors and this was considered a status symbol. However, the enterprise moved into a new building where not only executive offices were carpeted but also those of department heads. When this occurred the carpeted floors ceased to be as significant a status symbol. Organizational rank switched to the floor on which the office was located. Since the building was served by automatic elevators those offices on the highest floors were occupied by executives of higher level in the organization and connoted higher status. Also, these offices were closest to the president's office and the board of directors' meeting room which were located on the top floor.

The danger always exists that management will place too much emphasis upon status symbols. This can create a climate in the business enterprise that results in one status crisis after another. An overemphasis by an individual or a group of employees on status symbols may indicate a basic insecurity as to their position and function in the enterprise. This may result from an unclear definition of the responsibilities or inadequate authority vested in an individual or group. Though status and its symbols exist wherever people come together in organizations, management needs to see that these are not overemphasized.

DEVELOPING A HEALTHY WORK CLIMATE

A healthy work climate is developed in the business enterprise as the result of conscious effort on the part of management. Building high morale among employees requires day-to-day actions by supervisors based on sound human relations concepts. Little of lasting value will be achieved by crash programs to raise the level of morale and productivity if they are not accompanied by individual acts that show a genuine concern for employees. It is important for managers to develop an awareness of the implications of their attitudes and actions when dealing with persons in the daily conduct of business. To improve the manager's awareness of human relations the following suggestions should be helpful.

1. The superior sets the tone in the enterprise. The principal responsibility for determining the work climate rests with the superior. Subordinates will tend to follow this lead. This responsibility for promoting good human relations ranges from the president of the business enterprise down the management hierarchy to the first level of supervision. Each person who directs the activities of others should remember that subordinates will be watching to see what kind of an example is set.

Examples of ways in which a manager sets the tone for subordinates include the friendliness exhibited toward employees and how it is expressed, manner of dress, the degree of professionalism in associations with others, commitment to the enterprise as measured by the energy and time devoted to the job, the attitudes expressed toward the enterprise, and the prejudices which may be exhibited. The fact that the superior has primary responsibility for determining the work climate does not relieve subordinates of their responsibilities to behave in a manner that will be a positive contribution to the enterprise. However, when a poor example is set for employees by management there is little incentive for subordinates to do better.

2. Make deserved praise public; reprimand in private. The advice of "Praise publicly and reprove privately" is generally sound advice for the business manager. A private reprimand enables the individual employee to save face and may be more effective in changing behavior patterns than publicly criticizing the employee's actions or attitudes. Most people like to have deserved public recognition despite their modest protests that "it really doesn't make any difference" whether they receive public recognition. However, there are times when the most effective praise will be a quiet word of commendation by the person's boss for a job well done.

3. Remember the importance of listening in good communications. Avoid making judgments until the other person has told his or her story and you believe you fully understand the situation. Try to perceive the other person's view of the situation. It is very difficult to really listen if you are busy thinking of what your response will be.

4. When giving directions make sure that others understand what you expect. Do not expect persons to respond effectively if they are not properly prepared to carry out your instructions.

5. Preserve the dignity of the individual. It is important for each person to keep a good self-image. Management should avoid placing the individual employee in a position where he loses face. When this occurs the supervisor should expect a defensive, perhaps violent, reaction that is not likely to be constructive in arriving at a satisfactory solution to the issue at hand.

6. How a change is made may be more important than the change itself. While change is one of the characteristics of today's business scene, management should recognize that change tends to disrupt the lives and work habits of people. Most individuals prefer not to have patterns of behavior interrupted. Consider your own habits. Try dressing in a different order tomorrow morning; or in coming to class take a different route. If you are typical, you will resist such changes. In the work environment the same thing is true of individuals' habits. We resent changes that require us to establish new ways of doing things.

This natural resistance to change causes one of management's greatest challenges: to effect the changes necessary to improve enterprise operations with a minimum of disruption of good work habits.

In making changes it is important that management communicate to workers the reasons for the change. Management should recognize that changes in organization structure, location of offices and shops, product lines, and personnel have definite human relations implications. The more information management is able to pass along to employees regarding anticipated changes the less disruptive the change is likely to be.

Furthermore, to promote good morale management should undertake actions to lessen the personal impact of changes on employees. This would include such actions as helping employees to find new homes if the enterprise's location is moved to a different city. Management can work closely with industry and government employment agencies to provide new jobs for workers who were displaced by a change in the production requirements of the enterprise. What may seem to be a relatively minor, insignificant change to top management may be a major disruption somewhere in the organization. That is why managers down the line should be sensitive to the importance of the way in which the change is carried out. The proposed change which appears to be quite logical from a technical point of view may be difficult to make if consideration is not given to the human relations aspects of its implementation.

SUMMARY

Human relations consists of providing a work climate which will both satisfy the employees' needs and achieve the broad economic objectives of the business enterprise. People have physical and material needs which are met largely through wages and fringe benefits. However, employees also have nonmaterial needs both psychological and social which management should recognize.

Direction is the process of aiding an enterprise's employees in carrying out their work activities. To be effective in exercising direction, managers need technical, human, and conceptual skills. Generally, technical skill is required to a greater degree in first-line supervision, conceptual skill at the top management level, and human skills at all levels of management.

Leadership is the element of direction which causes subordinates to further the accomplishment of enterprise goals. Leadership can be exercised in two ways—authoritarian or participative.

Communication, the transmission of understanding, is essential in the process of direction. Two-way communication should occur vertically and horizontally in the business enterprise. Both written and spoken communications are used in business, and each method has its advantages and disadvantages. For there to be good communication, there must be both effective transmission and receipt of information, with the listener or reader understanding the frame of reference of the speaker or writer.

In the formal organization structure, each person occupies a particular status and is expected to fulfill the role associated with that status. These positions can be shown in a formal organization chart.

The informal organization is a self-grouping of employees in the work environment which depends upon the personalities of the individuals for its being. Informal work groups usually are made up of workers who perform the same general type of work in the same area and who hold similar values.

Status is a relative position in an organization. Status is achieved when a person earns it and ascribed when based on some inherited characteristic. Prestige is an abstract concept which refers to the recognition and regard that go with a particular status. Esteem refers to how well a person performs the role associated with that status position. Status symbols are visible evidence of a person's rank in the business enterprise.

There are a number of considerations for management to remember in developing a healthy work climate:

1. The superior sets the tone in the enterprise.
2. Generally, it is good to praise in public and reprimand in private.
3. Listening is important for good communications.
4. Make sure others know what is expected of them.
5. Preserve the dignity of the individual.
6. When a change is made, it is important *how* the change is made.

TERMS FOR REVIEW

human relations
psychological needs
social needs
technical skill
human skill
conceptual skill

authoritarian leadership
participative leadership
achieved status
ascribed status
prestige
esteem

QUESTIONS

1. What differences are there in enterprise goals and individual needs?
2. *a.* What examples of good human relations have you observed practiced in the organizations with which you have been associated?
   b. What incidents have you observed that indicated a lack of sensitivity to the importance of human relations?
3. What needs are most important to you in considering a job opportunity? What difference, if any, would it make if you were considering a summer position before returning to college instead of a permanent position?
4. Comment on the following statement by the owner of a medium-size department store: "I would like to have more participation by my supervisors and other employees, but I can't afford the time that is required for them to make a decision. Also, I feel that I know more about my business than anyone else."
5. What should you remember if you are to be an effective listener?
6. Prepare three statements that could be given opposite interpretations depending upon the frame of reference of the speaker and the listener. How could these statements be rephrased so the transmitted message would be what was intended?
7. "Since informal organizations are bound to arise within any business enterprise, a formal organization is really of secondary importance." Comment on this statement.
8. What kinds of status symbols have you observed in the organizations of which you have been a part? Are people serious about the importance of status symbols? Why or why not?
9. Why may the way in which a change is made be as important as the substance of the change itself? Give an example to illustrate such a situation.

Business briefs

Levi Strauss

Levi Strauss, the manufacturer of jeans, is a family-controlled enterprise which was founded in 1850 and still projects a family image. Its shares of common stock were sold to the public for the first time in 1971. One of its junior executives, in his twenties, stated that what he really likes about the company is that it is very people-oriented. This young man was impressed that on chance meetings with the president, the top executive would speak to him by his first name. Furthermore, the junior manager feels that management is open to suggestions. People are encouraged to cross departmental lines to discuss ideas. Pride is felt that Levi Strauss has been a leader in such projects as employment of minorities.

1. What insights into the human relations climate at Levi Strauss can be gained from this brief?

The hotline versus the grapevine

In Tacoma, Washington, the office employees of St. Regis Paper Company can dial a company hotline telephone for information on company developments. A recorded report provides information on local office and companywide developments. The hotline avoids the necessity of employees depending on the grapevine for rumors of changes at St. Regis. After the recorded telephone report, employees have an opportunity to record their comments to be heard by management.

1. What advantages does this telephone hotline have over the company grapevine?
2. What limitations does such a hotline have?
3. What possible problems might arise from such a hotline?

Cases

Merkley Company

The Merkley Company is an electronics manufacturing plant employing approximately 2,300 employees. Of this group, approximately 2,000 are production employees and about 300 are office employees composed of both clerical and administrative personnel.

Within this plant the company provides a modern, well-equipped cafeteria. Although the Merkley Company owns the facilities, an outside catering firm is contracted to prepare and serve the food. All menus are planned by the catering firm with the services of an industrial dietitian and approved by the Merkley Company plant personnel department.

Menus had always included a choice of two hot plate lunches and "ready-made" sandwiches, prepared earlier in the day and wrapped in cellophane. In addition, employees had the regular choice of beverages, desserts, and small dishes of salad which were also prepared earlier in the day. Both production and office employees made their food selection from the same menu—there was no executive dining room or special menu for executives.

The cafeteria can serve 500 employees at a time. Thirty-minute lunch breaks, starting at 11:15 a.m., are staggered over about two hours to accommodate the 2,300 employees. All employees eating in the plant are required to eat in the cafeteria, even though they may have brought their lunch from home. Since the lunch breaks have to be staggered, the production employees eat during the earlier lunch periods, and the office employees eat during the last lunch periods.

The plant had been in operation about one year when the personnel department began receiving complaints from the office personnel regarding the food in the cafeteria. The complaints didn't seem to come from the production employees, only from the office employees. Within a few days, more and more office personnel were complaining about the food and menus. Finally, a marked difference was noticed in the number of office personnel purchasing the lunches in the cafeteria. Although there were only 30 minutes allowed for lunch, more and more clerical people were leaving the plant to go out for lunch.

Conversations with various office employees seemed to indicate the complaint was not so much the quality of the food as the menu itself. The personnel manager began to think that office personnel tended to have different eating habits than production personnel. Since the production employees were exerting greater physical energy in the performance of their duties, perhaps they needed a heavier lunch, e.g., meat, potatoes, and beans. The office employees desired lighter lunches, e.g., sandwiches and large salad plates.

It had been the practice of the Merkley Company general plant manager to hold monthly office employee meetings to discuss general plant operations and to keep them up to date on such items as the latest developments of new products. One of these meetings was held at the time the personnel department was getting the most cafeteria complaints. During this meeting, the subject of the cafeteria menus was raised by several office girls. They all agreed that the lunches offered were too heavy. They would much prefer to have sandwiches or maybe a salad plate. It was pointed out to them that ready-made sandwiches were already available as were salads. The office employees argued that the salads were too small to make a complete lunch. Also, since they had to eat last, after all the production employees, there were few salads left and the sandwiches were usually stale.

Some employees suggested that the company put in a sandwich bar offering such items as "made-to-order" cold sandwiches, hamburgers, and malted milks, and also providing large salad plate lunches. Later that day, the general plant manager and industrial relations manager discussed the suggested new sandwich bar. However, they both hesitated installing the extra kitchen equipment necessary for such a bar, believing the expense would be too great unless more than just the office employees were interested. To determine this interest, they decided to conduct a survey to determine just how much interest there was in the plant for such a salad and sandwich bar.

The industrial relations manager asked the cafeteria manager to have his employees conduct a survey among the production employees to determine their interest in a light lunch menu. The light lunch would be offered in addition to the heavier hot lunch. The surveys were conducted the following Monday as the production employees filed past the serving counter collecting their noon lunch. They were shown a sample menu for the proposed sandwich bar including the prices and asked whether or not they would be interested in patronizing such an eating facility.

Of this group, 91 percent of the production employees surveyed indicated that they were not interested and that they preferred a hot plate lunch. Early the next day, the general manager called the industrial relations manager into his office to discuss the results of the survey. Although there was apparently little interest on the part of the production employees, they decided to go ahead and set up a short-order sandwich and salad bar anyway, but on a much less elaborate basis than would be necessary to serve the entire plant.

Since the vast majority of the production employees said that they were not interested in short orders, the new menu would be available only to the office personnel. Since it would take an additional person to operate the bar, it did not seem economically feasible to have it open for the production employees, especially since so few indicated an interest in patronizing it.

After the arrangements had been made the additional limited cafeteria equipment was installed. The new facility was opened one week later. On the opening day as the first few groups of production employees began coming into the cafeteria at 11:15, only the hot plate line was set up. But at 11:45 as other groups came into the cafeteria, the cafeteria employees were beginning to set up the sandwich bar in preparation for the office personnel who would be coming in at 12:10 and 12:20 p.m. As the last 30 to 40 production employees filed past the new sandwich bar, a few attempted to order a sandwich of their choice. Each was informed that this food was for office employees only. A few of these production employees expressed mild displeasure, but management heard very little about it during the rest of the day. The office employees were very well pleased with the new arrangements and voiced much appreciation.

The next day, 92 percent of all production employees boycotted the cafeteria. Each brought his own lunch from home. Although they all ate their home-prepared lunch in the cafeteria, they refused to buy food from the regular hot food serving line. As a result of this boycott much of the prepared hot food had to be destroyed at a cost of nearly $800. Later during the lunch period, employees began to explain to cafeteria personnel that they were protesting because they couldn't buy the sandwiches they wanted.

1. Why do you think the production workers boycotted the cafeteria after the survey had indicated their lack of interest in the sandwich bar?
2. What alternatives are open to management at this time? What would be the likely consequences of each of these alternatives?
3. What would you recommend?

"Lessons Learned"

Tom Jones eyed the correspondence and memos on his desk. The nearby calendar told him that ten months had passed since he had come to Falls City to help open a new plant (see Exhibit 1) for Acme Products Company, a nationwide packaging concern. Tom paused to reflect on how busy these past months had been. As a group leader, he had been confronted with a wide variety of problems. He had been constantly on the go in an effort to help get the plant into production on schedule. Only in the past month had things slacked up a little.

The ringing telephone summoned Tom from his thoughts and into the office of Mr. Jackson, his department head. Handing Tom a memo, Mr. Jackson said, "We have a request here from our general manager in Chicago. He'd like to have us submit to him some of the "Lessons Learned" by us during our new plant startup and shakedown. They'd

EXHIBIT 1
Acme Products Company (Falls City plant organization chart)

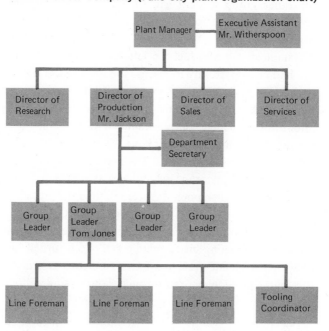

be of benefit in planning future expansions. Can you put together some ideas?"

Tom replied that several of the group leaders had already discussed the need for more detailed installation drawings. He then asked, "Should this be strictly technical or should it include other problems?"

"List anything serious that's confronted you fellows," was Mr. Jackson's answer.

During the next week, Tom sought out the other group leaders individually and acquainted them with his assignment. He asked for their thoughts and recommendations. Upon condensing and editing all the ideas, he found that they fell into three categories:

1. Facility installations and drawings.
2. Tooling tolerances and finishes.
3. Unclear personnel assignments and absence of an organization chart.

All three of these items had been subjects of discussions on numerous occasions in almost all the departments of the new plant.

Upon receiving the drafts back from typing, Tom reviewed them with the other group leaders. He then sent them for Mr. Jackson's consideration. On the following day, his draft copies were returned with Mr. Jackson's note, "Well Done."

The next day Mr. Jackson left for a conference in Dallas. Tom had not had an opportunity to discuss the final report on "Lessons Learned" with his boss before the departure. While Tom was on the telephone, the executive assistant to the plant manager, Mr. Witherspoon, stormed into the department office, slammed down a handful of papers and lashed out at the nearest secretary, "This rubbish is obviously incorrect. These conditions don't exist." The assistant continued, "This was written by a misguided, ignorant individual and is in poor taste without thought or fact." As Witherspoon departed he haughtily advised that the papers should be destroyed. As the secretary returned the papers to Mr. Jackson's mailbox, Tom saw the heading "Lessons Learned."

After completing his telephone call, Tom turned his thoughts on the executive assistant's reaction to the "Lessons Learned" report. Some of the following thoughts ran through Tom's mind: Should I speak to the executive assistant in an attempt to explain the report? Would it be better to go over the 'old-paper-shuffler's head and deliver the report directly to the plant manager? Had Mr. Jackson really studied the report or had he merely rubber-stamped it? Since the general manager in Chicago had requested the report he must have considered it important.

As Tom went to the water cooler for a drink he wondered what action, if any, he should take.

1. Discuss the central problems involved in this case.
2. *a.* What courses of action are open to Tom Jones?
   b. What do you recommend to Tom Jones? Why?

*Training is an important
part of personnel
management.*

Personnel departments were a logical development as American business enterprises became larger. They aid management in processing and maintaining the records required for a large work force. Also, managers became aware of the importance of the human factors in business and began to depend upon personnel departments for assistance.

By studying this chapter you will learn why the personnel function is important. The following questions are discussed:

> *What is the primary goal of personnel management?*
>
> *What specific responsibilities does the personnel department have in the management of the enterprise?*
>
> *What is the relationship between personnel management and labor relations?*
>
> *How is the personnel department organized?*

8

Personnel management

THE PERSONNEL MANAGEMENT FUNCTION

The primary goal of personnel management is a well-motivated and effective work force. Good personnel management places an emphasis on personal development of employees. It seeks to provide a climate in which individuals may use their abilities and obtain satisfaction in their work group. A successful personnel program will be able to integrate the individual objectives of employees with the objectives of the enterprise to achieve an efficient work situation.

The personnel department is in an excellent position to advise top management on the state of employees' morale. Personnel management can suggest methods of strengthening employee-management relations. In those enterprises where employees are unionized, the personnel department also assists in the conduct of labor relations.

Three groups carry out the personnel management function. The overall responsibility for personnel management should be assumed by top management. The president of an organization sets the tone of the work climate. The president is responsible to the board of directors for the establishment of the broad objectives and policies of personnel management. It is the president who appoints the director of the personnel department and other key executives.

The second group is made up of the supervisors throughout the enterprise. The first-line supervisors, department heads, district managers, and other managers actually put personnel policies into practice. It is important that these supervisors understand the personnel policies established by top management and actively support them.

The third group having responsibilities for personnel management is the personnel department. This department is generally established as a "staff" department. Its purpose is to provide service to other departments. The personnel department hires employees, trains them, and provides a variety of other services.

RESPONSIBILITIES OF THE PERSONNEL DEPARTMENT

Hiring and placement of employees

The responsibilities of the personnel department include the recruitment, selection, induction, and training of employees.

To provide for efficient and uniform hiring practices, employment activities should be centered in the personnel department. Here records can be kept up to date. Interviews and testing can be carried out. Specialists can be used to determine which persons qualify for positions that become available. The supervisor of the prospective employee should have the right to accept or reject any applicant recommended by the personnel department. However, centralized hiring relieves the supervisor of many details associated with hiring and placement of personnel.

Job specifications. The first step in hiring is taken when the supervisor turns in a request for personnel to fill certain jobs. Job specifications should be drawn up to describe accurately the requirements of the position to be filled. The specifications should be realistic and not call for someone who is superhuman. Neither should they disregard important parts of the job which require special abilities.

Recruitment. After the request for workers has been turned in, the personnel department undertakes the recruitment phase. Sources of candidates include former employees who are qualified but who have been laid off or have voluntarily left the enterprise. Also, candidates may apply as the result of advertising and contacts with groups such as schools, unions, private employment agencies, minority organizations, and correctional authorities. These groups all are interested in knowing when an enterprise has job openings. The local office of the public employment service is also a helpful source of employment information. Depending on the scope of the enterprise's activities, recruitment may extend over a wide geographic area and draw applicants from a great distance.

Employee selection. The selection of individuals who will be offered employment is a six-step process. This consists of a screening interview, application form, employment tests, physical examination, reference check, and comprehensive interview. Figure 8–1 illustrates the employment process.

The *screening interview* may be conducted by an assistant in the personnel department. It provides an opportunity to make a preliminary decision about the applicants' suitability for employment. Applicants may be turned down for employment for specific jobs not only because they are deficient in some respect, but because their education or intelligence are too high for the jobs which are currently vacant. If the applicants appear to be good candidates, then the screening interview may be used to explain the rest of the employment process.

The *application form* provides information about the candidate in writing. It acts as a simple test of writing ability and should contain items which the enterprise has found to correlate with job success.

The development of a *testing program* is a complex undertaking. Management should understand the limitations as well as the potential benefits from a thoughtfully devised program. A good testing program will measure applicants' abilities for a particular job and will provide an objective comparison between applicants.

The *physical examination* should be given to applicants who are considered seriously for employment to benefit both the enterprise and the individuals. Employees should not be placed in jobs which might be harmful to them or where they might endanger other workers. The enter-

FIGURE 8–1
The employment process

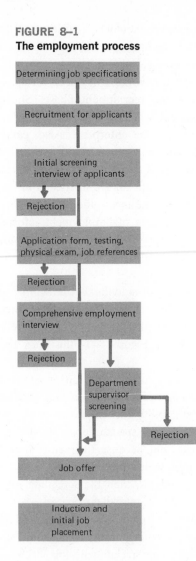

prise should be protected against the risk of claims from persons who have disabilities prior to employment.

The investigation into the *job references* provided by the applicant gives the enterprise a check on past work records. The reference checks also test the applicant's accuracy and honesty.

The main purpose of the *comprehensive employment interview* is to complete or to correct information on the applicant which has been provided by the previous steps. Qualities of the applicant may be drawn out by a skillful interviewer which in previous steps have not been covered. This is the opportunity to explain fully the requirements of the job. Also, one can seek to determine why the applicant wants this particular position (in addition to the paycheck which will go with the job).

If the applicants qualify in all respects they are accepted for employment, sometimes with a probationary period. The supervisor for whom they work may have met the employees before they are finally selected. The supervisor should have some authority in determining which workers come into the department, since the supervisor is responsible for the productivity of the department. However, in large enterprises the supervisor's most important function in the hiring process is to provide a realistic list of requirements for the positions to be filled. Then the personnel department should select the applicants who meet those requirements.

Employee induction

Before a new employee is placed in a specific job in the enterprise, he should be introduced into the organization. A good induction provides the new employee with useful information about the enterprise, and some idea of the policies affecting employees and the services which may be provided for them. First impressions are important in determining future employee attitudes toward the enterprise. A good induction program will maximize the benefit from the job training which will be given later.

A good program of employee induction has these three elements:

1. The personnel department provides introductory information to employees either individually or in groups.
2. Additional information is provided by the new employee's supervisor about the department and the requirements of the job.
3. After the employee's first days on the job, a follow-up interview is held either by the supervisor or by the personnel department. This can check on the employee's progress, answer additional questions, or repeat information provided earlier.

An initial tour of the factory is helpful in enabling new employees to relate their jobs to the entire operation of the enterprise. The induction program should give the newcomer a feeling of belonging to the organization. It should make clear that management is concerned about his welfare and success in the new job.

Employment outlook

Personnel workers

Attracting the best employees available and matching them to jobs they can do effectively are important for the successful operation of a business enterprise. Personnel workers interview, select, and recommend applicants who have the education and experience to fill vacancies. In addition to staffing, they counsel employees, plan training, develop wage and salary scales, and investigate methods to improve personnel operations.

The number of personnel workers is expected to expand very rapidly through the mid-1980s as employers recognize the need for trained personnel to maintain good employee relations. A college education is becoming increasingly important for personnel work. Many employers in private industry prefer applicants who have majored in business or personnel administration.

For some positions, specialized training may be necessary. Testing and counseling often require a bachelor's degree with a major or graduate degree in psychology. An engineering degree may be desirable for work dealing with time studies or safety standards. Training in industrial relations may be helpful for work involving employee management relations. An accounting background is useful for positions concerned with wages, pensions, and other employee benefits.

New personnel workers usually enter formal or on-the-job training programs to learn how to classify jobs, interview applicants, or perform other personnel functions. After training they are assigned to work in specific areas.

Personnel workers should speak and write effectively and be able to work with people of all levels of intelligence and experience.

Employee training

Besides the induction program, the employee may need specific training for the new job. There are four types of employee training:

1. *Apprenticeship training* is used in jobs requiring long periods of training and a high degree of skill. The new employee works under supervision of trained employees and is required to meet rigid performance standards. Employers may use apprenticeship programs in cooperation with trade unions.

2. *Vestibule training* is off-the-job training where workers are trained in an area of the plant physically separated from their workplace. Machinery and jobs similar to the conditions in the shop itself are duplicated as nearly as possible. This method of training provides an opportunity for teaching the best methods of doing a particular job. Employees may become accustomed to the job before actually entering the department. However, since vestibule training takes place in an artificial setting, some adjustment is necessary when workers move to the shop where they will work.

3. *On-the-job training* places the workers in the shop at a machine or workplace. There they will be trained by a supervisor, a special instructor, or an experienced employee. The effectiveness of this type of training depends upon the quality of instruction. Without good instructors the new employee is likely to find it frustrating. At best there will be little uniformity in the training of personnel.

4. *Vocational-school training* consists of courses outside the enterprise in areas such as welding, blueprint reading, or automobile mechanics. This training may precede employment or may supplement the training provided by the enterprise in its own plant.

Training represents a continuing responsibility for management. New methods, products, and individual abilities dictate that training is not finished after the worker is placed in a shop or office. The personnel department should stand ready to provide training programs for all employees, not merely those recently hired.

Job analysis

To maintain a satisfactory level of morale and employee efficiency, the wages paid employees should be adequate and fair. A good system of wage payments takes account of differences in jobs and also provides for individual differences in performance on the same job. The personnel administrator is also concerned with the level of wages paid for similar work in the community. Finally, the personnel administrator should be able to advise management on the best methods of calculating wages. This could be on the basis of time, productivity, or some combination of the two.

Job description. The first step in job analysis is to determine what jobs are performed in the enterprise. This is done by writing a *job description* that contains the essential elements of each specific job. This includes such factors as physical effort, skill, responsibility, mental effort, and working conditions.

Job evaluation. Once descriptions have been written for all jobs in the enterprise, the process of job evaluation begins. This consists of measuring the value of each job in relation to the other jobs in the enterprise.

The simplest method of job evaluation is to identify the factors to be singled out for the analysis and assign weights to each factor. For example, physical effort may be assigned a maximum of 40 points, while skills required may be assigned a maximum of 110 points. The determination of the maximum weights assigned each job depends on the type of jobs which the enterprise has. Next, the personnel administrator selects several jobs in the plant which are used as bench marks against which all other jobs will be measured. These bench-mark jobs are then evaluated according to the point scales established for each factor in the evaluation scheme. The bench-mark jobs should be those which employ a number of persons and which are widely known to all employees. For example, the job of a machinist first class might be assigned the following point spread: physical effort 20, skill 100, responsibility 60, and working conditions 20 for a total of 200; whereas a job of custodian might carry points as follows: physical effort 30, skill 10, responsibility 20, and working conditions 30 for a total of 90 points. Other jobs in the enterprise will be ranked in relation to the bench-mark jobs. A careful handling of the point assignments and relative rankings is necessary to maintain fairness.

Job evaluation provides management with a more desirable basis for wage determination than a haphazard scheme of wage payments. A carefully administered program of job evaluation will result in a logical scale of jobs which can be used as a basis for setting relative wage scales. However, such a system has limitations. No job evaluation system is completely scientific. Judgments on the relative worth of different jobs are difficult to make. Evaluators must determine the maximum points to be assigned to each factor in the analysis. Then they must assign factor points to each job according to some system of values.

Also, some jobs may be viewed by workers as of unequal attractiveness even though the point analysis makes them of equal value. Some jobs may seem to be stepping-stones to higher positions. Others are viewed as dead-end assignments. In some cases exceptions to the job evaluation system may be necessary to attract workers to a particular job where labor is in short supply.

You should remember that job evaluation rates *jobs,* not the *individuals* on the jobs. The evaluation of individuals is performance rating, which is discussed separately in this chapter.

Wage determination. After the job evaluation is completed, management must fit the scale of jobs to its wage scale. The wage scale in an enterprise will depend on the level of wages in the community for similar jobs, the ability of the enterprise to pay higher wages, the bargaining strength of the labor union if the company employees are unionized, and the industry of which the particular enterprise is a part.

In putting into effect a new job evaluation system, the best psychology is to do so at the time of a general wage increase. Then those jobs which have been paid at too high a rate can be brought into the scale without lowering those rates, merely by raising other rates. The implementation of a job evaluation plan may require a period of time before all jobs are "in line" with a fair scale.

Performance rating

Once a system of job evaluation and wage scales has been worked out, individuals must be selected to fill the various jobs. There should be a range of pay to provide room for supervisors to recognize individual differences in performance on the same job. An employee's performance on the job will determine the amount of pay within the range for that particular job. Therefore, the supervisor has a responsibility to keep employees informed about their progress. This is accomplished through a performance rating system, sometimes called a merit rating system. (See Figure 8–2.)

The performance rating system is used to make merit wage increases within job classifications and to guide management in selecting employees for promotion. Formal performance rating of employees reduces the practice of giving raises on the basis of quick judgment or favoritism.

The performance rating system provides managers with a means of

FIGURE 8–2

PERFORMANCE RATING REVIEW

Name:_____ Job Title: _____ Dept.:_____ Date:_____

Instructions to Supervisor: Summarize the individual's performance by checking each of the 4 evaluation factors below. Your ratings should reflect your judgment based on your observation of the employee. Use N/E (not evaluated) if you have insufficient evidence on which to make a rating. However, normally all items should be evaluated. These ratings should indicate what the employee has actually accomplished. Remember that personnel performance rating and development represents an important responsibility of management.

Rating System:
A– Exceeds Departmental Expectations
B – Meets Departmental Expectations
C – Below Departmental Expectations

Evaluation Factors — Ratings

	A	B	C
Quality of Work	Consistently does high quality and accurate work; creative with high degree of ingenuity and practicality.	Usually can be depended upon for good work; few mistakes; practical; some creativity.	Work performed in a careless and slip-shod manner; frequent mistakes; lacks creativeness.
Quantity of Work	Consistently high output; works rapidly.	Satisfactory production level; works steadily.	Below average in output; slow; wastes time.
Knowledge of Job	Expert knowledge of job and related areas; rarely requires instruction.	Good knowledge of job and related work; requires only normal instructions.	Has limited knowledge of job; requires frequent instruction and guidance.
Cooperation and Attitude	Enthusiastic and cooperative team worker; inspires confidence; loyal to company; solicits suggestions for improvement.	Responsive and cooperative; interested in job and company; accepts constructive criticism.	Lack of cooperation; little job interest; resents suggestions and constructive criticism.

Instructions: Check the appropriate block for the qualities listed below:

Capacity for Advancement: Qualifications	Is qualified for higher position with no further training or experience.	May be qualified for higher position with additional training and/or experience.	Qualified for present job, but has only limited potential for advancement.
Capacity for Advancement: Leadership Ability	Has demonstrated many of the qualifications for leadership; excellent supervisory material.	Has demonstrated some of the qualifications for leadership; possible supervisory material.	Has demonstrated few, if any, of the qualifications for leadership; not considered supervisory material.

	Yes	No
Is attendance satisfactory?	____	____
Is the employee punctual?	____	____

Remarks and/or Recommendations:

Rater's Signature_____   Supervisor's Signature_____ Date_____
   Title_____   Title_____

After Supervisor's signature, forward orginal copy of Performance Rating Review to the Personnel Office. Retain copy in local files. This Review is to be discussed with the employee before it is filed.

rewarding effective employees and furthering operating efficiency of the enterprise. Discussions with employees about their ratings should take a positive direction whenever possible. Morale and productivity are much easier to improve by pointing out positive elements in the employee's performance than by emphasizing weaknesses.

Performance rating is only one source of evidence for promotions or pay increases. Other information is provided by records of output, quality of work, and attendance.

Promotion

Promotion is the advancement of an employee to a better job with more responsibility, increased skill, or higher status. An important part of the promotion is that it results in an increased salary or rate of pay. A promotion may involve moving an employee to a more skilled job within the same basic job classification, such as from second-class machine operator to first-class machine operator. Or a promotion could be a major shift in jobs such as from a production worker to a supervisor.

Seniority and ability. There are two basic factors which affect promotion—seniority and ability. Labor unions usually believe that seniority should be the basis upon which promotions are decided. On the other hand, managements usually believe that ability should be the key factor in making promotions. In achieving a balance between seniority and ability the following considerations may be helpful.

The supervisor in a department is responsible for the productivity of the personnel. Authority should be delegated to the supervisor to select those employees for promotion who have the abilities needed for success in new positions. Promotion should be the reward for employees who increase their skills and exhibit capability for better jobs. To promote only on the basis of seniority places an unfair restriction of management in view of the supervisor's responsibility for results. Seniority should be taken into account when making promotions, but only when the other qualifications of two or more candidates for a better job are substantially equal.

If supervisors are to win the confidence of workers in their promotion policies, promotion should not be based on favoritism and personal relationships. Senior employees should be considered for promotion based on their abilities, performance ratings, objective production records, and personal interviews by management. The junior employee should be selected for the promotion only when he or she can be shown to be superior to the senior worker.

When seniority is used as one of the criteria for promotion the question arises as to how it is to be computed. Seniority may be determined by length of service in the enterprise, plant, department, or job classification. An employee's seniority can start from the time of hiring into any of the above units. The basis for determining seniority is critical because it will vary depending upon which unit is used.

For example, a long-time employee who has moved from one department to another has relatively little seniority on a departmental basis, but considerable seniority with the company. The question of how seniority is counted when an employee is transferred, laid off, or promoted is thus important for both employees and management.

Whatever system of seniority is adopted, seniority lists showing each employee should be publicly posted. Then all workers will have knowledge of their relative standing, and possible errors can be corrected.

Employee transfer

Promotion is an upward change in jobs. *Transfer* is the movement of an employee to another job at about the same pay and on the same level in the organization. The specific type of work done by the employee may change with a transfer. However, there is no significant change in responsibility. Employees may be transferred within the enterprise for a number of reasons including shift transfers, production transfers, and remedial transfers.

Shift transfers are used when the plant operates more than a normal eight-hour day. The evening shift usually runs from about four o'clock in the afternoon to midnight, and the night shift from midnight to eight o'clock in the morning. Most workers prefer to work the regular day shift. Workers on the night shift have their normal pattern of waking and sleeping hours reversed. However, if production needs require multiple shift operations, some workers will have to be hired for these extra shifts. From time to time transfers will be required from one shift to another. One positive aspect of shift work from the employee's point of view is that normally the unusual shifts carry a pay premium. Also, some employees prefer these shift assignments for personal reasons.

Production transfers are necessary when there is a change in the job requirements from one department to another. Some jobs may be eliminated, and other types of work require additional workers. In this case workers are transferred for production purposes to avoid laying off present employees and hiring new ones. Production transfers may also occur when replacements are needed because of retirement, dismissal, or promotion of other workers. The personnel department can be an effective clearinghouse for department supervisors in making production transfers.

Remedial transfers are made because of some problem with a particular person on a particular job. The worker may become too old to bear the physical burden of the job. Changing health conditions may require a transfer. A worker may become tired of a certain job. The initial placement of the worker in a particular job may have been at fault. Or the worker simply may not be getting along with the supervisor or the people in the department but may be useful in another part of the plant. Both the employee and the enterprise may benefit from a remedial transfer.

Downgrading and layoffs

Sometimes transfers, particularly production transfers, result in *downgrading*. This means that employees are moved to jobs requiring less skill than those previously performed. This may come about because the higher skills are no longer needed. When this situation arises the question is whether it is better to downgrade or lay off an employee. Generally neither solution is satisfactory. Downgrading may damage worker morale. However, if there is widespread unemployment in the industry the employee may be thankful for the chance to remain with his or her employer. When jobs are more plentiful, the employee may prefer a layoff to downgrading.

At times a company may be faced with reduced demand for its products. This means a layoff of workers, sometimes in large numbers. Although layoffs, like downgrading, may be only temporary, sometimes permanent changes in the size of the work force are required. This raises major problems for management. Should the hours of work be reduced before any employees are laid off? Many companies lay off probationary employees first and then reduce hours of work, before making large layoffs of permanent employees.

On what basis are workers to be retained? Normally seniority is a critical factor in determining which workers will be retained and which will be laid off. In unionized plants seniority is especially important.

However, sometimes consideration is given to the skill and ability of workers. For long-time employees whose work is satisfactory, morale is improved by knowing that seniority will keep them employed during bad times. Junior workers should understand the enterprise's policy regarding layoffs. This is one of the many things which should be explained during the induction of new workers into the business enterprise.

Discipline of employees

A good discipline policy provides for constructive, positive actions by supervisors carried out consistently under a clear set of regulations. Most employees are anxious to do what is expected of them. The enterprise's discipline policy should be administered so as to encourage self-discipline. At the same time, provision should be made for prompt action against the relatively small number of employees who do not conform to reasonable rules for plant conduct.

There are four essentials in every good disciplinary policy:

1. There should be a written list of clear and reasonable rules along with the penalties which will be applied for infractions.
2. All employees should be informed of plant rules and standards of work.
3. A means of informing employees how well they are meeting standards of conduct and work should be established.
4. A careful investigation of incidents prior to disciplinary action should be carried out. If and when guilt is established, this should be followed by prompt corrective action.

A partial listing of conduct which will not be permitted in the plant usually includes:

Gambling on company property.
Fighting or attempting to injure others except in self-defense.
Deliberate destruction of company property.
Drinking liquor on company property or drunkenness on the job.
Violation of safety regulations.
Smoking in prohibited areas.
Failure to wear safety glasses in machine shops.
Unexcused absences without notifying the company.
Refusal to accept a proper job assignment.

The above list indicates the wide range of rules used in industry. Usually the rules are drawn up in meetings with supervisors and employee representatives.

After an employee's guilt has been clearly established, the disciplinary action may include one or a combination of the following penalties:

1. Oral warning.
2. Written warning.
3. Suspension or disciplinary layoff for a specified period of time.
4. Demotion to a less desirable job.
5. Discharge from the enterprise's employ.

The penalty to be applied depends on the nature of the offense and whether there have been previous violations by the employee. Ordinarily for first offenses either a verbal or written warning is sufficient unless the infraction is serious enough for immediate discharge.

Safety and health

The personnel department frequently cooperates with supervisors and engineers in administering safety and health programs for employees. An important federal law went into effect in 1971 which affects every business enterprise not already covered by federal safety legislation. The *Occupational Safety and Health Act of 1970* is wide ranging. It requires employers to provide safety and health programs for the improvement of working conditions. The Occupational Safety and Health Administration (OSHA) was established to administer the legislation. OSHA has the power to set mandatory job safety and health standards. It can inspect business enterprises to determine if they are in compliance with the law. The personnel department can assist line managers in improving safety and health conditions and can maintain the records and reports required by OSHA.

RELATIONSHIP BETWEEN PERSONNEL MANAGEMENT AND LABOR RELATIONS

When the enterprise's employees are unionized the interaction between the union and management is called labor relations. The labor relations director usually is part of the personnel department. In some cases the personnel manager also will be designated as the labor relations director. The labor relations director acts to represent and to advise top management in the negotiation of the labor contract which spells out the terms under which union members will work. Labor relations personnel are involved in handling grievances by union members over disputes relating to the work situation.

When an enterprise's employees are unionized, the most significant change is in how personnel policy is formulated. When no union exists in an enterprise, personnel policy is usually determined unilaterally by management. Personnel functions such as hiring and placing employees, setting wage rates, establishing seniority rules, determining work standards, and taking disciplinary action can be carried out without consultation or approval of the labor force. The fact that personnel policies may be unilaterally determined and administered by management in the nonunion work situation does not necessarily mean that they are poor policies. An enterprise having no union can create a healthy work climate for employees. However, in the nonunion shop the employees usually have little or no chance to appeal actions taken by management which may affect their welfare.

When a union exists in an enterprise, personnel policies are bilaterally determined. Questions relating to employees' welfare are decided by management after consultation with union representatives, or they are jointly decided by management and the union. Supervisors must be able to justify their personnel decisions if disputes arise. Decisions must be within the language and meaning of the labor contract signed by management and the union.

The establishment of a union in the enterprise can have some benefits for management. A consistent pattern is developed for dealing with employee grievances. Management is forced to analyze its position on various issues affecting employee welfare and to weigh carefully the possible implications of proposed changes. Through seniority lists and established layoff procedures, management is spared having to make individual decisions as to which workers will be released if reductions in the work force become necessary. Where labor unions negotiate contracts with a number of employers for the same wage rates, the enterterprise is put on a par with other firms in the industry.

Because of the importance of unions in many industries today, the next chapter is devoted to a discussion of labor relations.

THE PERSONNEL DEPARTMENT

The personnel department acts in a staff capacity to the other departments of the business enterprise. This means that it provides certain

FIGURE 8–3
Partial organization chart of a personnel department

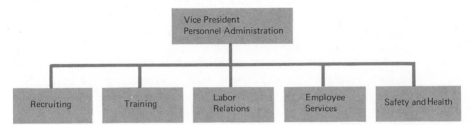

services along with advice and assistance, but is not responsible for giving orders to line supervisors in the production or marketing departments. Figure 8–3 illustrates the general organization of a typical personnel department.

Personnel manager

The head of the department usually has the title of personnel manager or vice president for personnel administration. The personnel manager normally reports to the president of the enterprise. Depending on the size of the enterprise and the number of employees there may also be labor relations personnel, recruiters, interviewers, training supervisors, and clerical assistants.

Employee services

In addition to the duties performed by the personnel department for line supervisors, most personnel departments administer a variety of employee services. These service programs include those relating to insurance and retirement. Also, the personnel department handles the sponsoring of company recreational activities, including athletic teams, picnics, and news bulletins with information of personal interest to employees. Community activities relating to the enterprise and its employees, such as United Way drives for local charities, may be handled in part by the personnel department.

Housekeeping duties

The personnel department performs a number of housekeeping duties for the business enterprise. Records are maintained on each employee. These include data on recruitment, employment, training, health and other personal information, pay history, disciplinary actions, and promotions or transfers. These records provide information for line supervisors when historical background is needed on an employee.

Advisory role

The personnel department cooperates with other departments in the business enterprise. It works with safety engineers to see that safety regulations are enforced and to improve safety of machinery and the production process. Personnel administrators can assist industrial engineers in motivating employees to better productivity. Personnel officials maintain contact with union officials to improve communication with management.

Finally, as advisor to top management, the personnel department can determine the level of employee morale through such data as absentee rates, labor turnover, complaints and grievances, accidents, and production efficiency. Once these data are analyzed, the department may make suggestions for improving the enterprise's work climate.

SUMMARY

The functions of the personnel department include providing staff assistance in the recruitment, selection, induction, and training of employees. The personnel department acts as advisor to management in matters of employee morale and employee-management relations. Top management and supervisors throughout the enterprise, as well as the personnel department, have important roles to perform in personnel management.

The personnel department, functioning as the center for employment activities, performs five basic steps in the hiring and placement of employees:

1. Working with line management in determining job specifications.
2. Recruiting job applicants.
3. Carrying out the selection process.
4. Performing induction of new employees.
5. Coordinating a program of employee training.

The personnel department normally performs the function of job analysis to determine that wages are fair. The first step in job analysis is to draw up a job description covering the essential elements of each specific job. Then job evaluation ranks each job in relation to other jobs in the enterprise. Following job evaluation, the wage scale is drawn up.

A performance rating system is used to evaluate an employee's performance. This is used to make individual merit increases in wages within job classifications and to guide management in selecting employees for promotion. Both seniority and ability are important considerations in promotion policy.

The personnel department should formulate policy on transfers of employees from one job to another, between departments, from one work shift to another, or for remedial reasons.

Downgrading and layoffs are important areas relating to workers and should be covered by formulated personnel policies.

A discipline policy should provide a clear statement of what is expected of employees and should be fairly administered.

When workers are unionized, the personnel department can assist management in developing positive policies and attitudes toward organized labor and can aid supervisors in the administration of those policies.

The personnel department functions in a staff capacity. Its organization structure includes a personnel manager and subordinates in the areas of recruiting, training, labor relations, employee services, and safety and health. The head of the personnel function should report to the president of the enterprise and be considered a member of top management.

TERMS FOR REVIEW

personnel management   *seniority*
job specifications   *employee transfer*
recruitment   *downgrading*
employee training   *layoffs*
job description   *discipline*
job evaluation   *Occupational Safety and Health*
performance rating   *Act of 1970*
promotion

QUESTIONS

1. Outline the steps that a personnel department might go through to add an additional shift of both skilled and nonskilled workers in a television manufacturing enterprise.

2. What types of training programs would be appropriate for the different kinds of workers hired as the result of the expansion outlined in Question 1?

3. Distinguish between job analysis and performance rating. What is the importance of each?

4. Assume the role of the owner of a small manufacturing enterprise and draw up a statement of your views of the relative importance of seniority and ability in making promotions or layoffs for production workers.

5. Assume the role of the labor union president in a small manufacturing enterprise and draw up a statement of your views of the relative importance of seniority and ability in making promotions and wage increases for production workers who are members of the union.

6. Why is a written disciplinary policy important for the business enterprise?

7. *a.* What changes occur in the development and administration of personnel policies when an enterprise's nonmanagerial employees become unionized?
   b. What positive and negative implications are there for management in such a development?

Business briefs

Turnover of college graduates

A personnel manager for a large midwestern manufacturing corporation recently voiced the following comment:

"We are hiring college graduates in business administration and paying them $10,000 a year and up. Top management has indicated that we are to hire more of these young people. However, we haven't been able to keep many of them more than a year. After an orientation period of two weeks they are rotated from one department to another for three-month periods in one of our factory locations. At the end of a year we put them in a spot which may be open and where the trainee expresses an interest. Then the supervisor takes over their work assignments. One problem is that many of our supervisors are getting very little more in salary than these college graduates even though they have been with the company for a number of years."

1. What personnel problems are implied in this statement?
2. What suggestions would you make to the personnel manager for reducing turnover in college graduates and for maintaining supervisors' morale?

PVC peril

Business is faced with controversy not only in the end uses of products such as "no-return" bottles but in the production process itself. An example of this conflict is that surrounding the manufacture of polyvinyl chloride (PVC). PVC is a plastic widely used in the auto industry in upholstery, dashboards, gaskets, mountings, and some engine parts. PVC is produced from a deadly gas, vinyl chloride monomer (VCM).

After the deaths from liver cancer of workers at a PVC plant in Kentucky many different parties expressed a variety of concerns:

The Occupational Safety and Health Administration (OSHA) demanded that certain respiratory equipment be worn by workers any time they were exposed to gas emissions of 25 parts per million in cleaning the reactor vessels used in the production process.

Respirator producers stated that much equipment wasn't available because the National Institute of Safety and Health (NIOSH) hadn't approved the cartridges used in masks to filter chemicals and gases.

NIOSH said that only two cartridges had been received to be tested for approval.

Some workers objected to wearing extra equipment and did not wear respirators unless a supervisor was present.

An industry executive stated that respiratory equipment decreases worker productivity and increases product cost.

A union official indicated that the decrease in worker productivity when using respirators is slight but that companies consider respirators an unnecessary expense.

Another industry executive declared that cost isn't a factor but safety is. This manager said that masks with air lines are a safety hazard where a worker moves up and down stairs.

Some union officials called for a shutdown of the industry unless PVC dangers can be controlled and also complained that at 25 parts per million of VCM, workers can be cancer seeded.

An industry official stated that shutdown of the entire industry would result in job losses of up to 2 million with production and sales losses of $60 billion. This claim was disputed by a union official who suggested that if PVC were banned a substitute material would be found or could be obtained from plants in other parts of the world.

1. As a personnel administrator in the plastics industry, what approach would you suggest in dealing with this controversy?

2. What factors will have to be considered in any solution to this situation?

3. Should a product which is banned because of safety considerations in the United States be produced by a multinational business corporation in another country with less strict safety standards?

Cases

Hedgepath Early American Furniture Company

The Hedgepath Early American Furniture Company is a family-owned and family-managed enterprise. It was started some 30 years ago by Ronald A. Hedgepath, Sr., who had developed the business into a successful furniture manufacturing operation employing some 250 production workers.

In 1975, Hedgepath's only son, Ronald Junior, was home for the summer from the state university where he was majoring in business administration. Ronald had worked in the factory in previous years. During the summer of 1975 he was employed in the main office doing general office work. Because of some of the personnel practices he observed, and in view of what appeared to him to be a high rate of employee turnover, Ronald persuaded his father that the company needed a director of personnel administration.

The elder Hedgepath had built up his business by depending heavily on his plant foremen to do the hiring, training, and firing of employees. The ten foremen had been personally picked by him. In the small southern town where the plant was located they had considerable prestige because of their positions with the company. Several of the foremen had been with the Hedgepath Company since its founding.

When the word got around that at young Ronald's insistence a new man was being brought in as "personnel director" and that all hiring and firing would now be centralized, there was considerable grumbling among the foremen. Particularly the old-timers declared that they understood Hedgepath personnel needs better than any outsider ever could.

Jim Curtis, age 29, was employed as the new personnel director. He had a bachelor's degree in business administration. He had worked five years as assistant personnel manager for a large automotive parts manufacturer in another city.

Mr. Curtis soon found that he had his hands full in trying to work out some uniform personnel policies for the Hedgepath plant. There was no union at the plant. For years each foreman had made his own "personnel policies," with considerable individual variation from foreman to foreman. The workers who had been employed for any length of time soon learned what to expect from their particular foreman. Hiring of friends and relatives was a common practice. When orders slowed down, there was no companywide policy for laying off workers. Each foreman determined who was to be laid off. Seniority was sometimes given consideration. However, more generally, foremen attempted to retain those employees who were the most productive, or who were relatives, or with whom they had special friendships. When Curtis questioned one of the foremen why a particular worker with a marginal attendance record was being retained the foreman replied, "I have known Bob Jones for 18 years and I am not about to let him go." From the tone of his remark it was obvious to Mr. Curtis that the foreman did not wish to be pressed further on the matter.

As part of his investigation of the labor turnover situation, Mr. Curtis began conducting exit conferences with employees who were leaving the company. These conferences revealed that these employees were disgruntled with such things as special friendships and nepotism in hiring and laying off workers. Also they felt there was unfair treatment in such matters as allocation of overtime, promotions, transfers from one department to another, and discipline.

As Curtis began to develop standardized personnel procedures, some of the foremen cooperated. However, he met resistance from a number of them. There was also a varied reaction from the workers. Some of the plant employees were glad to see the personnel director's actions since they thought they would get a "fairer shake." However, other employees resented the new personnel director, as they had things pretty well worked out with their foremen and didn't want this relationship threatened in any way.

Some of the employees who had complaints about the actions of their foremen began coming to Curtis to air their grievances. At the same time, several of the foremen began going to the plant superintendent whenever the new personnel director did anything which they felt threatened their power. Whenever a decision made by Curtis failed to work out in their departments, they were quick to blame the personnel director. Curtis, in turn, claimed that these foremen were not cooperating with his attempts to work out sound personnel policies that all departments could live with.

As a result of this situation, the plant superintendent found that much of his time was occupied in settling arguments between his foremen and the new personnel director. After several weeks of this he went to the senior Mr. Hedgepath with the statement, "You're going to have to do something with that personnel man if we're going to get any work done around here!"

A chart of the Hedgepath Company is given in Exhibit 1 showing

EXHIBIT 1
Partial organization chart of the Hedgepath Early American Furniture Company

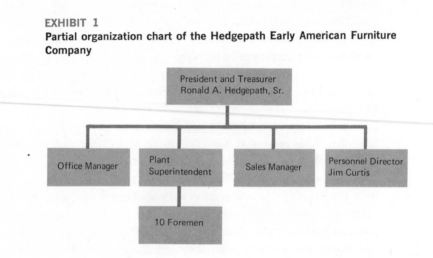

the major management positions in the company after the establishment of the personnel department in 1975.

1. What are the problems involved in instituting a personnel department in the Hedgepath Company where none previously existed?
2. What should be the nature of the authority of the personnel manager?
3. In what ways could the foremen participate in improving personnel policies and practices?
4. What should Mr. Hedgepath do in response to the statement by the plant superintendent?

Artwein Manufacturing Company

Ellen Walters was the personnel director of Artwein Manufacturing Company. One of her responsibilities was to provide notice to employees when new jobs opened up throughout the factory which made possible transfers and promotions. The vacancies or new jobs were posted on two bulletin boards convenient for the workers. An employee who saw a job posted that he or she wanted to try for would inform the management through a "bid" system. This bid system, which generally functioned smoothly, had been worked out with the union to which all production workers belonged.

The labor contract, which both management and the union had signed, was quite detailed regarding the selection of employees for a promotion when vacancies or new jobs developed. The agreement stated:

VI–3–B. Vacancies and openings will be filled on the following basis:
1. From the department in which the opening exists in order of departmental seniority, providing the ability of the applicants is relatively equal. The following factors will be considered in determining ability.
   a. The quality and efficiency of the employee's performance in his or her current job.
   b. Physical fitness (consistent with requirements of the vacancy).
   c. Background of education and experience, including experience in similar or related work (consistent with requirements of the vacancy).
   d. Record of unexcused absenteeism.
2. From other departments of the plant on the basis of plant seniority, provided the ability of the applicants, as defined in Paragraph VI–3–B—1 above, is relatively equal.

In November 1975, Ellen Walters posted a new job for bid in the shipping department. The new job was titled main sealer operator and maintenance person. It was placed in labor grade 7, that of semiskilled work, with a rate of $4.88 an hour. This job involved operating and maintaining a new carton-sealing machine through which ultimately 60 percent of the total production of the plant would go. Although at first the machine would be used only on the day shift, it was planned that eventually the machine would be in operation 24 hours a day. The employee first selected for this job would work the day shift and would have the responsibility of instructing other employees who would work the second and third shifts when the machine went into full production. The employee initially hired for the job would be trained in the operation and maintenance of the equipment by factory representatives of the manufacturer.

The carton-sealing machine the employee would be operating was a new type which cost approximately $50,000 including installation charges. On the advice of the manufacturer of the machine it was decided to use a combination operator and maintenance person for this equipment. The manufacturer advised that the person selected for the job be an individual who was familiar with machinery and who had mechanical training and experience. There were many minor, but critical, adjustments to be made on the machine. The equipment was more likely to break down and have failures if these adjustments were not properly made.

The personnel director prepared a list of all employees who had bid on the new job. There were 35 bids from throughout the plant. This included four men in the shipping department where the sealer machine would be used. The labor agreement required that first consideration be given to employees in the department where the opening exists in order of departmental seniority. These four men from shipping were interviewed by the personnel director and the assistant plant manager in charge of production and shipping. The purpose of the interview was to get additional information about the applicants' education and experience other than what might be shown on company records. All men were physically fit for the job.

On the basis of the interviews and the company's personnel records the following summaries were made concerning these four applicants for the new job:

Ray Jones was the employee with the greatest departmental seniority. His seniority date in the shipping department was June 18, 1966. His job classification was inside truck driver. Some years ago he had taken on-the-job training in dairy farming conducted by the Veterans Administration. In this program he had some training in the maintenance and use of farm tools and machinery. He was considered to be a satisfactory employee by his supervisor. Personnel records showed no unexcused absenteeism.

The employee who stood second in departmental seniority among the applicants was John Robertson. His seniority date was April 4, 1967. He had two years of college compared to the other three applicants who had only high school diplomas. Although Robertson did not claim any mechanical background or training, he was considered a reliable worker by his supervisor in the shipping department. His attendance record was good.

Tod Smith was the third man on the seniority list. He had a seniority date in the shipping department of July 19, 1969. His job classification was inside truck driver. In the interviews Smith indicated that he had had experience with tractors and combines in his farming work. He also indicated that he had taken four years of on-the-job farm training under the Veterans Administration program. His attendance was satisfactory.

Richard Carlson was the fourth man on the list and had a seniority date of July 31, 1972. He was also classified as inside truck driver. His personnel record showed that while in the Air Force he had attended radar school and served as radar crew chief for about six months. Carlson's high school program included machine shop courses and work in shop mathematics, blueprint reading, and shop theory and practice. He had machine shop training during 1973–74 at an evening course at the local high school. His work and attendance records were satisfactory.

The personnel director and assistant plant manager looked over the records of the most senior employees outside the department who had bid on the job. They decided that they would be able to select one of the four men interviewed from within the shipping department to fill the initial position of main sealer operator and maintenance person. The new job would be considered a promotion for any of the four men.

1. What are the issues relevant for management in this case?
2. As an assistant to the personnel director which employee would you recommend be selected for main sealer operator and maintenance person? Why?

A case of fighting

Walter Sloan and Tommy Burke were employed by the company as waste handlers on the graveyard shift to fill large bins with waste materials from the production areas of the plant and remove it to the rear of the factory for further disposal. Both men were union members. The following events occurred in the early morning of October 13, 1975.

According to reports obtained by questioning the two men, about 2:30 A.M. Tommy Burke passed Walter Sloan on his way to the storage room to pick up an empty bin. Burke made an obscene remark and gesture to Sloan who returned a remark. Then Burke grabbed the front of Sloan's coveralls and ripped them slightly. Before this could develop further, the supervisor, Mr. Kirby, appeared and ordered the men back to work. This broke up the incident. Sloan went on back to the department where he had been working. Burke picked up an empty waste bin from the storage room. At this point Mr. Kirby took no further action.

About an hour and a quarter later, at 3:45 A.M., Walter Sloan went to the storage room to get an empty bin. He found an empty bin and headed toward his department with it. However, as Sloan later told company officials, Tommy Burke came up to him and grabbed the bin, saying he was taking "that bin." Sloan allowed him to take the bin. Another employee, Jim Thomas, who was working in the area observed this incident and pointed out another bin which Sloan could use.

Sloan then went to get the one which had been pointed out but found that it was half full of waste. He then started for another bin which he thought was empty. Just as he was about to take this bin Burke ran up to Sloan, grabbed both his arms, and told Sloan he was not going to get that bin either. Sloan jerked his arms loose and shoved Burke back into the bin. Later Sloan said that he told Burke to leave him alone as he shoved him away.

Burke became angry and approached Sloan with his fists clenched. He told Sloan that he was "going to knock the hell out of him." When Burke was close enough to him, Sloan struck Burke with his fists at least twice. The blows were sufficient to knock Burke down for a few seconds. Burke sustained two cuts, one on his lip and one over his eye.

Then Sloan left the storage room area and obtained a bandage to place over a cut on his hand which he got from striking Burke. Sloan was reluctant to inform management of the fight. When he encountered the supervisor, Mr. Kirby, who had observed the previous incident, Sloan said he had cut his hand on a piece of wire.

In the meantime, Mr. Kirby had found Burke and noticed his injuries. Kirby took Burke to the first-aid room and later Burke was taken to the hospital where his cuts were treated by a physician. Sloan was sent home for the remainder of the shift. He was told to return at 7:30 A.M. when statements concerning the affair would be taken.

Further investigation revealed that the incident occurred substantially as has been reported.

1. What issues should concern management in this case?
2. If you were a member of management, how would you proceed in an investigation of an incident similar to this? What additional information would you find helpful in arriving at a decision in this case other than that which is given? How would you obtain this information?
3. As a member of the personnel department of the company, what recommendation would you make to management regarding disciplinary action, if any, for Sloan and Burke? Give the reasons for your position.

Courtesy United Steelworkers of America

*Contract negotiations
are an important part of
labor relations.*

9

Labor relations

*T*he importance of good human relations and the role of personnel administration leads to our discussion of a third area involving the work force— labor unions. When management deals with the work force through a union this is referred to as labor relations. The subject of labor unions produces strong emotional feelings in many persons. There is much public interest when a major strike occurs or when some other labor dispute is widely publicized. However, you should know that most day-to-day contacts between unions and managements take place in an atmosphere quite unlike that of these relatively infrequent events.

You should approach the study of labor relations with an open mind to examine how organized labor affects the operation of business enterprises. The following questions are discussed in this chapter:

How has significant national legislation affected labor relations?
What has been the growth of union membership?
Why do workers join unions?
How are labor unions organized?
What provisions are normally included in the labor contract?
How does the grievance process contribute to a healthy work climate?

LEGISLATION AFFECTING LABOR RELATIONS

To understand the relationship between labor unions and today's business enterprises you need to see how this relationship has evolved and how management's dealings with unions have been influenced by national laws. Many significant incidents, laws, and court decisions are important in the development of today's labor-management relations. However, there are three modern pieces of national legislation which must be included in our discussion. The first of these is the Wagner Act of 1935. It was followed by amending legislation in 1947 known as the Taft-Hartley Act and in 1959 by the Landrum-Griffin Act.

The Wagner Act ✕

The National Labor Relations Act of 1935, usually called the Wagner Act, represented a Magna Carta for organized labor in the United States. Prior to this law business had used many methods to suppress union activities and to discourage employees from joining unions. During the 1920s and earlier in the United States it was not unusual for employees to be fired from their jobs merely because they were suspected of union activity. Owners circulated *blacklists* to other employers with the names of former employees who had been discharged for union activities. Sometimes a worker was required to sign a *yellow-dog contract* agreeing not to join a union as a condition of employment.

Employers did not limit antiunion activities to economic pressure. They also used strikebreakers, labor spies, and armed guards in attempting to prevent unions from organizing their factories. All types of violence occurred including clubbing, shooting, and dynamiting by both business and workers in the battles over the employees' right to organize unions. During this period of American history the political and legal climate generally stressed property rights and favored management's attempts to avoid unionization.

Few employers were willing to recognize voluntarily the right of their employees to join a union and bargain collectively over wages and working conditions. In 1935 the Congress under the leadership of President Franklin D. Roosevelt passed the National Labor Relations Act. This act, known as the Wagner Act, declared that employees "shall have the right to self-organization, to form, join, or assist labor organizations, to bargain collectively through representatives of their own choosing."

To protect workers against the earlier antiunion practices the Wagner Act made illegal any interference or restraint of employees who engage in union activities. An employer cannot discharge an employee for union activity. No type of discriminatory action can be taken lawfully against an employee for joining a union. No company unions are permitted. These had been organized in the past by some managements to dominate the union organization and to avoid bargaining with an independent union. Also considered an unfair labor practice is an employer's refusal to bargain with a union selected by employees to represent them.

The administration of the Wagner Act is the job of the National Labor Relations Board originally composed of three members. Field examiners investigate complaints of unfair labor practices. Then trial examiners conduct formal hearings and pass their findings on to the board for affirmation. Decisions of the board can be appealed through the federal courts to the Supreme Court to determine if the board has jurisdiction in a particular instance or has overstepped its legal bounds.

Another function of the National Labor Relations Board is the conduct of elections to determine whether groups of workers in an enterprise desire a union. These elections are held if a union is able to certify interest by 30 percent or more of the employees the union would represent in an enterprise. Then the union must receive a majority of votes in the election to be certified as the workers' bargaining agent.

The Wagner Act marked a turning point in the growth of unions in America. In 1935, there were less than four million union members in the United States. By 1947, when the Wagner Act was significantly amended, more than 15 million American workers belonged to unions.

The Wagner Act minimized the industrial disputes stemming from whether employees shall be represented by a union. The NLRB election procedure is a better means for determining whether an enterprise is to be unionized than the strikes and violence which marked earlier representation battles.

However, the Wagner Act was not successful in reducing strikes in already organized industries. There were almost 5,000 strikes in 1946 involving more than 4.5 million workers. Excesses by unions and limitations of the Wagner Act started a movement to correct some labor abuses. The pendulum of public opinion and federal support for union activity began to swing the other way. The change in public opinion, combined with Republican control of Congress in 1946, set the stage for significant revision of the Wagner Act.

The Taft-Hartley Act

The Labor Management Relations Act of 1947, commonly known as the Taft-Hartley Act, was actually an amendment to the Wagner Act. In an attempt to correct some abuses by organized labor, the Taft-Hartley Act adds restrictions on the activities of labor organizations. It gives employers rights not spelled out in the earlier legislation. The administration of the act remains with the National Labor Relations Board, which was increased from three to five members.

The 1947 act defines unfair labor practices by an employer in essentially the same way as the Wagner Act. However, the Taft-Hartley Act goes further by outlawing certain labor practices by unions. There is to be no restraint or coercion of employees in determining which union will represent them. The union cannot interfere in the right of an employee not to participate in union activity. The union cannot force an employer to discriminate against an employee for nonunion membership unless the union shop is authorized. In a *union shop* the employer agrees that employees must join the union after they are hired, but union membership is not a prerequisite for being hired. It is an unfair labor practice for a union which has a union-shop agreement to charge excessive initiation or membership fees.

In a *closed shop* workers must be members of the union before they may be hired by an employer. The closed shop is illegal under the Taft-Hartley Act.

Under the Taft-Hartley Act employers or self-employed persons cannot be forced to join a union. This prevents unions from forcing independent businessmen such as plumbers to join a union even though their earnings and working conditions might affect those of unionized employees in the same occupations.

Secondary boycotts by unions were also outlawed. A *secondary boycott* occurs when employees of Company A with a grievance against their employer picket Company B or persuade Company B employees to strike because Company B uses Company A's products. A *primary boycott* is one in which employees refuse to use the products of their employer with whom they have a dispute. This is permitted since it involves direct action against their own employer. Although easy to define in a simple example, in practice the secondary boycott is often difficult to distinguish from direct action against an employer.

The Taft-Hartley Act also prohibits unions from forcing employers to recognize or bargain with one union if another union has already been certified by the NLRB as the bargaining agent. The purpose of this clause is to avoid the disastrous effects on both employers and employees resulting from conflicts among different unions. *Jurisdictional strikes* which grow out of disagreements over which craft has the right to perform particular jobs were outlawed. The building-trades unions were particularly affected by jurisdictional disputes because of overlapping of skills among their members. Another labor practice by unions defined as unfair is *featherbedding,* which requires an employer to pay for services not performed. However, the interpretation of this provision allows for payment of employees even though they do little or no productive work. An example would be the use of "standby musicians" during recorded broadcasts or when outside bands play in local theatres.

The Taft-Hartley Act also requires union officers to file affidavits that they are not members of the Communist Party and do not support any organization that advocates overthrow of the U.S. government by force.

Protection for the public. The Taft-Hartley Act protects the public from strikes which would cut off the flow of essential goods and services. Whenever the president of the United States determines that a labor dispute threatens the national health or safety, the attorney general can obtain an injunction from a federal court. This has the effect of postponing any strike for a period of 80 days. During this time workers cannot strike nor can management lock workers out of the plant. Terms of work and pay are frozen for the time, and the parties are obliged to make every effort to settle their differences. The Federal Mediation and Conciliation Service is available for assistance of both parties. Before the 80-day injunction period is over, if no settlement has been reached, the National Labor Relations Board is required to poll employees to see if they will accept the last offer of management. If no settlement is reached through this procedure the president submits a report to the Congress with or without recommendations for action.

The right-to-work controversy. A controversial part of the Taft-Hartley Act is Section 14b. This provides that individual states may outlaw union-shop contracts which require workers to join a union. In 1975, 19 states had these right-to-work laws.

A state right-to-work law substantially weakens unions in organizing new workers. Unless employees can be forced as a condition of employment by the labor agreement to join a union after being hired, it is difficult to promote a solid union membership. Unions maintain that all workers in a unionized factory should bear their share of the cost of benefits secured by the union.

The Taft-Hartley Act amending the Wagner Act by no means represented a perfect piece of legislation. Generally union leaders were critical of the restraints imposed on unions by the legislation. Business praised the act but felt it did not go far enough or provide sufficient penalties for what some considered wrongdoing by unions. Some of these problem areas were dealt with in the next major piece of labor relations legislation which was passed in 1959.

The Landrum-Griffin Act

The Labor-Management Reporting and Disclosures Act of 1959 is commonly known as the Landrum-Griffin Act. It placed the federal government for the first time in the position of policing the internal affairs of labor unions. The need for new controls over labor organizations and their leaders came to light as the result of congressional investigations. These disclosed irregularities and questionable practices in some unions and on the part of some managements in their relations with union officials.

Some of the principal provisions of the Landrum-Griffin Act are as follows:

1. All labor organizations are required to have a constitution and bylaws which spell out matters such as membership eligibility, fees and dues, handling of union funds, and procedures for collective bargaining and strike authorizations.

2. Regardless of the union's constitution, union members have certain inalienable rights. These include safeguards against improper discipline, protection against unreasonable dues and initiation fees, and democratic controls over union officials. Union members may have these rights enforced by appealing to the federal courts if necessary.

3. Unions and union officials must file reports with the Secretary of Labor regarding their activities and finances. These reports are similar to those previously required of corporations under the Federal Securities Act. This put on record many of the internal workings of unions which had previously not been subject to review by any outside agency.

4. Limitations were placed on union organizing tactics and on employer countermeasures to union organizing activities. The purpose of these limitations was to restrict these activities on both sides to peace-

ful persuasion of workers. The Taft-Hartley Act restriction against secondary boycotts was strengthened. Picketing by unions hopeful of persuading nonunion shop employees to vote for the union was limited.

The Landrum-Griffin Act was wide sweeping in its scope and detailed in its requirements. The chief limitations were imposed upon unions.

TABLE 9–1
Summary of major labor relations legislation

Wagner Act (1935)

Gave employees the right to organize unions and bargain collectively with employers.

Prohibited an employer from discriminating against an employee for union activity.

Prohibited company unions.

Required employer to bargain with the union certified as employees' bargaining agent.

Established NLRB to investigate unfair labor practices and supervise union representation elections.

Taft-Hartley Act (1947—amended Wagner Act)

Outlawed these practices by unions:

Coercion by employees in determining which union would represent them.

Union interference with the right of an employee not to participate in union activity.

Forcing an employer to discriminate against an employee for nonunion membership unless union shop is authorized.

Charging excessive initiation or membership fees when a union shop exists.

Forcing self-employed persons to join a union.

Closed shops.

Secondary boycotts.

Forcing employers to recognize or bargain with one union if another union has already been NLRB certified.

Featherbedding.

Union officials required to file non-Communist affidavits.

President of the U.S. could obtain 80-day injunction to postpone a strike which threatened the national welfare.

States were permitted to have right-to-work laws outlawing union shop contracts.

Landrum-Griffin Act (1959)

Required unions to have a constitution and bylaws.

Guaranteed certain rights to individual union members.

Required unions to file financial and activity reports with Secretary of Labor.

Limited unions and employers to peaceful persuasion of workers in organizing campaigns.

Many of the provisions in the act of 1959 were framed to deal with specific union problems brought to light by the congressional investigations at the time.

GROWTH IN UNION MEMBERSHIP

The union movement has had variations in growth depending upon economic, political, and social factors along with the shifting tide of public opinion and legal decisions. Figures 9–1 and 9–2 show how the strength of union membership has varied from 1930 to 1974.

As Figure 9–1 indicates, there was a spectacular growth in union membership between 1936 and the end of World War II. The passage of the Wagner Act in 1935 plus a keen rivalry between the AFL and the CIO stimulated the organizing efforts of the unions. The number of union members increased during World War II as the result of higher employment levels and wider union recognition.

Following the end of World War II in 1945 a wave of industrial unrest and work stoppages began. In the year following V-J Day more than 10 million men and women were demobilized from the armed forces. Thousands of factories had to retool to make the change to a peacetime economy. Some factories shut down either temporarily or permanently. Hours of work were cut back and unions fought to keep take-home pay at wartime levels, which had often included overtime pay at premium rates. Numerous strikes occurred and the prestige of unions was damaged. The Taft-Hartley Act was passed in 1947. This period was one of leveling off in union growth.

The Korean emergency in 1950 stimulated union growth. With the merger in 1955 of the AFL and CIO the groundwork was laid for achievement of union membership of 17.5 million workers in 1956. However, the merger did not solve all of organized labor's problems. The Landrum-Griffin Act passed in 1959 put pressure on unions to "clean house."

By 1974 union membership had reached an all-time high of 21.6 million workers. However, as Figure 9–2 shows, the proportion of union members in the total labor force actually slipped from a 1956 high of 25 percent to about 22 percent in 1974. This can be explained in part by the changing nature of the work force. Automation has decreased the number of blue-collar workers who were most likely to be union members. An increasing percentage of the work force is made up of women and white-collar workers who have traditionally been less interested in union membership.

FIGURE 9–1
Membership of national and international unions, 1930–1974

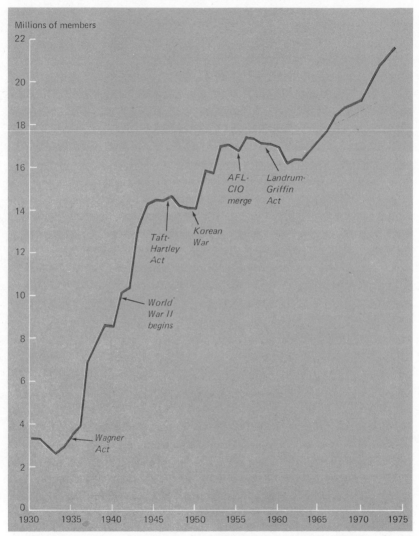

Millions of members

Wagner
Act

World
War II
begins

Taft-
Hartley
Act

Korean
War

AFL-
CIO
merge

Landrum-
Griffin
Act

Source: U.S. Bureau of the Census, *Statistical Abstract of the U.S.: 1974* (95th ed.) and
U.S. Department of Labor.

Unions have increased their efforts to organize professional and
technical, clerical, and sales employees. White-collar attitudes toward
unions are changing. Many white-collar workers believe their wages
have lagged behind the higher prices of goods and services. Teachers,
police, and firefighters are becoming increasingly interested in union

FIGURE 9–2
Union membership as a percent of the labor force, 1930–1974

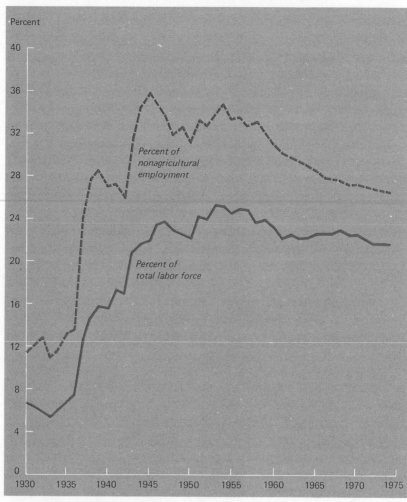

Source: U.S. Department of Labor.

organization as they face more pressures in carrying out their responsibilities.

WHY WORKERS JOIN UNIONS

Contrary to the belief of some managers, the desire for more pay is only one of the reasons workers become union members. Usually a variety of economic and noneconomic considerations determine why workers join unions.

Economic motives for union membership

The three main economic factors which motivate workers to join labor unions voluntarily are wages, fringe benefits, and security in employment and wage income.

The prospect of higher wages does motivate workers to join a union. However, fringe benefits such as health insurance, disability benefits, life insurance, pensions, and paid vacations are becoming increasingly important. Workers also want security in employment and wage income to protect them against layoffs due to seasonal and general declines in business activity.

Noneconomic motives for union membership

Noneconomic motives influencing employees to establish or to join a union may be stronger than the economic motives. Eight noneconomic motives for union membership can be identified.

1. Employees want protection against arbitrary action by supervisors in discipline and discharge. The union provides a procedure for dealing with grievances to try to insure fairness by management.

2. Workers desire a voice in making the decisions which affect them. Employees like to participate in decisions such as how overtime will be distributed, how layoffs will be carried out, and how increased compensation will be divided between pay raises and fringe benefits.

3. There is a need to establish channels of communication between employees and top management. This becomes increasingly important as the enterprise grows and the line between employees and management sharpens. The union organization with its grievance procedure provides an avenue of communication between workers and management.

4. The union offers an opportunity for increased individual satisfaction associated with the work experience. The employee who becomes active in the union organization frequently feels a sense of accomplishment and purpose in holding a union office or participating in union activities. The union provides an opportunity to satisfy the worker's psychological needs for self-realization. This is especially true when the

work environment is routine and monotonous and the employee has more than average capabilities.

5. In today's complex industrial society most individuals feel a need for identification with some group. Group identification tends to reduce feelings of insecurity in the individual employee. Union membership can provide an important kind of group identification.

6. Individual workers are motivated to join a union by the social pressure of the informal work group. Employees with negative or indifferent attitudes may become union members in order to conform to the attitudes of the work group. The worker who refuses to join may encounter hostility from his fellow workers and not be accepted in the informal organization of the enterprise.

7. Unions sometimes provide for the recreational, social, cultural, and educational needs of workers. Particularly in certain industries or in large urban areas, the labor organization plays a large part in meeting these needs of employees.

8. The employee may be motivated to union membership because of his family ties. Studies have shown that a worker with a family background of union membership is more likely to become a union member than a worker from a nonunion family.

Union membership required for employment

Where a union shop has been lawfully agreed to by an employer and an existing union, all members of the work force covered by the labor agreement will be required to join the union within a specified time after being hired. In the union shop an employee has no option of whether or not to join a union. It is a condition for continued employment.

THE STRUCTURE AND ORGANIZATION OF THE LABOR UNION

Craft and industrial unions

Unions are customarily organized on a craft or an industry basis. *Craft unions* draw their members from a particular trade or occupation. An example of the craft union is the International Brotherhood of Electrical Workers, which includes electricians whether they are employed in factories, the building trades, or shipyards. The *industrial union,* typified by the United Automobile Workers, organizes the workers in a particular industry regardless of the kind of work they do. Sometimes the line between craft and industrial unions is blurred as each reaches beyond its original scope of skills or industry to organize other workers.

Local unions

The local union is the unit which deals most directly with individual union members. In some respects, the local union is analogous to municipal government. The local usually includes members from one enterprise or geographical area and has its own officers. Sometimes the local will have a business agent or secretary-treasurer who takes care of the affairs of the union and will be paid from the local union treasury. Local unions may draw assistance from a business agent appointed by the national union who serves more than one local in an area.

Important members of the local union organization are the shop stewards. These individuals are usually elected by the union employees with whom they work. Although shop stewards are full-time employees of the enterprise, they represent union members and discuss grievances with first-line supervisors.

In some instances stewards may collect dues for the union treasury. Just as first-line supervisors have a great influence in determining the human relations climate, so union stewards tend to set the tone for union activities in the enterprise.

National union organization

The local union is generally affiliated with a national or international union. Since the organization of the labor union is essentially political in character, local union leaders must meet the needs of workers who compose the local membership. If these local leaders are not able to "deliver" on issues of importance, they are likely to be replaced by new officers at the next union election. The same is true with the national labor organization. The national union has to meet the needs of its local affiliates if the national leaders are to retain their offices for any period of time.

Representatives from the national organization assist local unions in negotiations either for contract agreements or in grievances which have not been settled at lower levels. They also act as organizers to reach nonunion employees of enterprises in their areas. The national union may provide its locals with financial aid during a strike.

Most national and international unions having locals in the United States are affiliated with the AFL–CIO, the combined organization of the American Federation of Labor and Congress of Industrial Organizations. Today the AFL–CIO unions, which were united in 1955, represent the majority of American union members. However, there are significant unions which are not affiliated with the AFL–CIO. These independent unions include the Teamsters, the Automobile Workers, and the United Mine Workers.

There is a heavy concentration of membership in a few unions. Table 9–2 lists the unions reporting membership in excess of 200,000.

TABLE 9–2
National and international unions reporting more than 200,000 members, 1972 (in thousands)

Union	Members	Union	Members
Teamsters (Ind.)	1,855	Engineers, operating	402
Steelworkers	1,400	Paperworkers	389
Automobile Workers (Ind.)	1,394	Clothing workers	365
Electrical (IBEW)	957	Musicians	315
Carpenters	829	Government (AFGE)	293
Machinists	758	Electrical (IUE)	290
Retail clerks	633	Teachers (AFTC)	249
Laborers	600	United transportation	248
Meat cutters	529	Postal workers	239
State, county workers	529	Railway, steamship clerks	238
Service employees (SEIU)	484	Letter carriers	220
Hotel and restaurant	458	Mine workers (Ind.)	213
Communications workers	443	Painters	208
Garment, ladies'	428		

Source: U.S. Bureau of Labor Statistics, *Directory of National Unions and Employee Associations,* 1973.

The teamsters', automobile workers', and steelworkers' unions each have over one million members. Together these three unions account for almost one fourth of union membership in the United States.

THE UNION CONTRACT

When the management of a business enterprise bargains collectively with its employees through union representatives over conditions of employment the result is a contract agreement. Union contracts customarily run for two or three years. Despite the unique nature of each union contract, there are certain issues dealt with in most contracts. These issues, discussed in the following pages, form the framework within which labor relations are handled in the individual enterprise.

The bargaining unit

One of the first elements of a union contract is the *recognition clause* which states that management acknowledges a certain union as representing a designated group of employees. The *bargaining unit* defines the employer and the employees covered by the union contract. On the employer side, the bargaining unit may be one business enterprise. Or it may include a number of firms dealing with the same union, which is called *industrywide* bargaining. On the employee side, the bargaining unit may include employees in certain job classifications or in a particular factory if the enterprise is a multiplant operation. When job classification is the basis for definition of the bargaining unit, management may have to bargain with more than one union. These could represent different crafts such as electricians, pipefitters, and carpenters.

Union security

Customarily the contract will spell out the provisions for union security. In most instances this means that all employees covered by the contract will be required to join the union within a specified time after being employed and will be required to maintain their membership in the union. Frequently, a *checkoff* clause in the contract authorizes management to deduct union dues from the employee's pay and turn this sum directly over to the union treasury.

Grievance procedure and arbitration

Almost all labor contracts contain procedures to be followed in dealing with complaints by union members against management. Grievance procedures spell out a succession of steps through which complaints may be processed from lower to higher levels of management and union officials. If a dispute cannot be settled by the parties themselves, an impartial third person called an *arbitrator* is called upon to settle the issue.

Because of the importance of the grievance process and arbitration to labor relations, this area is discussed in detail following the remaining union contract provisions.

Wages and hours

Hours of work and wage rates are a subject of major importance in collective bargaining. General wage scales are outlined in the contract with detailed wage scales for various job classifications listed in appendices to the basic contract. Such elements as overtime premiums, bonuses, wage incentive systems, automatic wage adjustments, and wage reopening discussion clauses are usually a part of this section of the labor contract.

Pay or work guarantees

The inclusion of a guarantee of pay represents a relatively new, but important, feature of the collective bargaining agreement. As recently as 15 years ago *supplementary unemployment benefit* plans were virtually unknown. These SUB plans consist of payments made by employers to a fund that is used to pay employees who have been laid off. This money supplements unemployment benefits paid under state plans. Unions which have negotiated unemployment benefit plans include the United Auto Workers, the steelworkers, and the rubber workers.

In contrast to the relatively recent guaranteed pay plans, some guarantee of hours of work for employees over a given period has been in existence for years. Such work guarantees include the 36-hour-week guarantee in the meat-packing industry, weekly hours guarantee in various transportation enterprises, and a minimum hours-per-week guarantee in sugar refineries.

Holidays and vacations

Almost all labor contracts include a statement regarding holidays. On a paid holiday employees are paid for a workday even though they do not work. Those employees who may be required to work on designated holidays are paid a premium, such as time and a half (i.e., they receive one and a half times their regular hourly rate) or double time. The number of days recognized as holidays has increased over the years with the number now ranging from six to nine.

Paid vacations are part of the labor contract with the length of the vacation based on the employee's years of service with the enterprise. Paid vacations usually run from one to four weeks.

Employee benefits

Employee benefits cover a broad range of insurance and pension provisions. Employee benefits have increased considerably in recent years and are an important part of the union contract. Most contracts call for some of the following types of insurance for employees: life insurance, medical and hospitalization coverage, and accidental death and disability insurance.

The majority of union contracts provide for pensions for employees retiring from the enterprise. The tendency in recent years has been for the amount of pension benefits to increase and for the retirement age to be liberalized. It is important whether or not the employee has a *vested interest* in pension benefits. When benefits are vested employees are entitled as a matter of right to the contribution after a specified period whether or not they are still in the employment of the enterprise at retirement age. The present tendency is to provide for vested pension rights. This increases the mobility of employees since they need not remain with one employer in order to qualify for retirement benefits in addition to federal social security.

Discipline and discharge

Union contracts include mention of the measures of discipline an employer may undertake for certain activities of employees. A broad reference to disciplinary measures is made in a general management rights clause. Discipline short of discharge includes oral and written warnings, suspension, transfer, demotion, or pay penalties. This section of the contract usually requires that some form of notice to employee and union be given. Frequently a hearing must be held before disciplinary action can be taken.

Discharge is the strongest form of disciplinary action an enterprise can take against an employee short of court action in a civil suit or supporting criminal prosecution. Almost all contracts have a section on discharge. This includes the grounds for dismissal and procedures for notification, action, and appeal. Chapter 8 discusses personnel policies dealing with discipline, plant rules, and employee conduct.

Management and union rights

It is not unusual to find a statement regarding management's rights in the labor relations contract. The general statements of managerial rights customarily contain provisions relating to the right to direct the working force and the right to conduct the business. Frequently, a statement is made that the management retains all its rights except those specifically detailed in the contract as subjects for collective bargaining.

Sometimes limitations will be placed on management's rights to contract work, including restrictions on subcontracting. A common provision is that subcontracting is prohibited if it would result in a layoff of employees or if some employees are already in a layoff status. Other restrictions may limit changes in production methods and the type of work performed by supervisors.

Union rights may include access of union representatives to the plant, control of the union label such as in the apparel industry, and permission for union bulletin boards. Also, the contract may call for management to collect union dues automatically from employees' pay through the *checkoff system*.

Unions may be restricted by the contract in such matters as the number of union stewards in the plant, conduct of union activities on company time, and solicitation of union members during company time.

Seniority provisions

Nearly all union contracts cover seniority as it affects employees in matters of job retention, promotion, and transfers. Ordinarily employees with greater length of service with the enterprise get preference over those with lesser seniority.

There are different degrees of emphasis on the role of seniority for purposes of promotion. The most weight is given to seniority when the clause "seniority shall prevail" is the basis for determining which employee shall be promoted. Or the contract may indicate seniority shall prevail with the promotion given to the most senior candidate "if qualified." The "if qualified" clause places relatively less weight on seniority. The most senior employee could be passed over if not qualified for the promotion. Management has the most latitude in promotions when the "if equal" clause is included. The "if equal" clause means that the most senior employee will be given the position if ability and qualifications are equal to other competing candidates.

Management usually prefers to have as much latitude as possible in selecting personnel for promotion, transfer, or layoff. However, seniority systems can aid management in dealing consistently with a large work force and the many jobs which do not require a high degree of skill.

Strikes and lockouts

Nearly all union contracts provide for a no-strike clause—either unconditional or conditional. An unconditional clause bans work stoppages for the life of the contract. A conditional clause may permit strikes but only if the grievance procedure is not effective or a deadlock occurs during bargaining on a new contract or the old one has expired.

A *strike* is action taken by workers to cease work. Picketing usually follows by union members to prevent other personnel from entering the struck plant. A similar action by management is called a *lockout,* when union members are not permitted by management to enter the enterprise's facilities because of a dispute. Customarily management will give a no-lockout pledge in the labor agreement when the union accepts a no-strike clause. Contracts with no-strike clauses may specify disciplinary penalties ranging up to discharge for individual participants in unauthorized or wildcat strikes.

The majority of strikes in recent years have been over wages. Other strikes occurred because of dissatisfaction over factory administration, union security, fringe benefits, or job security. Many strikes occur while management and union officials are bargaining over terms of a new labor agreement after the old contract has expired. In 1974 the number of strikes in the United States reached an all-time high of 5,900.

Working conditions and safety

A variety of guarantees are made against discrimination by either management or union toward individual employees on account of race, creed, sex, age, or some other ascribed status. Employee health and safety is referred to in the contract in clauses such as those covering union-management safety committees, safety equipment and who shall pay for it, first-aid provision, and physical examinations. Sometimes services and working conditions such as company dining rooms, parking lots, rest rooms, and locker and shower facilities are included in this section of the contract.

This lengthy discussion has only outlined the most frequently encountered provisions in the typical union contract. It should be apparent that a great deal of time and effort by both management and the union go into its development. The union contract is an important part of the American industrial scene.

THE GRIEVANCE PROCESS AND ARBITRATION

The grievance process

The grievance process is one of the major contributions of American unionism to industrial human relations. The grievance process is customarily a three- or four-step procedure with a decision by an impartial third party if management and labor cannot settle the grievance at an earlier stage. A typical grievance procedure would include the following four steps.

First, the employee or employees with a complaint would present the grievance in writing to the first-line supervisor. It would be discussed by the aggrieved, the union steward or a member of the union grievance committee, and the supervisor. If the grievance is settled at this first step to the satisfaction of both management and labor, the remaining steps are unnecessary. If the grievance is not settled then the written complaint is signed, dated, and sent to the second step.

Second, the written grievance is discussed by the union grievance committee and the next higher level of management, perhaps the factory superintendent. At this stage a staff member of the industrial relations department may advise or represent management in attempting to settle the grievance. Most grievances should be settled in the first or second steps.

Third, if the grievance is not settled in the second step it is sent to a committee composed of a representative of the local's national union and the factory superintendent or some higher member of management. At this stage the local union has national assistance and the enterprise's industrial relations director is probably involved on the management side. Each side will investigate the complaint and attempt to establish a basis for settling the dispute.

Fourth, if top management and the national union representative are unable to agree on a solution to the grievance, the issue may be dropped if the aggrieved and the union wish, or it may be submitted to a third, impartial party for arbitration. The contract will provide that issues taken to arbitration are final and binding on both parties. The arbitrator is selected with the mutual consent of both parties with each side bearing the expenses necessary to prepare and present its own case. Customarily the cost of the arbitrator is borne equally by the business enterprise and the union.

The role of arbitration in the field of industrial relations is sometimes confused with conciliation and mediation. *Arbitration* is a judicial process with the arbitrator assuming the role of a judge. The parties are required to submit evidence and cross-examine each other's case. After the arbitrator has heard both sides and has had a period of study and deliberation, a decision is rendered.

Conciliation is the action of a third party to bring together management and labor when a dispute exists between them. The conciliator's role is merely to get the parties to talk over their dispute in the hope of reaching a settlement. On the other hand, *mediation* is the process whereby a third party brings the two sides together and *also* actively participates in the discussions. The mediator attempts to bring about a compromise which will be acceptable to both parties. This may involve talking first to one side and then to the other privately, or mediation may take place in a three-way discussion.

Benefits of the grievance process

There are several functions that a good grievance process performs in the modern industrial enterprise. First, it provides an orderly procedure for resolving disputes in the administration of the labor contract. Second, by raising a complaint on an issue, the employee brings dissatisfactions to the surface where they may be evaluated and resolved. This gives the employee an emotional release for dissatisfactions and frustrations. Even though the grievance may ultimately be lost, the employee feels at least it has been called to management's attention.

Third, the nature of the grievance process enables higher management to locate poor first-line supervision. If an unusual number of grievances originate among the employees of a particular supervisor there should be an investigation of the quality of management in that department. The existence of the grievance process is a check on arbitrary actions by supervisors. If the supervisors' actions are subject to review they are likely to be more careful in making decisions which may have to be justified.

Finally, the adjustment of grievances tends to prevent future complaints. As management seeks the underlying problems causing a grievance, corrective action may be taken that will lead to a better work climate. Management should always ask the question, "What can we learn from the fact that this grievance was filed?" A properly functioning grievance process is an important tool in developing a good labor relations climate. It can improve the human relations understanding of supervisors throughout the organization.

This discussion of the grievance process has been in the context of a unionized situation. Management may also establish a grievance procedure where no union exists, except that in the final stage arbitration normally will not be included. For the grievance process to be effective, the machinery must be used. In a nonunionized enterprise the management must encourage employees to use it. There should be a human relations atmosphere in which employees will not fear reprisal if they bring a grievance to management's attention.

SUMMARY

When management deals with the work force through a union this is referred to as labor relations.

The National Labor Relations Act of 1935, commonly known as the Wagner Act, represented a Magna Carta for organized labor in the United States. The Wagner Act prohibits employers from interfering with employees engaging in union activities. The act is administered by the National Labor Relations Board, which hears complaints of unfair labor practices and conducts union representation elections.

The Labor Management Relations Act of 1947, commonly known as the Taft-Hartley Act, was an amendment to the Wagner Act and outlawed certain unfair labor practices by unions. The Taft-Hartley Act gave power to the president of the United States to cause a postponement in any strike threatening the national health or safety.

The Labor-Management Reporting and Disclosures Act of 1959, known as the Landrum-Griffin Act, gave the federal government the role of policing certain internal affairs of labor unions.

Total union membership reached a high in 1974, although as a proportion of the labor force it slipped from the 1956 high.

Economic motives for joining a union include higher wages, fringe benefits, and security in employment and wage income. Noneconomic motives for union membership include protection against arbitrary action of supervisors, a voice in decision making, the need to identify with a group, and family ties which are prounion.

Unions are usually organized on either a craft or industry basis with local and national organization structures.

The union contract normally includes a wide variety of provisions, such as statements on wages and hours, union security, grievance procedures, holidays and vacations, and working conditions and safety.

The grievance process provides a means whereby complaints of employees can be resolved in an orderly manner.

TERMS FOR REVIEW

National Labor Relations Act of
1935 (Wagner Act)
Labor Management Relations
Act of 1947 (Taft-Hartley
Act)
union shop
closed shop
right-to-work laws
Labor-Management Reporting
and Disclosures Act of 1959
(Landrum-Griffin Act)

union or shop steward
union contract
strike
lockout
grievance procedure
arbitration
conciliation
mediation

QUESTIONS

1. Summarize the economic, political, and social conditions that preceded the passage of the National Labor Relations Act in 1935.
2. Discuss the union shop from the point of view of:
   a. The superintendent of a factory.
   b. The local union president.
3. What are the functions of the National Labor Relations Board?
4. How do you account for the recent increase in the unionization of professional, technical, clerical, and sales employees?
5. What conditions might influence an inidvidual to join a labor union? Consider the relative importance of economic versus noneconomic motivations.
6. Why is the labor contract an important document for both management and the union?
7. Examine current publications reporting business and economic news for labor contracts which are in the process of negotiation. What issues seem to be most important to each side in arriving at a satisfactory agreement?

8. After a study of materials available in the library, write a 300-word summary either supporting or opposing the application of compulsory arbitration by the federal government to labor-management disputes which affect the public welfare.

Business briefs

Layoff of minority workers

In the recession of 1974–75 a number of business enterprises and labor unions were faced with the dilemma of choosing between the layoff of newly hired women and blacks or of white males with long seniority records.

In the spring of 1975 nationwide unemployment edged toward 10 percent. In some metropolitan labor markets one worker in eight was unemployed. Reduced demand for products and rising inventories caused business enterprises to lay off both production workers and supervisors.

In one manufacturing corporation 15 percent of the work force was laid off based on seniority of employment with the company. The result was that more than 25 percent of the blacks and a higher percentage of the women employed by the corporation lost their jobs. These employees had relatively little seniority. In 1965 only 2 percent of the corporation's employees were blacks. By late 1974 this proportion had risen to 11 percent. Women rose from 6 percent of the manufacturer's work force to 14 percent over this same time.

One solution to the wholesale layoff of minority employees is to give preferential treatment to women, blacks, and other minorities and bypass the seniority system for them when layoffs have to be made. Such a course of action usually gets a strong reaction from union officials. One local union officer stated, "There is no way I would stand for bypassing seniority. That's how the union was built." On the other hand, the EEOC and some minority spokespersons are concerned about past discrimination and the massive layoffs of minorities from newly hired positions.

1. What are the possible consequences for a unionized business enterprise of following a union contract which calls for seniority in layoffs and recalls of workers?

2. What are the possible consequences for a unionized business enterprise that bypasses the union contract to protect minority workers in layoffs?

3. What possible solutions might be found for the dilemma of seniority rules versus minority employment in a business enterprise faced with increasing inventories and lower sales?

A new approach to labor relations

The Federal Mediation and Conciliation Service has developed an experimental program, "Relations by Objective," designed to improve labor relations, raise workers' morale, and prevent strikes. If the work climate in an enterprise can be improved, greater productivity may result.

The Federal Mediation and Conciliation Service, an independent agency created by the Taft-Hartley Act, has traditionally worked to solve labor-management crises after they developed. The Relations by Objective (RBO) program seeks to improve the basic relationship existing between management and the unions in the business enterprise before a crisis erupts.

The RBO approach requires that union and management personnel analyze their problems, define what they would like to see in an ideal relationship, and discuss how to achieve these goals. One difficulty often found is that agreements reached at the top level by management and union officials have not been communicated throughout the organization.

The RBO program emphasizes training first-line supervisors and union stewards to deal more effectively with each other and with the problems faced by the work force. The RBO approach has been used at one of Georgia-Pacific Corporation's pulp and paper mills with an improvement in labor relations.

1. What attitudes will management and the union have to take if an RBO program is to be initiated in a business enterprise?

2. How does the RBO approach differ from more traditional labor-management relations?

3. What benefits can be achieved for workers from greater productivity?

Cases

Forty minutes of overtime

The management of Amalgamated Manufacturing Company became involved in a dispute with the union over an incident which occurred on May 18, 1974. An important customer of Amalgamated had given the company short notice that it wanted certain production units revised. The customer wanted shipment on May 18 on a given number of the modified units. There was a deadline of 6 P.M. that day for production of these units in order to meet the airline shipping schedule.

The changes on this model required special arrangement for tooling, gauging, and precise measurements along with some modifications in the methods of assembling the units. Amalgamated's management started on these changes early on the morning of May 18. Certain women employees were selected from other assembly lines to work on this particular assembly line. They were instructed in the methods of assembling the units for the special rush order. Work was started on this assembly line at approximately 3 P.M. The work was not completed at the end of the shift at 4:30 P.M.

At this point management made a decision to go ahead with the same girls on the assembly line. These were the assemblers who had already been instructed on the changed methods. Had management brought on other employees to complete the work additional time would have been required to instruct the new employees, which might have prevented the order from being shipped on time. Ten employees worked overtime for 40 minutes on May 18 and completed the assembly work at approximately 5:10 P.M. The units were boxed and reached the airport in time for the 6 P.M. deadline.

The labor contract between Amalgamated and the union contained a provision regarding the equalization of overtime among employees. One paragraph of the contract states:

> All overtime work shall be rotated equally among the employees on seniority in a classification. If extra employees are needed, the overtime shall then be offered on a seniority basis to employees who formerly worked in that classification.

In actual practice the way this provision had been applied every employee in a classification did not wind up with an equal number of overtime hours. Overtime had been equalized on the basis of *opportunities* for overtime rather than on the basis of equalization of overtime hours actually worked. Each employee who had seniority in a classification was given the opportunity for overtime work on a rotation basis regardless of her accumulated period of overtime. If an employee turned down the offer for overtime work when it was her turn according to the seniority list, that employee was passed over and the next most senior employee was asked. The employees who worked 40 minutes overtime on the project of May 18 were not the employees who would have been entitled to work this overtime on such a rotation basis. However, to meet the emergency the management decided to go ahead and assign the overtime work to these ten employees.

In the past, in similar emergency situations, the rotation of overtime opportunities had also been departed from. One specific incident was on record when a shop steward had agreed that the overtime could be assigned on the basis of production requirements in an emergency situation.

The next day when union officials were informed of the company's action by some of the workers, the union filed a grievance on behalf of the ten employees who would normally have been granted the opportunity for overtime under the contract and according to company rotation practice. The union requested that the company pay each of these ten employees for the 40 minutes of overtime they had been deprived of on the previous day. The union referred to the contract provision and alleged that the management had violated the labor agreement by assigning this overtime to the ten employees who were already working on the specially-set-up assembly line.

1. What action would you recommend for company officials in response to this grievance by the union? Why? Discuss both the possible immediate and long-run consequences of the action you suggest.
2. Would you suggest any changes in the manner in which the company has been handling overtime? If so, what changes and why?

Grievance over disciplinary action

On October 15, 1975, Walter Sloan and Tommy Burke were given 15-day suspensions from work without pay by the factory management. This was a disciplinary penalty for the fighting incident of October 13, described in "A Case of Fighting" (see Chapter 8, Cases). A statement of the disciplinary action taken, which included a detailed account of the incident and a warning, was placed in the personal history record of each employee. The statement indicated that both Sloan and Burke were informed that any future incident of fighting involving either man would result in his immediate and final dismissal from employment.

On October 20, Walter Sloan filed a grievance complaining that the disciplinary action was not fair to him and that he had acted only in self-defense. Sloan asked that the disciplinary suspension be lifted and that the warning letter be removed from his personal history record. The other employee involved, Tommy Burke, did not file a grievance.

The grievance was processed through the various steps according to the union's contract with the company. However, no settlement of the issue could be reached that was satisfactory to both the union and the management. Therefore, the case was submitted to an arbitrator for hearing and disposition. By the time of the hearing both men had served their suspensions and had returned to work.

In addition to the description of the incident given in the earlier case, the following information was brought out by testimony during the arbitration hearing. The account of the facts of the case came largely from the testimony of the grievant, Walter Sloan. The one witness to the incident beginning with the taking of the first bin from Sloan by Tommy Burke was Jim Thomas, who was operating a machine in a nearby area. Thomas was in a position to observe the events, although he could not hear all that was said. Thomas's testimony in the arbitration hearing agreed in all important points with that of Sloan's.

Burke had been questioned regarding the incident by supervisors and by the personnel director. Burke did not appear to testify at the arbitration hearing, but other witnesses testified that he was very vague in his account of what happened. Burke had stated the fight started over a bin, but that he didn't remember anything more until he was in the hospital. He did remember the obscene incident which occurred an hour before the fight. Burke indicated he was only kidding with Sloan.

During the arbitration hearing Sloan testified that Burke had bothered him since the incident in question, once by shouldering him, and once by pulling a power dolly out in front of him. He said that he had brought this to the attention of the personnel director.

There were several union witnesses who testified at the hearing that Burke was known among the employees as a bully, that he was given to frequent horseplay, that he had had trouble with other employees, that he had been in two fights shortly before the incident in question, and that he had bothered women employees. Apparently, none of this had ever been reported by employees to supervisors. Nor had it been witnessed by supervisors, or at least if observed by supervisors it had not been reported. Much of this testimony was based on hearsay.

The basis for the company's position that Sloan was due a penalty was summarized by the personnel director in his testimony at the hearing. The company's decision to penalize Sloan as well as Burke was based upon four reasons:

1. Sloan had not reported the fight to a supervisor.
2. Sloan had made no attempt to avoid engaging in fighting.
3. Sloan had concealed the true cause of injury to his hand.
4. Sloan's actions were responsible for the company becoming involved in costs of $88 under workmen's compensation.

After the hearing the arbitrator told the company and the union that he would inform them in writing of his decision and the reasons for it.

1. Assume the role of the arbitrator who was asked to decide this industrial dispute. State how you would decide the case and give the reasons for your decision.
2. Assume the role of the personnel director. Frame a policy statement for management's discussion and ultimate approval of disciplinary penalties for fighting.

☆☆☆☆☆☆☆☆☆☆☆☆☆☆☆☆☆☆☆☆☆☆☆☆☆☆☆☆☆☆☆☆☆☆☆☆☆☆
☆☆☆☆☆☆☆☆☆☆☆☆☆☆☆☆☆☆☆☆☆☆☆☆☆☆☆☆☆☆☆☆☆☆☆☆☆☆

section four

The provision
of goods and
services

*Products are displayed
in a variety of ways to
stimulate consumers'
needs.*

10

The consumer and the marketing concept

G reater attention is being paid to the consumer today! There are a variety of reasons for the increased importance of the consumer. First, there has been a rising level of consumer income. Second, consumers are becoming more vocal about the nature and quality of goods and services being offered by business. Third, protection of the consumer is being given more recognition by government through the political process.

No longer do we hear statements attributed to past business leaders such as, "Any customer can have a car painted any color that he wants, so long as it is black," or, "What's good for the country is good for General Motors, and vice versa." Now statements from corporate headquarters emphasize an interest in meeting consumers' needs, dealing fairly with complaints, and generally acting in a socially responsible manner.

This chapter discusses the marketing concept of business and the role of the consumer in today's economy. The following issues are considered:

What is the marketing concept of business?

What are the factors which influence consumer behavior?

How is the consumer changing?

Why has consumerism developed?

What are government and business doing to protect consumers?

THE IMPORTANCE OF MARKETING

Marketing has been described as both the creation and delivery of America's standard of living. This imaginative definition does not tell us exactly what is the process of marketing in the business enterprise. However, it does give the flavor of the exciting nature of marketing in today's affluent American economy. Marketing may also be defined as the activities that move goods and services from producers to consumers to satisfy needs. You will recall from Chapter 1 that goods have utility when they have the power to satisfy human wants. Marketing imparts place, time, and possession utility to goods. The production function, discussed in Chapter 12, directly imparts form utility to goods. However, even the nature of the form utility provided by production is influenced by what can be marketed to consumers.

Marketing is as vital in today's economy as is the production of goods and services. It has been estimated that about 50 percent of the consumer's dollar is spent for marketing activities. Our market economy is directed by the spending decisions of all types of consumers. These range from the teenager spending money earned on a part-time job to the Department of Defense which spends over $75 billion yearly. Despite some poverty in the United States, today the vast majority of our families are faced with decisions on how to spend incomes which have risen significantly over the past several years. For most American families the question is not whether there is sufficient food on the table, but what luxury goods and leisure-time activities they will purchase.

THE MARKETING CONCEPT OF BUSINESS

Increased emphasis on the consumer in recent years has led to the development of the marketing concept of business. The essence of *the marketing concept of business* is recognizing a consumer need, developing a product to satisfy this need, and in the process earning a profit for the business enterprise. This means that management thinking throughout the enterprise must be oriented to the importance of the consumer. Marketing becomes everybody's job, not just the responsibility of a few marketing managers.

The General Electric Company provides an example of an enterprise oriented toward the marketing concept of business. In an annual report to its stockholders General Electric stated:

> Marketing, through its studies and research, will establish for the engineer, the designer, and the manufacturing man what the customer wants in a given product, what price he is willing to pay, and where and when it will be wanted. Marketing would have authority in product planning, production scheduling, and inventory control, as well as in the sales distribution and servicing of the product.

When the marketing approach covers all areas of the enterprise, the actual act of selling a product is the last step in a sales effort which starts when the product is first conceived. Consumer appeal is built into each product from the design stage through to final markets. The marketing manager is part of the cycle of activity from the very beginning of the process.

The marketing concept of business emphasizes the importance of consumers. The objective is to produce consumer satisfactions. Goods and services have no value in or of themselves. Only when they are desirable to consumers do they take on value.

The enterprise must have a market for the goods and services it hopes to produce. A market consists of consumers who are willing and able to buy the goods produced by a particular business enterprise. These markets must be created and stimulated by managers. In today's rapidly changing economy the creative management does not wait for customers to seek out their product. Management woos the customers and actively tries to attract them to its products in competition with other enterprises.

TRANSLATING CONSUMER NEEDS TO WANTS

A basic objective of marketing is to translate consumer needs into wants. To need something is to depend upon it to carry out a way of life. People need all kinds of goods and services to carry on an established pattern of living. However, they are not always fully conscious of their needs. The challenge of creative marketing is to focus consumers' attention on their needs and to suggest products that will meet these needs. Through the marketing process needs are translated into wants. To want a product is to recognize it is available and can satisfy a need.

There is no shortage of needs in our world today even in the United States. People need more than they have in food, clothing, shelter, health and safety, education, and the many conveniences of life. In many instances, however, these needs are not clearly understood. Creative marketing can bring such general needs into sharper focus. It can translate a dimly perceived need into a want for a specific good or service.

Marketing is sometimes criticized on the grounds that it results in the production of goods the American people really do not need. This charge is not based on an understanding of the close relationship between needs and wants. Wants arise from needs. It is not possible to stimulate persons to want a product when they do not feel some need for it. At the same time it is clearly recognized that not all needs have the same priorities. Certain essentials of food and shelter are basic to life while the need to see television shows in color is not. However, even gadgets such as electric toothbrushes meet a need. They do serve a useful function. The fact that people could survive without a particular good or service does not mean these products are not needed to achieve a certain standard of living.

Once a need has been turned into a specific want of the consuming public, the American standard of living is never the same again. Consider how much different and less productive American business would be without air conditioning. At one time air conditioning was virtually unknown except by primitive methods available to a few. Protection from the summer's heat and humidity was a latent need. Today it has been translated into a want of most Americans. We want air conditioning in our homes as well as at work. Out of this want has grown a new industry. New jobs have been created, new investment opportunities opened up, and new managerial challenges provided as the result of the translation of this consumer need into a clear-cut want.

The process of translating a need into a want is a job for marketing management. The consumer's attention must be called to the nature and the significance of the need. Many needs have an emotional rather than a rational basis. A good marketer learns when to appeal to emotion, to reason, or to a combination of both.

It is possible for consumers to react negatively to a new product because of unconscious emotional factors. This happened when instant coffee was first introduced. The use of instant coffee saves time and is more convenient than the preparation of regularly brewed coffee. However, some women were unwilling to use the instant product because they subconsciously felt it reflected on their self-image as good housewives. To change consumer attitudes various advertising programs were designed to show how instant coffee contributes to gracious living, which presumably is a goal of every woman. One television advertising series pictured an experienced household domestic servant showing an attractive young wife how she could improve the quality of her meals by serving a particular brand of instant coffee which the husband proclaimed tasted "better than fresh perked" coffee.

THE CONSUMER

Ultimate consumers

With the marketing concept placing the emphasis upon the consumer, it is important that the consumer be defined and analyzed. *Ultimate consumers* are individuals or households who use goods or services for the satisfaction of personal needs. *Industrial users* buy products for use in producing other goods or services and are discussed in the next two chapters. When the term "consumer" or "consumers" is used in this book it applies to individual or ultimate consumers.

Individual consumer behavior

Consumers buy particular goods and services for a variety of reasons. We do not know exactly why an individual makes a buying decision at a given time. A consumer is influenced by a variety of stimuli out of which comes a response either to purchase or not to purchase some product or service. The factors affecting the consumer's behavior can be classified as economic, psychological, and social.

Economic factors. Economic considerations affecting consumer behavior center around people's rational use of scarce resources to satisfy their needs. Thus, the level of consumer income, whether incomes are rising or falling, personal savings, and the availability of credit are important economic determinants of behavior. The increase in the American consumer's income is so important that it is discussed in detail later in this chapter. Price of the good, its durability, and expense of operation and repair are all factors relating to economics which may influence the consumer. The price of competing goods or goods that could serve as substitutes is also an economic consideration that may influence the consumer's decision. However, important as they are, economic factors are not the sole determinants of consumer behavior. Psychological and social influences also affect consumer decision making.

Psychological factors. Psychologists are not in agreement as to what provides the best explanation of consumer behavior. What may explain one individual's motivations would not necessarily explain another's behavior. Also, the marketing manager is interested in actions of groups or classes of consumers since marketing programs usually must appeal to numerous individuals. However, the research and concepts of psychologists can be helpful in providing insights into buying motives.

One theory of motivation is provided in Maslow's hierarchy[1] of needs which arrays five needs in the order in which an individual tends to seek their satisfaction:

1. Physiological needs—for food, drink, sex, and shelter.
2. Safety needs—for security, order, protection, and family stability.
3. Belongingness and love needs—for affection, belonging to a group, and acceptance.
4. Esteem needs—for self-respect, reputation, prestige, and status.
5. Self-actualization needs—for self-fulfillment, doing what one is best fitted for.

In addition, Maslow suggested two other classes of needs for those individuals who may have satisfied the first five needs:

1. The need to know and understand.
2. The need for aesthetic satisfaction—beauty.

Theoretically a person tends to try to fulfill all needs at one level before moving on to a higher level of needs. In actual practice most people attempt to fill needs on different levels at the same time, probably never completely satisfying the needs at any one level. However, people do have some priority of needs even if every individual does not have the same priority. For example, a college student who enjoys good music may habitually skip lunch (a physiological need) while spending money to build an extensive record collection (an aesthetic need). The business manager must recognize people have different levels of needs. For consumers to spend their income for particular goods they must be convinced that some need will be satisfied. Also, people tend to feel those needs most strongly which have not yet been satisfied. What are your most strongly felt needs?

Social factors. Marketing managers have traditionally used income as a means of predicting buying behavior. Today about half of the American families have incomes of $12,000 and above. This group includes blue-collar workers as well as professional and white-collar employees. These families tend to vary in their spending patterns depending partly upon the social class with which they identify.

This is illustrated by Coleman's example[2] comparing three families

---

[1] A. H. Maslow, *Motivation and Personality* (New York: Harper & Row, Inc., 1954), pp. 80–97.

[2] Richard P. Coleman, "The Significance of Social Stratification in Selling," in *Marketing: A Maturing Discipline,* ed. Martin L. Bell (Chicago: American Marketing Association, 1961).

from different social classes having the same relatively high income. An upper-middle-class family (perhaps headed by a lawyer) would likely spend a relatively large share of its income on a home in a prestige neighborhood, expensive furniture, quality clothing, and club memberships or cultural entertainment. A lower-middle-class family (perhaps headed by a salesperson) would probably spend the same income on as good or better house in a less fancy neighborhood, more on furniture and clothing but not from such expensive stores, and have a larger savings account. In comparison, the upper-lower-class family whose support might come from a welder has a smaller house in a less desirable neighborhood but the family may have a larger, newer automobile; newer television set; and the husband spends more on sports.

In addition to the social class with which they identify, other groups in society influence the consumers' behavior. These include the clubs to which they belong, schools they attend, and labor unions, athletic teams, or church groups in which they participate. The values of these formal groups along with informal groups in society influence their members. Young people tend to seek approval from their peers by dressing, behaving, and buying as others do. Business managers generally act and spend in patterns which gain the approval of their associates. Even college professors are influenced by their colleagues in buying decisions.

The marketing manager should be aware of the differences which exist in the consumer market based upon social groupings. When a product has special appeal to a particular group in society the advertising and sales promotion program should take this into account. Beverage manufacturers, magazine publishers, and fashion designers have all found their markets may be segmented, at least partly, depending upon various social classifications. Different forms of advertising may be necessary to reach these segments of the market.

THE CONSUMER OF THE 1970s

The 1970s mark a time of dramatic change for consumer markets in the United States. In economic terms the proportion of high-income families has increased significantly. Changes are occurring in the population in the age, education, and composition of the work force which also affect spending patterns. Some of these economic, demographic, and social factors which affect business are discussed below.

Employment outlook

Marketing research workers

Managers of business enterprises require a great deal of information to make sound decisions on how to market their products. Marketing research workers provide much of this information by analyzing available data on products and sales, making surveys, and conducting interviews. They prepare sales forecasts and make recommendations on product design and advertising.

Although a bachelor's degree is the usual entry requirement for marketing research trainees, graduate training is becoming important for some specialized positions and for advancement to higher level positions. Knowledge of data processing is helpful because of the growing use of computers in sales forecasting, distribution, and cost analysis.

College graduates trained in marketing research and statistics will find favorable job opportunities in this occupation through the mid-1980s. The growing complexity of marketing research techniques also will expand opportunities for psychologists, economists, and other social scientists. Job opportunities for those who hold master's and doctor's degrees will be excellent.

The demand for marketing research services is expected to increase very rapidly through the next decade. Existing marketing research organizations will expand and new marketing research departments and independent firms will be set up. Business managers will find it increasingly important to obtain the best information possible for appraising marketing situations and planning marketing policies.

Higher consumer income

The U.S. consumer market is changing. In past decades we moved from a nation of predominantly low-income families to one of middle-income mass markets. Now the move is into an era of high-income mass markets with one half of families having an income exceeding $12,000 per year. Figure 10–1 shows the changing nature of American families'

FIGURE 10–1
Number of families by family income in 1947 to 1973 (in constant 1973 dollars)

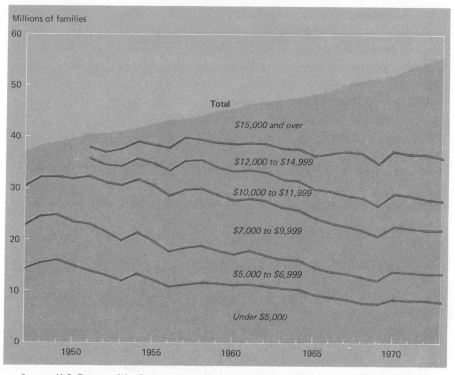

Source: U.S. Bureau of the Census, *Current Population Reports,* Series P-60, no. 97, January 1975.

income over the past 26 years. Over the past 26 years median family income in real terms has increased 100 percent.

The distribution of families by income class has changed dramatically over the past 20 years. Figure 10–2 illustrates the increase in the proportion of families having incomes of $15,000 and above and the substantial reduction of those with incomes below $5,000 annually.

FIGURE 10-2
The changing pyramid of family income (total families each year = 100 percent; based on 1974 dollars)

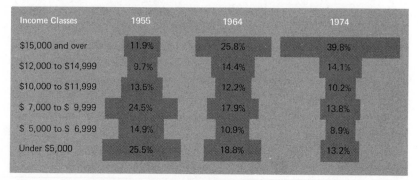

Income Classes	1955	1964	1974
$15,000 and over	11.9%	25.8%	39.8%
$12,000 to $14,999	9.7%	14.4%	14.1%
$10,000 to $11,999	13.5%	12.2%	10.2%
$ 7,000 to $ 9,999	24.5%	17.9%	13.8%
$ 5,000 to $ 6,999	14.9%	10.9%	8.9%
Under $5,000	25.5%	18.8%	13.2%

Source: U.S. Bureau of the Census, *Current Population Reports*, Series P-60, no. 99, July 1975.

Factors contributing to higher family income

Educational achievement. Contributing to the rising income level of American families is the rising level of educational achievement. Figure 10-3 shows the increasing proportion of the adult population which has attended high school and college. The number of college graduates has increased and is projected to become even greater in the 1980s.

Generally the greater the level of educational achievement the higher the person's lifetime income. Figure 10-4 compares the estimated lifetime income for adult men depending upon whether their highest educational achievement was elementary school, high school, or college graduation.

Working wives. The increased number of households having two wage earners also has contributed to higher family incomes. From 1950 to 1974 the overall percentage of husband-wife families with the wife in the paid labor force increased from 19 to 37 percent of all families. The median family income where the husband and wife were both in the paid labor force was $15,240 in 1973. This was 33 percent higher than the median family income where the wife was not in the work force.

More discretionary income

Discretionary income is the income left over after covering the family's spending for necessities. Discretionary income may be spent for

FIGURE 10–3

Educational attainment of adults 25 years and over, 1950–1970, projected to 1985

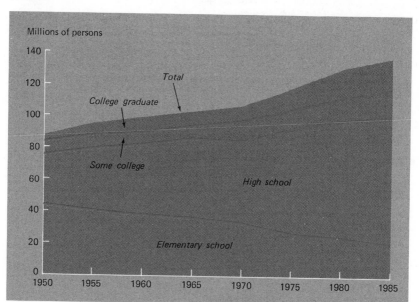

Source: U.S. Bureau of the Census, *Current Population Reports*, Series P-20 and unpublished data.

luxuries or saved and invested. The rising real income of Americans provides additional discretionary income. This increases the challenge for marketing managers. They must attract the consumer's discretionary spending dollars in competition with a wide variety of goods and services. For example, more consumers are now able to make large discretionary purchases and will choose between such items as a vacation home at a lake, a trip to Europe, or a second car. Once basic transportation is provided, the auto manufacturer competes not only with other automobile manufacturers but with the vacation home industry, foreign travel agencies, art dealers, and producers of many other goods and services.

The job of marketing is complicated further by the fact that what one family considers necessities may be considered luxuries by another. Also, with higher standards of living the definition of what is considered a necessity will change. What were previously luxury goods will become necessities, opening up new areas for luxury spending. The consumer durable goods industries offer many examples of this concept. Twenty-

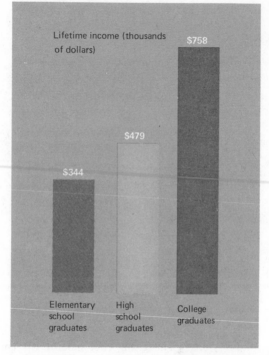

FIGURE 10–4

Estimated lifetime income in 1972 for men 18 years and over in the U.S., depending upon educational achievement

Source: U.S. Bureau of the Census, *Current Population Reports,* Series P-60, no. 92, March 1974.

five years ago television was considered a distinct luxury. Today most families think of television as a necessity.

In the early 1950s the color television industry was in it infancy but grew until it became the exotic consumer appliance of recent years. Figure 10–5 shows the degree of saturation of color television and other consumer durable goods owned by American households. These statistics do not include renters who have appliances such as refrigerators furnished by the landlord.

Figure 10–5 illustrates that there are still opportunities for further sales both to expand the market for durables and to replace present models in use. However, industry is challenged to develop new products which will meet or expand consumers' needs. It remains to be seen whether mass markets will develop for items such as microwave ovens, home trash compactors, instant home movies, or color video recorders.

FIGURE 10–5
Percent of total U.S. households owning selected consumer durable goods, 1971

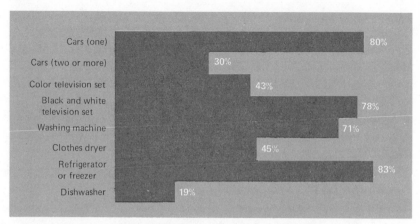

Cars (one)	80%
Cars (two or more)	30%
Color television set	43%
Black and white television set	78%
Washing machine	71%
Clothes dryer	45%
Refrigerator or freezer	83%
Dishwasher	19%

Source: U.S. Bureau of the Census, *Current Population Reports,* Series P-65, no. 40, May 1972.

Demographic changes

To predict better the kinds of goods and services that consumers will need, alert marketing executives study changes in the size and composition of the population. Figure 10–6 shows the U.S. population and growth rate since 1945 and its projection to 1990. While the total population continues to increase, the growth rate began a steady decline in the early 1960s until 1974 when it was projected to increase slightly into the 1980s. The decreased growth rate may be attributed to a declining birth rate. The lower birth rates may be caused by a number of factors. These include the desire by couples for a higher standard of living which can result from postponing or having fewer children and having the wife work outside the home. The cost of rearing a child to college age has been estimated by the Institute of Life Insurance to be $23,000 for the average family. When another $16,000 per child is added for those who go on to college it is apparent that the reduction in family size from three or four to one or two children significantly reduces the economic cost of children to the family.

In addition to total size, the composition of the population is changing during the 1970s, as is illustrated by Figure 10–7. There is a substantial increase in the 25 to 34 age group of the population along with a significant increase in the 20 to 24 age bracket. This increase in these two age groups means a larger work force with increasing competition

FIGURE 10–6
U.S. population and growth rate, 1945–1990

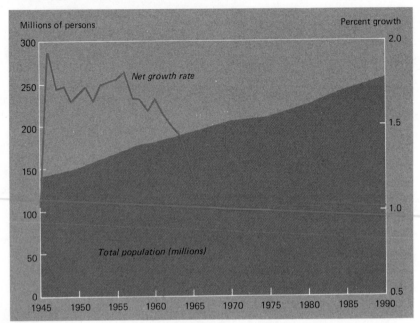

Source: U.S. Bureau of the Census, *Current Population Reports,* Series P-25, no. 442, no. 448, and no. 521.

FIGURE 10–7
Population growth by age groups

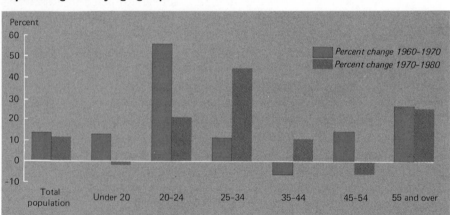

Source: U.S. Bureau of the Census, *Current Population Reports,* Series P-25, no. 448.

for jobs. Furthermore, these workers do not have as great an advantage in educational qualifications over older age groups as had been the case in earlier generations.

The changes in the size and composition of the population have varied meanings to different manufacturers and service enterprises. For example, the larger proportion of the population in the 25 to 34 age group will provide increased sales opportunities for manufacturers of appliances and furniture. However, increasing competition for jobs in these populous age groups may mean that both husband and wife will seek jobs. They may have fewer or later children. They may feel less free to spend their income fully or to go into debt. If these actions should become widespread, then the impact of the post–World War II baby boom will not be as expansive for the economy as had once been predicted.

CONSUMERISM AND CONSUMER PROTECTION AGENCIES

Consumerism

Despite the importance of the consumer to American business and the fact that most business enterprises attempt to serve consumer needs well, complaints by consumers about products and service continue to be heard. In the 1960s consumer protest against some products and business practices became a force to be reckoned with both by business and politicians. The protest has been labeled *consumerism.* Today's consumers are making themselves heard to an extent previously unknown by American business. They express concern about poor quality products, lack of proper service, use of food additives which may be harmful, products which are unsafe, misleading advertising, and practices by business which are wasteful or contribute to pollution.

Consumerism as a movement gained focus with the publication in 1965 of Ralph Nader's *Unsafe at Any Speed.* This book, critical of the Corvair auto, became a best seller. Following the book's publication, sales of General Motor's Corvair dropped. In 1969 GM ceased production of this rear-engine car. Nader has continued his consumer-oriented activities. He and his followers are credited with significant influence in the passage of federal legislation intended to protect consumers in such areas as auto safety and food processing.

Government protective agencies

A number of government agencies have been created over the years to protect consumers' interests. Federal government agencies with important consumer-protection responsibilities include the Federal Trade Commission, the Food and Drug Administration, and the Consumer Product Safety Commission.

The Federal Trade Commission and the Food and Drug Administration were both created before World War I. Their consumer protection authority was strengthened in the late 1930s. The Federal Trade Commission has responsibility for policing advertising and marketing practices. Also, it enforces a variety of legislation including labeling acts for wool, fur, and textile products. These responsibilities are in addition to the FTC's duties in enforcing the antitrust laws discussed in Chapter 2. The Food and Drug Administration is charged with regulation in areas such as maintenance of drug standards and evaluation of new drugs, food purity, and cosmetic products.

The FTC and advertising

In the early 1970s the Federal Trade Commission responded to increasing complaints by consumers about the honesty of information contained in advertising. A program was announced in 1971 requiring advertisers to be able to support advertising claims of product performance, safety, quality, or comparative price. The FTC's objectives in this program were education and deterrence. Hopefully the additional information provided by advertisers would enable the consumer to make better purchasing decisions. Also, advertisers would be deterred from making claims which could not be backed up with facts.

An industry-by-industry approach has been taken by the FTC in this truth-in-advertising campaign. Since 1971 the FTC has requested supporting data from many industries. These include manufacturers of automobiles, tires, color television sets, cold remedies, pet foods, hearing aids, and air conditioners. The FTC has adopted a "reasonable basis" test in deciding if advertising claims are supported. When no "reasonable basis" for the claim exists, the advertising claim is assumed to be unfair and deceptive.

Evidence must be available to support objective statements such as "averages 26 miles per gallon." Subjective claims must also be documented. An example of a subjective claim is the statement by an auto manufacturer that a particular model "is the best-handling passenger car ever built in the United States."

The FTC has several ways of dealing with enterprises which do not live up to government standards in advertising. First, cease-and-desist orders may be issued requiring the business to stop the questioned advertising. These orders may include fines. Second, the enterprises may be required to provide additional information in future ads. For example, the FTC ordered that advertising for a swimming-aid device disclose that the device is not a life preserver and should be used only in shallow water. Third, the FTC may require corrective advertising. In its first such order the FTC required Continental Baking Company to spend 25 percent of its advertising budget for one year on FTC-approved corrective advertisements that Profile bread is not effective for weight reduction as earlier ads had claimed.

The Consumer Product Safety Commission

In the late 1960s Congress established a study commission on product safety to examine the extent to which product hazards constituted a public safety problem. The study indicated that 20 million Americans were injured annually in the home as the result of accidents associated with consumer products. Of this number 110,000 persons were permanently disabled and 30,000 were killed. Economic cost in damage claims and time lost amounted to more than $5.5 billion annually.

Following this study legislation was passed in 1972 authorizing the establishment of the Consumer Product Safety Commission (CPSC). This body began work in 1973 to carry out the Consumer Product Safety Act to improve the level of safety in product design. Also, the act holds manufacturers accountable for the safety of their products which are sold to ultimate consumers.

The Consumer Product Safety Commission's responsibilities include the development of safety standards for various industries, evaluation of the safety of products, collection of injury statistics, and coordination of governmental safety enforcement. Manufacturers or distributors are required to notify the commission within 24 hours of discovery of any "substantial product hazard" in goods available to the public. In the first two years of its existence the CPSC received notices for potentially hazardous products ranging from spray paint to color television sets.

The commission has responsibilities under several other recently passed laws. These include the *Poison Prevention Packaging Act* which requires dangerous substances to have safety containers with caps which are difficult to remove. Also included is the *Flammable Fabrics Act* which requires children's night clothes to be flame retardant. The 1970 *Child Protection and Toy Safety Act* provided increased protection from toys which might have mechanical or electrical hazards.

A number of actions can be taken by the commission to improve product safety. It can order a manufacturer, wholesaler, or retailer to recall, repair, or replace any product which the commission considers "unreasonably" risky. The commission can seize the product or ban its sale. Managers who refuse to abide by commission rulings can be fined and jailed up to one year. However, the general approach of the CPSC has been to seek cooperation with industry to improve product safety and not to emphasize penalties.

Other legislation

The following legislation passed in recent years is also important to consumers:

The *National Traffic and Motor Vehicle Safety Act of 1966* requires auto manufacturers to notify first purchasers of cars by certified mail of any safety defects discovered after manufacture and delivery. This law also provides for the issuance of safety standards for motor vehicles and for other programs to improve highway safety.

The *Wholesome Meat Act of 1967* updated and strengthened the standards for inspection for red meat animals. Two thousand of the 17,000 slaughter and packing houses in the country which produce 85 percent of the meat eaten in the United States had been subject to federal meat inspection since 1907. Now, in cooperation with the states, the remaining 15 percent of the meat produced by small or seasonal plants is subject to standards designed to improve the quality of meat products.

In 1968 the *Wholesome Poultry Products Act* was signed into law. This act extended federal inspection standards to poultry sold intrastate.

The *Truth in Lending Act of 1968* requires creditors to furnish individuals to whom credit is about to be extended a statement of the amount of financing charges and the percentage rate of interest charged annually. Before this law was passed, practice had varied considerably regarding the degree of disclosure to consumers of actual annual interest rates.

The *Fair Credit Reporting Act* passed in 1970 contained a number of provisions to protect consumers in credit matters. This act requires that all agencies reporting consumer credit rating data follow reasonable procedures to assure the accuracy of their information. Any user of credit information who rejects a consumer for credit, insurance, or employment must inform the individual of the source of the credit report. Also, consumers may use the courts to obtain identification of the sources of information behind the credit reports.

Also in 1970 the 1965 *Cigarette Labeling and Advertising Act* was amended to strengthen the warning on cigarette packages to read "Warning: The Surgeon General Has Determined That Cigarette Smoking Is Dangerous To Your Health." The act also regulated cigarette advertising, with television advertising of cigarettes ceasing after January 1, 1971.

Private groups aiding consumers

There are two nonprofit organizations which test and rate products for the benefit of consumers. They are Consumers' Research and Consumers Union. Both organizations issue monthly publications reporting the results of their studies.

Consumers can also be helped by Better Business Bureaus which are sponsored in metropolitan areas by business enterprises. The Better Business Bureaus encourage responsible business practices. They will answer consumers' questions about a particular enterprise and provide information as to whether they have received complaints about the business.

A recent development is the sponsorship by some Better Business Bureaus of arbitration service to handle consumer complaints against a particular enterprise. When the individual customer and a business enterprise agree to arbitration, an impartial person hears both sides of the story, checks claims and counterclaims, and renders a decision on the dispute. The procedure is conducted at no charge to the consumer. It can reduce court case loads and act as a local small claims court. The early experience with the BBB arbitration program indicates that the decisions are about equally divided between complainants and businesses.

Business aid to consumers

Many business enterprises have been concerned with consumer satisfaction and product safety for years. Enterprises such as General Electric, Zenith, Sears, 3M, and RCA had product safety programs long before the passage of the Consumer Product Safety Act. However, increased consumer sensitivity and government regulations are stimulating business to do even more.

A number of enterprises including Whirlpool Corporation have installed toll-free telephone lines to answer customers' questions and complaints about their products. Enterprises such as Standard Oil of Indiana and Mobil Oil are giving increased attention to consumer inquiries about computer-billed charges.

A good handling of consumer complaints is the 1970 example of Calgon Corporation. The company faced charges that its Calgonite detergent caused suds to overflow in a particular type of dishwasher. The result was sometimes damaging to floors and furniture. Calgon reformulated the detergent to correct the sudsing problem and compensated consumers for known damages.

Additional business enterprises are moving toward the approach of Zenith Radio Corporation's stated philosophy that "it isn't enough to claim that 99%—or even 99.9%—of the company's products are satisfactory." A dissatisfied consumer should be able to expect that the enterprise "sincerely wants to make an adjustment if the customer has been disappointed." The chairman of American Motors stated that an auto buyer "doesn't expect every car to be trouble-free, but he does want the troubles fixed—fixed completely, fixed without cost and fixed carefully." American Motors adopted a "buyer protection" guaranty plan which has received positive consumer reaction.

J. C. Penney is known for its emphasis on the importance of customer satisfaction. In 1974 the J. C. Penney Company's Management Conference reaffirmed the longtime commitment of that enterprise to the consumer:

The Penney Idea
1. To serve the public as nearly as we can to its complete satisfaction.
2. To expect for the service we render a fair remuneration, and not all the profit the traffic will bear.
3. To do all in our power to pack the customer's dollar full of value, quality and satisfaction.

4. To continue to train ourselves and our associates so that the service we give will be more and more intelligently performed.
5. To improve constantly the human factor in our business.
6. To reward the men and women in our organization through participation in what the business produces.
7. To test our every policy, method and art in this wise: "Does it square with what is right and just?"

Adopted: 1913

SUMMARY

The marketing concept of business involves recognizing a consumer need, developing a product to satisfy that need, and in the process earning a profit for the business enterprise. The marketing concept means that the thinking of managers throughout the business enterprise must be oriented around the importance of the consumer. A basic objective of marketing is to translate consumer needs into wants.

Customers of business may be either ultimate consumers or industrial users. Individual consumer behavior is influenced by economic, psychological, and social factors.

The consumer of the 1970s has a rising level of real income resulting in increased amounts of discretionary spending power. Since 1947 median family income has increased 100 percent in real terms. This higher family income is attributed to higher educational achievement and an increase in the number of families which have both husband and wife working. More discretionary income and changes in the size and composition of the population will present challenges for marketing managers in the future.

Consumerism is increasing in importance with both government and private groups becoming more insistent that business avoid deceptive practices and unreliable products. Federal government agencies with important consumer protection responsibilities include the Federal Trade Commission, the Food and Drug Administration, and the Consumer Product Safety Commission.

Legislation passed in recent years to protect the consumer includes the Poison Prevention Packaging Act, the Flammable Fabrics Act, the Child Protection and Toy Safety Act, the National Traffic and Motor Vehicle Safety Act, the Wholesome Meat Act, the Wholesome Poultry Products Act, the Truth in Lending Act, the Fair Credit Reporting Act, and the Cigarette Labeling and Advertising Act.

TERMS FOR REVIEW

marketing	*family income*
marketing concept of business	*discretionary income*
market	*demographic changes*
want	*consumerism*
need	*Federal Trade Commission*
ultimate consumer	*Consumer Product Safety Com-*
industrial user	*mission*
Maslow's hierarchy of needs	

QUESTIONS

1. Is the application of the marketing concept of business more important today than at some other period in our economic history, such as in the depression of the 1930s or the period immediately following World War II? State the reasons for your answer.

2. Explain why consumers do not always act in a rational manner when buying goods and services.

3. Cite ten examples of products advertised in the mass media to illustrate where an appeal is made to one or more of the five basic needs in Maslow's hierarchy.

4. Give five examples of items that you feel are purchased by college students in which the motivation is more psychological or social than economic.

5. What are the implications for business in the changing nature of the income distribution pyramid illustrated in Figure 10–2?

6. What do the statistics in Figure 10–5 imply for the future product development and sales promotion by durable goods manufacturers?

7. What are the implications for business in the changing nature of the population as illustrated in Figures 10–6 and 10–7?

8. How do you account for the interest in consumerism at a time when the incomes of American families generally are at historically high levels?

9. Outline the important consumer legislation passed by the Congress in recent years.

10. From current periodicals examine statements by consumer groups that American business and governmental bodies are not living up to consumers' expectations. Also examine statements in defense of business's actions. Write a 300-word paper summarizing your conclusions from this study.

Business briefs

Computerized checkout counters

A revolutionary new system is being introduced to speed up the checkout at supermarket counters and to eliminate hand stamping of individual prices on an estimated 170 billion cans, bottles, and packages annually. The system is made possible through the use of a Universal Product Code.

The UPC marking on each container is a computer-language symbol which identifies the manufacturer and the specific product. When the specially marked containers are brought to the checkout counter, the clerk passes each UPC symbol over a laser scanner or uses a wand which reads the symbol and transmits it to a computer in the store. The computer matches the coded symbol to the correct price, product type or brand name, and size. The computer sends the data back to the checkout counter where it is printed on a receipt and flashed on a display board. The entire process takes only a fraction of a second.

Industry studies estimate savings might amount to $35,000 yearly for stores with grocery sales of $60,000 a week. (The system would not result in cost savings for the store with sales of less than $10,000 weekly.) In addition to cost savings for marking containers and faster checkouts, stores would gain through better inventory control.

The advocates for the system suggest the following advantages for consumers:

1. Waiting time at checkout lanes will be reduced by one third or more because the scanner can read the symbols faster than a clerk can operate a cash register.

2. Assuming the computer is properly programmed, there is less chance of being charged the wrong price for an item.

3. The grocery receipt will be more detailed by including brands and specific item designations. The system allows items to go through in a random manner with price breaks being calculated automatically on specials. For example, if corn is 39¢ a can or 3 for $1.00 the computer system will print out 39¢ for each of the first two cans. The third can will automatically be priced at 22¢ to complete the 3 for $1.00 deal.

Opponents of the UPC system include some consumer advocates and labor unions. Consumer advocates point to these objections:

1. Even if shelves were marked with prices, an unethical merchant

could post low prices on the shelves but program the computer with higher prices.

2. No easy means would be available to consumers to measure higher food prices by comparing prices of newly purchased goods with those already on kitchen shelves.

3. The $100,000 or more cost per store of installing scanners and the computer system would put smaller grocery stores at a disadvantage compared to large supermarkets.

Grocery clerks' unions generally oppose UPC and computerized checkouts because the system would reduce the need for grocery employees by about 20 percent. Although most union contracts protect jobs of present employees, the long-run effect of this change would be savings in wage costs for merchants.

Legislation has been sponsored in Congress and a number of state legislatures requiring each item to be individually priced. Such legislation if passed would reduce cost savings from a computerized checkout system by about 25 percent.

1. Discuss the advantages and disadvantages of UPC and computerized checkouts from the point of view of (*a*) supermarket management, (*b*) consumers, and (*c*) retail clerks.
2. If you were a legislator, what position would you take on such a system? Why?

Can the spray

Americans purchase nearly 3 billion cans of aerosol spray products each year. We can be deodorized, painted, cleaned, and have our hair set, bugs killed, and medications applied by using the appropriate aerosol spray can.

In 1974 a theory was presented by scientists that the fluorocarbons which give spray cans their fine-spray punch are depleting the vital ozone layer in the earth's stratosphere. The ozone layer filters the sun's rays, providing protection of those on earth from an overdose of ultraviolet radiation. Scientists claim that if the ozone is damaged or destroyed the higher radiation levels would increase the incidence of skin cancer, ruin crops, and alter the world's weather.

Because of this theory, some scientists, environmentalists, and government officials are calling for an immediate ban on the use of fluorocarbon propellants. Manufacturers of products which use spray cans generally oppose a ban until the ozone-depletion theory is subjected to further research and definite proof. Environmentalists reply it is better to be safe than sorry with a question of such importance. Some scientists have predicted flourocarbons could deplete the ozone layer by 16 percent within 25 years. This could result in 100,000 or more additional cases of skin cancer annually.

Government groups concerned with the issue include the Consumer Product Safety Commission, the Environmental Protection Agency, the Council on Environmental Quality, and committees of the Congress. Industry scientists, including those at Du Pont which produces fluorocarbon under the trade name Freon, are studying the matter and seeking substitutes for fluorocarbons. In June 1975, Johnson & Johnson, a major user of aerosol cans for consumer products, announced it was discontinuing use of aerosol cans. The State of Oregon passed legislation banning the sale of such products by 1977.

1. *a.* At what point should government ban the use of products such as fluorocarbons, DDT, or cyclamates?
   b. Who is responsible for providing evidence of a product's safety or danger?
2. How should the trade-off between an industry's economic health and the public's environmental welfare be determined?
3. Should manufacturers and retailers voluntarily remove products which *may* be harmful to the environment or to people before being required by government to do so?

Business listens

In the summer of 1974 a Weslaco, Texas, couple and their daughter checked into a motel of a national chain in a nearby state. They went into the motel's restaurant 30 minutes before closing time and were served a second-rate meal which included instant mashed potatoes and a warmed-over entree. The couple wrote a complaining letter to the chain's home office. Shortly afterward they received a letter of apology from the motel manager and an invitation to spend a night as the management's guests the next time they were in the area. Such incidents, while not necessarily commonplace, indicate that more managements are listening to customers.

Numerous large corporations have staffs to deal directly with customer complaints and inquiries. For 40 years General Motors has had an owner relations department which now consists of nearly 500 employees. GM managers and quality control personnel receive copies of letters sent to this department. When a GM auto owner complains, the zone office receives the letter and contacts the dealer. If the complaint is not resolved by the dealer or the zone office to the customer's satisfaction the Detroit office reviews the complaint to see whether everything possible was done to satisfy the customer. Because of the emphasis in the auto industry on repeat business, GM is interested in equitable handling of customer concerns.

Several hundred business enterprises now have consumer relations departments. A few of these consumer affairs managers hold the title of vice president and report directly to top management. However, the vast majority of consumer affairs officers are removed from management's direct contact.

Not all consumer relations officers have much influence on enterprise policy or decisions concerning consumer complaints. Some consumer advocates charge such positions are simply for public relations purposes with little genuine concern for consumers' welfare.

1. How important is it for an enterprise to have a consumer affairs department?
2. If a consumer affairs department is to be effective, what should its role be?
3. How would you answer the statement by one manager, "If an enterprise's manufacturing department does a good job and if products are honestly advertised, a consumer affairs department is simply a needless expense which results in higher prices for consumers"?

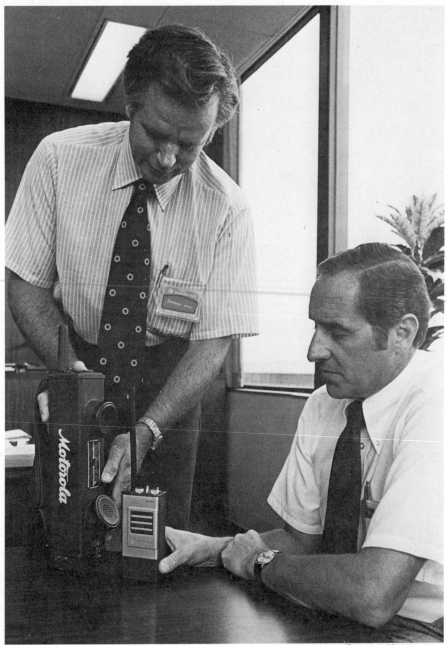

Courtesy Motorola inc.

Alert managements seek to improve products to better meet consumers' needs.

O nce consumers' needs and wants have been determined, management must create a marketing program to satisfy the needs of the firm's target customers. The marketing program is composed of four important variables which constitute the marketing mix. These variables can be abbreviated as Product, Promotion, Price, and Place and are often called the "four Ps of marketing."

Each of the four Ps is considered in this chapter which includes a discussion of the following issues:

What factors are considered in determining the right product for the target customers of the business enterprise?

What means can be used in the promotion program to communicate effectively with the target customers?

At what price should the product be offered to target customers?

How shall the business enterprise place the goods where they can reach target customers?

11

The marketing mix

THE MARKETING MIX

The four variables which make up the marketing mix are symbolized in Figure 11–1 with their focus on the consumer. The management which truly adopts the marketing concept of business concentrates on its target consumer group. An enterprise's management attempts to gain a competitive advantage over other firms by distinguishing its product in some way for the consumer. All the enterprise's marketing activities are carried out with the goal of surpassing its competitors in fulfilling consumer needs.

FIGURE 11–1
The marketing mix

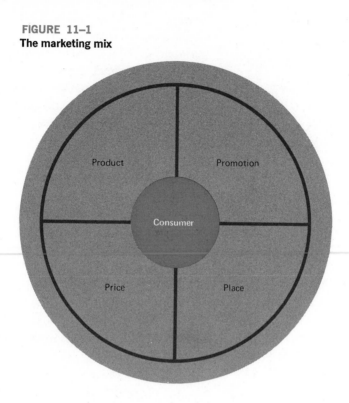

A discussion follows on each of the variables of product, promotion, price, and place. Although each is considered separately, the marketing mix of a business enterprise consists of the total of all these elements. There is a close relationship among the four Ps. Decisions made in one dimension of the marketing program affect the other variables. There are many trade-offs to consider in determining a marketing mix that will be effective in profitably meeting consumers' needs.

For example, a manufacturer of lawn mowers might consider selling its total production to Sears where the mowers would be marketed under Sears' Craftsman label. Such a decision would relieve the manufacturer of promotion and place decisions and expenses. However, with only one major customer the manufacturer may lose control of the pricing decision and have to accept a lower price for lawn mowers than if they were sold to numerous wholesalers or retailers. If the manufacturer decided to sell to many smaller distributors, it would require promotional expense and more place decisions.

PRODUCT

Product defined

A simple definition of a product is a physical object with certain characteristics. A better definition from the marketing viewpoint is that a *product* is whatever satisfies a consumer's need. Thus, when a homeowner buys a new carved-wood front door the family is actually obtaining several different satisfactions for a variety of needs—shelter, security, and architectural beauty.

Products may be tangible such as a house or clothing. They may be intangible such as realtors' activities or school teaching. Intangible products are usually called *services.* Although they do not have physical characteristics, services provide very real consumer satisfactions. Medical advice and treatment, hair styling, and legal counsel are examples of different services that produce consumer satisfactions. The inclusion of services as products is important since a large proportion of the labor force is engaged in this sector of the economy. Since World War II consumers increased their spending for services more than for tangible goods.

Tangible products may be classified as durable or nondurable goods. *Durable goods* have physical qualities and uses which usually last over a relatively long period of time. Automobiles, tape players, and golf clubs are examples of durable consumer goods. *Nondurable goods* have physical characteristics and uses which limit their use to once or only a few times. Hamburgers, perfume, flowers, and newspapers are examples of nondurable consumer goods.

Making consumer satisfaction an important criterion of a product enables us to distinguish between different physical goods. Features such as brand name, color, packaging, the manner of distribution, price, and service provided differentiate one product from another.

For example, a color television set may be sold by a department store which provides credit, delivery, servicing, and a large inventory selection. This is not an identical product with the same television model purchased on a cash-and-carry basis from a discount house with a limited selection of models and no service technicians. Which of these television sets you purchase will depend upon the satisfactions you obtain from the extra services provided by the department store compared with the lower price at the discount house. This consumer trade-off between extra service and price can be used by the management of each television outlet in deciding upon their target customers.

Classification of consumer products

The distinction between products for ultimate consumers and industrial users was made in Chapter 10. Marketing of consumer goods is discussed in this chapter. Industrial goods and the process by which they are purchased are discussed in Chapter 12. Consumer goods may be classified according to consumer buying habits as convenience goods, shopping goods, and specialty goods.

Convenience goods. *Convenience goods* are purchased with a minimum of effort at the nearest available location. Convenience goods are low-price items about which the consumer has considerable knowledge. Usually brand identification is not so strong that consumers will not accept a substitute brand if their first choice is unavailable.

Convenience goods may be classified further as staples, impulse goods, and emergency goods. *Staples* are bought and used frequently without much consideration being given to their purchase. Many food products and nonprescription drug items are staple goods. Brand identification may have some weight in the buying decision. Usually easy availability will be more important than the brand. Items such as bread, milk, and aspirin are considered staples and easy availability to consumers is important in their distribution.

Impulse goods are items which customers buy on sight without having gone out specifically for their purchase. Their unit price is usually low. The purchase of an impulse good satisfies a need which is strongly felt at the moment. Retail stores frequently place items near doors or at cash registers which will be bought by customers on an impulse. Candy bars, chewing gum, cigarettes, and magazines are frequently displayed in this way.

A good may be either a staple or an impulse item depending on the purpose of the good's use and whether it was purchased because of an immediately felt need. Candy bars purchased for lunch boxes as part of a weekly grocery shopping trip may be considered staple goods. A candy bar might be viewed as an impulse item if it were purchased and eaten on the spot because the person just happened to see it.

Emergency goods are bought only when an urgent need is felt. In this situation price is not too important. The customer needs the goods at once. Tire chains purchased at a turnpike service station during a snow storm or ambulance service for a victim of heart attack are examples of emergency products.

Shopping goods. *Shopping goods* are compared with competing products for price, quality, style, or service by the customer before purchase. Frequently the customer lacks complete knowledge about shopping goods before arriving at the store. This presents an opportunity for personal selling by sales personnel. Shopping goods typically have a relatively high unit price and are bought less frequently than convenience goods. Examples of shopping goods include men's and women's apparel, jewelry, and furniture.

Since the customer likely will want to compare shopping goods with the competition, retail stores selling these goods find it desirable to be located close together. The manufacturer of shopping goods has fewer retail outlets than the producer of convenience goods. In some cases the name of the retail store is more important to the customer than the name of the manufacturer. Therefore, the retailer has considerable opportunity to increase sales of shopping goods through promotion.

Specialty goods. Specialty goods are identified by customers with strong brand preference or particular features which justify a special buying effort. The customer usually has knowledge of the product before the buying trip and is willing to go out of the way to find a certain brand. Examples of specialty goods include photographic equipment, expensive clothing, stereo sets, and health foods. An automobile may be considered a specialty good by the customer who has a strong preference for a particular manufacturer's models.

Although specialty goods may have a high unit price, this is not always the case. Even an inexpensive item may be considered a specialty good if the customer has a strong brand preference for it. Thus for many persons Kodak film and processing are specialty goods since they will use no other brand even though film and processing of other manufacturers may be priced lower.

Blurred classifications. The classification of consumer products can be useful to marketing managers. However, it is not an inflexible system nor do all products fit neatly into the scheme. Items may be considered in different categories by customers under varying circumstances. Customers' shopping habits may change over time. For example, people now buy many products in supermarkets which they formerly purchased in drugstores or variety stores. As incomes rise families may buy products as convenience goods which formerly were shopping goods. Changes in the buying habits of customers require enterprise managers to be alert to necessary changes in the marketing mix.

Importance of new products

New product development is a major element in the marketing program of the business enterprise. Business must continually give consumers new and improved products to hold old customers and to win new ones. In today's markets manufacturers cannot prosper without new products. Many corporations have 50 percent of their sales in products which did not exist ten years ago. Marketing research experts have estimated that within the next three years approximately 75 percent of the economy's growth in sales volume can be expected to come from new products and new brands of merchandise. In such industries as electrical machinery, chemicals, and textiles, more than 50 percent of sales growth in recent years has come from newly marketed products. Those enterprises with the research programs necessary to develop new products will experience the greatest growth in sales and profits in the future.

Products tend to have a life cycle of sales and profit margins as shown in Figure 11–2. Both the sales and profit margin curves slope upward, reach a peak, and then decline. However, there is a significant difference in the timing of their peaks. The sales curve continues to rise after the profit margin curve has already reached its peak. This can be partially explained as the result of competitive enterprises producing

FIGURE 11–2
Product life cycle for sales and profit margin

Sales dollars and profit margin percentages

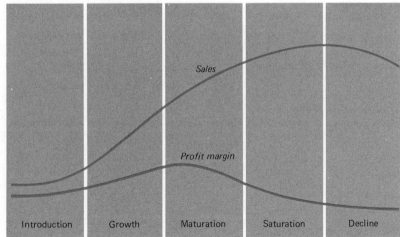

similar goods, reducing prices and therefore forcing profit margins down. To insure continued high profit margins on total sales the business enterprise must develop new products to take up the profit slack on products which are still increasing in sales volume. This emphasis on profits rather than sales volume is an important aspect of good marketing management.

New product development is complicated by the actions taken by an enterprise's competitors. A business firm must be ahead of the competition with at least some of its products unless management is willing to operate with lower profit margins than those enterprises which emphasize research and development.

Developing the product

The development of a new product should be undertaken only after a market analysis of the probable demand for the product. A market analysis enables the manufacturer to develop a product prospective customers want with the necessary quality to sell in a given price range. There are four stages in the typical product development program:

1. The idea stage.
2. The development stage.
3. The improvement stage.
4. The evaluation stage.

During the idea stage creativity is encouraged. The research group should be bound as little as possible by tradition or conventional thinking. While some people have more creative ability than others, this can be developed through practice. Frequently, helpful results have come from new personnel who are able to face a problem without "built-in" thinking that limits the range of imaginative new solutions.

Once the idea for a new product has been accepted, the product enters the development stage. This calls for designing the product and constructing a working model. At this stage it is important to determine what the product will look like, how it will operate, and to obtain preliminary cost estimates. Management makes frequent appraisals during the development stage. The project can be closed out if problems are encountered which cannot be solved satisfactorily.

After the development phase, the product is tested in the field to see if there are any "bugs" in it. Generally design simplifications and other improvements are discovered during field tests. Modifications are made in the product, and the model that will be placed on the market takes shape.

In the evaluation stage the final tests and modifications are undertaken. Production drawings and final cost estimates are made up. The final production models are constructed. All production details are worked out before the production lines are set up. In practice, improvement never ends. Modifications will take place even after commercial production begins. However, changes are more costly the further along they occur in the development of the product. The use of a pilot production program and careful evaluation in the final stage of product development reduces the number of changes.

Not all new products are successful. As a matter of fact, failure is far more common than success in new-product invention. For every five products developed to the point where they are ready for mass production, only one is ever actually produced and distributed. Of those new products which are placed on the market only about half are commercially successful.

PROMOTION

Promotion of the enterprise's product to encourage the potential customer to buy is another important element of the marketing mix. Promotion is the communications dimension of marketing. Target customers are informed and persuaded regarding the product or the enterprise. Feedback from promotion makes management aware of the consumers' needs and reactions to a specific product. Business enterprises compete to fulfill the expanded needs and wants of consumers. Creative promotion programs can be useful in meeting this challenge. Three methods of promotional activities are discussed here—personal selling, advertising, and sales promotion.

Personal selling

Personal selling is almost always an important method of promotion. In some enterprises it is the only form of promotion. Selling involves some method of communication with the customer. The most direct and effective form of communication is a personal presentation. This has the advantage of tailoring the sales effort to each particular customer, but the disadvantage of a high cost for each personal communication.

Employment outlook

Manufacturers' salesworkers

Practically all manufacturers, whether they make computers or can openers, employ salesworkers. Manufacturers' salesworkers sell mainly to other businesses—factories, railroads, banks, wholesalers, and retailers. They also sell to hospitals, schools, and other institutions.

Most manufacturers' salesworkers sell nontechnical products. They must be well informed about their firms' products and also about the special requirements of their customers.

Salesworkers who deal in highly technical products, such as electronic equipment, often are called sales engineers or industrial salesworkers. In addition to having a thorough knowledge of their firms' products, they must be able to help prospective buyers with technical problems.

Beginning salesworkers take specialized training before they start on the job. Some companies, especially those that manufacture complex technical products, have formal training programs that last two years or longer. College graduates increasingly are preferred as trainees.

The number of manufacturers' salesworkers is expected to rise moderately through the mid-1980s as a result of general economic growth and the greater emphasis manufacturers will place on their sales activities. Among the factors expected to influence employment growth in the occupation are the expansion of markets for technical products and the resulting demand for trained salesworkers.

In addition, the increased volume of business transacted with some customers—modern industrial complexes, chain stores, and other large institutions—will heighten competition among manufacturers supplying these organizations and intensify the need for effective selling. Manufacturers are expected to be selective in hiring. They will look for ambitious young people who are well trained and temperamentally suited for the job.

Salesmanship.   The heart of personal selling is salesmanship. This involves contact with prospective buyers and preparation of appeals to influence them to buy. Modern salesmanship provides the buyer with information to aid the customer in making the best decision as opposed to using high-pressure tactics. Most enterprises depend heavily on repeat business for their sales. Today's salesmen and saleswomen are equipped with knowledge regarding competitors' products as well as their own. They are trained to provide prospective customers with product information and service.

Personal selling is important to the entire economy as well as to the individual business enterprise. According to the U.S. Bureau of the Census about 10 percent of the total labor force in the United States is engaged in sales work.

Special types of sales representatives.   To assist the salesperson who takes orders and makes specific sales there are two types of specialists—missionary sales representatives and technical specialists. *Missionary sales representatives* work for a manufacturer to develop goodwill and generally stimulate demand on the part of potential customers. Normally they do not take orders or make specific sales. They may assist with sales promotion programs or provide training assistance for the customer's sales force. The *detail representative* who works for a drug manufacturer and calls on physicians and pharmacists is one type of missionary sales representative. Activities include promoting the company's reputation and the quality of its products as well as providing information on new products and distributing professional samples.

Technical specialists usually have scientific or engineering training and knowledge of an enterprise's products so they can talk with the customer's technical personnel. They may provide solutions to particular problems and suggest special applications of equipment or products which will be helpful to the customer. The technical specialist is usually called in by the regular sales person after a particular problem has been discovered.

To develop an effective sales program, management must provide programs for selecting training, compensating, and controlling its sales force. Sales personnel should work closely with others in the marketing department to relate sales activities to other promotional programs.

Advertising

Enterprises serving wide markets must carry on some of their promotional activities on a broad basis if they are to achieve mass distribution. Therefore, advertising becomes an important selling tool. *Advertising* is the communication of a group message by an identified sponsor regarding a good, service, or idea. Through advertising it is possible to communicate ideas about a product to many persons at once.

Advertising media. The marketing manager can select from a variety of advertising media. The most widely used media include newspapers, television, direct mail, magazines, radio, and outdoor advertising.

Newspaper advertising provides a flexible and timely medium which can be used to provide coverage in a specific city or trade territory. It is adaptable to local conditions. The costs per prospect are relatively low, based on the newspaper's circulation.

Television is the newest and fastest growing of major advertising media. It appeals to both the eye and the ear of the potential consumer. Television can be geared to a geographic market or to a particular time when a desired segment of target customers is most likely to be watching television. Television advertising is relatively expensive unless large audiences are reached by its message.

Direct mail can reach the exact market an advertiser desires and therefore may be highly selective. Its copy and form of presentation are flexible. Direct mail is costly on the basis of prospects reached. However, if the mailing list is current and contains the proper target customers, the message goes to the hands of interested parties.

Magazines can reach nationwide markets with a relatively low cost per prospect. Regional editions may be used for more limited geographic coverage. Specialized magazines and trade journals can reach audiences who represent clear-cut prospects for the advertiser's product.

Radio advertising offers the flexibility of saturation coverage for a limited geographic area or wider coverage on the networks. The radio ad's message and life are brief but can be repeated a number of times during an advertising campaign at a relatively low cost.

Outdoor advertising signs, if properly placed, reach a large number of people. They are generally used for products with a wide market. The outdoor ad's message must be short. A particular sign's cost may be relatively low per person contacted, but the cost of placing these ads over a wide geographic territory can be high. Outdoor signs are often used to advertise tourist facilities and to give information to travelers.

Advantages of advertising. While advertising is less direct and less flexible than personal selling, it has the advantage of lower cost per customer contacted. Also, advertising may provide information to the target customers which will cause them to seek out the product. It may

Employment outlook

Advertising

Many specialties are found in advertising work. Advertising managers direct a firm's advertising program. They decide policy questions such as the type of advertising, the advertising budget, and the agency to employ.

Account executives, who work in advertising agencies, study a client's sales and advertising problems, develop a plan to meet the client's needs, and seek approval of the proposed program. Research directors and their assistants assemble and analyze information for advertising programs. They study possible uses of a product, its advantages and disadvantages compared to competing products, and ways of reaching potential buyers.

Advertising copywriters create the headlines, slogans, and text that attract buyers. Artists and layout workers plan and create visual effects in advertisements. Media directors negotiate contracts for advertising space or time.

Employment of advertising workers is expected to increase moderately through the mid-1980s, as the volume of consumer goods and competition among manufacturers increase. Although opportunities should be favorable for highly qualified applicants, those seeking entry jobs will face stiff competition.

put prospects in a more responsive mood when contacted personally by a sales representative. Thus, advertising can support the personal selling program of the enterprise.

Advertising reaches individuals who may be inaccessible to sales personnel. Even though a sales representative cannot get an appointment with an executive or consumer, the advertisement can reach the desk or home to convey its sales message.

Advertising by a manufacturer can strengthen the position of its dealers, attract new dealers, or enable the manufacturer to enter new geographic or customer markets.

The promotion campaign for a new product usually includes advertising to inform and interest potential customers. Advertising campaigns may also be used to increase sales of a product through more frequent replacement, such as motor oil changes; or to lengthen the selling season, such as encouraging consumers to buy flowers at other times than holidays or special occasions.

Product and institutional advertising. Advertising may be classified as product or institutional. *Product advertising* has the objective of providing information and selling a specific good or service. *Institutional advertising* seeks to develop goodwill for an enterprise or an industry rather than directly selling a particular product. Institutional advertising's objective is to improve the long-term relationships with the various publics with whom the enterprise has contact.

Product advertising may be aimed at developing consumer demand for a general product rather than a specific brand, especially in the introduction phase of a product's life cycle. Thus, in the early stages of color television the theme for advertising campaigns by RCA, the pioneer of today's color television system, was the general idea of color television instead of black and white.

In the growth and maturity stages of the product life cycle the emphasis of product advertising normally turns to promotion of a specific brand. In the growth stage of color television RCA, Zenith, Magnavox, and other manufacturers tended to stress the merits of their own brands. RCA emphasized its long experience in color television. Zenith emphasized handcrafting in its chassis and Magnavox stressed its hand-finished cabinet quality and design.

As the product matures and reaches the saturation or sales decline phase in its life cycle, advertising may turn to reminder advertising which reinforces the product in the customer's mind. An enterprise with a dominant industry position may use this type of advertising to maintain its market position.

Institutional advertising may be used to develop a community's confidence in an enterprise. For example, banks and savings and loan associations often use institutional advertising to create an image of strength and integrity without promoting a specific service. Large worldwide corporations may use institutional advertising to emphasize the quality and research behind all their products. General Motors Corporation uses the GM "Mark of Excellence" in much of its advertising. General Electric uses the phrase "Progress Is Our Most Important Product" as part of its institutional advertising. At times an advertising campaign may contain elements of both product and institutional advertising.

Institutional advertising can also be used to counteract negative publicity or consumer reaction to a particular event. For example, an oil company wished to reduce criticism stemming from oil discharges from tanker ships which polluted beaches. The company ran a series of television advertisements stressing the positive things the company was doing which protected or enhanced the environment.

Spending on advertising. Figure 11–3 shows the amount of advertising expenditures as a percentage of sales for several major industry groups. Although in total dollars the amount spent for advertising is great, advertising spending is relatively small when compared to sales. For example, automobile manufacturers spent over $500 million for advertising in 1971, but this amounted to less than one percent of sales dollars. For manufacturing industries in 1971, 1.3 percent of sales was spent for advertising. In contrast to this, many enterprises spend more than 10 percent of sales for personal selling.

Sales promotion

Sales promotion acts as a link between personal selling and advertising to make each more effective. Personal selling aims at specific customers, and advertising is directed at large numbers of potential consumers. The function of sales promotion is to fill the gap between these extremes by focusing selling efforts on selected small groups. Targets of sales promotion efforts may be the enterprise's own sales force, wholesalers, retailers, or consumers. Sales promotion includes preparing displays and other sales aids, developing materials for training sales per-

FIGURE 11–3
Expenditures for advertising in selected industries, 1971, expressed as percent of sales

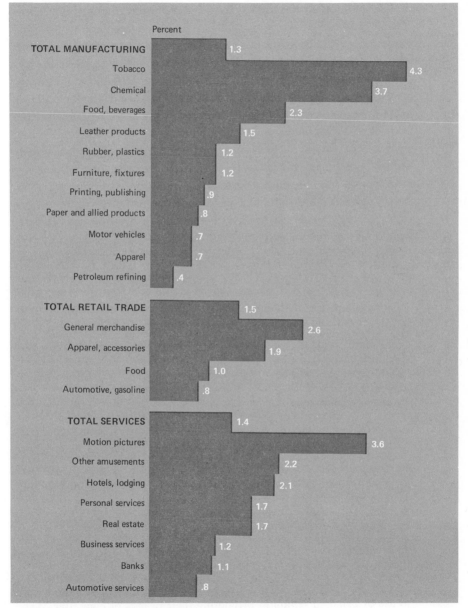

Percent

TOTAL MANUFACTURING	1.3
Tobacco	4.3
Chemical	3.7
Food, beverages	2.3
Leather products	1.5
Rubber, plastics	1.2
Furniture, fixtures	1.2
Printing, publishing	.9
Paper and allied products	.8
Motor vehicles	.7
Apparel	.7
Petroleum refining	.4
TOTAL RETAIL TRADE	1.5
General merchandise	2.6
Apparel, accessories	1.9
Food	1.0
Automotive, gasoline	.8
TOTAL SERVICES	1.4
Motion pictures	3.6
Other amusements	2.2
Hotels, lodging	2.1
Personal services	1.7
Real estate	1.7
Business services	1.2
Banks	1.1
Automotive services	.8

Source: U.S. Internal Revenue Service.

sonnel, and conducting contests and premium programs for customers.

An example of a sales promotion effort directed at the sales force is the sales contest with expense-paid trips for winners to places such as Hawaii or Mexico. Sales promotions aimed at consumers may give away free samples of toothpaste or soap or bonus trading stamps. Premiums such as silverware redeemable by mail for boxtops or coupons are another approach. Sales promotion to consumers may be through price incentives using coupons, refunds, or cents-off-package deals. Rexall Drug made famous the one-cent sale where the buyer gets two items for the price of one, plus one cent. Popular promotional devices include giving away specialty items such as calendars, pens, balloons, or paperweights with the name and address of the advertiser. Another promotional approach is to have manufacturers' representatives come into the retail store to give demonstrations of new foods, cosmetics, or fashions. The variety of these examples indicates that sales promotion activities are limited only by the imagination.

The key to good sales promotion is flexibility and ingenuity to improve the effectiveness of personal selling and advertising. Sales promotion may be carried on by the sales force or by the advertising department. It may be handled by a separate unit in the marketing department. Outside consultants in sales promotion are sometimes used especially to suggest new ideas or to conduct certain promotions such as contests.

Total promotion mix

Different combinations of personal selling, advertising, and sales promotion efforts may be effective in successfully marketing a particular product. One type of promotional activity may be used as a substitute for some other type of promotion. For example, consumers can be reached through both personal selling and advertising. If an enterprise uses little advertising probably it will have to rely heavily upon personal selling. The Fuller Brush Company spends very little for advertising. However, each product in its line is sold personally door-to-door through use of sales promotion samples and small catalogs. On the other hand, the tobacco companies have large advertising budgets and make almost no use of personal selling in promoting their brands of cigarettes. Avon Products has introduced television advertising to support its door-to-door personal selling campaign for cosmetics. A key marketing decision is the determination of the best combination of promotional efforts.

PRICE

Pricing is one of the major elements in the marketing of an enterprise's product. Price directly affects both sales volume and profits. However, the degree of control exercised by a management over the prices charged for its products varies widely. At one extreme are sellers who exercise almost no control over the price received for their goods. In these cases of pure competition the seller accepts the going market price and is not able to influence price. There are few examples in industry but there are some in agriculture that approximate this situation. The American farmer who raises commodities such as wheat is in this marketing position.

At the other extreme is the monopolist who is the only supplier of a particular good or service and can establish the selling price. Here too, examples in American economic life are difficult to find since our national policy is to limit the monopolist. Where natural monopolies do exist, as in the case of public utilities, the prices charged customers are regulated by public commissions. In regulated industries the objectives are to provide a fair return to the enterprise for providing the service and yet to protect consumers by keeping rates reasonable.

Between these extremes of pure competition and monopoly lies the pricing situation of most enterprises in American industry. Varying degrees of imperfect competition lead to a wide variety both of pricing practices and emphasis upon price and nonprice competition.

Practical pricing considerations

Economists have outlined important theoretical foundations underlying pricing in industry. With increasing knowledge and the use of high-speed computers, marketing managers are improving their pricing decisions. However, in most instances the manager in a business enterprise still does not have the detailed knowledge of the market necessary to construct a sophisticated price structure model. Therefore, there are several practical pricing considerations which should be taken into account by marketers. These include consumer demand, importance of nonprice competition, costs, pricing strategy, and government controls.

Consumer demand

The marketing manager would like to know how important price is to the consumer relative to other factors such as quality, service, reliability, and sales promotion. Sometimes price is an important determinant of consumer demand. When changes in the price of a good result in substantial changes in consumer demand the good is said to have a high degree of *elasticity of demand.* When price changes bring about little or no change in demand for a product the good has *inelasticity of demand.* An example of a good with a relatively high degree of demand elasticity is beefsteak. When the price of steak goes up many people switch from steak to roasts and hamburger. As the price of steak declines these same consumers switch back to steak. The classic example of a product which has high inelasticity of demand is table salt. Most people would not use more salt even if the price were reduced substantially. Neither would they decrease their consumption of salt if the price doubled or tripled.

There are three tests which may be applied to determine the elasticity of demand for a product. Generally the demand elasticity is greater when many substitutes are available, when the product is a luxury good and can be dispensed with fairly easily, or when it is a big-ticket item such as a car or a home.

Importance of nonprice competition

Where there is a tendency in an industry toward uniformity of price, market share is determined largely through nonprice competition. Nonprice competition includes promotion, quality and service competition, and fashion. Nonprice competition may reduce the importance of the pricing decision.

In the tobacco industry the chief emphasis for cigarette sales is on nonprice competition through advertising. Prices of different brands of cigarettes are essentially the same. An attempt is made by each manufacturer to distinguish its product in the mind of the consumer from other competing tobacco products. This is done mainly by advertising which appeals to the emotions.

Quality and service are important nonprice considerations for a variety of products. Brand names such as Maytag, Cadillac, Texaco, Omega, and Hart Shaffner & Marx reflect an image of quality or service. This reduces the importance of price competition for these products.

Fashion is the style of a particular product which happens to be popular at a given time. Improved methods of communication and better use of advertising have contributed to an increased emphasis on fashion. Alert purchasing and selling efforts by retailers are necessary when fashion is an important factor in merchandise lines. Out-of-fashion goods may be difficult to dispose of unless large price markdowns are made resulting in reduced profit margins. Today's consumer is more fashion minded. The recognition of this is important in selling consumer goods. If an enterprise can emphasize the fashion aspect of its products, price becomes less important.

Costs

An obvious consideration in pricing is the cost associated with producing and distributing the products of the business enterprise. Over the long run the manager must cover all costs of doing business if the enterprise is to avoid operating at a loss. In fact, it is necessary that all business costs be covered with some revenue remaining for profit. You are reminded of the discussion of the role of profits in Chapter 4.

It is easy to state that all costs should be covered over the long run in pricing decisions. However, the application of cost analysis to immediate or short-run pricing decisions is considerably more complicated. It is difficult to calculate the total cost in producing and distributing a product. Costs vary depending on factors such as the quantity of goods produced, the nature of fixed and variable costs, spending for research and development, and the amount spent for sales promotion. The problems involved in determining costs for pricing decisions have led to the development of cost accounting systems. A discussion of the nature of costs is covered in the chapters on Production and Control. An important responsibility of the marketing department is to provide top management with information regarding probable consumer reaction to different prices. Expected consumer reactions can be considered in setting product prices as well as production and marketing costs.

Pricing strategies

A range of pricing strategies may be used in the business enterprise. Skimming the cream and market penetration represent two extremes in pricing strategy.

Skimming the cream pricing. A policy of *skimming the cream* results in setting a price at the high end of the possible range of prices for a product. Such a policy is likely to be used with a distinctive product in the introduction stage of its life cycle or for products where nonprice competition is emphasized. Early in the product's life demand will probably be less elastic in response to price. Also, competition is not as intensive as later. High prices at the introduction stage may generate greater profits. These can be used to cover development costs. Also, if a mistake is made in initial pricing of a new product it is easier to lower the price than to raise it. Later in the product's life cycle, a series of planned price reductions can broaden the market to increase sales and meet price competition.

Market penetration pricing   In *market penetration pricing* the price is set relatively low to achieve mass market acceptance quickly. This strategy can be successful if demand for the product is highly sensitive to price and if considerable competition is expected as soon as the product is introduced. Also, lower costs per unit of production may be achieved when a large volume of goods is produced. This is especially true of products having high fixed costs that can be spread over volume production. An enterprise with a large investment in plant and equipment may profit from mass marketing early in the product life cycle. Also, a low initial price may achieve a degree of product acceptance in the market which will help meet competition better in the future.

Government controls

In some instances prices charged by a business enterprise are directly controlled by government. This is especially true for public utilities where rates to be charged for service within a state are established by state regulatory commissions. Interstate utility services are controlled by federal government agencies. Governments also directly affect prices when they buy goods from business enterprises. In many instances contracts for government purchases are on the basis of competitive bidding. Or profits may be limited by cost plus a fixed fee or percentage of the contract.

The antitrust laws set the ground rules to which business pricing practices must conform. These laws include the Clayton Act and the Robinson-Patman Act which were discussed in Chapter 2. Generally price fixing in an industry is illegal as are other restraints on competition. It is unlawful to practice price discrimination in interstate markets among purchasers of products of similar grade and quality where the result may tend to injure competition. Differences in price to different purchasers must be based on cost differences or on the need to meet competition. Government generally has attempted to prevent large enterprises from setting prices so low as to drive out smaller competitors.

The fear is that once competition has been eliminated the larger, surviving firms will raise prices even higher than before the predatory price cutting.

PLACE

Place is an important dimension of the marketing mix. Place includes the factors which provide time and place utility to satisfy customers. Place decisions have to be made regarding channels of distribution for a product and transportation and storage systems. Services as well as tangible goods have place considerations.

Channels of distribution

Channels of distribution determine the route a product takes from the producer to the ultimate consumer or industrial user. Thus, channels of distribution include enterprises and individuals active in the transactions associated with the movement of goods or the provision of services. Channels include the producer and the final customer along with any middlemen involved in the transfer of title to the goods.

Functions performed in channels

In recent years there has been a tendency to reduce the number of middlemen between the producer and ultimate consumer. However, there are certain marketing functions which must be performed in moving goods from producers to consumers. If one institution in the channel of distribution does not perform or bear the cost of a particular function someone else must do so.

Wholesalers perform the economic function of storage, imparting time and place utility to goods. The wholesaler usually buys and sells in larger quantities than does the retailer. For example, a food wholesaler purchases canned goods by the carload and sells to the grocery stores in case lots. The retailer sells to the household in quantities as small as a single can. Other marketing functions to be performed include transporting, grading or sorting, financing, and risk taking by holding title to the goods. When the middleman is bypassed or eliminated from the channel of distribution, either the manufacturer or consumer must perform or share the cost of these functions.

Marketing functions can be shifted forward or backward in the chan-

nel of distribution or shared but not eliminated. In deciding which channels to use the choice should be treated as a system. The objective is to
reduce total distribution costs and to improve service for the benefit of
consumers as well as business.

   Channels for industrial users. Channels of distribution vary depending partially on the nature of the customer. Frequently goods for industrial users will be marketed directly by the producer to the user. In
some instances a middleman may take title to industrial goods and in
turn sell them to industrial users. Figure 11–4 illustrates typical channels
for products of industrial users.

FIGURE 11–4
Channels of distribution for industrial products

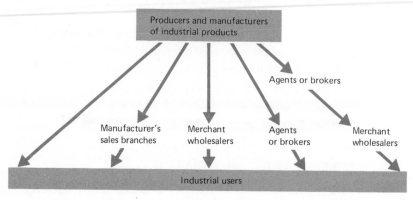

   Channels for ultimate consumers. Channels of distribution to ultimate consumers vary considerably in their complexity. The most simple
channel is from the manufacturer of goods directly to the consumer.
More complicated channels of distribution include one or more middlemen between the producer and the consumer. Figure 11–5 illustrates the
range of channels for consumer products.

Institutions of distribution—wholesalers

   There are three principal types of wholesalers used by manufacturers
to distribute their products to retailers or industrial users. These are the
merchant wholesaler, manufacturer's sales branch, and the agent or
broker. In making the decision as to which system is best for distribution
of their products manufacturers must analyze the alternatives in view of
their products, the services to be provided, and the customers they wish
to reach.

FIGURE 11–5
Channels of distribution for consumer products

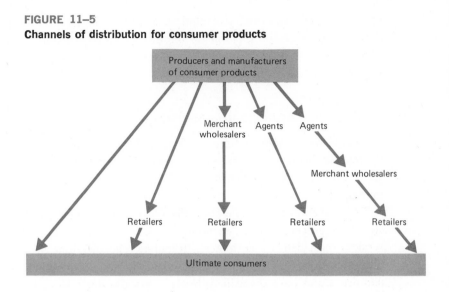

Merchant wholesalers perform several important functions for manufacturers. They purchase merchandise from manufacturers, take title to the goods, and assume the risks associated with selling them. The merchant wholesaler stores the product, delivers it to retail or industrial customers, handles the collection of accounts, and may provide service facilities and sales promotion.

Jobbers, drop shippers, and cash-and-carry wholesalers are other types of wholesalers which normally take title to goods as they move through the channel of distribution but usually do not provide all the services performed by the merchant wholesaler.

A *manufacturer's sales branch* or office may be desirable if the product is complicated and requires considerable technical knowledge or is not widely known. Sales branches are owned and operated by manufacturers separate from their factories. They may or may not carry inventories from which orders are shipped directly. The sales branch enables the manufacturer to control the selection of retail or industrial customers. With sales branches the manufacturer performs the wholesale functions of storage, shipping, credit financing, and servicing.

Agents and *brokers* constitute the third class of wholesalers. The distinguishing characteristic of agents and brokers is that they customarily do not take title to goods but negotiate the purchase or sale of merchandise. For this service they are paid a fee or commission. They may represent specialized product lines as in the case of processed foods brokers or building supplies manufacturers' agents. Customarily the agent or broker is in close communication with potential customers and is able to provide information on the demand for goods at any time. This permits the manufacturer to avoid the expense of a sales force. A large area can be covered by a network of independent sales agents.

Institutions of distribution—retailers

Retailers sell goods and services to the ultimate consumer. This puts the retailer in a key position to test consumer acceptance of the product, gauge whether it is priced correctly, and assist customers in making their purchases.

No longer can retailers be easily classified as department stores, drugstores, or grocery stores depending on the merchandise sold and the services provided to customers. Retailing classifications have been blurred with the development of discount houses. Also, supermarkets and drugstores have diversified their merchandise lines so as to appear as small department stores. Today retailing ranges from highly impersonal vending machines to small specialty shops dealing in luxury merchandise with much personal service. Some manufacturers such as Firestone, Singer, and Rexall have moved into the retail field with their own stores designed to serve the consumer directly.

What kind of retailing do you think will prevail in the future? Obviously no one has the final answer. New products are brought onto the market. Consumer wants and shopping habits change. Retailers must meet these challenges! In the past 25 years retailing methods have changed dramatically. First came discount houses, then shopping centers, and most recently enclosed shopping malls. The retailer who can sense new ways to fulfill consumer wants will be the one who will prosper. Retail institutions in which no imagination or creative marketing is used will likely fade from the American scene. At best they will linger in the shadows of retailers who are able to meet aggressively the opportunities in today's markets.

Physical distribution

Physical distribution consists of moving and handling goods through channels of distribution. For goods to have possession utility they must be at a location where they are available to the consumer at the proper time. The physical distribution system includes the transportation of goods and their storage.

Transportation of goods is critical to business and consumers in our interdependent society. This is highlighted during a major truck or railroad strike. Transportation systems are so important that some economists have traced the economic development of the United States by analyzing the impact of new means of transportation over the years. In selecting a form of transportation for their products, today's managers can choose among railroads, trucks, waterways, pipelines, and airlines.

Railroads. As Figure 11–6 indicates, railroads carry more intercity freight than any other single means of transportation in the United States. Railroads are well suited for long hauls of products which are bulky and have a low value relative to their weight such as coal, steel, and building materials.

Railroads have faced stiff competition from other forms of transpor-

FIGURE 11–6
Freight traffic by mode of transportation, 1972

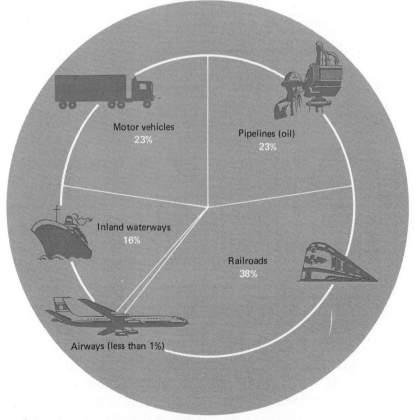

Source: Interstate Commerce Commission, *1973 Annual Report.*

tation in recent years. To counter this competition, mainly from trucks, railroads have provided a number of services to meet the needs of specific shippers. For example, when faced with the loss of the shipping of new cars from assembly plants to dealers the railroads designed a triple-deck car carrier. This won back a considerable amount of the business from truck transport operators. With the development of subcompact American automobiles the railroads devised a carrier which would stack these minicars vertically. Now more can be carried per freight car than by traditional horizontal stacking.

Another innovation by railroads is "piggyback" service, in which loaded truck trailers are carried on railroad flatcars. The transported goods can be packed at the shipper's site and not handled again until they are unloaded at the buyer's freight dock. This provides additional flexibility for the railroads since the loaded truck trailers can be driven directly to the buyers' locations even if they are not on a rail siding. Also, with less handling the goods are not exposed to as much risk of damage or theft.

Trucks. Truck transportation has more than doubled its proportionate share of freight carried over the past 30 years. This growth has been achieved because of the flexibility of trucking operations, the improvement in the nation's highway system, and truck freight rates that are competitive with railroads.

Waterways. The coastal and inland waterways in the United States are used by ship and barge traffic to haul a considerable amount of bulky, nonperishable products such as mineral ore, sand, coal, cement, and petroleum products. Water transportation is the cheapest method of moving goods but also is the slowest, and some waterways are closed by ice in the winter.

Improvements have been made in water transport with the development of containerization. Ships are designed to take standard-size containers directly from freight cars or trucks without repackaging. "Fishyback" service using truck trailers similar to rail piggyback service has been developed to increase the flexibility of water transportation.

Pipelines. Pipelines are used primarily to carry products such as crude oil and natural gas. While water transportation is less costly for refined petroleum products, pipelines are used extensively for natural gas and to carry oil from the fields to refineries.

Airlines. Airlines are the newest, fastest, and most expensive means of transportation. Air freight rates are lower now than just a few years ago. However, they are still higher than rail or truck rates. This has

Employment outlook

Industrial traffic managers

An industrial traffic manager arranges the transportation of materials and finished products. Industrial traffic managers analyze various transportation possibilities and choose the most efficient type for their companies' needs—rail, air, road, water, pipeline, or some combination. Then they select the route and the particular carrier.

Activities of industrial traffic managers range from checking freight bills to deciding whether the company should buy its own fleet of trucks rather than contract for services. They route and trace shipments, arrange with carriers for transportation services, prepare bills of lading and other shipping documents, and handle claims for lost or damaged goods.

Employment of industrial traffic managers is expected to increase slowly through the mid-1980s as more businesses centralize their shipping and receiving activities in separate departments. Growth in this occupation will stem from an increasing emphasis on efficient management of traffic activities and from the trends toward procuring materials over greater distances and distributing products in wider markets. There will be a strong demand for specialists who can obtain the lowest possible freight rates. A college education is becoming increasingly important in this field.

caused shippers to analyze the total cost of physical distribution in justifying this type of transportation.

The speed of air transportation has opened up new markets for products which are fragile or perishable. Orchids and other tropical flowers
can be shipped from Hawaii to the mainland. Electronics parts can be
less expensively packaged. Inventories can be reduced as the result of
speedy availability through use of air transport.

Storage.   The storage function is the holding of goods from the time
they are produced until their final use. For the business enterprise this
involves a system of warehousing, materials handling, and order processing.

Warehousing.   Warehousing, or physical storage of goods, may be
done by the manufacturer, wholesaler, or retailer. The ownership of
warehouse space is an added cost of doing business. Unless there is a
continuing need for permanent warehouse space, the business enterprise
may find it desirable to rent space in a public warehouse.

Public warehouses are located across the country and overseas. They
provide storage space and other services associated with storage to public customers. These warehouses may be prepared to receive goods in
large quantities and repackage them for smaller shipments to customers.
A public warehouse may assist in financing inventories held by them by
issuing a warehouse receipt that can be used as security for a loan from
a bank. The public warehouse company assumes responsibility for damage or loss of goods placed under its custody. Storage facilities for per-
ishables and agricultural commodities are maintained by some public
warehouses.

Materials handling.   The efficient movement of goods into warehouse facilities, their placement, storage, and subsequent removal from
the warehouse provide a challenge for materials handlers. The handling
of materials is a major part of storage cost.

Generally the movement of goods in a vertical plane is more expensive than horizontal movement. Therefore, older warehouses with several floors connected by slow-moving freight elevators are being replaced
with new one-story warehouses.

Much mechanization is being applied to materials handling. This includes forklift trucks, conveyor belts, and hydraulic ramps to make un-
loading and loading easier. Pallets, which are wooden racks that hold a
number of boxes or items for easy storage or movement, are widely used
in warehousing today. Containerized packaging of standard sizes is being
used for easier handling, storing, and transporting. Some grocery and

drug warehouses use automated order-filling and radio-controlled equipment for greater efficiency.

Order processing. Once an order from a customer has been received it must be processed. Processing includes the flow of paperwork covering the transaction and the physical shipment of goods. Order processing should be done accurately and promptly to maintain customer goodwill. Mistakes in order handling or delayed shipments can undo the favorable image of the enterprise and its product which has been created by earlier steps in the marketing mix.

ORGANIZATION OF THE MARKETING DEPARTMENT

When an enterprise adopts the marketing concept of business it emphasizes the profitable fulfillment of consumer wants. Perhaps the most important aspect of applying the marketing concept is orienting the thinking of all personnel to improved customer service. Once top management has accepted the marketing concept of business it must be communicated and implemented throughout the business enterprise.

The top marketing executive normally reports directly to the president of the enterprise. Figure 11–7 shows a partial organization chart of a marketing department. Each manager will have authority and responsibility for certain functions and a number of subordinates depending on the size and needs of the enterprise.

FIGURE 11–7
Partial organization chart of a marketing department

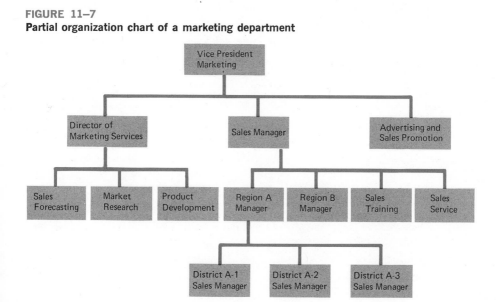

SUMMARY

The marketing program of a business enterprise can be thought of as being composed of four variables which constitute the marketing mix. These variables are Product, Promotion, Price, and Place. They all focus on the consumer, which is consistent with the marketing concept of business.

Consumer products may be classified as convenience goods, shopping goods, and specialty goods. Consumer buying habits for each class of products differ.

New products are the lifeblood of many business enterprises since the typical product life cycle reaches a peak after which profitability and then sales begin to decline.

Promotion consists of personal selling, advertising, and sales promotion. Advertising is the process by which the enterprise's marketing message is communicated to potential consumers through a visual or oral medium. Sales promotion acts as a link between personal selling and advertising.

Pricing considerations include consumer demand, the importance of nonprice competition, costs, pricing strategy, and government controls.

Channels of distribution, transportation, and storage systems all relate to the factor of place in the marketing mix. The channels of distribution vary depending upon the nature of the customer, the product, and who is to perform the economic functions associated with moving the product from the producer to the consumer.

Transportation systems include railroads, trucks, waterways, pipelines, and airlines. The choice of a means of transportation requires careful study by marketing managers.

The storage function includes a system of warehousing, materials handling, and order processing.

The marketing department is an important part of the business system and functions to fulfill consumer wants resulting in a profit for the enterprise.

TERMS FOR REVIEW

marketing mix	*advertising*
product	*sales promotion*
services	*nonprice competition*

convenience goods   *skimming the cream pricing*
shopping goods   *market penetration pricing*
specialty goods   *channels of distribution*
product life cycle   *wholesaler*
personal selling   *retailer*

QUESTIONS

1. Interview a retail store manager in your area to determine what products his store now sells that were not on the market five years ago. How would you classify these new products based on consumers' buying habits?

2. *a.* Based on Figure 11–2 what are the implications for the enterprise which does not market new products?
   b. How does the nature of the product line influence the need for new products?
   c. Give examples of products which have different length product life cycles.

3. Evaluate the relative importance of the 4 Ps for small specialty shops and large department stores as they compete in the same enclosed shopping mall.

4. What long-term changes may occur in the consumer's shopping habits as the result of the development of the enclosed shopping mall? What are the implications for the older, established retailers in downtown locations?

5. Select examples of product and institutional advertising which you found appealing. What made these ads effective for you? Give an example of how your buying behavior for a particular item was influenced by advertising.

6. By examining the nature of the promotion program for a product, try to determine the general nature of the pricing strategy being followed by the retailer or manufacturer. To what extent is nonprice competition a factor in selling the product you selected for study?

7. Comment on the following quotation by a manager of a discount store in a suburban location: "We have eliminated the wholesale middleman and buy direct from the manufacturer. Since we do our own warehousing and servicing we are able to pass these savings on to the consumer." How would you test the manager's statement?

8. After a study of materials available in the library, write a 300-word paper either supporting or opposing the statement that advertising simply adds to the cost of goods without adding to the value received by consumers.

Business briefs

"Avon calling"

Since World War II American retailing has changed from emphasis on downtown department store selling to the discount house, to the suburban shopping center, to the enclosed shopping mall. Now there is an increased interest by business enterprises in direct selling in the customer's home.

Door-to-door selling has long been a part of the American retail scene. Fuller brushes and Electrolux vacuum cleaners (both now owned by Consolidated Foods) are familiar products to many housewives. Avon Products is the world's largest manufacturer of cosmetics and toiletries. Avon has added costume jewelry which is sold directly in the customer's home to its product line. Avon sales more than tripled from 1966 to 1974 and profits doubled. Encyclopedias and other books and magazines are widely sold on an in-home basis. Tupperware (part of Dart Industries) effectively utilizes neighborhood gatherings of housewives, called Tupperware parties, to sell its kitchenware and other products. Other retailers are also using the idea of neighborhood hostesses where company representatives display and demonstrate a variety of products.

1. How do you account for the continued success and growth of in-home selling?
2. Why will consumers permit strangers to come into their homes to extol the virtues of products ranging from cosmetics to vacuum cleaners?
3. What types of goods are particularly suited for direct sale in the customer's home?

National Airlines

In the spring of 1975 National Airlines announced a new promotional air fare designed to attract more persons to fly on its huge Boeing 747 and DC-10 planes. The new ticket prices provided air service between certain cities below the cost of bus or train travel.

This no-frills service seated passengers in a special third-class compartment at the rear of the airplane. No free meals were provided passengers. In fact, no meal or liquor service was available except that soft drinks could be purchased. Passengers desiring to eat during the flights had to bring snacks or box lunches with them onto the plane.

Costs for these flights were much lower than on previous economy air fares. For example, the new no-frills day coach service between New York and Miami was $61 one-way compared with the earlier economy air fare of $98. Service by bus was $63 and by train $72.

In order to get these lower fares passengers had to pay for tickets at least seven days in advance. The no-frills service was not available on weekends, some holidays, and during certain summer periods.

1. Why would National Airlines institute such flights?
2. As a marketing manager of National Airlines how could you justify these discounts of almost 40 percent to the financial officer of the airline?
3. What is National Airlines attempting to provide the public?
4. What would you expect National's competitors to do?

Baskin-Robbins ice cream

While many merchants are finding consumers to be price conscious, one ice cream shop chain is thriving on a premium-priced product. Baskin-Robbins ice cream stores, a franchise chain with home offices in California, has more than 1,400 shops in the United States, Canada, and Japan. This chain now sells more "hard" ice cream than any other chain store operation—including Howard Johnson's.

Baskin-Robbins stores carry at least 31 flavors of ice cream and sherbet with exotic names such as Red, White & Blueberry; Pink Bubble Gum; and Baseball Nut. Flavors are changed frequently with several new ones introduced monthly throughout the year. Although many new ice cream flavors are concocted in the company's research laboratory, only a handful are deemed appealing enough to be marketed across the country.

Unlike other ice cream chains which also sell coffee, sandwiches, and other snack items, Baskin-Robbins stores sell only ice cream products. Their ice cream is of high quality, with some flavors containing twice as much butterfat as the minimum federal standard.

Prices for Baskin-Robbins ice cream range from 23¢ a scoop up (depending on the store's location) to $4.50 a gallon. In contrast some supermarkets sell ice cream for as little as $1.09 per half gallon.

1. How do you account for the success of Baskin-Robbins despite the relatively high price of their product?
2. How important is the location of a Baskin-Robbins ice cream store in a community?
3. What advantages would a Baskin-Robbins retail franchise have over a local ice cream shop selling a similar quality product?

Enjoying it more

"Warning: The Surgeon General has determined that cigarette smoking is dangerous to your health." This required statement is displayed for smokers on every cigarette ad and package sold in the United States. American Cancer Society officials are calling for an even stronger statement to be required by the Congress.

More than 10 years after the Surgeon General's 1964 report claiming that smoking causes cancer, heart trouble, and other diseases, the cigarette industry is switching its advertising emphasis from low tar and nicotine brands to "full-flavor" brands.

Marketing analysts suggest that low tar and nicotine brands have not been successfully marketed. Only two of these brands are among the top 20 sellers.

In general the full-flavor cigarettes have relatively high tar and nicotine content. The chairman of R. J. Reynolds Tobacco Co. stated, "Full flavor is what people want, and that's what Reynolds is going to give them." Reynolds' Winston and Phillip Morris' Marlboro, the nation's two biggest selling brands, are both relatively high in tar and nicotine content. Reportedly these two manufacturers are spending some $60 million promoting their top sellers.

1. Why have cigarette manufacturers switched their advertising emphasis to full-flavor cigarette brands?
2. Examine current cigarette advertising. Bring a copy of an ad to class and be prepared to discuss what needs are being appealed to by the ad.
3. In 1971 cigarette advertising was banned from radio and television. Should it also be banned from magazines, newspapers, and other printed media?

Case

The Sure-Cover Company

Jack Holby, marketing manager of the Sure-Cover Company, listened as members of the company's marketing committee discussed a new type of wallpaper which was being considered for marketing.

Jack realized that there was a temptation to grab at this new product as a possible solution to the company's declining sales. Sure-Cover, a major producer of wallpaper, had been able to maintain its share of that market in recent years. However, the total industry sales had been steadily declining. The reason for this was the increasing use of paint as a substitute for wallpaper. Economy was apparently the chief consideration. The cost of having a professional apply wallpaper was not much greater than the cost of having a room painted. However, with the cost of professional application of both paint and paper rising, more home owners were turning to do-it-yourself projects. In almost every case, the do-it-yourself customers were using paint because of the mess associated with hanging wallpaper.

The new product now being considered consisted of the standard Sure-Cover line of paper with a pressure sensitive adhesive applied to the back. The paper was to be called "Ready-Stick."

"With this paper," Jerry Forbes of the product development department stated, "any amateur can do a professional job of paper hanging with little trouble or mess." Forbes also pointed out that, based on his conversations with personnel in production and purchasing, it was clear that production costs would run at least 50 percent higher than the cost of producing standard paper.

As Forbes concluded his remarks, Jack Holby reflected on some of the views which his subordinates, members of the marketing committee, had previously expressed concerning the new product. Although he was their superior, Holby realized that these persons, because of their experience and individual perspectives, could contribute a great deal toward the effective solution of this top management problem.

Jack had discussed this problem with Tom Monroe, director of market research, a few days earlier. Tom's biggest concern was the reaction of customers to the price of Ready-Stick. If normal retail margins were allowed, the paper would have to be sold at $5 a roll compared to the $3 price on the standard roll. Past experience had shown that consumers are very responsive to changes in the price of wallpaper, partly because there is little preference for one brand over another. (Most consumers cannot even name a brand of wallpaper.) Furthermore, the price of Ready-Stick would seem even further out of line when compared with paint. The cost of standard wallpaper per square yard was already in excess of the cost of paint necessary to cover the same area. At a higher price, Ready-Stick would be more than double the cost of a comparable amount of paint.

Jack Holby shared Tom Monroe's concern over the high price of Ready-Stick. He agreed that the consumer's reaction to this price would be an important factor in the product's success. He was not certain, however, that it was helpful to compare the price of Ready-Stick with the price of either standard paper or paint. He wondered whether either of these was a comparable substitute for Ready-Stick. Were there not features about Ready-Stick that would justify its higher price in the consumer's mind?

Tom Monroe went on to say that if the product were introduced, he believed it should be marketed through different retail outlets than those now being used. "Sure-Cover presently distributes their paper only through 5,000 stores which specialize in wallpaper. This provides for a rather limited exposure, especially as compared with paint which is sold through about 40,000 hardware stores as well as in most wallpaper stores. Since this is a new product it is important that it receive maximum exposure to the consumer."

Monroe recommended that the new product be sold through supermarkets. This, he explained, would provide the necessary exposure to the consumer. The high markup on wallpaper should be especially attractive to supermarkets. Furthermore, he thought the product would not seem "out of place," considering the increasing trend toward "scrambled merchandising" in supermarkets. Many supermarkets now carry nonfood lines ranging from cosmetics to lawn mowers. Holby was intrigued by this idea. As he turned the idea over in his mind he tried to imagine how the purchase decision was normally made for this kind of product and whether the consumer would accept a supermarket as the place to buy it.

Holby had also talked recently with Jill Mason, director of advertising. Jill was enthusiastic about the product. However, she said it might require an entirely different promotion program than that being used for the standard line of paper. Jill pointed out that since brand preference among consumers was not significant, only a small proportion of the promotion budget had formerly been designated for consumer advertising. The average consumer tended to select the store and then select the paper from among those which were shown. For this reason, Sure-Cover had found that promotion efforts directed at the dealer had better results than those directed at the consumer. The dealer could be influenced to (1) stock the paper and (2) "push" the Sure-Cover brand, if convinced of the quality of the paper. Accordingly, more than 80 percent of the promotion budget was spent on trade journal advertising, mailers, catalogs, and samples. The remainder was devoted to consumer advertising.

Jill Mason felt that this strategy would have to be revised considerably for Ready-Stick.

Paul Fiedler, the sales manager, saw possible problems in distributing the new product. If the Ready-Stick were marketed through the present dealers, he felt they would not actively support it. "These dealers derive much of their income from the application of wallpaper," he explained. "They are not likely to be enthusiastic about a paper which does not require professional application." If alternative outlets were chosen, Fiedler also anticipated difficulties. "Almost all of our present sales are of paper which is applied professionally. If our present dealers feel we are taking away from their sales by selling Ready-Stick through other outlets, there could be serious repercussions." He went on to emphasize that dealer support was essential to the sale of the firm's standard wallpaper. Even though Sure-Cover was a leader in the industry, this position depended upon the continued support of the dealers. Since brand recognition was lacking, dealers would feel no necessity to retain the line if they felt they were being treated unfairly.

Jack Holby turned his attention back to the discussion now taking place among the members of the marketing committee. Although he had had prior conversations with each person on this problem, this was the first opportunity for them to discuss it as a group. Jack realized that he would have to make a recommendation to the company president within the next few days as to whether the product should be produced. Furthermore, if the decision was made to introduce the Ready-Stick paper, he and his subordinates would have to develop a detailed plan for marketing the new product.

1. Would you recommend that Sure-Cover proceed with the production of Ready-Stick? Justify your recommendation.
2. If a decision were made to proceed with this product, recommend a program of promotion and distribution.

*Sophisticated machine
tools improve worker
productivity and product
quality.*

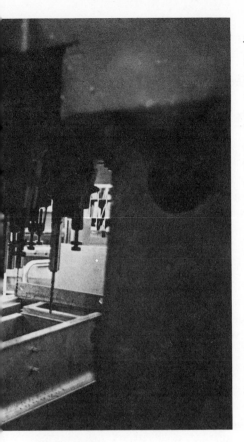

12

Production

*I*f you want a sports car you are not interested in sheets of steel, glass plates, synthetic fabrics, and unprocessed rubber. Unless these materials are combined in the proper way into a completely assembled automobile they will have little value for the typical consumer who wants a car. Production provides goods with form utility by turning raw materials and semifinished products into finished goods for either consumer or industrial use.

Great strides have been made in the production process in the United States during the past 50 years. The ability to mass-produce goods at prices which make them available to millions of people is one of the outstanding accomplishments of the private enterprise system. The increased productive capacity of our economy in part stems from the improved productivity of workers, from increased investment in capital equipment, and from the application of improved production techniques and management methods.

For a better understanding of the production function you need to answer the following questions:

How does management determine the location of new production facilities?

What factors must management consider in setting up the production system?

Why is production control and scheduling so important?

What is the role of purchasing in the production process?

How does automation relate to production?

How may the production department be organized?

THE LOCATION OF PRODUCTION FACILITIES

The importance of factory location

The selection of a factory site is a decision of major importance for any business enterprise which engages in manufacturing operations. The location of production facilities is normally a long-term commitment. It is usually not easy to dispose of large amounts of machinery and buildings if a mistake is made in the factory's location. The initial location of a plant or a proposed change in factory location involves consideration of the following factors.

Nearness to raw materials. When raw materials used in the manufacturing process are bulky and expensive to transport it is wise to locate the factory near the source of these commodities. Iron and steel plants are frequently located near sources of iron ore or coal because of the bulkiness of these raw materials. When many different parts go into the manufacture of a product, it is not possible to locate the factory near all raw materials. Management must decide whether the advantage of being close to some raw materials sources outweighs other factors which influence factory location.

Nearness to markets for finished products. To achieve economies in distributing its products a manufacturer may select a plant location close to significant users of its goods. This involves an analysis of future expected markets as well as present distribution patterns. With nationwide and international distribution of product lines this may mean having multiple-plant operations to serve geographical areas where the enterprise's products are sold.

Quality and cost of labor available. An important question in deciding plant location is whether there is an adequate supply of workers available for the new factory. Management must determine what skills are required and whether the area can supply the workers in a satisfactory cost-quality relationship. If enough skilled workers are not already available, are there persons in the community who can be trained for the new jobs? Are wage rates in the area in line with what management will encounter in other areas and with what its competitors are paying? If prevailing wages in the area are higher than elsewhere in the industry, especially without increased skills or productivity, management may be at a competitive disadvantage in its cost of production.

Sometimes enterprises relocate manufacturing facilities in an attempt to avoid unionization of the work force. Examples of this are seen by the location of manufacturing plants where traditional attitudes toward unions have been less positive than in heavily industrialized areas. However, with the protection given union members and organizers by national legislation, managements cannot depend upon plant location to avoid unions.

Access to transportation facilities. Because of the importance of time in delivering manufactured products to customers, access to good transportation facilities should be considered in factory location. The transportation facilities used depend on the nature of the product and the importance of speed. An example of locating a factory with access to transportation can be seen where an electronics plant is adjacent to an airport. Air transportation is convenient for both company products and personnel.

Many railroads are willing to provide railroad spurs alongside new factories to encourage greater use of rail freight. Some railroads are developing industrial parks located near important rail junction points with attractive lease or purchase plans.

Availability of utilities. A management interested in a new factory site wants to know if enough electricity, gas, and water are available at economical rates for manufacturing. This is especially important when the manufacturing process consumes large quantities of utility services.

Satisfactory tax situation. There are several state and local taxes which business enterprises must pay. One of the most important is the real estate and property tax imposed by local and state governments on factories, equipment, and inventories. This is based on assessed valuation which is usually less than full market value. The property tax usually varies between three and six percent of the assessed value of business property. There may also be state and local sales or income taxes which business must pay.

The cost of local and state taxes is a minor portion of an enterprise's costs of doing business. Therefore, these taxes are usually not too important unless other factors are virtually equal in the choice among several locations. A more important consideration than the amount of taxes is whether the community is providing a satisfactory level of municipal services.

Miscellaneous factors. A variety of other factors influence factory location. These include the quality of the community measured by its schools, colleges, cultural programs, and churches, along with the attitude of its people toward new enterprise. The availability of land for factory sites, adequate zoning, and up-to-date building codes are necessary to encourage new industrial development.

With the many elements influencing factory location it is impossible for management to consider each factor equally. Management's problem is to determine those elements which are most important and then select the best location under the existing conditions. Information regarding possible plant locations is available from local chambers of commerce, state industrial development commissions, industry trade associations, railroads, and utility companies. Management can use much of this information but should recognize that each locality is certain to picture itself in the most favorable light. The final decision for factory location must be made by management from its own analysis in light of the enterprise's requirements.

THE PRODUCTION SYSTEM

At its best the production system of a modern business enterprise operates as a smoothly functioning unit. Through the design of efficient production systems we have achieved mass production of goods priced within the reach of millions of consumers. One example of improved production processes which have lowered costs is the development of color television. When color television was a new product a set cost about $1,000. Technology and improved production have reduced costs. Now a color television set is down by 50 percent or more of its initial price. The elements of the production system include research and product design, process design, production control, purchasing, and automation.

Research and product design

Research in most manufacturing enterprises is directed primarily toward *applied research*. This involves practical application of scientific knowledge to definite problems or needs. Applied research is wide-ranging in scope. It may be directed toward the development of new products or toward discovering ways of reducing costs of established product lines. In contrast, *pure research* extends our frontiers of knowledge without regard to the immediate application of its findings.

In many industries up to 10 percent of annual sales is directed toward research and development. Corporations such as Du Pont, Merck, and

IBM are noted for both pure and applied research in the fields of chemistry, pharmaceuticals, and computers. Government agencies also conduct research both alone and in cooperation with universities and private enterprises. Both pure and applied research are important to us in today's economy.

Research and product design may be done by the production, engineering, or marketing departments. Sometimes a separate research department is organized. The final product developed for manufacture should be the result of close cooperation between marketing and production personnel.

The objective in *product design* is to develop a product that will perform properly, appeal to consumers, and be sold at a price that will be profitable. Performance relates to how the product works, its reliability, mechanical design, and ease of repair. Consumer appeal relates to the form and appearance of the product. Automobile designers have to consider both performance and appearance to come up with a successful model. A particular model may not sell well, but by redesigning its appearance it may be successful even with little change in performance qualities. But good styling alone is not enough for a product to be successful. Because of mechanical or performance difficulties an auto model may be labeled as a "lemon." Sales may suffer even though the styling is good. Successful product design results in a product which rates high both in performance and appearance.

Process design

Whereas product design has to do with the product's characteristics, *process design* is the development of the means of producing it. The objective of good production management is to have the most efficient method for manufacturing a given product. Essential elements in process design include the factory layout, the type of machinery used, and the development of prototypes.

Factory layout. How machines and production lines are arranged in a factory makes a great deal of difference in the cost of production. Materials should move through the manufacturing process in the quickest and most direct manner. Transportation, handling, and clerical expenses should be held to a minimum. A good factory layout makes the most efficient use of available machines and manpower.

There are two basic types of factory layout. The factory may be laid out according to product or process. *Product layout* is the arrangement of machinery and assembly lines by chronological steps in the manufacture of the product. As the product moves through a plant organized on a product layout basis there is a gradual buildup of the product from raw materials or parts to the finished product.

Product layout is especially economical when the articles being produced are of standard specifications and required in large volume. In product layout the use of automatic equipment, continuous production lines, and conveyors results in low costs per unit produced even though the total investment is large. The product layout moves materials through the factory rapidly with a minimum of handling and transportation.

The advantages of product layout also provide the basis for its weaknesses. As nearly as possible all machines must be kept operating with a minimum of idle time. When something goes wrong along the product layout it is frequently necessary to shut down the entire assembly line until the trouble is remedied. The product layout therefore requires numerous maintenance and setup personnel, materials suppliers, and engineers to back up the workers tending the machines. Attention must be given to balancing production facilities so that backlogs of materials do not pile up at any one point along the layout. Once the product layout is set up it probably will be costly to change.

Process layout occurs when different types of machines or functions are located together regardless of where the process comes in the production of a product. In process layout the same kind of machines are grouped together. This means that all grinding is done in one location, all polishing in another, all drilling in another, and so on through the various steps in the manufacturing cycle. Process layout provides a great deal of flexibility. Products requiring specialized manufacturing operations can be scheduled into the different areas. Machinery can be fully occupied if scheduling is well done.

A breakdown of one machine is not as critical with process layout as with product layout. If a machine breaks down its work can be transferred to a similar machine in the area. With no continuous production line, such as in product layout, the balancing of production time for machinery is not as important. Process layout is used when a variety of products are produced with the same machines and with job-lot orders in small quantities.

However, process layout also presents some problems for production managers. Transportation and materials-handling costs are usually high because the conveyors and mechanized handling used with product layouts are not present. Goods in process of manufacturing move more slowly, resulting in higher inventories and greater financial costs. The scheduling routine of materials and the accounting for costs of production are different for every order. This is in contrast to the more standardized procedures in product layout.

Process layout and product layout each have advantages and disadvantages. In practice most manufacturing enterprises use elements of both depending on the nature of the product, the variety of goods produced, the length of production runs, and the importance of flexibility.

Machinery selection. The machines used in production are either general-purpose or special-purpose machinery. *General-purpose machines* can be used for a variety of different jobs requiring the same kind of work. A drill press is an example of a general-purpose machine. A drill press can be used to drill one or many holes, of different sizes, to different depths, and into different materials by simply changing the drill bit. General-purpose machinery is fairly well standardized and available from a number of different manufacturers.

The general-purpose machines found in many factories include shapers, lathes, drills, presses, grinders, polishers, boring machines, and milling machines. While each of these machines performs a different function, in general they change the form of raw materials or semiprocessed goods by removing material, cutting holes, smoothing, bending, or shaping. Because of standardization the general-purpose machine is likely to be less expensive than the special-purpose machine.

General-purpose machines are usually slower than special-purpose machines. They may require skilled operators if the parts are hand-fed into the machine. Goods produced on general-purpose machines may require more inspection as there is no guarantee that every part will be the same with hand-fed machinery. However, general-purpose machines can be fitted with special automated controls to insure greater uniformity. Or highly skilled operators may be used to assure greater conformity to quality standards.

General-purpose machines are especially useful when the work in the factory is varied and the volume for any single product is small. Skilled machinists are able to operate more than one type of general-purpose machine. This provides flexibility which is necessary for the job-lot shop. However, it also results in somewhat higher unit costs than when long production runs and standardized products permit the economical use of special-purpose machines.

Special-purpose machines are designed for a particular job and have the right tools and adjustments built in. Once the special-purpose machine is calibrated and in operation a semiskilled worker can be used to tend the machine. In some instances all a worker has to do is to supply raw materials to the machine, remove the parts which have been produced, and occasionally check to see that the machine is producing to established standards. Special-purpose machines are desirable when long production runs of a part justify a large investment in a machine for that one job.

Prototypes. Frequently before production begins on a new product or before a new factory is built, a prototype is constructed. A *prototype* is a model or pattern which will be used as the basis for subsequent production. A prototype may be made of the product or the production process. A good example of a product prototype is the clay model of an automobile made during the design process to show its styling and appearance in three dimensions. Later hand-tooled auto models will be put together, complete with mechanical work. These models will be tested extensively before the final production-line car will be decided upon.

A prototype of the production process consists of a scale model of the complete factory or the production line and is called a *pilot plant.* Engineers carefully check every detail of the pilot plant. They try to anticipate and eliminate as many problem areas as possible before the factory is built. The construction and testing of a pilot plant may cost thousands of dollars. However, this money is spent to reduce the risks involved in the investment of millions of dollars in the new factory and equipment.

Once the product and process designs have been settled management must place orders for the tooling necessary to start production. *Tooling* consists of items such as cutting and grinding attachments, clamps, gauges, loading devices, and other fixtures. Tooling is designed to adapt machinery and assembly lines to the production of a particular product. It may cost from a few hundred dollars to millions of dollars depending on the complexity of the product and the amount of new tooling required. The automobile industry spends hundreds of millions of dollars annually for new model tooling. Tooling is only part of the expense of gearing up for a new product. New machinery may be required or a factory building may be constructed to house the new production facilities.

The final step before full-scale production begins is to put the new production facility through a series of test runs. Production personnel and engineers will iron out difficulties and eliminate "bugs" which may appear despite all the precautions that have been taken. During this time the personnel department will have recruited and trained any additional workers necessary for the production process. Prior to this time the marketing department will have completed its analysis of the expected market for this product. Pricing and distribution decisions will have been made. Top management will be coordinating the efforts of the various departments for a smooth introduction of the new product to the consumer.

PRODUCTION CONTROL AND SCHEDULING

The heart of the modern factory system is production control. *Production control* consists of a wide variety of activities including authorization of orders, scheduling, routing, and maintaining production schedules. Production control personnel coordinate and control the production process to meet delivery schedules. Production control personnel must maintain good communications with the marketing department as well as with production supervisors.

A master schedule of anticipated production is normally prepared to provide a general basis for control. This master schedule is based on the factory's capacity and the sales forecast for the demand for the enterprise's goods. You will recall the process of sales forecasting discussed in Chapter 6.

Orders and authorization of production

Orders for specific customers are sent by the marketing department to production control, which has the responsibility for scheduling these orders so delivery dates can be met. The sales department has a responsibility for coordinating its efforts with production control so unrealistic delivery dates will not be promised customers. In some instances the sales department is not permitted to give a firm delivery date until it has been cleared with production control.

The specific orders coming from the sales department constitute the authority to the factory to produce the goods. Once an order has been placed the authorization to produce the goods is prepared by the scheduling section of production control. The specific scheduling assignment takes into account the status of other orders already in the production process, the present utilization of factory capacity, and the promised delivery date. A master schedule is used as an overall control device to summarize units produced, orders on the books, and the available productive capacity for the future.

Production scheduling

Production scheduling covers the time orders are received from the sales department until finished goods are shipped to customers or to the warehouse for future shipment. The objectives of good production scheduling are to assure that delivery schedules are met and that the most efficient utilization of production capacity is achieved.

Before setting up production schedules an important factor to be considered is *lead time.* This is the time necessary for all arrangements before production can begin. In the case of simple or repeat production orders the lead time may be measured in days. With model changes in automobiles, appliances, and other complex goods the lead time is measured in months. Several years of lead time is required with items such as new aircraft or aerospace products where new technology must be developed.

Scheduling and the follow-up is a valuable control device in the modern factory. A complex system of production scheduling is required today because of the thousands of parts which go into many products we take for granted. The complexity of scheduling systems can be illustrated by the manufacture of a portable typewriter which has more than 1,750 parts. Each part must be available at the right place, in the proper quantity, at the time it is required in the assembly of the typewriter. This scheduling is further complicated when more than one typewriter model is being manufactured, and in different colors with different type faces. Scheduling systems become even more complex when you consider the problems involved in the production of aerospace products which have a multitude of parts and may require coordination among a number of manufacturing plants.

Routing. An important part of production control and scheduling is routing. *Routing* includes detailed instructions as to how a particular order will move from department to department, which machines will be used, and when inspections will be made. The routing sheet provides the man or woman who is foreman in each department with specific information regarding the order, how it is to be processed, and where the materials go after each department has completed its particular operations.

Employment outlook

Foremen

Men and women who are employed as foremen supervise skilled, semiskilled, and unskilled blue-collar workers. Supervision is the most important part of the foreman's job. Many blue-collar workers never work for supervisors higher than foremen. It is through their foremen that they get work orders, recognition, and discipline. Foremen interpret and communicate company policy to the workers. They also train newly hired workers and advise experienced workers on the proper way to handle jobs. In unionized plants foremen may meet with union representatives to discuss work problems and grievances.

Employment of foremen is expected to increase moderately through the mid-1980s. Growth of business and government organizations will create a demand for more foremen. Demand also will be stimulated by the trend toward more complex production processes that require greater supervision.

Although fewer than one tenth of all foremen are college graduates, a growing number of employers are hiring foremen trainees with college backgrounds. This practice is more prevalent where production processes are highly technical such as in the chemical, oil, and electronics industries. Employers generally look for college graduates with backgrounds in business administration, industrial relations, mathematics, engineering, or science. Foremen trainees undergo on-the-job training until they are able to accept supervisory responsibilities.

Foremen with outstanding ability, particularly those with college education, may move up to higher management positions. For example, in manufacturing they may advance to jobs such as general foreman, department head, and plant manager. In some instances, as in the construction industry, foremen may use the experience and skills they gain to go into business for themselves.

Maintaining production schedules. There are a number of means available to see that production is on schedule. A variety of charts are used. These charts show the detailed operations required for an order, when they should occur, and what the state of actual production is. Visual control boards also are available to measure the status of orders. All these devices require constant revision to check on production and to reflect changes in schedules.

In many instances the electronic computer has replaced these charts and control boards. The ability of computer systems to provide instant information on the status of orders and machine use has been of great benefit to production managers in efficient scheduling. Computers are used on a continuous basis to receive information from the factory machinery for constant control of the production process. Machinery or reporting stations in the factory are connected electrically to the computer. Information on jobs underway or completed is fed immediately into the computer for analysis and reporting.

PURCHASING INDUSTRIAL GOODS

In many manufacturing enterprises the value of purchased materials makes up 50 percent or more of the cost of the final product. In most manufacturing operations the materials that are purchased are the largest single expense in the manufacturing process.

Purchasing is defined as the procurement of industrial materials and supplies for use or for further processing, not for immediate resale. This excludes buying merchandise for sale to the consumer without changing its form, as is done by retail and wholesale merchants.

Steps in the purchasing process

The essential steps in the purchasing process are outlined below. This is to provide you with a broad understanding of purchasing. Therefore, no attention is given to the details of forms and records. The steps in the purchase of industrial goods are as follows:

1. The need arises for specific industrial goods. For maximum efficiency, purchasing schedules should be planned in advance. However, at times emergencies, such as breakdowns or sudden changes caused by shifts in demand, may necessitate rush orders.

2. An accurate description of the goods is drawn up on a purchase requisition form.

3. Once the requisition has been drawn up and filed with the purchasing department, the negotiations with possible sources of supply are undertaken.

4. After negotiations and analysis of the different vendors, the purchasing department selects a particular vendor and places an order for the goods. The purchase order contains data such as precise merchandise description, quantity, price, delivery date, and the signature of the purchasing officer.

5. Prior to the anticipated delivery date, a follow-up on the order is carried out by the purchasing department to confirm that the promised delivery date will be met.

6. Upon receipt of the vendor's invoice, an itemized statement of merchandise shipped by the seller, the purchasing department checks that the goods shipped match the description on the purchase order.

7. When the industrial goods arrive they are inspected for quantity and quality and to see whether damage has occurred in transit. After the merchandise has been received and inspected, the invoice is approved for payment. The departments are then notified that the needed goods are available.

Price and quality considerations

Purchasing agents are expected to negotiate and to buy at the most favorable prices obtainable. However, invoice price is but one element of cost. Delivery costs also must be considered. A low price paid to a supplier a great distance away may result in high transportation charges so that the delivered cost of a low-priced item is actually much higher. At times a lower invoice price may be obtained through quantity purchasing. However, the expense of handling and storage may outweigh this price differential by the time the materials have been issued and put to use. These examples illustrate that low unit prices on invoices do not always mean the lowest total cost to the purchaser.

Quality as well as price must be taken into account in the purchase decision. Quality is a relative term. *Quality* may be defined as the possession of the necessary criteria which fit a product to a given use. The purchasing enterprise must define the minimum standards of quality suitable for the intended purpose. Qualities superior to these minimum standards may be desirable but are not essential. For an enterprise to purchase materials below the minimum necessary standards represents potential waste. However, there is no reason to spend additional money

Employment outlook

Purchasing agents

The purchasing agent's job is to maintain an adequate supply of items a firm needs for its operations. Purchasing agents and their assistants obtain goods and services of the required quality at the lowest possible cost. They buy when stocks on hand reach a predetermined reorder point, or when a department in the organization requisitions items it needs.

Once an order has been placed with a supplier, the purchasing agent makes periodic checks to insure that it will be delivered on time. This is necessary to prevent work flow interruptions due to lack of materials. After an order has been received and inspected, the purchasing agent authorizes payment to the shipper.

A moderate increase in the employment of purchasing agents is expected through the mid-1980s. Major factors underlying this growth include the continued increase in the size of business and manufacturing firms and the development of new products and sources of supply such as foreign markets. In particular, the ever-increasing complexity and specialization of business functions and products will spur demand for purchasing agents with knowledge in specific areas.

to purchase a product or raw material of higher quality than is necessary to accomplish a specified purpose.

Selecting sources of supply

In the process of selecting the sources of supply for the enterprise, the purchasing department normally goes through four successive stages before it chooses a particular vendor with whom to place a purchase order. These stages include:

1. The information or survey stage, when possible sources for a product are considered.
2. The inquiry stage, when the relative qualifications and merits of potential suppliers are determined.
3. The analysis and selection stage, when the initial order is placed.
4. The administration or experience stage, when the vendor-customer relationship is established or when the selection process is repeated to search for a more satisfactory source of supply.

MAKE-OR-BUY DECISION

There are times when the question arises as to whether it is better to manufacture a component part in one's own plant or to buy from an outside vendor. To help top management with the make-or-buy decision, comparisons should be made in the areas of costs, quantity desired, and necessary quality.

The *cost of purchased goods* may be determined rather easily. The complete cost up to the time of use is the figure which should be used. This cost includes the invoice price of the purchased goods plus transportation charges and costs of handling and storage. Against this purchased cost must be balanced the total estimated cost of producing the goods in the enterprise's own shops. This cost calculation should include not only the cost of materials and labor, but the investment including depreciation on necessary equipment, utilities, supervision costs, and normal waste and spoilage. All these costs of production must be included for a fair comparison with the cost of purchasing the product.

The *quantity of goods* required is an important consideration. Are the potential cost savings large enough to justify producing the component part? Is the quantity needed great enough to realize economies of mass manufacturing by spreading the fixed costs over many units of production?

Quality control of an item may be better if it is produced in your own plant rather than purchased outside. This becomes an important consideration when strict quality control and exacting requirements are needed. The production of the good in your own plant may make it easier to guarantee the desired quality. On the other hand, if quality standards are significantly greater for the new product than plant employees have been accustomed to dealing with, quality may be improved by purchasing the component from a manufacturer accustomed to such high standards.

There are other problems associated with the self-manufacture of a component part. Once the enterprise is committed to such a policy, especially where special equipment is necessary, an element of inflexibility is introduced. Freedom of selection is sacrificed, despite subsequent cost savings available through outside purchase. Frequently, the decision to manufacture a component rather than to purchase from an outside vendor is made without taking into account these considerations.

INVENTORY CONTROL

Inventories typically represent a substantial part of a manufacturing enterprise's assets. Inventory control is important to three different departments in the business enterprise. The production department must be assured of an adequate supply of materials on hand to manufacture goods when needed. The marketing department must be able to fill sales orders and meet customers' delivery dates. The finance department is concerned with the need to minimize the amount of funds invested in inventory at any given time. Smaller inventories reduce storage costs and reduce the risk of losses from obsolete merchandise or falling prices.

The items to be carried in inventory are determined by the enterprise's needs based on production and sales estimates. This requires coordination between production and marketing personnel. The quantity of inventory should be considered both in the total dollars invested in inventories and on individual classes of goods.

Manufacturing inventories are classified as raw materials, goods in process, or finished goods. *Raw materials* include unprocessed commodities and purchased component parts to be assembled into the finished product, Once the inventories have been placed in the production cycle they become *work in process*. Here their form is changed or other parts are added to them to increase their value and to move the materials nearer to product completion. When the manufacturing process is completed and the goods await distribution to consumers they are *finished goods*. Finished goods inventories represent the buffer between immediate sales needs and the ability of the factory to produce goods. Inventories are carried on the accounting records of the enterprise at the cost of the materials plus the costs added during the manufacturing process.

The administration of inventories includes the receipt of goods, their storage, the issuance of materials to production departments, and shipment of finished goods to customers. A system of records provides for accountability of goods, information on inventory turnover, and reorder points. The analysis of inventory turnover is discussed in Chapter 13. Today inventory control is improved by computer systems and mathematical models.

PURCHASE OF CAPITAL EQUIPMENT

The purchase of major equipment, or capital equipment, such as machinery, transportation equipment, or office equipment requires different analysis than the purchase of materials which go into the manufacture of a product. *Capital equipment* lasts longer than a year, is used to manufacture other goods, and does not become part of the product being manufactured. New capital equipment may result in greater speed of output, less variation in the product, lower costs, or greater dependability.

Special problems arise in the purchase of capital equipment because of its characteristics:

1. Capital equipment usually involves large amounts of money which may require some special form of financing. The purchase of capital equipment is generally a decision of major importance for the enterprise.

2. In view of the long life of most capital equipment items, the purchase of major equipment is an infrequent occurrence. The type of capital equipment purchased will likely vary from year to year. This makes the purchase of this equipment difficult to routinize.

3. The total costs of capital equipment are more difficult to determine with a high degree of preciseness than are raw materials costs. In addition to the initial cost, the cost of capital equipment includes obsolescence, maintenance and repair, and idle time.

4. The characteristics of capital equipment produced by different manufacturers are seldom identical. A machinery manufacturer normally has different features and options for a particular line of equip-

ment. Therefore direct comparison of machines and prices is difficult.

5. Because of its long life, in the purchase of capital equipment management may commit itself to a series of other decisions with long-run consequences. These decisions include the type of product to be manufactured, the method of production, and the costs of operation. It is easier to change to new raw materials or component parts than it is to change capital equipment in a factory.

6. Consideration must be given as to how the proposed capital equipment will fit into the plant layout. Extensive changes may be required in the production process when new capital equipment is introduced.

OTHER ELEMENTS OF THE PRODUCTION SYSTEM

Other important elements of the production system include motion and time analysis, quality control, and maintenance.

Motion and time analysis

Motion and time analysis is done by industrial engineers to provide a basis for production standards on factory jobs. Actually the establishment of standards is a twofold process. First comes the motion analysis to determine the best way of doing a particular job by reducing waste effort to a minimum. The methods engineer studies the job and breaks it down into its essential elements, eliminating unnecessary movements and establishing a pattern for efficient production.

Once the motion analysis is completed, the worker is trained in the new method. Then the industrial engineer conducts a time study analysis, using a stopwatch, to determine how much time is necessary to carry out the job under actual factory conditions. A number of observations will be required to determine fairly the amount of time necessary for a particular job. Variations in the employee's work pattern caused by chance or unusual circumstances might make one or a very few observations result in an unrealistic work expectation. This time study will be the basis for setting the work standard after allowances are made for worker fatigue, production delays, and necessary personal time. These factors are added to the average observed time in setting work standards.

Time study is based on the assumptions that the skilled industrial engineer can determine the best method for performing a job and can judge what a normal pace is for doing that job. These assumptions are sometimes questioned by labor unions, and work standards are often the subject of bargaining between management and organized labor.

With experience workers are often able to reduce the original time required for the job as they become more skilled, discover shortcuts, and improve on the original method which was developed for the job. These improvements are referred to as "creeping methods changes." The result of this improvement in job performance is that the workers are able to earn a somewhat higher rate per hour if they are paid by the number of units produced. Or workers will have more leisure time if they are paid on an hourly basis and expected to produce only so many units per hour. When management notes this it will often restudy a job and tighten up the work standard by reducing the allowable time for a given job. As you would expect, workers generally object to this!

In establishing work standards a desirable psychological practice is to set an expected rate of production which the average worker can exceed by 10 to 15 percent by exerting a bit more than normal effort. The establishment of piece rates or hourly production standards is a tedious job. Management seeks to strike a balance between fairness to the workers and at the same time hold down production costs so the enterprise can be competitive and earn a profit.

Quality control

An important element in the production system is the maintenance of the desired quality in manufactured products. Once standards of quality have been established a means of inspection must be devised. Many different types of inspections can be carried out on manufactured goods. These range from a skilled cook tasting a vat of soup to pronounce it fit for canning to a test driver putting a new car off the assembly line through a series of tests before shipment to a dealer. A good quality control system not only includes final inspection, but also prevents continued production of unsatisfactory goods.

Inspection can occur as goods move along the production lines or at central inspection facilities located away from the production process. When inspection is done on the production lines there is an opportunity to prevent the buildup of an excessive number of defective products.

Central inspection facilities may act as receiving stations for products from all over a factory. This may be a laboratory where detailed inspections are made under carefully controlled conditions. Central inspection facilities permit more objective inspection since the inspector is not standing by the production worker who may be responsible for the unsatisfactory work.

Sometimes every product in a factory will be inspected. However, often some form of partial inspection is used based on a statistically selected sample.

Maintenance

The work of the *maintenance* force is to keep the factory in efficient operating order. This involves a wide variety of activities including lubricating moving parts, repairing machinery, or fixing a plumbing breakdown. All the physical facilities in a factory start wearing out the day they are installed. Therefore, a sound maintenance program must be instituted if production is to continue uninterrupted by breakdowns.

Hiring skilled maintenance personnel, providing them with proper tools, and keeping an inventory of spare parts is costly. However, a breakdown which stops production causing workers and machinery to be idle is even more costly. This means *preventive maintenance* should be part of the maintenance program in a factory.

In recent years there has been a move toward the use of machines and tooling designed to last only for a model run. These machines are sold at a price which makes substantial overhauls uneconomical. This tends to reduce the cost of maintenance, not only by cutting down on the number of maintenance personnel but also by reducing the spare parts inventory. Less money is invested in expensive machinery which may become obsolete. However, careful analysis is required to determine if the total costs of production are lower by adopting such a policy.

AUTOMATION

We have heard a great deal about automation in recent years. It means something different to different people, depending upon their frame of reference. To planners it may mean the promise of a world of factories producing huge quantities of goods requiring little human physical effort. Workers may look upon automation as a threat to their employment, with labor unions seeking to protect the jobs of their members. Owners may view automation as a means of lowering the cost of production, thereby increasing profits. And idealists may see automation as a means for improving living standards through greatly increased production. Actually automation contains all these dimensions.

Automation today represents an extension of mechanization which began in the latter half of the 18th century with the invention of the steam engine by James Watt. *Mechanization* is the application of power-driven tools in factory production and results in a saving of both human energy and time. The textile industry was the first to be mechanized. Mechanization represents the first phase in the process of automation.

The second phase in automation is the use of the *continuous process assembly line* where goods are moved from one stage of the production process to another by use of automatic conveyors. The continuous production process can be seen today in such industries as steel, glass, and nonferrous metals.

The third phase in automation is sometimes is called the *fully automated process.* It consists of the feedback of information from the machine as it inspects it own output and actuates controls to correct deviations from established standards. This type of automation is already in use in the metalworking industries, in oil refining, and in hydroelectricity production. Automatic feedback and control systems are made possible through electronic data processing equipment and controls. The result of the use of electronic computers and increased automation is the elimination of many routine production and clerical jobs in industry. Workers with increased technical knowledge are required to program, check, and maintain these automated processes. With the application of electronic computers managament is finding that information is available more rapidly, in greater quantities, and in wider variety than ever before. Because of the importance of computers today, Chapter 16 is devoted to a discussion of this subject.

ORGANIZATION OF THE PRODUCTION DEPARTMENT

In a manufacturing enterprise the production department is a line department since it contributes directly to the main function of the enterprise. The complexity of the organization of the production department depends on the size of the enterprise and the nature of goods produced. The organization for the production function in a typical manufacturing enterprise is illustrated in Figure 12–1.

Manufacturing management

The executive in charge of manufacturing has a title such as vice president for manufacturing. The line organization directly responsible for production goes through the production manager to the division superintendents and then to the foremen and their assistants. The maintenance department headed by a master mechanic or superintendent of

FIGURE 12–1

Partial organization chart of a typical production department

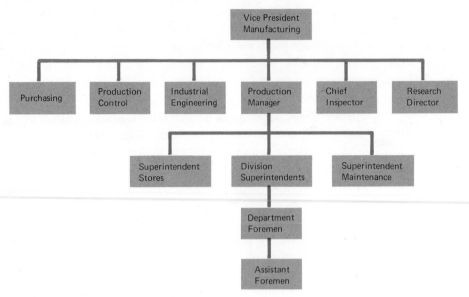

maintenance reports to the production manager, as does the inventory or stores superintendent.

A number of production staff departments assist line managers by performing functions which support manufacturing operations. These typically include production control, industrial engineering, inspection, purchasing, and research. Other departments, particularly personnel and accounting, play an important staff role in the production function. The legal department may assist by assuring that manufacturing processes and products are properly protected by patents and that the enterprise is not infringing on patents of other firms.

The factory foreman

The role of the foreman is extremely important in manufacturing operations despite the increased use of automation and staff persons in the modern factory. Men and women who serve as foremen must be trained in the technical requirements of their departments. While they need not necessarily be more highly skilled technically than any of the workers under their direction, they should have some technical skill. The foremen need to understand how the work of their departments relates to the total operation of the factory.

As important as technical skill is for the foremen, they should also have an awareness of the importance of good human relations in dealing with the workers. This usually requires some training and a thorough understanding of the enterprise's policies and operating rules.

As first-line supervisors the foremen represent the point at which management comes into direct contact with the workers. They must interpret and administer enterprise policies as they affect employees. It is their responsibility to communicate the enterprise's position on questions raised by employees. The typical factory worker views the foremen as being the management. Therefore, the impressions created by them will significantly influence workers' attitudes toward the business enterprise.

SUMMARY

Production consists of providing goods with form utility by turning raw materials and semifinished products into finished goods for either consumer or industrial use.

The location of production facilities involves consideration of such factors as closeness to raw materials and markets for finished goods, access to transportation, availability of labor and utility services, and a satisfactory tax structure.

The first steps in the production system are research and product design and process design. This involves factory layout, machinery selection, and building of prototypes. Production control and scheduling, purchasing, and inventory control are also important elements in production. Other significant elements in the production system are motion and time analysis, quality control, and maintenance. The purchase of capital equipment involves a number of special problems.

Automation progresses from mechanization to the continuous process assembly line to the fully automated process which has a control system to correct deviations from established standards.

The vice president of manufacturing customarily is in charge of the production system. In large factories an extensive organization is necessary to support the foreman, which is the point at which management is in direct contact with the work force.

TERMS FOR REVIEW

production	*finished-goods inventories*
product design	*capital equipment*
factory layout	*motion and time analysis*
production control	*quality control*
production scheduling	*maintenance force*
purchasing	*automation*
raw materials	*foreman*
work in process	

QUESTIONS

1. *a.* What advantages does your area have for the location of manufacturing enterprises? Talk with Chamber of Commerce personnel, public utilities managers, and realtors to develop this information.

    b. What type of manufacturing activities would be particularly desirable for your community?

    c. What negative as well as positive implications are there for a community as the result of a new factory?

2. Examine current publications and find specific examples of research which has resulted in new industrial or consumer products.

3. If possible, arrange with the personnel or public relations department to tour a factory in your area. Observe the type of factory layout and the machinery which is used.

4. What are some various examples of the application of "quality" to a product? Why would quality specifications be quite different for a product depending upon its intended use?

5. If a manufacturer is able to produce a component part for less than its purchase price would you advise the enterprise to go ahead and produce it? Explain your answer.

6. Why is the purchase of capital equipment an important decision in most enterprises?

7. What factors make the position of factory foreman an important and difficult one? What does this imply for the top management of a manufacturing enterprise?

8. After a study of materials in the library, write a 300-word summary either supporting or opposing the statement that automation results in the elimination of jobs and causes higher levels of unemployment.

Business briefs

Float the glass

In its first-quarter 1975 report to shareholders, PPG Industries announced a new "float" method for producing flat glass which reportedly yields more uniform, higher quality glass than the previously used production process. The new process has been installed in PPG's Wichita Falls, Texas, factory where it is expected to result in lower operating costs. The production capacity of the new line will be equal to the plant's initial production line which was 200 million square feet of glass yearly.

The original "float" process for manufacturing flat glass was developed more than 20 years ago by Pilkington Brothers, Ltd., in England. This method produced flat glass at lower cost than earlier methods which involved a complicated roller system. Following Pilkington's development of the float process, PPG and other glass manufacturers paid license fees to the English enterprise for a number of years for use of the technological process.

The new PPG float process consists of mixing and melting raw ingredients for glass in a high-temperature furnace. A "stream" of molten glass of the desired production width, normally 160 inches, is formed at the refining or exit end of the melting furnace. By a novel delivery system the stream then flows as a production-width layer of glass onto molten metal in a sealed chamber or bath. The ribbon of molten glass, supported by the perfectly flat molten metal, flows through the bath and gradually cools until its undersurface is hard enough to be conveyed by rollers without marring the finish. Then the glass is cooled, washed, and cut into desired sizes with automatic equipment.

PPG indicates that the new process is covered by basic patents in the United States and many foreign countries. Possibilities exist for converting existing float glass production facilities to the new process. PPG may license other flat glass manufacturers to use the process for a fee.

1. What benefits can PPG expect from this new manufacturing process?
2. *a.* What risks did PPG take in attempting to develop the new float process?
   b. What alternative course of action could PPG have taken regarding development of a new production process?
3. What possible benefits for the general public may float from this new process?

Metrication mayhem

Metrication, the transition to the metric system of weights and measures, is not only an issue of concern to the public in general but also to business managers, purchasing agents, and skilled laborers such as machinists. For example, machinists who provide their own tools might spend as much as $4,000 each for a new set of metric-measure tools. Opposition to metrication has come from some labor unions unless government subsidies are provided.

Many U.S. business enterprises are resisting the switch to the metric system. This was especially true during the 1974–75 recession. Costs of retooling, training, and product redesign place short-run pressures on profits in many enterprises.

However, conversion to the metric system can streamline industrial measurements and specifications resulting in reduced costs over the long run. As an example, the American National Standards Institute (ANSI) states that the new Optimum Metric Fastener System calls for 25 standard thread sizes instead of the present 59. Product lines could be streamlined, inventories could be reduced, and other benefits of standardization could be realized such as longer production runs. American industry could save an estimated $500 million annually through production economies stemming just from the new fastener system.

For several years Congress has considered legislation to provide federal subsidies to reduce the expense of conversion to the metric system. Proposed legislation would establish a federal metric board to evaluate subsidy requests.

In 1975 most nations except the United States, Yemen, Liberia, Burma, and Brunei were on the metric system. Many multinational business enterprises such as General Motors, IBM, and International Harvester are establishing metric standards without waiting for government to require or subsidize the shift.

1. Should metrication be pushed for the United States in view of the costs of conversion?
2. Should government provide subsidies to business and labor for metrication? Why or why not?

Cases

The Drivewell Corporation

The Drivewell Corporation has been in business for one year. It is engaged in the design and manufacture of devices and component parts for manufacturers in the trucking industry. The founder of Drivewell, Jim Schollenbach, had been a successful engineer in the industry for a number of years. He had considerable experience in the invention of new products and had supervised the establishment of a new manufacturing plant for a former employer. Schollenbach organized his company after he became dissatisfied with the management of the firm where he had been associated. He had long dreamed of going into business so he could be his own boss. He felt his products were simpler, more efficient, and could be sold profitably for the same or slightly lower prices than competing products.

During the early months of the Drivewell Corporation most of Schollenbach's time was spent in handling the many varied details necessary to starting a new enterprise. Finances had been a limiting factor although he had been able to negotiate a major borrowing arrangement with a local bank to go along with limited equity funds. A draftsman, sales manager, and a few general machinists were hired along with a part-time clerical girl who kept the company's books with the assistance of a local certified public accounting firm.

Manufacturing operations and office work were carried out in a small plant which was rented on a monthly basis. Emphasis was placed upon developing pilot models which could be used for samples to be tried out by prospective customers. These pilot models met with a good response in the industry. Within a few months some limited orders were being produced and shipped.

However, Schollenbach was disappointed that things were not moving along as rapidly as he had hoped.

He was discussing his problems with Herb Johnston, a friend who had been helpful in organizing the enterprise.

"Even though we planned for a period of time in getting operations started," began Schollenbach, "I never dreamed it would take so much of my time in dealing with details. Also, we have encountered numerous delays in obtaining parts. For example, one of our main products requires a particular type of rubber bushing which is not standard in the industry at present. As is the customary practice we paid for a special mold which we put in the hands of a large rubber manufacturer when we placed our initial order. As it turned out, we had to contend with a strike in the rubber industry. Then when production started again our order must have been pushed back down the line. The bushings arrived over seven weeks later than the date I had been promised. As we get into volume production we can afford to place large quantity orders on these bushings. However, we really were delayed getting out pilot models and on an initial order for a customer because of the failure to get the first batch of bushings."

"How about other raw materials," asked Johnston, "do you have this problem with other suppliers?"

"Partially," answered Schollenbach. "Since we are a small purchaser we aren't able to command much respect by the big companies in getting any special treatment for our orders. We have been able to buy steel from a local distributor. Much of our steel fabrication has been done in our shop for the pilot models. Later on we will place special tooling in the hands of a particular steel manufacturer which will cut down on our fabricating costs. However, this tooling will cost several thousand dollars and we aren't ready for that now either in terms of volume of production or finances.

"Another problem we have had is getting delivery on the proper kind of springs. One of the spring manufacturers we have been dealing with shipped us an order of the wrong spring. We were able to adapt our models to this spring because of the necessity of getting our orders out. But this has been time consuming and somewhat more costly than we had anticipated.

"The most encouraging part of our business so far has been the excellent reception that our pilot models have received when they have been placed in operation in the field. The reports have been good from the first. Enough pilot models are now in use that we can begin to expect some substantial orders in the near future. Morale is high among our employees because we all believe in the product, but it will be good to get some profitable contracts under our belts."

1. What are the major problems facing Jim Schollenbach in expanding the Drivewell Corporation's operations?
2. What, if anything, can Schollenbach do to deal with these problems?
3. From the point of view of a purchasing agent for a large manufacturer, at the present time what would be the strengths of selecting the

Drivewell Corporation for an order of component parts? What weaknesses would the Drivewell Corporation present from the point of view of a large manufacturer who might like to use its parts?

The Sunflower Dairy

The purchasing agent for the Sunflower Dairy was reviewing the sales proposals of manufacturers of metal tanks which were needed to equip an expansion of Sunflower's milk-processing facilities. The purchasing agent recalled the conversation he had had with the salesman from the Walter Monroe Container Company. The product line of the Monroe Company was more expensive than top management of Sunflower Dairy initially had in mind. However, the purchasing agent had consented to visit the Monroe manufacturing plant along with the chief engineer of Sunflower Dairy who was responsible for the expansion project.

Upon arriving at Monroe's plant the purchasing agent and the chief engineer were greeted by Monroe's sales manager, Tom Huntington, who quickly got down to business. "Gentlemen," he said, "we have invited you here to show you first hand what our capabilities are for producing stainless steel tanks that will meet your needs for a quality product."

The sales manager and the two visitors toured the company's manufacturing facilities. Sunflower's chief engineer was impressed with the cleanliness of the manufacturing plant which fabricated metal products and the apparent industry of the workmen as they went about their production duties. When he asked the sales manager about this general attitude of productivity on the part of the work force the sales manager replied, "We have had seven expansions of our plant in the past ten years. Our work force is well paid by local labor market standards. Management emphasizes high quality on all work. This attitude goes right down to the first-line supervisors and to the men who are doing the work on the floor. The success we have enjoyed with our products by emphasizing quality workmanship and being willing to pay for it has justified the higher prices we have had to charge."

Using a medium-size container the sales manager pointed out the attention given to finishing the outside of the tanks with final grinding and polishing by hand. The purpose of this extra work was to give a pleasing appearance to the product. Special attention was given in the design phase of such equipment to provide more safety features than were customarily required. "We realize," the sales manager indicated, "that many of the purchasers of our products have plant tours by their customers and the general public. We think an attractive, well-designed piece of machinery is important from a public relations viewpoint as well as from the point of view of the production manager."

The sales manager of Monroe Company also showed them how the fillets[1] on the inside of the tanks were carefully filled in and finished to eliminate the possibility of residue building up in the close corners of the tanks. This feature not only represented a health and safety feature, but made it easier for the tanks to be cleaned and reduced maintenance costs for the user.

After the plant tour the sales manager discussed the product which the Monroe Company hoped to sell to the Sunflower Dairy for their expanded facility. He pointed out how some of the specifications of the Monroe product exceeded those called for in the initial request for price quotations on the part of Sunflower. He then outlined why his company felt these changes were desirable. Monroe engineers had made some design changes which they believed improved the product and made it easier to service. The sales manager frankly stated that Monroe's price was as low as was possible in view of the product and quality. In spite of this, the purchasing agent for Sunflower Dairy knew that the price was some 10 percent higher than competing products which would lack some of the quality features but which would probably provide satisfactory service.

Upon their return to the home office, as the two Sunflower executives discussed their trip, the chief engineer concluded by saying, "I am very impressed with the Monroe operation. They have given me some good ideas on equipment design. However, their price is higher and you know what the president said at the last management meeting about costs on the new expansion."

1. What issues face the purchasing agent at this point?
2. How should he proceed to deal with these issues?
3. Appraise the production and marketing philosophy of the Walter Monroe Container Company in the light of a competitive market for their products.

---

[1] A fillet is a concave junction formed when two surfaces come together. In this case two metal pieces come together to form the edge of a tank creating a concave surface inside the tank.

section five

Accounting
and finance

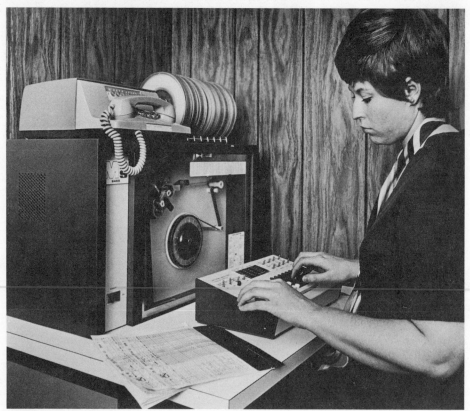

An enterprise's accounting system can include recording business transactions on magnetic tape for computer processing.

13

Understanding accounting statements

*A*ccounting has been called the language of business. It provides the basis for reporting profits or losses and for presentation of the economic picture of the enterprise. You should understand the basic accounting statements whatever your role in the organization. Because an understanding of accounting is so important to management, the following issues are discussed:

How is accounting information used by management?

Why are financial statements important for groups other than management?

What are the basic accounting statements?

How are these statements analyzed?

THE USE OF ACCOUNTING INFORMATION

Accounting consists of recording, measuring, analyzing, and reporting the results of enterprise transactions in monetary terms. An enterprise's accounting system should be designed to evaluate the financial implications of decisions and to assess the possible consequences of future courses of action. Accounting statements should be prepared on a consistent basis from one time period to the next to make comparisons meaningful.

The information provided by the enterprise's accounting system is of interest to groups both inside and outside the business enterprise. To be effective management needs financial progress reports made on a periodic basis. Groups outside the company which make use of financial statements include stockholders, bankers, and governmental agencies.

Management uses of accounting

An essential use of an enterprise's accounting system is to determine operating results. Accounting provides the basis for determining profits or losses over a given period of time. The measurement of income and the statement of an enterprise's financial position are important to the management process, especially for control.

For control purposes accounting provides a basis for establishing quantitative standards, for measuring performance, and for analyzing variations from expectations. Accounting reports are helpful for communicating plans throughout the organization. Standards set in financial terms are easily understood and provide a basis for evaluating subsequent performance. These evaluations may be helpful in determining promotions, commendations, or salary increases, as well as corrective action, demotions, or possible dismissals.

Outsiders' use of accounting information

Information derived from the enterprise's accounting system is useful to individuals and organizations outside the enterprise. Outsiders who make use of accounting data include stockholders, government agencies, banks, and creditors of the enterprise.

Stockholders' use. In the small enterprise organized as a proprietorship or a partnership where the owners are active in the business there is no need to publicize financial results for the benefit of the owners. The owners are already aware of the enterprise's profitability and financial condition. However, in today's large corporations there is a separation of ownership and management. The thousands of stockholders who are the owners of the corporation have no direct voice in the management of the enterprise. They have no knowledge of results unless published financial reports are made available to them. The managements of widely owned corporations provide this information to their shareholders through regularly published financial statements. This information is made available to the general public. It is of interest not only to present stockholders of the corporation but also is necessary for analysis by those who may be considering the purchase of stock in the corporation. Thus both present and prospective shareholders are vitally interested in the financial statements of large corporations.

Governmental use. The reporting of financial information is required by numerous governmental agencies. Tax authorities require detailed financial reports from business enterprises to accompany the payment of a wide variety of local, state, and federal taxes. In recent years there has been a move toward greater cooperation between state and federal income tax authorities to assure better conformation with tax regulations of both. Public disclosure of the financial standing of widely held corporations is required by the Securities and Exchange Commission, an agency of the federal government established in 1934. The SEC requires that corporations provide adequate information to investors about new security issues and reveal dealings in their own stock by enterprise executives. Stock exchanges and investment advisors are also subject to SEC regulations to protect stockholders.

Banks' and creditors' use. Accounting information about enterprise operations is required by banks and other financial institutions before they lend money to the enterprise. The business manager should be prepared to provide complete information, not only about past results of the enterprise but also a financial projection of future plans. This information is needed before a banker will lend funds. Financial planning should include evidence that management has considered its needs carefully and has estimated when the loan can be repaid if it is granted.

A *trade creditor* supplies merchandise or services to an enterprise and is willing to ship merchandise without requiring cash payment upon delivery. Before a trade creditor will ship merchandise to a firm for the first time, it is customary to analyze the accounting statements of the customer to determine that the chances are good that the merchandise will be paid for according to the terms of the credit. The terms of trade credit vary with the industry and local circumstances. Customarily, trade credit is granted for periods of 30 to 60 days with cash discounts of 1 or 2 percent of the billed price being given for prompt payment, such as within ten days from the date on the invoice. Whatever the credit terms, the purchasing enterprise should observe them to maintain its good credit rating.

THE BASIC ACCOUNTING STATEMENTS

The balance sheet and the income statement are the two most widely used accounting statements. They provide much information about the enterprise's financial condition and operations. An understanding of these statements is essential for financial analysis and control. A third accounting statement called the statement of changes in financial position is now prepared. Owners and creditors find it a useful tool in addition to the balance sheet and the income statement.

The balance sheet

The *balance sheet* is a financial picture of the enterprise at the close of business on a particular date, usually at the end of a month, a quarter, or a year. It is a statement of the assets which the enterprise owns and the claims against those assets. The claims against the enterprise's assets are either claims by outsiders, called liabilities, or claims by the owners, called owners' equity or net worth. It is this balancing of the assets of the business enterprise against the claims to the assets that gives the balance sheet its name. Therefore, the equation which represents the balance sheet is:

$$\text{Assets} = \text{Liabilities} + \text{Net Worth}$$

Assume that a new enterprise is started by a person who set aside $5,000 to initiate the business. The balance sheet of this new business enterprise after this initial act would be:

$$\text{Cash \$5,000 (assets)} = \text{Owner's equity \$5,000 (claims)}$$

Next assume the owner-manager went to a bank and borrowed $3,000 to provide funds to begin operations. After this transaction the balance sheet of the enterprise would be:

Assets		Liabilities	
Cash......................	$8,000	Bank loan....................	$3,000
		Net worth	
		Owner's equity..............	5,000
		Total liabilities and	
Total assets................	$8,000	net worth..............	$8,000

The balance sheet will continue to reflect changes in the accounts of the business enterprise as additional transactions occur. The balance sheet lists only those assets which are owned by the enterprise on a specified date.

The balance sheet in Figure 13–1 illustrates the simplified year-end statement of assets, liabilities, and net worth for a typical retail corporation. A discussion of each item on the balance sheet follows.

Assets. Current assets are those assets which are cash, realizable in cash, or expected to be sold or consumed during the year. Current assets are customarily listed on the balance sheet in order of liquidity. The liquidity of an asset is measured by how readily it can be turned into cash.

Cash is listed first since it is easiest to transfer into other assets or to use in paying what is owed by the enterprise. Normally cash is held in bank accounts, although small amounts may be kept in the enter-

FIGURE 13–1

JEANS, INCORPORATED
Balance Sheet
As of December 31, 1975

Assets		Liabilities	
Current assets		Current liabilities	
Cash....................	$ 6,000	Accounts payable........	$ 4,900
Accounts receivable......	3,000	Wages payable...........	1,200
Inventories.............	9,000	Taxes payable	1,000
Prepaid insurance.......	600	Miscellaneous payables..	300
Total Current Assets..	$18,600	Total Current Liabilities..........	$ 7,400
		Long-term liabilities	
Fixed assets		Bank loan, due 1980......	7,000
Fixtures and equipment..	$15,000		
Less: Accumulated depreciation...........	1,500	Total Liabilities.....	$14,400
Net Fixed Assets...	$13,500		
		Net worth	
Other assets		Common stock............	$10,000
Trademarks.............	$ 500	Retained earnings.........	8,500
Miscellaneous assets....	300	Total Owners' Equity.............	$18,500
Total Other Assets.	$ 800	Total Liabilities	
Total Assets........	$32,900	and Net Worth...	$32,900

prise's cash drawer for making change in retail transactions or for small expenditures.

Accounts receivable are amounts owed to the enterprise by customers who have purchased goods on credit. Accounts receivable are considered to be relatively liquid since they normally should be collected within a few weeks or months.

Inventories are the cost of the stock of goods the enterprise has available for sale to customers. The varied nature of inventories in a manufacturing enterprise is discussed in Chapter 12 on production.

Prepaid expenses are expenses which have been paid for and not yet used. A typical example is a fire insurance policy where the premium is paid for two years at a time and provides insurance protection next year as well as during the current year.

Fixed assets, sometimes called capital assets, represent long-term assets such as land, buildings, and equipment which will not be turned into cash but which are necessary for the operation of the enterprise. The gross amount of the fixed asset account represents the acquisition cost of such assets. *Depreciation* is the accounting charge to reflect the decline in the value of fixed assets over a period of time. *Accumulated depreciation* is the total amount of the cost of fixed assets which has been charged as an expense of using those assets over the years. The accumulated depreciation is subtracted from the fixed asset accounts to derive a book value of fixed assets as of the date of the balance sheet.

Other assets is a "catchall" category that includes all assets not listed either as current or fixed. Other assets are sometimes intangible in nature, such as patents and trademarks. *Patents* are exclusive rights to a product or process conferred by government authority to the holder. *Trademarks* are words or symbols which identify a particular brand of merchandise. Registered trademarks are protected by legal restrictions against their use by unauthorized persons or enterprises.

Liabilities. *Liabilities* are amounts owed by the business enterprise to its creditors. *Current liabilities* are those obligations which will fall due within a short period of time, customarily within the coming year.

Accounts payable are amounts owed to suppliers for purchases of inventory goods. Sometimes *notes payable* are signed to recognize formally the financial obligations to banks, to other financial institutions which supply money, or to vendors which supply merchandise.

Wages payable represents amounts owed to employees for their work efforts. This obligation is paid each payday. The amount which accrues will depend upon the level of wages paid and the frequency of their payment, such as weekly or monthly.

Taxes payable is the size of the enterprise's current tax liability to various governmental bodies. Customarily, a large proportion of this figure is to cover income tax liabilities which build up with profitable operations. This must be paid according to the tax schedules set by federal and state authorities. Sometimes the taxes payable account on the balance sheet will be broken down into the types of taxes payable, such as income taxes, social security taxes, and property taxes.

Miscellaneous payables is another "catchall" account for any outsiders' recognized financial claims against the enterprise which have not been listed elsewhere. The *total current liabilities* is the amount of debts which management expects to have to pay within a year.

Long-term liabilities are those financial obligations which do not have to be paid off during the coming year. These may arise from a variety of borrowing arrangements. In the Jeans, Inc., balance sheet there is one long-term liability, a bank loan due in 1980.

Net worth. The *net worth,* or owners' equity, section of the balance sheet shows the amount of the owners' claims to the assets of the enterprise. The net worth section of a corporation is divided into various accounts such as preferred stock, common stock, and retained earnings. These divisions are for legal or accounting purposes and do not have much financial significance except for preferred stockholders who constitute a different class of owners.

Preferred stock, of which there is none in Jeans, Inc., is the class of ownership shares in a corporation which has preference over common stock as to a stated amount of cash dividends each year. Preferred stockholders also have priority over the common stockholders if the corporation should be liquidated. If the corporation's assets were sold, the preferred stockholders would have a claim to a stated amount of funds after all liabilities had been paid. After the preferred stockholders' interests were satisfied, the common stockholders would divide the remainder of the funds from the sale of the corporation's assets in proportion to the number of shares of common stock each held.

When a corporation's common stock is sold, the proceeds are recorded in the *common stock* account. This account reflects the amount of funds received by the corporation for the common stock which has been issued. A detailed balance sheet would normally indicate the number of shares of common stock held by the corporation's owners. In the case of Jeans, Inc., the number of shares of common stock outstanding is 1,000.

The *retained earnings* account, sometimes called *earned surplus,* shows the amount of profits earned by the enterprise over the years and kept in the business to strengthen and expand operations. The amount of retained earnings varies each year depending upon annual profits or losses and the amount of earnings paid to the owners in dividends.

The balance sheets for corporations, partnerships, and proprietorships are similar in the listing of assets and liabilities. The accounts will be designated differently for ownership interests among these different forms of business organization. However, each type of enterprise has a net worth section which shows the owners' claims to the assets of the enterprise.

The income statement

In contrast to the balance sheet which portrays assets, liabilities, and net worth as of a certain date, the income statement summarizes the revenues and expenses that have occurred in the enterprise's operations between two points of time. Thus, the income statement is drawn up to cover a period such as a year or some other period of time over which

An introduction to the American business enterprise

management wants to measure its operations. The income statement is sometimes called the profit and loss statement or the operating statement. It can be expressed in the following simple equation:

$$\text{Revenue} - \text{Expenses} = \text{Net Income}$$

or stated using different terminology,

$$\text{Sales} - \text{Costs} = \text{Profit}$$

Example of a corporation's income statement. Figure 13–2 is an illustration of a simplified income statement, or profit and loss statement, of Jeans, Inc., for the year's operations ending December 31, 1975.

FIGURE 13–2

JEANS, INCORPORATED
Income Statement
For the year ended December 31, 1975

Net sales			$80,000
Less: Cost of goods sold			
Inventory beginning January 1, 1975	$ 6,000		
Add purchases for the year	40,000		
Cost of merchandise available for sale	$46,000		
Less ending inventory Dec. 31, 1975	9,000		
Total cost of goods sold			37,000
Gross income on sales			$43,000
Less: Operating expenses:			
Selling expenses			
Salesclerks' wages	$11,000		
Advertising expense	3,000		
Depreciation expense-fixtures and equipment	800		
Supplies expense	500		
Miscellaneous expenses	100		
Total selling expenses	$15,400		
General and administrative expenses			
Manager's wages	$ 8,400		
Rent	9,000		
Insurance	700		
Miscellaneous taxes	1,800		
Miscellaneous expenses	400		
Total general and administrative expenses	$20,300		
Total operating expenses			35,700
Operating income			$ 7,300
Financial expenses:			
Interest expense			500
Profit before income taxes			$ 6,800
Income taxes			1,400
Net Profit			$ 5,400

Each item on the statement is discussed as an example of a typical retailer's income statement.

Net sales means that all cash discounts given for prompt payment of goods and credits for returned merchandise have been deducted from the gross sales.

Cost of goods sold is the value of merchandise sold calculated at its costs rather than the price for which it is sold. For a retailer or wholesaler that does not change the form of the goods it sells, the calculation of cost of goods sold is relatively simple. The cost of all purchases made by the retail enterprise is added to the value of its inventory at the beginning of the year. This gives the cost of goods available for sale. Then the value of the inventory at the end of the year is subtracted to give the cost of the goods sold during the accounting period.

In a manufacturing enterprise the cost of goods sold includes the costs added during the manufacturing process. Thus, a calculation of cost of goods manufactured is made by adding the costs of raw materials used during the year, direct labor, factory expenses such as utilities and supplies, insurance, and depreciation on plant and equipment. The cost of goods manufactured is added to the beginning inventory. This sum represents the total amount of manufacturing costs. From this total subtract the value of the inventories at the end of the accounting period, and the difference is the cost of goods sold. Although in actual practice the determination of cost of goods sold is somewhat more complicated than this because of different types of inventories and problems of allocating various costs, this is the essence of the process.

Gross income is found by subtracting the cost of goods sold from net sales and is the amount from which all other expenses must be deducted.

Selling, general, and *administrative* expenses are deducted from gross income to give operating income.

Operating income is the profit generated from the operation of the enterprise before interest payments and income taxes are deducted.

Interest expense is the cost of borrowed money and is deducted from operating income in Figure 13–2. Then federal income taxes are calculated based on the *profit before taxes.*

The bottom figure on the income statement represents the *net profit* for the period. If this figure is negative the enterprise has suffered a loss during the accounting period and the owners' equity shown on the balance sheet is decreased by that amount. If profits have been earned the owner's equity is increased.

Supporting records. Each of the accounts shown in the balance sheet and income statement is a summary of detailed accounting records which reflect individual business transactions and provide specific information about the account. For example, on the balance sheet of Jeans, Inc. the accounts receivable total of $3,000 is substantiated by an accounts receivable ledger showing each customer who has received credit from the retailer. These individual accounts show the value of merchandise sold, the date of the transaction, and the amount and date of payments received from the customer along with other identifying information which could be used to check the details of the enterprise's relationship with its customers.

The manager has more accounting information available than the balance sheet, the income statement, and the statement of changes in financial position. However, these statements provide a summary of the enterprise's operations and a basis for further analysis.

Statement of changes in financial position

A third accounting statement, that of *changes in financial position,* draws information from both the balance sheet and the income state-

FIGURE 13–3

JEANS, INCORPORATED
Statement of Changes in Financial Position—Cash Basis
For the year ended December 31, 1975

Cash sources (inflows):		
From operations:		
From sales..	$80,000	
Decrease in accounts receivable......................	500	
Total sources from operations......................	$80,500	
Less: Cash used for expenses.......................	73,800	
Cash generated from operations.....................		$ 6,700
From other sources:		
Investment by owners (new stock issued)............	$ 3,000	
Bank loan..	7,000	
Cash received from other sources...................		10,000
Total cash sources during the year (inflows).......		$16,700
Cash applications (outflows):		
To purchase new store fixtures.......................	$ 9,000	
To increase inventories.............................	3,000	
To reduce accounts payable..........................	2,700	
Total cash applied during the year (outflows)......		$14,700
Change—Increase in Cash Balance during the Year.......		$ 2,000

ment. This statement summarizes the funds generated from operations and other sources and reveals the use of these funds to show the changes in the enterprise's financial position occurring over the period. Sometimes this presentation is called a *source and application of funds statement. Funds* may be defined in several ways. Two common ways of defining funds are as cash or as working capital (current assets minus current liabilities). In this chapter we define funds as cash.

Figure 13–3 presents a simplified statement of changes in financial position. The figures shown were taken from the income statement, the balance sheet, and other accounting data. In the interest of simplification the example will not trace through their derivation.

This statement shows the changes which occurred in the enterprise's cash position during the year. Sometimes such a statement of funds is called a "where got—where gone" statement regarding cash.

The three basic accounting statements can be summarized as follows:

1. The income statement shows the profits which were earned over a period of time.
2. The balance sheet shows the financial position of the enterprise at a specific point in time.
3. The statement of changes in financial position reflects funds flows over a period of time.

THE FINANCIAL ANALYSIS OF ACCOUNTING STATEMENTS

Once the basic accounting statements have been compiled from information provided by the enterprise's accounting system, the analyst must interpret these statements. The absolute figures contained in these accounting statements can be used to compute ratios which can be compared with previous years or with other enterprises in the same industry. Ratios measuring an enterprise's liquidity, profitability, and solvency are helpful tools of financial analysis.

Measures of liquidity

Liquidity is the ability of the enterprise to meet its current financial obligations when they become due. Measures of enterprise liquidity are widely used in analyzing short-term financial strength and operating efficiency.

Current ratio. The current ratio is the relationship of current assets to current liabilities. The current ratio for Jeans, Inc., is:

$$\frac{\text{Current assets}}{\text{Current liabilities}} = \frac{\$18,600}{\$7,400} = 2.5 \text{ times or 2.5 to 1}$$

This means that current assets are 2.5 times the amount of current liabilities. The larger this ratio, the stronger is the enterprise's current financial position. A widely-used rule of thumb for a satisfactory current ratio is 2 to 1. The current ratio is the most commonly used balance sheet ratio.

Acid test ratio. The acid test ratio is the measure of *quick assets* to current liabilities. Quick assets consist of cash, short-term investments which are held instead of cash, and accounts (or notes) receivable. For Jeans, Inc., the acid test ratio is:

$$\frac{\text{Quick assets}}{\text{Current liabilities}} = \frac{\$9,000}{\$7,400} = 1.2 \text{ times or 1.2 to 1}$$

The acid test ratio is a measure of short-term liquidity like the current ratio except that inventories and prepaid expenses are excluded from the assets which may be turned into cash. This makes the acid test ratio a more severe test of enterprise liquidity. A widely-used rule of thumb for a satisfactory acid test ratio is 1 to 1.

Inventory turnover. Because much of an enterprise's current assets are typically invested in inventory, the inventory turnover ratio can be a useful calculation for management. This ratio indicates the number of times that merchandise moves through the enterprise during the period under study. Inventory turnover is computed by dividing the cost of goods sold by the average inventory on hand over the period.

Average inventory is commonly determined by adding the beginning and ending inventories for the accounting period and dividing by 2. The inventory for Jeans, Inc., on January 1, 1975, was $6,000 and on December 31, 1975, was $9,000. Therefore the average inventory was $7,500 for 1975. The average inventory turnover during the year was:

$$\frac{\text{Cost of goods sold}}{\text{Average inventory}} = \frac{\$37,000}{\$7,500} = 4.9 \text{ times.}$$

Since a profit normally is earned each time inventory is sold, a relatively high inventory is desirable. However, too large an inventory turnover may mean that sales are being missed if inventories are too small in relation to potential sales. On the other hand, a lower inventory turnover may mean sales are down or that some inventory is no longer attractive to customers. At times inventory turnover may decline if management builds up inventory to anticipate greater sales in the future.

Collection of credit sales. The *average collection period* may be calculated to analyze how promptly credit customers are paying their accounts. This is sometimes called *days' sales outstanding in receivables* and is calculated by taking the ratio of accounts receivable to average daily credit sales.

In most manufacturing enterprises nearly all sales are made on some type of credit. In retailing enterprises the accounting records will show which sales are for cash and which are on credit. The average daily credit sales for Jeans, Inc., during 1975 amounted to $110 a day. Thus, the calculation of the average collection period for 1975 is:

$$\frac{\text{Accounts receivable}}{\text{Average daily credit sales}} = \frac{\$3,000}{\$110} = 27.3 \text{ days' credit sales}$$

outstanding in
accounts receivable

Since the clothing store's credit terms are for payment within 30 days, it would appear that on the average credit customers are paying their accounts promptly.

Measures of profitability

Overall measures of profitability may be derived from the income statement and the balance sheet. The ratios of net profit to sales and net profit to net worth are discussed with the vertical analysis of the income statement.

Vertical analysis of income statement. The *vertical analysis* of the income statement consists of a percentage relationship of all items in the income statement to sales. Vertical analysis is useful when comparing the enterprise's current operations with past periods or with industry statistics. The percentage breakdown of Jeans, Inc.'s income statement derived from Figure 13–2 is:

Vertical analysis, income statement For the year ended December 31, 1975		
Net sales..		100.0%
Less: Cost of goods sold..................		46.3
Gross income on sales......................		53.7%
Less operating expenses:		
Selling expenses........................	19.2%	
Gen. and adm. exp.....................	25.4	
Total operating expenses.................		44.6
Income from operations....................		9.1%
Less: Interest expense....................		.6
Profit before income taxes.................		8.5%
Income taxes.............................		1.7
Net Profit................................		6.8%

The vertical analysis of the income statement highlights the relative importance of the various expenses. By comparing changes in expense percentages from one year to another, management can diagnose areas which need improvement to raise profitability.

Net profit margin. The last item in the vertical analysis shows the *net profit margin*. This important measure of profitability is the ratio of net profit to net sales. For Jeans, Inc., in 1975 the net profit margin was:

$$\frac{\text{Net profit}}{\text{Net sales}} = \frac{\$5,400}{\$80,000} = 6.8\%$$

If this ratio seems too low, an examination of the different expenses shown in percentage form in the vertical analysis can be made to determine which expenses are out of line.

Return on owners' investment. Since the profits earned by an enterprise represent the return on the owners' investment, another important measure of profitability is that of *net profit to net worth* (owners' equity). For the clothing store in 1975 this ratio was:

$$\frac{\text{Net profit}}{\text{Net worth}} = \frac{\$5,400}{\$18,500} = 29.2\%$$

This ratio shows the rate of return on the owners' investment. It is a measure of how efficiently the corporation is using the funds provided by the stockholders.

Measures of solvency

Liquidity, which was discussed earlier, refers to the ability of the enterprise to meet its cash needs for current business operations. *Solvency* refers to the enterprise's ability to pay long-term financial obligations when they fall due as well as to meet the interest payments on outstanding debt. By borrowing more money the owners of the enterprise assume more risk since these debts will have to be repaid in the future. Measures of solvency include the ratio of owners' equity to total debt, long-term debt to total assets, and the number of times interest is earned.

Owners' equity to total debt. The ratio of *owners' equity to total debt* measures the owners' investment compared with the claims against the enterprise by creditors. This is an important measure of how much protection creditors have against shrinkage of the value of the assets of the enterprise. For Jeans, Inc., the ratio is:

$$\frac{\text{Owners' equity}}{\text{Total debt}} = \frac{\$18,500}{\$14,400} = 1.3 \text{ times or } 1.3 \text{ to } 1$$

This means for each $1 of liabilities outstanding on December 31, 1975, there was $1.30 of net worth. The larger this ratio the greater the protection for creditors and the less risk that the business enterprise will be faced with insolvency.

Long-term debt to total assets. The ratio of long-term debt to total assets measures the proportion of debt which falls due more than a year in the future in relation to the total assets of the enterprise. For the clothing store this ratio is:

$$\frac{\text{Long-term debt}}{\text{Total assets}} = \frac{\$7,000}{\$32,900} = 21.3\%$$

This ratio shows what proportion of the enterprise's assets are being financed by long-term debt. Both interest and principal repayments must be made according to a schedule agreed upon when long-term funds are borrowed. Since future business conditions cannot be forecast with extreme accuracy, the prudent management is unwilling to finance too great a proportion of total assets by use of long-term debt. To do so might jeopardize the enterprise's solvency at some time in the future as the result of circumstances which arise subsequent to the borrowing. Management should analyze the nature of its anticipated cash inflows over future years before undertaking long-term borrowing.

Times interest earned. The *number of times interest is earned* is a measure of the enterprise's ability to meet current interest charges on borrowed funds. For Jeans, Inc., this ratio is:

$$\frac{\text{Operating income}}{\text{Interest}} = \frac{\$7,300}{\$500} = 14.6 \text{ times}$$

In this instance the annual interest charge is covered 14.6 times by operating income. The more times interest charges are covered by operating income the safer the situation from the viewpoint of both lender and borrower.

SUMMARY

Accounting is the recording, measuring, analysis, and reporting of enterprise transactions in monetary terms. Management uses accounting

Employment outlook

Accountants

Accountants prepare and analyze financial reports. Those in the field of management accounting provide the financial information that executives need to make intelligent business decisions. They may specialize in taxes, budgeting, investments, or internal auditing (examining and appraising their firms' financial systems and management control procedures).

Employment of accountants is expected to increase rapidly through the mid-1980s as businesses and government agencies continue to expand in size and complexity. Greater use of accounting information in business management, changing tax systems, and growth of large corporations that must provide financial reports to stockholders, all point to excellent opportunities for accountants.

Accountants with college degrees will be in stronger demand than those who lack this training. In addition, the trend toward specialization will create opportunities for persons trained in a specific phase of accounting.

As data processing systems continue to replace manual preparation of accounting records and statements, the need for some lower-level accountants may be reduced or eliminated. On the other hand, many highly-trained accountants will be required to prepare, administer, and analyze the information made available by these systems.

data to determine operating results and for control purposes. Accounting statements are also used by present and potential owners of business enterprises, by governmental agencies, and by present and potential creditors.

The balance sheet presents a financial picture of the business enterprise's assets, liabilities, and owners' equity at a given point in time. Typical current assets include cash, accounts receivable, and inventories. Fixed assets are represented by land, buildings, and equipment. Other assets include patents and trademarks.

Current liabilities usually include accounts payable, wages payable, taxes payable, and miscellaneous payables. Long-term liabilities may be items such as bank loans which do not fall due during the next year.

Owners' equity, or net worth, shows the amount of the owners' claims to the assets of the enterprise.

In contrast to the balance sheet which portrays assets and claims against those assets as of a certain date, the income statement summarizes what has occurred in enterprise transactions between two points of time. The income statement, or the profit and loss statement, shows the revenues during a given period and the expenses for the period. The difference between revenues and expenses is the profit for the period.

The statement of changes in financial position summarizes the funds generated from operations and other sources and reveals the way in which these funds were used between two points of time.

In financial analysis, measures of liquidity analyze the ability of the enterprise to meet its current financial obligations when they become due. The current ratio and the acid test ratio are common measures of liquidity. The average collection period for accounts receivable and the inventory turnover ratio are measures calculated to analyze current operations.

The vertical analysis of the income statement consists of a percentage relationship of all items in the income statement to sales. This shows the relative importance of various expenses.

Measures of overall profitability include the ratios of net profit to sales and net profit to net worth.

Solvency measures the enterprise's ability to pay the principal as well as to meet the required schedule of interest payments on long-term financial obligations. Measures of solvency include the ratio of owners' equity to total debt, the ratio of long-term debt to total assets, and the number of times that interest charges on borrowed funds are earned.

TERMS FOR REVIEW

accounting
balance sheet
owners' equity (net worth)
current assets
fixed assets
current liabilities
long-term liabilities

income statement (profit and loss
statement)
statement of changes in financial
position
liquidity
solvency

QUESTIONS

1. In addition to managers and owners, why are outside groups interested in accounting statements of corporations?
2. Explain the accounting equation.
3. Indicate how changes in assets, liabilities, or net worth sections are reflected in the balance sheet.
4. What information does the income statement provide?
5. Examine either *Moody's Industrial Manual* or *Standard & Poor's Corporation Records* in the library for examples of balance sheets and income statements. In what ways do these vary from the examples in Figures 13–1 and 13–2?
6. Select a balance sheet and income statement of a corporation and suggest changes which would make it more meaningful to the average stockholder.
7. What is the purpose of ratio analysis? Explain the usefulness of the specific ratios relating to liquidity, profitability, and solvency to (*a*) management and (*b*) a potential investor.

Business brief

Fight or switch?

Certified public accountants act as auditors of business enterprises' accounting statements and certify to interested parties that these statements conform with generally accepted accounting principles. However, corporations and public accountants do not always agree over specific issues concerning accounting. Sometimes these disagreements are resolved. In some cases the CPA firm will give the enterprise's accounting statements a qualified opinion.[1] Management prefers not to have a qualified opinion since this reveals to outsiders not only disagreements but sometimes potentially serious financial difficulties. On occasion a business enterprise will dismiss its CPA firm and hire a different outside auditor. Also, CPAs have withdrawn as auditors when conflicts could not be resolved satisfactorily.

An example of a disagreement between a major CPA firm and a client is the case of the enterprise which sold a large tract of Florida real estate. The enterprise wanted to realize profits on the sale immediately. However, the auditors maintained that part of the profits should be deferred until after certain improvements for which the selling enterprise had obligated itself were completed. These improvements included the building of roads, sewers, and a golf course. The CPA finally agreed to let the land sale be reported as a completed transaction after the enterprise's management obtained agreement from the buyers that the buyers would assume responsibility for completion of the improvements.

A variety of disagreements have arisen between CPAs and enterprises over such matters as how to compute tax deductions for subsidiary operations, how to determine tax liabilities in disputes with the Internal Revenue Service, and how to figure the economic life of computer equipment. In addition to friction over accounting practices, enterprises change auditors because they are unhappy with the fees charged by CPA firms. Switches in accountants also occur when a CPA firm believes the extensive use of other CPAs by a corporation's subsidiaries gives the parent corporation's CPA too little control over auditing practices.

Since 1971 the Securities and Exchange Commission has required business enterprises and CPA firms which part company because of disagreements over accounting practices to file public 8-K reports indicating the reasons for the break in relations.

1. What is the purpose of requiring a CPA opinion of a business enterprise's accounting statements?
2. Should the government prohibit a business enterprise from changing its CPA firm when a disagreement between the two arises?
3. When a change of CPAs occurs should the nature of the disagreement be revealed to stockholders in the corporation's annual report?

---

[1] A qualified opinion briefly states the nature of the disagreement which the CPA has with the enterprise's accounting practices.

Cases

The Chocolate Heart Candy Store, Inc.

The Chocolate Heart Candy Store was opened in the new Parkwood Mall, an enclosed regional shopping center, in the summer of 1974 and soon became very popular. In addition to prepackaged assortments the store carried quality candy which was boxed to the individual customer's specification.

In January 1976, the owners of the shop, Mr. and Mrs. James Ford, were reviewing the first full year's operations. Up to that point the only formal accounting statements which they had used had been the balance sheets and income tax returns which were prepared by a tax accounting service. The Fords felt that the candy store was a success, but they believed that some additional analysis would help them make a better judgment in the matter.

In addition to the balance sheet for the year ended December 31, 1974, the records of the Chocolate Heart Candy Store included a record of all checks paid during 1975 and a file of unpaid invoices which were owed to suppliers. All candy sales were for cash.

EXHIBIT 1

Beginning

CHOCOLATE HEART CANDY STORE, INC.
Balance Sheet
December 31, 1974

Assets			Liabilities		
Current assets			Current liabilities		
Cash		$ 900	Wages payable		$ 300
Merchandise inventory		4,100	Accounts payable		2,600
Supplies		300	Income taxes payable		250
		$ 5,300			$ 3,150
Fixed assets			Long-term liabilities		
Fixtures	$8,000		Bank loan, due 1981		3,200
Less: Accumulated			Total liabilities		$ 6,350
depreciation	400	7,600			
			Net worth		
			Common stock	$6,000	
			Retained earnings	550	6,550
			Total Liabilities		
Total Assets		$12,900	and Net Worth		$12,900

Sale for yr *p + L.*

EXHIBIT 2
Taken from the cash records of Chocolate Heart Candy Store, Inc. for 1975

Cash receipts		Cash disbursements	
Cash sales...............	$48,250	Wages paid..............	$11,000
		Rent.....................	5,000
		Advertising..............	2,500
		Utilities..................	1,200
		Insurance................	200
		Interest..................	300
		Income taxes, 1974........	250
		Miscellaneous cash	
		expenses..............	350
		Supplies.................	500
		Paid on accounts payable	
		for merchandise during	
		1975...................	23,600
		Total expenditures....	$44,900
Cash balance,		Cash balance,	
Dec. 31, 1974..............	900	Dec. 31, 1975......	4,250
	$49,150		$49,150

+ *a/c Pay is down 400*

EXHIBIT 3
As of Dec. 31, 1975

Inventory on hand.....................	$3,700
Supplies on hand......................	300
Accounts payable.....................	2,200
Wages payable.......................	300

Ending

Annual depreciation rate on fixed assets is 10 percent of original cost.
Income tax rate is estimated to be 20 percent of taxable income.

1. From the information given in Exhibits 1, 2, and 3 determine:
   a. Sales for 1975. *48250*
   b. Cost of merchandise sold. *23600*
   c. Total expenses for 1975. *46,010*
2. Prepare an income statement for 1975 and a balance sheet as of December 31, 1975.
3. How can these statements be useful to the Fords? What measures could they use to determine how successful they were in their first full year of operation?

Bradley Cafeterias, Inc.

Richard Knight was a loan officer at a Dallas bank. For some time he had been interested in Bradley Cafeterias, Inc., which is an operator of cafeterias and industrial food services.

Knight was one of the stockholders of Bradley Cafeterias. In February 1975 he received the company's annual report for the year ended December 31, 1974, which was mailed to all stockholders. The annual stockholders' meeting would be held in approximately three

EXHIBIT 1

BRADLEY CAFETERIAS, INC.
Balance Sheets
As of December 31
(millions of dollars)

Assets	1974	1973
Current assets		
Cash	$ 5	$ 6
Accounts receivable	6	4
Inventories	8	7
Prepaid expenses	1	1
Total Current Assets	$20	$18
Fixed assets		
Buildings, equipment, and land	48	43
Less: Accumulated depreciation	18	16
Net Fixed Assets	$30	$27
Other assets		
Investments, deposits, etc.	$ 3	$ 3
Total Assets	$53	$48
Liabilities		
Current liabilities		
Accounts payable	$ 5	$ 4
Wages payable	2	2
Taxes payable	2	2
Current loans payable	1	1
Miscellaneous payables	3	2
Total Current Liabilities	$13	$11
Long-term liabilities		
Long-term debts	10	10
Total Liabilities	$23	$21
Net worth		
Common stock	$15	$15
Retained earnings	15	12
Total Owners' Equity	$30	$27
Total Liabilities and Net Worth	$53	$48

weeks. Mr. Knight did not plan to attend the stockholders' meeting. However, he wanted to analyze the company's annual report to see what progress had been made over the year and to compare the results with 1973.

Exhibits 1 and 2 are summaries of information taken from the annual report which Mr. Knight used in his analysis.

EXHIBIT 2

BRADLEY CAFETERIAS, INC.
Income Statement
For Years Ended December 31
(millions of dollars)

	1974	1973
Net sales...	$120	$90
Less: Cost of goods sold*...........................	100	74
Gross income..	$ 20	$16
Selling, general, and administrative expenses...........	10	8
Operating income...................................	$ 10	$ 8
Financial expense—interest.........................	1	1
Profit before income taxes...........................	$ 9	$ 7
Income taxes..	4	3
Net Profit...	$ 5	$ 4

* Depreciation included in cost of goods sold of $3 million for each year.
Note: Cash dividends on common stock were $2 million in 1974 and $1 million in 1973.

1. Compare sales, profits, and total assets shown in the 1974 Bradley statements with those for 1973.

2. Prepare a financial analysis for 1974 using the measures of liquidity, profitability, and solvency developed in Chapter 13. Compare 1974 ratios with those for 1973.

3. What significant changes occurred in the company's financial picture during 1974?

4. As a stockholder what additional financial information would make your analysis more meaningful?

*Banks perform many
financial services for
consumers and business
enterprises.*

Courtesy Valley National Bank of Arizona

F *inancial institutions have an important influence on business. Without an effective means in the economy for regulating the money supply and for providing debt and equity funds, business would not be able to operate. The financial institutions of this country direct savings into investment by making money available for business, consumers, and government. Either directly or indirectly every business enterprise's success depends on the money and capital markets. This chapter deals with the following issues:*

What is the nature of our system of financial institutions?

What are the roles of the U.S. Treasury and the Federal Reserve System in influencing the financial markets?

How do the different financial institutions serve the private enterprise system?

What services are performed by investment bankers?

OUR SYSTEM OF FINANCIAL INSTITUTIONS

Financial institutions regulate the money supply and serve as channels for savers' funds to business enterprises, individuals, and governmental bodies which need them. Although business can expand by reinvesting profits, frequently additional money from outside the enterprise is required. These external funds are obtained through financial institutions either as debt by borrowing or as equity funds by selling additional shares of stock in the corporation.

Besides providing funds for business

14

Financial institutions

enterprises, financial institutions loan money to various governmental units and to individual consumers. The federal government, states, counties, cities, and school districts borrow money through the sale of bonds. Other financial institutions specialize in providing individual consumers with funds which we may use to buy goods and services. Financial institutions act as intermediaries between those who have savings to be invested and those who want to spend the funds for goods or services.

There is a wide range of financial institutions. The U.S. Treasury and the Federal Reserve System are active in determining the money supply. Investment bankers act as intermediaries for channeling both debt and equity funds to business enterprises. Commercial banks, life insurance companies, savings and loan associations, mutual savings banks, pension funds, and other specialized institutions fulfill particular financial needs. You need to understand the role of each of these financial institutions.

ROLE OF THE U.S. TREASURY

The U.S. Treasury provides part of the money supply and manages the debt of the federal government. The money supply in the United States consists of two elements—currency and demand deposits. Currency is the token coin and paper money in circulation. Demand deposits in commercial banks in the form of checking accounts represent most of the public's money supply. As of July 1975 the money supply

TABLE 14–1
Ownership of direct and fully guaranteed securities of the U.S. federal government as of June 30, 1975 (billions of dollars)

Held by:	
U.S. government agencies and trust funds	$145
Individuals	87
Federal Reserve banks	85
Commercial banks	69
Foreign and international	66
State and local governments	30
Other miscellaneous investors	27
Corporations	13
Insurance companies	7
Mutual savings banks	4
Total	$533

Source: *Federal Reserve Bulletin,* September 1975.

consisted of $72 billion of currency and $222 billion of demand deposits.

The U.S. Treasury is also an important borrower of money. It provides an opportunity for investors who desire a high degree of safety for their funds. The gross direct debt of the U.S. government amounted to $533 billion at the end of June 1975. The ownership of direct U.S. Treasury debt which is fully guaranteed by the federal government is shown in Table 14–1. Notice the wide range of lenders to the federal government.

This U.S. Treasury debt arises out of an excess of spending over receipts by the federal government over the years. A large portion of our federal debt was incurred during wars in which the United States participated. When government spending exceeds tax collections it is called *deficit financing*. If revenues exceed spending in a given period the government has a surplus of funds which may be used to reduce its indebtedness.

THE FEDERAL RESERVE SYSTEM

The basic purpose of the Federal Reserve System is to provide for a flow of money and credit to foster orderly economic growth and stable prices. The system was established in 1913 although its powers and functions have continued to evolve over the years. The United States is divided into 12 districts with a Federal Reserve bank located in each district to meet regional needs. Figure 14–1 shows the boundaries of the Federal Reserve districts in the continental United States.

The Federal Reserve System is controlled by the Board of Governors located in Washington, D.C., which consists of seven members appointed by the president of the United States and confirmed by the Senate. The Board of Governors is the most powerful body in the System. It is highly influential in determining the level of bank reserves, credit conditions, and rules affecting commercial banks which are members of the Federal Reserve System.

All nationally chartered commercial banks are required to belong to the Federal Reserve, and state chartered banks may belong. About three fourths of the deposits in the commercial banking system in this country are in banks which are members of the Federal Reserve System. The stock in the 12 regional Federal Reserve banks is owned by commercial banks which are members of the system. In essence the Federal Reserve

FIGURE 14–1
The Federal Reserve System: Geographic boundaries

Source: *Federal Reserve Bulletin*, June 1975.

System is the U.S. central banker. It acts as a banker's bank where member commercial banks which deal with the public can maintain reserve balances, borrow when necessary, and receive advice and direction concerning the economy's movement. However, unlike commercial banks which are private financial enterprises interested in making a profit along with serving their customers, the 12 Federal Reserve banks are not profit-oriented. Any excess income of Federal Reserve banks is turned over to the U.S. Treasury after providing for reserves and paying a fixed percentage return on the banks' stock.

Functions of the Federal Reserve System

Federal Reserve influence upon bank reserves. The availability of money and credit is a significant determinant of economic conditions. When the economy is expanding and the demand for goods and services is great the money supply must expand to facilitate the economic growth. On the other hand, if too much money and credit is made available the excessive demand will drive up prices and result in inflation. When the economy is in a recession, providing a sufficient supply of money and credit with lower interest rates tends to stimulate the economy toward recovery. The Federal Reserve through its influence on commercial banks has the important and delicate function of carrying out a constructive monetary policy for the country.

The Federal Reserve influences the supply of money and credit in our economy by regulating the reserves of commercial banks in three ways:

1. Setting the reserve requirements for commercial banks.
2. Determining the discount rate.
3. Carrying out open-market operations.

Required reserves. The Federal Reserve's Board of Governors has the power to set the specific reserve requirements which commercial banks must maintain to back up their deposits. With higher reserve requirements, more funds have to be held in reserve by commercial banks against deposits and less funds are available to be loaned out. As reserve requirements are lowered, this frees some bank reserves and permits bankers to expand their loans to business enterprises and individuals. In 1975 the required reserve ratio for demand deposits in large commercial banks was 16.5 percent.

Discount rate. The Federal Reserve has the authority to change the discount rate. The *discount rate* is the interest rate that member commercial banks pay to obtain funds from the Federal Reserve bank in their district. These funds are obtained from the Federal Reserve to strengthen a commercial bank's reserve ratio in relation to deposits. The higher the discount rate the less encouraging it is for commercial banks to obtain reserve funds from the Federal Reserve. When the discount rate is lowered it is more attractive for commercial banks to utilize Federal Reserve funds to increase their reserve positions. This enables the banks to grant more credit to their customers.

Open-market operations. The third method used by the Federal Reserve in influencing commercial bank reserves is *open-market operations.* This is the purchase or sale of federal government securities.

When the Federal Reserve buys government securities in the bond market the result is an increase in the commercial banks' reserves. This tends to increase the money supply and has an expansionary effect on the economy. When the Federal Reserve sells government securities, commercial banks' reserves are decreased and the money supply is reduced. This has a deflationary effect on the economy which is desirable when inflationary pressure is present. Through open-market operations the Federal Reserve can make more gradual changes in bank reserves than is the case with a change in the reserve requirements for commercial banks or a change in the discount rate.

Other functions of the Federal Reserve System. Additional functions of the Federal Reserve System include the provision of certain services for member banks, the federal government, and the public. Services for member banks consist of handling member bank reserve accounts, furnishing currency for circulation, acting as a central agency for clearing and collection of checks, and lending to member banks. For the U.S. Treasury and other governmental agencies the Federal Reserve System acts as fiscal agent, custodian, and depository for government funds. Services for the general public include collecting and interpreting economic data, working with business and academic economists, and undertaking research on monetary and general economic problems. The Federal Reserve also examines its member banks for good banking practices and cooperates with other bank supervisory agencies of the federal and state governments.

SPECIFIC FINANCIAL INSTITUTIONS

Financial institutions serve different financial markets. One way of classifying financial markets is by the length of time for which debt funds are loaned. The short-term or *money market* consists of debt which matures in one year or less. Longer-term financial markets are referred to as *capital markets.* There are four types of financial institutions which are very significant in the money and capital markets. These institutions are commercial banks, savings and loan associations, life insurance com-

TABLE 14–2
Total assets of selected financial institutions as of June 1975 (billions of dollars)

Commercial banks..............................	$898
Savings and loan associations....................	318
Life insurance companies.......................	276
Mutual savings banks..........................	117

Source: *Federal Reserve Bulletin*, September 1975.

panies, and mutual savings banks. Their relative size is shown in Table 14–2 which gives the total assets for each group.

In addition there are several other financial institutions of a more specialized nature which are also discussed in this section.

Commercial banks

The commercial banking system is the keystone of the American monetary and financial system. The 14,600 commercial banks in this country are the only financial institutions which accept demand deposits from the public. Commonly called checking accounts, these deposits permit the customer to request currency from the deposit at any time or direct that it be paid to someone else.

Also, the commercial banking system is capable of creating money through loans from its presently held checking accounts. This is possible because the commercial banking system is a *fractional reserve system.* This means that each bank is required to keep only a portion of its deposits in reserve form and may lend out those funds which are in excess of the required deposit reserves.

The multiple effect of fractional bank reserves. The following illustration shows how the fractional reserve concept may be used to expand the money supply for the commercial banking system as a whole. Suppose that a commercial bank receives $10,000 in currency from a customer to establish a checking account. We will assume the bank is required to maintain a 20 percent reserve against these accounts. Reserves may be either in the form of deposits with the Federal Reserve or in cash in the bank's vaults. This means that a commercial bank must have 20 percent of its demand deposits in reserves but may create additional

TABLE 14–3
The multiplying effect of new deposits in a fractional reserve banking system

Transactions	Amount deposited in checking accounts	20 percent required reserves	Excess reserves loaned out
Initial currency deposit in checking account.................................	$10,000	$ 2,000	$ 8,000
2nd transaction (deposit of amount just loaned).............................	8,000	1,600	6,400
3rd transaction.............................	6,400	1,280	5,120
4th transaction.............................	5,120	1,024	4,096
5th transaction.............................	4,096	819	3,277
6th transaction.............................	3,277	655	2,622
7th transaction.............................	2,622	524	2,098
8th transaction.............................	2,098	420	1,678
9th transaction.............................	1,678	336	1,342
10th transaction............................	1,342	268	1,074
11th transaction............................	1,074	215	859
12th transaction............................	859	172	687
13th transaction............................	687	137	550
14th transaction............................	550	110	440
15th transaction............................	440	88	352
Plus all additional transactions necessary to complete the cycle....................	1,757	352	1,405
Total for all transactions..............	$50,000	$10,000	$40,000

demand deposits by lending out the remaining 80 percent. Also, assume that the checks drawn on all additional demand deposits created by commercial banks are immediately deposited back into some bank in the system. As the result of all these transactions a total of $50,000 of demand deposits will be created including the initial $10,000 deposit of currency which started the cycle.

How this expansion occurs is demonstrated by Table 14–3 which shows a total of $50,000 in demand deposits. This includes the required $10,000 in reserves plus a total of $40,000 excess reserves which were loaned out and create the additional deposits. To achieve this maximum multiple effect permitted by fractional bank reserves, we assumed that each bank in the system would loan out all of its excess reserves. Furthermore, we assumed that all deposits were left in the banking system by the public with none being withdrawn for currency or for transfer outside the United States.

No single bank can lend more than its excess reserves at any one time.

Therefore, each bank depends upon additional deposits for the funds to create additional loans. However, the fractional reserve system permits the entire banking system to achieve the multiple expansion effect of the money supply. What is loaned to a person by one bank becomes a demand deposit in that bank or other banks, thereby creating additional reserves for further loans.

Activities of commercial banks. The commercial banking system is unique among financial institutions which deal directly with business and consumers in its ability to create money through the fractional reserve system. All other financial institutions must use funds received from deposits, premium payments, the sale of shares in the particular institutions, borrowing, or retained profits. Equity funds from stockholders provide a relatively small proportion of the typical bank's funds. More than 80 percent of the typical bank's sources of funds are provided by demand deposits or time deposits. Since such a large proportion of bank funds must be available for payment "on demand," bankers must walk a narrow tightrope in putting money to work profitably and at the same time with safety.

A term often used in the news media is the *prime rate of interest* which is the borrowing rate that commercial banks charge their most creditworthy customers. Other interest rates for business borrowing are generally scaled up from the prime rate. The prime rate is raised when the demand for loans is the greatest and when loan funds are in the shortest supply. Banks lower the prime rate to attract more borrowers when demand for money lessens and they have a surplus of lendable reserves.

Commercial banks are the largest single class of financial institutions according to total assets. They are the principal source of short-term credit for business enterprises. It has been estimated that over 90 percent of all short-term business loans in this country are made by commercial banks. Commercial banks are also important sources of funds for mortgage and consumer loans, such as for the purchase of a home or an automobile. Commercial banks hold large amounts of federal, state, and local government debt issues.

Commercial banks also provide such services as time and savings deposits, safety deposit boxes and vaults, and correspondent relationships with other institutions for national and international financial transactions. Nearly all commercial bank depositors' accounts are protected by insurance provided by the Federal Deposit Insurance Corporation. This governmental agency insures accounts up to $40,000 each. Commercial

Employment outlook

Bank officers

Because banks offer many services, a wide choice of careers is available in the field of banking. Loan officers evaluate the credit and collateral of individuals and businesses applying for a loan. Trust officers are responsible for investing funds as they administer trusts and estates.

Operations officers plan, coordinate, and control the work flow as they strive for bank efficiency. They also train and supervise a large number of people.

A correspondent bank officer is responsible for relations with other banks. A branch bank manager oversees the functions of a branch office. An international officer advises customers who have financial dealings abroad. Other career fields for bank officers are auditing, economics, personnel administration, public relations, and operations research.

Through the mid-1980s, employment of bank officers is expected to increase rapidly. Computers will be used to expand banking activities, and additional officers will be required for sound management and control. Although college graduates who meet the standards for executive trainees should find good opportunities for entry positions, many senior officer positions will be filled by promoting people already experienced in banking. Competition for these promotions, particularly in large banks, is likely to be keen.

banks provide loan funds to other financial institutions such as finance companies and investment bankers as well as to business enterprises and to individual consumers. The commercial bank has been called the institution prepared to provide a "full range" of financial services.

Savings and loan associations

Savings and loan associations constitute the second largest class of financial institutions. They act as financial intermediaries between individual and business savers and borrowers. Most borrowers use the credit for financing real estate construction.

Over 80 percent of the assets held by savings and loan associations are mortgages on real estate. Most of these funds are committed to the financing of one-to-four family homes. Savings and loan associations hold 44 percent of the mortgage loans outstanding on homes. This demonstrates their importance as institutions which finance home construction.

Savers who place their funds with savings and loan associations technically become shareholders in the savings and loan rather than depositors. Therefore, they actually receive dividends on their savings rather than interest. Legally savings and loan shareholders could be required to wait up to 30 days before withdrawing their savings. However, in recent years associations have customarily been willing to cash in a saver's account on demand. The vast majority of savings and loan associations are members of the Federal Savings and Loan Insurance Corporation, a government agency which insures each account up to $40,000.

Life insurance companies

Life insurance companies constitute the third largest class of financial institutions. Many people think of the life insurance company only as an institution which sells insurance protection and savings programs to individuals who pay premiums for this coverage. This underwriting of insurance risks does represent an important aspect of life insurance companies' operations since policy premiums constitute their major source of funds.

However, there is another important side to the life insurance business besides selling insurance protection. The premiums which are received are invested. The earnings from these investments are used to

Employment outlook

Actuaries

Actuaries assemble and analyze statistics to calculate probabilities of death, sickness, injury, disability, unemployment, retirement, and property loss from accident, theft, fire, and other potential hazards. This information is used to determine the expected insured loss. An actuary calculates premium rates and policy contract provisions for each type of insurance offered. Most actuaries specialize in either life and health insurance or in property and liability (casualty) insurance.

Employment of actuaries is expected to rise very rapidly through the mid-1980s. Job opportunities should be favorable for new college graduates who have passed one or two of the actuarial examinations while still in school and have a strong mathematical and statistical background. However, with the increasing number of students taking actuarial examinations, competition for beginning jobs could intensify.

The growing number of group health and life insurance plans and of pension and other benefit plans will require actuarial services. Government regulatory agencies will need additional actuaries. The widespread use of electronic computers has also made more actuarial studies possible. There will be a need for actuaries capable of working with electronic computers.

meet future payments to policyholders and beneficiaries, to generate income for operating expenses, to increase reserves, and to pay taxes and dividends.

Life insurance companies have a huge portfolio of investments to manage. Whereas commercial banks provide funds mostly for short-term loans, life insurance companies are active in providing long-term loans because of the difference in the demands upon their cash reserves. Life insurance companies are able to program rather accurately the cash they will need for payments to their policyholders through statistical analysis of accident and death rates. These actuarial studies enable the managements of life insurance companies to set premium rates, policy benefits, and reserves so as to permit the investment of funds in the long-term or capital markets.

Life insurance companies provide funds in significant quantity to all kinds of business enterprises. This includes industrial corporations, public utilities, and railroads, as well as mortgage money for all types of construction. In 1975 the major investments of life insurance companies fell into the following categories:

Corporate bonds	36%
Real estate mortgages	32
Corporate stocks	10
Policy loans	9
Government bonds: Federal, state, and local	4
Miscellaneous investments	9
Total Investments	100%

Mutual savings banks

Mutual savings banks are financial institutions which encourage individual savers to establish deposit accounts. They are the oldest class of strictly savings institutions in the United States. All but a few are located in New England and the Middle Atlantic states.

A mutual savings bank has no shareholders. All depositors have a "mutual" interest in the enterprise's operations. Thus payments for savings accounts are dividends in the strict sense of the word and not interest payments. Mutual savings banks are governed by boards of trustees which appoint their own successors. Many wealthy individuals serve as trustees for little or no compensation. They consider it an honor to be asked to be a trustee. This concept goes back to the founding of mutual savings banks when they were viewed as providing the common man

with a place and the encouragement to save money in good times to provide for himself when times were hard.

About 65 percent of the assets of mutual savings banks are invested
in mortgages. The balance of mutual savings bank investments is mostly
in corporate and government bonds.

OTHER FINANCIAL INSTITUTIONS

Besides the four previously-discussed financial institutions, there are
a number of others active in particular markets. These financial institutions include finance companies and credit unions which provide funds
directly to businesses and individuals. Institutions in the financial markets for stocks and bonds include personal trust departments, pension
funds, fire and casualty insurance companies, and investment companies.
Following a description of each of these institutions, the role of the investment banker is discussed.

Finance companies

There are a variety of enterprises which fall under the general category of finance companies. Finance companies borrow large amounts of
money from commercial banks and other lenders. In turn they make
smaller loans to business enterprises and individuals at higher rates than
the interest paid on their borrowed funds. The differential between the
borrowing and lending rates for finance companies provides for operating expenses and profits. At the end of June 1975, finance companies
had installment loans outstanding of $38 billion.

Finance companies which specialize in direct loans to individuals are
called *consumer finance* or *personal finance companies*. A consumer
finance company makes installment loans directly to you for the purchase of an automobile, major appliances, a television or stereo set, or
as a personal loan. Consumer finance companies provide a significant
amount of installment credit.

Sales finance companies also specialize in installment loans. However,
they do not make loans directly to individuals or business enterprises.
Instead they purchase installment receivables from merchants who sell
such products as autos, appliances, industrial equipment, and other durable goods. Sales finance companies also loan money to retailers and
wholesalers to finance their inventories. Usually installment loans and
inventory loans are secured by the merchandise on which the loans are

made. These financial institutions provide substantial amounts of credit to business enterprises.

Commercial finance companies provide loans to business enterprises, many of which would have difficulty obtaining credit from commercial banks because of the small size of the enterprise or the risk involved. Most of the loans by commercial finance companies are secured by accounts receivable of the borrowers, although loans based on equipment and inventories are also made. Interest rates are generally higher than those charged by commercial banks because of the additional risks involved and the increased costs of handling such loans.

Another highly specialized type of business financing is called factoring. *Factoring* is the purchase of a business enterprise's accounts receivable by a finance company, which then collects the accounts. Factoring is used widely in the textile industry and is a relatively expensive form of short-term financing. However, the factor (which the financial institution is called) provides a variety of services when it purchases the receivables of a business enterprise. These services include credit investigation and collection as well as assuming the loss for any bad debts which result from failure to collect the accounts.

Credit unions

Credit unions are cooperatives which promote saving on the part of their members. They also provide personal loans to members at relatively low interest rates. Credit unions are organized and sponsored by fraternal groups, labor unions, or by business enterprises for the benefit of their employees. Therefore, membership in a particular credit union is limited to those individuals who are part of the sponsoring group. Because of their cooperative nature, credit unions are normally managed by their members who serve on a part-time basis with little or no compensation. Some credit unions have paid secretary-treasurers or receive clerical support from the sponsoring organization. This type of financial institution is important in the consumer credit market with $23 billion in installment credit outstanding at the end of June 1975.

Personal trust departments

Personal trust departments of commercial banks and trust companies take legal possession of personal assets and manage them for the benefit of the person creating the trust or for some other designated person.

The trust department of a commercial bank (called the trustee) will take possession of funds provided by a person (the trustor) and provide investment management of the money. The income from this trust fund will be paid to whomever the trustor designates; perhaps it will also be paid to the person's family upon his death. Personal trust departments also act as executors and administrators of estates, receivers in bankruptcy, and trustees of private pension funds.

Personal trust departments control vast sums of wealth. Their funds are invested primarily in corporate stocks, state and local government bonds, and corporate bonds. As a class of institutions they have developed a reputation for responsible financial stewardship of the funds placed under their control.

Pension funds

Pension funds have become important sources of investment in all sectors of the capital markets since World War II. Pension funds basically are accumulated out of the contributions of employers and employees. These funds are invested in stocks, bonds, and other types of investments, such as mortgages. They are administered so as to provide retirement income for the individual beneficiaries and their families in their old age.

There are two general types of pension funds—private and government. Private pension plans provide retirement benefits for employees of business enterprises, union members, and employees of nonprofit organizations such as educational and religious institutions. Private pension funds invest heavily in common stocks of corporations and corporate bonds with smaller holdings of mortgages and U.S. government securities.

Government retirement plans also provide significant sources of funds for the capital markets. State and local government retirement monies are heavily invested in U.S. government bonds, state and local government securities, corporate bonds, and mortgages. Many states prohibit the investment of these funds in common stocks of corporations. However, a number of states now permit investment in high-grade common stocks.

A second class of government retirement plans is that of the federal government. The U.S. Treasury acts as the fiscal agent for a number of governmental retirement funds. These include the Old Age and Survivors Insurance Trust Fund, National Service Life Insurance Fund, Unemployment Trust Fund, and Railroad Retirement Fund. These trust funds are obtained from taxes such as social security payments by employees and employers, premiums, and contributions to specific fund accounts. After benefits are paid out to recipients, the balance in these funds is invested in U.S. government securities.

Fire and casualty insurance companies

Fire and casualty companies sell insurance service to their clients to cover destruction of property by fire or other hazards. Some also provide personal liability insurance and other types of insurance protection. Whereas the life insurance company guarantees a fixed dollar return for its policyholders, the fire and casualty insurance company assumes contingent liability and pays its policyholder only if a loss actually occurs. The fire and/or casualty policy has a limited amount of dollar protection depending upon the terms of the policy. Payments to policyholders may be no higher than the amount of the loss.

The fire and casualty insurance company's funds come mainly from premium income from policyholders and from investments made by the company. These funds are invested in a manner which will provide reserves to underwrite the risks assumed by the company in the policies which it has issued. Normally most companies are able to meet expenses and losses on policies from new premium income. This provides some flexibility for the insurance company's investment policies. However, in order to be able to meet calamitous losses from natural and human-caused disasters the insurance company must provide a cushion of readily marketable securities in its investment portfolio. This need is met by holding large quantities of U.S. government securities. Fire and casualty insurance companies also hold substantial quantities of corporations' common stocks and state and local government securities. Unlike the life insurance companies, the fire and casualty insurance companies do not invest heavily in the mortgage and corporate bond markets.

Investment companies

An important purchaser of corporate securities, especially of common stocks, is the class of financial institutions called investment companies. *Investment companies* obtain funds by selling shares of their stock and using the proceeds to purchase securities of other corporations. The usual purchasers of shares in investment companies are individuals who

Employment outlook

Underwriters

Underwriters appraise and select the risks their company will insure after analyzing information in insurance applications, reports of safety engineers, and actuarial studies (reports that describe the probability of insured loss). Some routine applications that require very little independent judgment are handled by computers. Generally, however, underwriters use considerable personal judgment in making decisions.

Underwriters have great responsibility. The insurance company may lose business to competitors if an underwriter appraises risks too conservatively or have to pay many future claims if the underwriting actions were too liberal.

The employment of underwriters is expected to grow moderately through the mid-1980s as insurance sales continue to expand. Higher personal incomes should stimulate purchases of life insurance, especially policies which provide retirement income and money for children's education. Property and liability insurance sales should expand as purchases of automobiles, pleasure boats, and other consumer durables increase.

The American public's growing security consciousness should contribute to demand for more extensive insurance protection. Expanding businesses will need protection for new plants and equipment and insurance for workmen's compensation and product liability. Heightened competition among insurance companies and changes in regulations affecting investment profits also are expected to increase the insurance industry's need for competent underwriters.

have relatively small amounts of money to invest but yet would like the benefits of a diversified investment portfolio. Investment companies are either *closed-end* or *open-end* depending upon whether the shares in the investment fund can be increased routinely.

Closed-end investment companies have a fixed amount of capital outstanding. When an individual investor wishes to buy stock in a closed-end company it must be purchased in the open market from someone who already owns the stock. The managers of the closed-end investment company buy and sell securities to improve their income and capital gains record with the funds provided when the company's shares were originally sold to the public.

Open-end companies, commonly known as *mutual funds*, do not have a fixed number of shares outstanding. They issue more shares whenever an investor desires to purchase shares in the fund. Shares are purchased at the net asset value. This is computed twice daily based on the market value of the securities in the portfolio plus a "loading charge" to cover the sales commission and other expenses of the sale. When the individual investor desires to sell his shares in the mutual fund they are sold back to the fund at the then-current asset value, minus a small redemption charge on some funds.

Some mutual funds, known as "no-load" funds, are sold to the public at net asset value without a loading charge. In these mutual funds there are no salesmen. Therefore, the individual investor saves the cost of the sales commission (loading charge). However, in order to purchase the fund the investor must contact the fund's management directly. This is usually done by responding to an advertisement in a financial newspaper or magazine.

FUNCTIONS OF THE INVESTMENT BANKER

The investment banker performs many valuable services as a middle-man between corporations and investors in the capital funds market. The investment banker is active in both the primary and secondary securities markets.

Primary and secondary securities markets

The *primary securities market* channels funds directly to corporations or governmental bodies in exchange for their securities. In the primary market the sale of new stock or bond issues increases the financial resources of the particular corporation issuing the securities. When selling new security issues an investment banker is participating in the primary securities market.

Secondary securities markets are those where stocks and bonds which are already outstanding are bought and sold among investors. The organized trading markets for corporate stocks and bonds are examples of secondary markets. These include the New York and American stock exchanges. In the secondary markets none of the proceeds from a securities transaction go to the corporation which issued the stocks or bonds since the corporation received funds when the securities were originally sold. An investment banker participates in the secondary securities market when acting as a broker for the transfer of securities among investors.

Although the secondary markets do not channel any additional funds directly into the business enterprises, an active secondary market for corporate obligations is important since it provides liquidity for commitments made in the primary markets. This liquidity makes investors more willing to participate in the primary securities markets since they can sell their securities to other investors should circumstances make this desirable or necessary.

Role of the Investment Banker

In primary securities markets

1. Underwrites new issues of stocks and bonds.
2. Sells new securities issues without underwriting (best efforts).
3. Sells new securities issues through private placements.

In secondary securities markets

1. Acts as broker in purchase and sale of securities for clients on organized exchanges and over-the-counter markets.
2. Buys and sells securities for own portfolio.

Underwriting

The sale of a new issue of stock or bonds is relatively rare for most corporations. Therefore, when this is necessary the investment banker can provide corporate management with useful assistance. The investment banker has knowledge of current market conditions and can help with the timing of the issue's sale, pricing, and other terms.

As underwriters, investment bankers assume the responsibility for the sale of a corporation's stock or bonds. They guarantee a specified amount of money for the securities to be sold. This puts the investment banker in the position of being a merchandiser of corporations' securities. The delicate job of the investment banker is to set an offering price so the issue will be well received by the investing public and at the same time bring as much as possible for the issuing corporation.

Underwriting security issues involves financial risk on the part of the investment banker because of rapidly changing conditions of supply and demand in the capital markets. Therefore, frequently a group of investment bankers will cooperate in the underwriting and sale of security issues. This grouping of investment bankers is called a *syndicate*. It is formed only for marketing a particular security issue. After the issue has been sold, the syndicate is dissolved.

When the investment bankers underwrite an issue they are paid a fee to cover their expenses. They also sell the securities for a markup over what the issuing corporation receives for the securities. This is to compensate them for their services and the risk borne in the transaction. An unexpected downturn in the stock or bond market immediately after the issue comes to market may result in the securities being left on the investment bankers' shelves. This leaves the choice of selling the issue at what it will bring (with a probable loss for the bankers) or holding the issue in the hope that market conditions will improve so it can be sold satisfactorily.

Best-efforts offering

The investment banker may also sell securities for corporations without underwriting the issue. This is known as a *best-efforts* offering. The investment banker assists with the planning and details connected with the issue and sells the stock or bonds, but does not assume the risk for their sale. Under these circumstances the business enterprise takes the risk of the sale of its securities, and the investment banker is compensated with a fee.

Private placements

In addition to their function as underwriters of securities to be sold to the public, investment bankers may assist enterprises in the sale of their securities through private placements. A *private placement* is the sale of an entire issue of securities to a single or small number of investors. A number of corporate debt issues in recent years have been through private placement to institutions such as life insurance companies and private pension funds. The investment banker's role in the private placement is to advise the business enterprise during the negotiation process and to handle various details associated with the issuance of the debt instruments.

Brokerage function

The brokerage function of the investment banker is the one which is probably best known to the public. Brokerage operations are carried on by the marketing organization of the investment banking house. As a broker the investment banker buys and sells securities, acting as an agent for customers. For this agency service the broker receives a commission on each transaction. Commissions for most sales or purchases on the stock exchange or the over-the-counter market vary from about 6 percent on small transactions down to about 1 percent on amounts of several thousand dollars. The role of the broker is illustrated in the discussion of the stock market in the appendix at the end of this chapter.

The investment banking firm also may buy and sell securities for its own portfolio or for those of its partners or officers. The transactions of investment bankers are policed by industry groups and also by the Securities and Exchange Commission. The commission's objective is to prevent manipulation of the securities markets and protect the interests of the investing public.

Investment banking houses are financed by equity capital provided by the individuals who own the firms. The traditional form of business organization for the investment banking house has been the partnership. However, in recent years a number of investment bankers have incorporated their operations. In 1971 the largest investment banking house, Merrill Lynch, Pierce, Fenner & Smith, Inc., sold a portion of its common stock to the public to increase its capital and broaden its ownership.

SUMMARY

Financial institutions regulate the money supply and channel savers' funds to the business enterprises, individuals, and governmental units which want to borrow these funds.

The U.S. Treasury provides currency for the money supply and manages the federal debt.

The Federal Reserve System is made up of 12 regional Federal Reserve banks and is controlled by a seven-member Board of Governors. The Federal Reserve System is influential in determining the money supply, the level of interest rates, and the banking system's ability to provide credit to its customers.

The level of commercial bank reserves is regulated by the Federal Reserve through its purchase and sale of government securities, changes in the percentage of deposit reserves required of member banks, and changes in the discount rate for member banks in their dealings with the Federal Reserve.

Commercial banks, the largest class of financial institutions, accept demand deposits. They have the ability to create money through the use of a fractional reserve system.

Savings and loan associations, the second largest class of financial institutions, receive savings mostly from individuals. In turn they make loans for the financing of real estate, mainly one-to-four family homes.

Life insurance companies constitute the third largest class of financial institutions. The premiums they receive for underwriting insurance risks are invested primarily in the long-term capital markets.

Mutual savings banks, consumer finance companies, sales finance companies, and commercial finance companies are all financial institutions which serve particular segments of the borrowing market.

Personal trust departments of commercial banks and trust companies take legal possession of personal assets and manage them for the benefit of the trustor or designated beneficiaries.

Pension funds are accumulated out of the contributions of employers and employees and are invested to provide retirement incomes for the beneficiary individuals.

Fire and casualty insurance companies sell insurance coverage for fire and other hazards. They invest in U.S. government securities, corporate common stocks, and state and local government securities.

Investment companies obtain funds by selling shares and purchase securities of other corporations. Open-end investment companies, commonly known as mutual funds, are a medium of investment for the small investor who wishes a diversified portfolio of corporate securities.

The investment banker performs such services as underwriting new issues of stocks and bonds for corporations, acting as a broker in buying and selling securities for clients in the secondary securities markets, and providing advice to business enterprises in the timing and details for long-term financing.

Appendix

The stock market and investing in securities

THE STOCK MARKET

Organization of stock markets

A great deal of the trading of corporate securities in the secondary market takes place on organized exchanges such as the New York Stock Exchange and the American Stock Exchange. Indeed, when people talk about "the stock market" they normally are referring to the New York Stock Exchange (NYSE), or the Big Board as it is informally called. The NYSE accounts for the majority of trading volume on organized exchanges.

A corporation's management must apply to have its securities listed for trading in the New York Stock Exchange. In order to qualify for trading the exchange has set certain minimum requirements as to demonstrated earning power, value of corporation assets, number of shares of stock outstanding, and the number of shareholders. The purpose of these requirements is to provide an active marketplace for well-established securities.

Trading on the floor of the organized exchanges is carried out by individuals and brokerage firms which hold membership in the particular exchange. On the NYSE there are about 1,400 memberships or "seats" which permit the holders to buy and sell securities on the floor of the exchange. These memberships may be sold to other qualified individuals or firms with the approval of exchange officials.

About one fourth of the members of the NYSE are specialists who perform the function of "making a market" for one or more stocks. This means they carry an inventory of shares in the issues in which they specialize and are willing to deal with other exchange members who are trading for themselves or their customers.

Buying and selling stock through an organized exchange

If you wished to purchase 100 shares of General Motors common stock on the New York Stock Exchange you would relay that order to your broker. The order would be sent by wire to the firm's New York office where it would be relayed to the trading member on the floor of the exchange. The member on the NYSE floor would take the order to the place, called a trading post, where the specialist dealing in General Motors stock is located and would carry out the transaction.

The purchase and sale of stocks on the Big Board is accomplished through the specialist who conducts a continuous two-way auction-type operation. The specialist quotes prices for buying and selling stock of a given corporation. The "bid" price is the price at which the specialist is willing to buy stock. The "ask" price is the price at which the specialist is willing to sell. The difference between these is called the "spread," which is the specialist's margin.

A variety of different types of orders for securities may be placed with brokers by members of the public. Usually orders to buy or sell securities are placed either at a particular price or "at the market," which means the transaction will be executed immediately for the best price your broker can obtain. Each broker who acts for a customer is charged with the responsibility of obtaining the best price for the customer. Stocks may be bought and sold in round lots which normally consist of 100-share units. Smaller orders are called "odd-lots," which in most stocks consist of from 1 to 99 shares. You will recall that brokerage fees range downward from about 6 percent depending upon the amount of the transaction.

After the broker on the floor completes the transaction both the broker and the specialist make a written notation of the deal. This information is sent back to the New York brokerage offices and then wired out to the branch office from where the order came. At the same time, a report of the transaction is relayed to the exchange reporting service where it is sent out across the country on a wire service. The transaction is reported on the visual tape, called a broad tape, which virtually every brokerage office has in continuous operation during the hours when the market is open for trading. This public report gives the symbol which represents the name of the corporation's stock, the number of shares in the transaction, and the price per share of stock. Likewise, brokerage officers may use their wire services or other reporting devices to obtain quotations of the bid and ask prices for their customers direct from the trading floor of the exchange in a very short time. It is possible for you to receive a quotation, place an order, have it executed on the floor of the stock exchange, and receive the report back in your broker's office in a period of less than ten minutes.

An introduction to the American business enterprise

FIGURE 14–2
How to read stock market reports

Many newspapers carry stock market reports similar to this sample taken from New York Stock Exchange transactions which occurred on June 26, 1975.

1   *The abbreviated name of the company issuing the stock. In this case it is Addressograph-Multigraph Corp. The stock is common stock unless the company name is followed by "pf," which indicates that the issue is a preferred stock.*

2   *These columns show the highest and lowest prices paid for a given stock on the exchange during the year. In this case it is $24.62½ and $18.87½ per share.*

3   *Figures following company names indicate the annual dividend rate estimated on the basis of the latest quarterly or semiannual payment. Here the annual rate is $1.80 per share. Letters following the dividend numbers indicate other data regarding dividends. For example, "b" indicates that, in addition to the cash dividend that is shown, a stock dividend is issued. Other symbols are explained in a footnote on the market reports page.*

4   *This column shows the stock's price/earnings ratio based on the closing price of the day divided by the latest 12 months reported earnings per share. For Allied Stores the P/E ratio is 9.*

5   *This column shows the number of shares traded for the day, expressed in hundreds. In this instance 150,300 shares of American Airlines stock changed hands during this day on the New York Stock Exchange. A "z" indicates the actual number of shares traded.*

6   *These two columns show the stock's highest price of the day and the lowest price that day at which the stock traded. In this case the stock hit a high of $31.50 and a low of $31.00.*

7   *These final two columns show the closing price of the day and the change from the previous day's closing price. For American Cyanamid the closing price was $27.25 per share or a decrease of $0.25 per share (¼) from the previous day's close.*

The prices of individual securities are determined by the relative supply and demand for them as received by the specialist. The specialist is charged with maintaining an orderly market for stocks. However, the willingness to buy or sell on the part of institutions and individuals interested in securities ultimately will determine the price at which transactions are completed.

Stock market averages

In addition to reports on price changes of individual stocks illustrated in Figure 14–2, there are reports on the general movement of stock prices at a given time. The most publicized of these stock-market price averages is the Dow-Jones average. Actually the *Dow-Jones average* is composed of four series of calculations of stock prices—one series for 30 industrial stocks, one for 20 transportation stocks, and one for 15 utility stocks, and a composite of the total 65 stocks. The Dow-Jones Industrial average is composed of some of the country's leading corporations including American Telephone & Telegraph, Du Pont Chemical, Eastman Kodak, General Electric, General Motors, Sears Roebuck, Texaco, and U.S. Steel.

The Dow-Jones averages are made up of "blue-chip" or high quality stocks. There are more broadly based stock market price averages such as the 500-stock average by Standard & Poor's Corporation, a securities research organization. The Standard & Poor's 500-stock average covers most of the value of all common stocks listed on the New York Stock Exchange.

Over-the-counter markets

In addition to the securities trading which takes place on organized exchanges, there is the *over-the-counter* market (OTC). On the OTC security dealers buy and sell stock through informal dealings, usually by telephone, rather than in a central place such as an organized exchange. Many security dealers maintain inventories of the stocks which trade over the counter. Their quotations for bid and ask prices are circulated in the investment community. When a member of the public places an order with an investment banker's brokerage office, the customer's representative will buy the stock where it can be purchased for the best price, usually after contacting two or three dealers.

Security issues which are traded in the OTC market include the stocks and bonds of typically small or medium-sized business enterprises. Also, the common stocks of nearly all commercial banks are traded in the OTC market along with many insurance company stocks.

While some U.S. government bonds are listed on the New York Stock Exchange, most federal government securities are traded in the OTC market. Municipal securities are traded exclusively over the counter. *Municipals* include the bonds of states, municipalities, school districts, and other local governmental units. Most corporate bond trading occurs over the counter, although some corporation bonds are listed on the stock exchanges.

INVESTING IN SECURITIES

Investment objectives

Investors in stocks and bonds, whether institutions or individuals, should establish their investment objectives and determine the type of securities needed to achieve these objectives. Then they are ready to select the specific securities to be included in their investment portfolios.

While the general objective of investing is to provide a monetary return on capital, there are several specific factors to be considered in judging the suitability of a particular investment. Investors need to determine the relative importance of current income, growth of the investment, and the degree of risk they are willing to assume. Current income can be provided from bond interest or dividends on corporate preferred or common stocks. Capital growth results from an appreciation in the market value of securities. Safety of principal is also an important factor in establishing investment objectives since some investments carry a much greater risk than others. Table 14–4 summarizes the general characteristics of bonds, preferred stocks, and common stocks in relation to these three objectives.

Despite the generalizations outlined in Table 14–4, there are excep-

TABLE 14–4
Securities characteristics and investment objectives

Objectives	Bonds	Preferred stocks	Common stocks
Current income	highest	medium	lowest
Capital growth (appreciation)	lowest	medium	highest
Safety of principal	highest	medium	lowest

tions to this classification. For example, some low-quality bonds have less safety of principal than high-quality preferred or common stocks. This emphasizes the importance of the final selection of specific stocks and bonds.

Selection of common stocks

In attempting to judge the future market-price performance of the common stock of a given corporation a number of measures are used by investment analysts. These include a corporation's earnings and earnings growth, cash dividends, market price of the common stock, the price/earnings ratio, and the quality of management.

Earnings and earnings growth. Net profit is divided by the number of shares of common stock outstanding to determine earnings per share. If the corporation has preferred stock in its capital structure, the cash dividends paid on preferred stock are subtracted from net profit before the earnings per share for common stockholders are calculated. The earnings per share and their rate of growth in past years are important determinants of common stock prices, especially as this may reflect the likely continued growth in earnings in the future. Most analysts feel that earnings for at least the past five years should be studied.

Cash dividends. The amount of cash dividends per share paid to stockholders and the trend of cash dividend payments are also factors in evaluating a common stock. The trend of cash dividend payments over recent years should be considered along with the proportion of earnings paid out in dividends.

Market price of the common stock. The present market price per share of common stock and the price trend over the years enables the analyst to determine whether there has been an increase in the value of corporate shares in the past. Generally an upward trend of market-price action is viewed more positively by analysts than a downward trend unless there is some valid reason for believing the price trend is about to reverse itself.

Price/earnings ratio. An important measurement which takes two key factors into account is the price/earnings ratio. The current market price per share of stock is divided by the past 12 months' earnings per share. This measure can be compared with the stock's P/E ratio in previous years and with other corporations' stocks in the same industry. Price/earnings ratios vary widely among different common stocks as they reflect investors' expectations of future corporate earnings.

FIGURE 14–3

DOW CHEMICAL NYSE-DOW

| RECENT PRICE | 55 | DIV'D YIELD | 2.5 % (NORM 3.0%) | P/E RATIO | 8.7 (NORM 16.5) | 568 |

| High→ | 27.4 | 26.0 | 30.6 | 29.2 | 26.9 | 24.9 | 39.8 | 55.7 | 67.9 | 70.0 | 1976 | 1977 | 1978 |
| Low→ | 22.0 | 18.0 | 20.1 | 23.5 | 21.5 | 19.6 | 24.1 | 39.0 | 46.5 | 49.9 | | | |

Price Stability 90 Scale from 100 to 5
Growth Persistence 75 Scale 100 to 5
"See inside back cover for Definition of Terms"

9.5 X "Cash Flow" p sh

$5 $4 $3 $2 $1 0 -1

12 MOS EARNINGS (A) Per Share Quarterly

INDEX of INSIDER DECISIONS

| | 1968 | 1969 | 1970 | 1971 | 1972 | 1973 | 1974 |

Shares Held by Investment Companies

12/31/73	3/31/74	6/30/74	9/30/74
3,112,310	3,571,290	3,685,557	3,941,557
(55 funds)	(63 funds)	(71 funds)	(79 funds)

Range Est'd Avg Prices 82 (+50%)

PERFORM'CE Next 12 Mos **2** Above Average

SAFETY **1** Highest
(Scale 1 Highest to 5 Lowest)

BETA 1.10 (NYSE Avg = 1.00)

Jan. 31, 1975 Value Line

$40 Sales per sh $20
Book Value per sh $5 "Cash Flow" per sh $3 $2
Earnings per sh $1

HISTORICAL GROWTH TREND .50 .30 .20

	1964	1965	1966	1967	1968	1969	1970	1971	1972	1973	1974	1975	© Arnold Bernhard & Co. Inc	77-79 E
	11.91	13.00	14.59	15.32	18.22	19.82	21.09	22.62	26.19	33.25	53.85	57.05	Sales per sh	62.35
	2.13	2.47	2.72	2.96	3.23	3.60	3.75	4.11	4.62	5.79	9.80	9.80	"Cash Flow" per sh	9.45
	1.04	1.20	1.36	1.45	1.50	1.64	1.46	1.70	2.06	2.94	6.40	6.00	Earnings p sh (yr-end)	5.50
	1.04	1.19	1.35	1.45	1.50	1.64	1.46	1.70	2.07	2.94	6.40	6.00	(A)Egs p sh as reported	5.50
	.59	.60	.67	.73	.80	.85	.87	.89	.90	.95	1.20	1.40	(B)Div'ds Decl'd per sh	2.40
	1.84	2.74	2.69	2.13	3.38	4.09	3.84	4.02	3.91	4.35	8.55	10.85	Cap'l spending per sh	6.50
	8.42	8.99	9.54	10.32	10.69	11.22	11.37	12.34	13.61	15.67	20.85	25.55	(C)Book Value per sh	35.25
	90.48	90.48	89.76	90.24	90.69	90.65	90.61	90.75	91.79	92.26	92.60	92.00	(D)Common Shs Outst'g	93.00
	22.9	20.8	16.6	18.3	17.6	14.6	15.4	19.3	22.3	18.5	9.5		Avg Ann'l P/E Ratio	16.5
	2.5%	2.4%	3.0%	2.8%	3.0%	3.6%	3.9%	2.7%	2.0%	1.8%	2.0%		Avg Ann'l Div'd Yield	2.4%
	1077.5	1176.2	1309.7	1382.7	1652.5	1797.1	1911.1	2052.7	2403.7	3067.9	4985	5250	Sales ($mill)	5800
	23.6%	24.8%	24.9%	25.1%	23.0%	23.2%	24.5%	24.5%	24.7%	25.1%	29.5%	26.0%	Operating Margin	22.5%
	98.7	115.6	122.6	136.0	157.2	177.9	207.7	218.8	234.9	263.1	315	350	Depreciation ($mill)	370
	93.8	108.1	121.7	130.9	136.0	148.7	132.3	154.4	189.0	271.2	593	552	Net Income ($mill)	510
	7.3%	7.6%	7.3%	7.8%	7.6%	7.7%	8.2%	8.0%	7.9%	8.0%	7.7%	6.9%	Depreciation Rate	7.7%
	42.2%	40.5%	39.5%	39.6%	39.7%	34.6%	39.3%	36.4%	39.2%	41.9%	48.5%	45.5%	Income Tax Rate	42.0%
	8.7%	9.2%	9.3%	9.5%	8.2%	8.3%	6.9%	7.5%	7.9%	8.8%	11.9%	10.5%	Net Income Margin	8.8%
	239.2	454.6	552.3	551.6	684.6	798.0	969.8	1010.1	1095.0	1225.9	1250	1500	Working Cap'l ($mill)	1500
	761.9	813.5	856.4	930.9	968.8	1017.5	1030.4	1119.7	1249.6	1445.7	1930	2350	(C)Net Worth ($mill)	3280
	234.5	266.5	289.0	207.9	204.5	172.0	248.5	214.4	383.8	554.9	590	600	Working Cap'l ($mill)	950
	10.4%	10.2%	10.5%	10.6%	10.6%	10.8%	9.9%	10.5%	11.4%	13.3%	21.0%	17.0%	% Earned Total Cap'l	13.0%
	12.3%	13.3%	14.2%	14.1%	14.0%	14.6%	12.8%	13.8%	15.1%	18.8%	30.5%	23.5%	% Earned Net Worth	15.5%
	57%	50%	49%	50%	53%	52%	59%	52%	44%	33%	18%	23%	% All Div'ds to Net Inc	44%

ANNUAL RATES of change (per sh)
	Past 10 Yrs	Past 5 Yrs	Est '71-'73 to '77-'79
Sales	10.5%	11.5%	14.5%
"Cash Flow"	10.0%	10.5%	12.0%
Earnings	11.0%	9.0%	16.0%
Book Value	6.0%	6.5%	17.0%

CURRENT POSITION ($mill.)
	1972	1973	9/30/74
Cash Assets	162.5	317.7	288.9
Receivables	583.4	722.9	1174.9
Inventory (LIFO)	423.9	497.5	675.8
Other	12.0	21.9	——
Current Assets	1181.8	1560.0	2139.6
Accts Payable	218.9	354.8	1333.7
Debt Due	307.3	253.0	186.5
Other	271.8	397.3	——
Current Liab'ties	798.0	1005.1	1520.2

CAPITAL STRUCTURE as of 12/31/73
Debt $1225.9 mill. Interest $89.9 mill.
Leases Uncapitalized; rentals about $51.4 mill. a year.
Pension Liab'ty None
Pfd Stock None Pfd Div None
Common Stock 92,259,853 shares

Cal-endar	QUARTERLY SALES ($ Millions)				Full Year
	Mar. 31	June 30	Sept. 30	Dec. 31	
1971	486.7	526.3	522.7	517.0	2052.7
1972	550.2	607.2	604.2	642.1	2403.7
1973	702.8	747.4	784.0	833.7	3067.9
1974	1017	1325	1346	1297	4985
1975	1150	1200	1400	1500	5250

Cal-endar	EARNINGS AS REPORTED (per sh)				(A) Full Year
	Mar. 31	June 30	Sept. 30	Dec. 31	
1971	.37	.46	.47	.40	1.70
1972	.45	.57	.57	.48	2.07
1973	.63	.86	.81	.64	2.94
1974	.77	1.79	2.45	1.39	6.40
1975	1.25	1.25	1.65	1.85	6.00

Cal-endar	QUARTERLY DIVIDENDS PAID				(B) Full Year
	Mar. 31	June 30	Sept. 30	Dec. 31	
1971	.216	.216	.225	.225	.883
1972	.225	.225	.225	.225	.90
1973	.225	.225	.25	.25	.95
1974	.25	.25	.30	.30	1.10
1975	.35				

BUSINESS: The Dow Chemical Company is the third largest U.S. chemical producer. Sales (and earnings) breakdown: chemicals and metals, 50% (41%); plastics and packaging, 33% (44%); bioproducts and consumer items, 18% (15%). Company leads in polystyrene (Styron); makes polyethylene, magnesium, pesticides, Saran Wrap,
pharmaceuticals; services oilwells. Foreign business accounts for 46% of sales, 58% of profits. Has 49,800 employees. 88,849 shareholders. Employee costs, 23% of sales; R&D, $118 mill. in 1973. Directors control 3% of stock. Chrmn.: C.A. Gerstacker. Pres.: C.B. Branch. Incorporated: Delaware. Address: Midland, Mich 48640

Dow has raised the dividend for a second time in a year. This will be the 16th consecutive year of higher dividends. Even so, the stock would hardly appeal to the income-oriented investors. Rather it is an equity offering moderate long-term growth potential at minimum risk. Its Safety is rated 1 (Highest), and over the short term it may perform better than the market averages.

The plastics industry is weakening, and Dow is big in plastics. Polyethylene is doing well so far, but polystyrene and urethane intermediates are moving more slowly. Chemicals and metals are still basically strong, although benzene derivatives are slowing and chlorine — which was in extremely short supply a few months ago — has moved into a balanced position. Agricultural chemicals, in the consumer and bio products area, are and probably will continue to be strong. Despite the industrial downturn and its surrounding uncertainties. . .

We expect Dow's earnings to do about as well as in 1974. The reason: Last year, when profits were soaring, Dow elected to absorb
many expenses of a non-recurring nature: it awarded an employee bonus, it charged accelerated depreciation, and expensed accrued taxes on foreign income for prior years. Therefore, even if net operating income should decline by $1 a share, reported income would still be equal to last year's. And net income will likely be reported on a fewer number of shares, thereby boosting share earnings. The company proposes to purchase 725,000 shares by the end of this year.

Dow isn't letting the recession crimp its expansion. It invested close to $800 million last year in new plant and equipment, and this year's spending is budgeted at $1 billion. In addition to the $200-million feedstocks unit in Texas and a $165-million unit in Louisiana, including a naphtha cracker, Dow will expand its capacity for polyethylene and acrylonitrile-butadiene-styrene plastics. H.C.E.J.

CASH POSITION	5-Year Av'g	9/30/74
Current Assets to Current Liabilities:	139%	141%
Cash & Equiv's to Current Liab'ties:	19%	19%
Working Capital to Sales:	13%	12%

(A) Based on avg. shs. outstanding. Excludes extraordinary gain: '71, 1¢, '73, 5¢. Loss: '70, 64¢. Includes special gains: '68, 15¢; '69, 14¢. Loss: '66. 11¢. (B) Next div'd meeting about Mar. 6. Goes ex about Mar. 24. Div'd payment dates: Jan. 30, April 30, July 30, Oct. 30. Plus 2% stock div'd in '65. ■ Div'd reinvestment plan available. (C) Excludes intangible assets of $83.8 mill., 90¢ a sh in '73. (D) In millions, adjusted for stock splits and div'ds.

For example, in 1975 the common stock of Mobil Oil, one of the leading international petroleum companies, was selling for a price/earnings ratio of only approximately six times. This very low P/E ratio reflected investors' fears over the status of Mobil's international oil sources in the Middle East and the prospects of increased taxes on the oil industry. On the other hand, at the same time the common stock of Merck, a top-grade drug manufacturer, was selling at a price/earnings ratio of 25. This high P/E ratio reflected investors' confidence in this enterprise's ability to continue its record of research and higher profits.

Quality of management.   One of the most important judgments, and perhaps the most difficult for the analyst to make, is an evaluation of the quality of the management of a corporation. The effectiveness of management in developing, producing, and marketing new products should be judged. Also, an evaluation is made of the enterprise's accounting statements with tests similar to those discussed in Chapter 13.

A number of investment advisory services provide analysis of stocks and bonds. Some of the widely known services include *Standard & Poor's Outlook* and the *Value Line Investment Survey*. Such advisory material plus studies of different corporate stocks made by stock brokerage firms provide a variety of reference material for the potential investor. Figure 14–3 from the *Value Line Investment Survey* illustrates the information that advisory services provide.

The fact that advisory services as well as investors differ about the desirability of a corporation's common stock at a given time is what makes an active market for publicly held securities. Considerable study and analysis should precede the investment decision if investors wish to manage their capital prudently. Although the long-run trend in common stock prices has been upward, significant price declines have occurred from time to time. Also, the price movement of an individual corporation's stock may not follow the general market trend.

TERMS FOR REVIEW

financial institutions
Federal Reserve System
reserve requirements
Federal Reserve discount rate
open-market operations

fractional reserve banking system
prime rate of interest
mutual fund (open-end investment company)
investment banker

money market	*primary securities market*
capital market	*secondary securities market*
commercial banks	

QUESTIONS

1. What functions do financial institutions perform in the economy?

2. Outline the role of the Federal Reserve System.

3. Explain how the Federal Reserve regulates the public's supply of money and credit.

4. Outline the services performed by commercial banks which justify calling them "the keystone of the American monetary and financial system."

5. *a.* Given an initial bank demand deposit of $10,000, what would be the maximum amount the commercial banking system could expand demand deposits if the required reserve ratio were 16⅔ percent?

   b. What conditions would have to prevail for such a maximum expansion to occur?

6. List the major types of investments made by each of the following financial institutions:

   a. Savings and loan associations
   b. Life insurance companies
   c. Mutual savings banks
   d. Consumer finance companies
   e. Sales finance companies
   f. Commercial finance companies
   g. Credit unions
   h. Personal trust departments
   i. Pension funds
   j. Fire and casualty insurance companies
   k. Investment companies

7. What specific functions does the investment banker perform?

8. Assume you have $4,000 of your own money to invest in the stock market. Select a corporation's common stock from *Moody's Industrial Manual, Standard & Poor's Corporation Reports,* or some other source. Plot the common stock's market fluctuations reported in the daily newspaper over a one-month period. How do you account for the changes in the stock's market price? What seemed to be happening in the stock market as a whole over this same period of time?

9. What are some of the important elements in a person's overall financial position that he should examine before deciding to invest money in the stock market?

Business briefs

Supermarket savings and loans

Savings and loan associations are going out from their quiet, dignified office buildings to reach savers where they shop. Western Savings & Loan of Phoenix has established branch offices in 11 Smitty's Big Town stores. San Antonio Savings & Loan has branches in 15 Handy Andy supermarkets. The Fred Meyer stores in Oregon which sell products ranging from food to building supplies started S&L branches in 1974.

S&L branches in stores have created a stir in the industry. Supermarkets are customarily open 12 to 14 hours a day, six or seven days a week. Such branch offices perform some of the services already handled in supermarkets such as approving or cashing checks and selling money orders, stamps, and fishing licenses. In addition, the retail customers are potential borrowers as well as savers with the savings and loans.

1. Why would supermarkets and discount department stores be a good location for savings and loan branches?
2. What advantages would there be for the stores which have such S&L branches?
3. What problems might arise from this development from the point of view of:
   a. The public's image of S&Ls?
   b. S&Ls not having such branches?
   c. Commercial banks?

More conservative lending?

After inflation, recession, and the failure of three national banks in the early 1970s, many bankers in the United States are reconsidering their easy-lending policies to business enterprises.

There was a tremendous growth in business loans in the 10 years from 1965 to 1975. Business loans by commercial banks increased from $70 billion in 1965 to $180 billion in 1975. Also, banks made major investments in nonbanking operations through bank holding companies. Numerous banks invested in REITs (real estate investment trusts) which helped finance the building boom over this 10-year period. Many REITs have fallen into difficulty as some of their commercial building investments have failed to pay off.

Failures of the U.S. National Bank of San Diego, Franklin National Bank in New York, and Security National on Long Island caused other American bankers to review their operations closely. The international banking community was shocked by the 1974 failure of Germany's Bankhaus I. D. Herstatt.

The result of these bank failures was that many bankers are attempting to upgrade the quality of their loans. This means some individuals and business enterprises without blue-chip quality credentials and substantial net worth will not find bank credit available. Few experts expect bankers to return to the degree of conservatism exhibited toward borrowers during the 1930s and 1940s. However, the free-wheeling lending of the 1960s by many bankers has come to a screeching halt.

1. What factors have contributed to the move toward more conservative lending policies by commercial banks?
2. What will be the likely result for individuals and business enterprises of this switch in bank lending practice?
3. What may be the result for other financial institutions such as savings and loan associations, commercial and personal finance companies?

How much to reveal?

Should the Securities and Exchange Commission require publicly held corporations to reveal the effects of their operations on the environment? How much would it cost a corporation to stop polluting the environment? These questions and others relating to social issues are being considered by the SEC as the result of a court suit by an environmental protection group.

Since its establishment in 1934 the SEC has emphasized disclosure of financial information by corporations so investors could be better informed in deciding whether to buy or sell stock based on financial criteria. Now the SEC is faced with the question of whether there are sufficient investors concerned with the social responsibility of a corporation as well as its profits to require disclosure of such information.

Also to be considered is how much and what kind of nonfinancial information investors want in making decisions. The list of nonfinancial information business might be required to provide seems endless. Disclosure about environmental pollution, equal employment opportunity programs, political contributions by corporate executives, energy conservation programs, samples and gifts to customers, and international activities are a few of the areas an annual report might cover.

Proponents of more nonfinancial revelations by business suggest that modern legislation such as the National Environmental Protection Act of 1969 requires the SEC to demand disclosure in new areas. Opponents of added disclosure by industry maintain that even investors who consider themselves socially responsible are still mainly interested in a profitable return on their investments and therefore rely primarily on the financial data in annual reports.

1. What are the advantages and disadvantages of requiring business corporations to reveal more nonfinancial data to the investing public?
2. *a.* What specific nonfinancial information would you like to see provided by:
   1. General Motors?
   2. Bank of America?
   3. Exxon?
   4. Dow Chemical Company?
   b. What would be the purpose of having the above information revealed by these corporations?
3. What criteria should be used to determine which activities of business enterprises are socially significant?

Case

Family financial planning

Tom McCormick graduated two years ago from a well-known university with a degree in electrical engineering. While in college he took no courses in business administration or economics. He was married during his senior year and employed upon graduation by a large corporation which makes about 30 percent of its sales to various federal government agencies.

During a vacation trip to his home town he raised the following question with his uncle who was a stock broker. "Uncle Max," Tom began, "Jane and I have saved $5,000 over the past two years since we've both been working. We were wondering if you could give us some tips on investing this in the stock market. I'm afraid we're not too sophisticated about money matters, but we seem to be living pretty well and still saving some money."

The uncle replied, "Well, Tom, each person or family should develop an overall financial program for savings. Two elements of this plan, insurance and an insured savings account, should be considered before investments in stocks are made.

"Insurance is a separate subject in itself. However, we can make a few pertinent observations here. Especially if you and Jane plan to start a family soon, you will want to make sure you have sufficient life insurance to provide for family financial security in case of early death of one or both parents. You probably already have a certain amount of life insurance. I would guess it would be *whole life* insurance. Whole life provides both insurance coverage and cash surrender values for the policy owner built up from payment of premiums which are invested by the insurance company. Many young families also buy relatively low-cost *term* insurance to have added insurance protection in the child-rearing years. Term insurance provides insurance coverage for a specified period of time but has no cash surrender value. Your family should also be protected with health and disability insurance."

Tom commented, "Right now we have whole life insurance but no term insurance. However, we haven't really analyzed whether our coverage is sufficient. I have health insurance which is provided by my employer as a fringe benefit at a very reasonable rate. However, this group insurance is available only while I'm employed by the company."

Uncle Max went on, "Of course, you also have government social security insurance which would provide benefit payments to you if you became disabled or to your widow or children under specified conditions in addition to providing retirement benefits. However, social security payments are considered by most persons as supplementary minimum amounts and should not be considered sufficient to provide for all of a family's insurance or retirement needs.

"The second element in a person's savings program is the establishment of a savings account in a bank or savings and loan association. This account can provide money to meet unexpected needs which arise on short notice. A recommended amount in such a savings account would cover three to six months' living expenses. Such accounts should be placed only in financial institutions which are insured up to $40,000 for each account by the FDIC or FSLIC.

"Once these two financial keystones to a personal financial program are established, then other investment media may be considered. For many families the purchase of a house on monthly payments is an important part of their investment program as well as providing for living quarters. Before the purchase of a house is undertaken, factors to be considered include the family's preference for home ownership versus

renting a house or an apartment; location of the house under consideration; the total costs of home ownership, including taxes, insurance, and
maintenance; and the length of time the family expects to live in the
area. Only after some of these factors have been considered would I
recommend that you begin to invest in common stocks.

"I don't mean to make this a long lecture, Tom. But if you'll indicate
how you stand on these factors, then we can talk about your investment
objectives, and I'll make some suggestions for your study."

1. Make a list of the important questions Tom and his wife need to
   consider as they plan their family financial program.
2. Assume that Tom has adequate insurance and insured savings so
   that he could consider investing through the stock market. What
   investment objectives would you recommend to him and his wife at
   this time? What kind of securities would you suggest to achieve these
   objectives?

Courtesy Continental Illinois National Bank and Trust Company of Chicago

*Financial markets
facilitate the provision
of funds to finance
enterprise operations.*

*T*he finance function is vital to the profitable management of every business enterprise. The impact of financial decisions is felt throughout the enterprise. Whenever a new product line is added, a new factory built, labor contracts negotiated, or dividend payments considered, questions relating to finance must be resolved. Are the funds available to undertake the proposed course of action? Will the project make good use of resources? How should the undertaking be financed? This chapter analyzes the following questions relating to the financial management of the business enterprise:

What is the finance function?
What are the responsibilities of the finance department for the profitable management of the enterprise?
What is the specific role of top management in the finance area?
How is the finance department organized?

15

Financial management

THE FINANCE FUNCTION

The financial aspects of management should be viewed as an integrated part of the total management of the enterprise rather than as a narrow, specialized activity concerned mainly with writing checks and collecting accounts. Certainly it is a responsibility of the finance department to disburse funds for financial obligations and to supervise the granting of credit and the collection of accounts receivable. However, this is not the heart of the finance function. The basic elements of the finance function are the profitable use of funds and the selection among alternative sources of funds to finance enterprise activities at the most economical cost.

Financial managers have a responsibility to analyze the proposals by production and marketing managers for promoting the profit objective of the enterprise. The finance department must be sure that funds will be available to undertake the specific projects selected by management. This does not mean that the finance department makes all the critical decisions as to which investments will be undertaken by the enterprise. The proposals for production and marketing programs still originate in those departments. Production and marketing executives should have the necessary expert knowledge to decide which equipment will do a particular job or what product is likely to sell best. However, the finance department should perform the task of review and control when major decisions are made as to whether the enterprise should commit funds to new or continuing projects.

RESPONSIBILITIES OF THE FINANCE DEPARTMENT

In its role of decision making in both the use of funds and the acquisition of funds, the finance department should develop certain guidelines:

1. To determine the optimum size of the enterprise.
2. To select the best balance among different types of assets.
3. To provide the funds necessary to finance these assets.
4. To deal with the dilemma of profitability versus liquidity.

Size of the business enterprise

The size of a particular enterprise depends upon the nature of the industry of which the enterprise is a part, the legal form of enterprise organization, and the policies which are adopted regarding specific practices.

In some industries there is not much choice as to size of the enterprise. The management of a steel mill has no alternative except to provide large amounts of capital for the elaborate plant and equipment necessary to produce steel. Even the smallest steel mill requires an investment of many million dollars. On the other hand, there are industries which have a greater variation in size and financing requirements. The retail grocery industry is an example of this. Some grocers seek the economies associated with large multistore supermarket operations. This requires much capital. Other food retailers operate a single store profitably on a minimum investment.

The size of the enterprise also depends on the legal form of organization which is chosen. The corporate form of organization lends itself to raising large amounts of capital. The partnership and proprietorship normally do not have access to many of the sources of funds available to the corporation.

Specific asset management

Once the general size of the enterprise has been established, specific policies must be selected to determine the proper balance among the different classes of assets necessary for business operations. Policies relating to the following classes of assets contain key elements of financial management:

1. The size of cash and near-cash balances.
2. Credit policies—shall the enterprise extend credit to its customers, and, if so, what should be the terms of credit?
3. What shall be the size and composition of inventories?
4. Which fixed assets shall be acquired?

Size of cash and near-cash balance. One of the important operating responsibilities of financial management is the maintenance of cash and near-cash balances sufficient to pay the bills of the enterprise as they fall due. The cash account usually consists of money on deposit in commercial banks, although some funds may be held in a small *petty cash fund* for minor disbursements in cash. In the case of retail enterprises, working balances of currency and coin are kept on hand to make change for customers. *Near-cash* is any asset which is immediately transferable into money without risk of loss of value in the process. The customary form of near-cash for many financial managers is the 91-day U.S. Treasury bill. Although the interest rate on Treasury bills is usually relatively low, this type of investment does provide some interest on funds which are in excess of immediate cash needs. At the same time the funds so invested can be turned into cash on short notice. The determination of the proper level of cash and near-cash balances may be complicated and difficult. Such factors as the fluctuation in the enterprise's scale of operations, the ability of management to predict cash receipts and disbursements, and the ability of the enterprise to depend on other sources of funds such as bank credit should all be taken into account before setting the desired level of cash balances.

Credit policies.   The decision as to how much is to be invested in accounts receivable depends upon the extent to which credit sales are an important part of the sales effort and the way in which credit is managed. Management may decide that sales will be made on a cash-only basis. This policy would avoid the problems associated with extending credit and making collections. Funds would not be tied up in receivables from customers. The possibility of bad debt losses would be eliminated. However, a no-credit policy may result in a much lower level of sales with lower profits than if the enterprise granted credit to its customers. When credit is extended, terms are usually quoted in an abbreviated form such as "2/10, n/30." This means that a 2 percent cash discount is allowed the customer who pays within 10 days from the date on the merchandise invoice statement or the bill is to be paid with no discount within 11 to 30 days.

Although each enterprise's management is theoretically able to set its own credit terms, credit practices are strongly influenced by those which prevail in the industry. Such policies as the terms of credit and the volume of credit sales will likely be similar to those which exist throughout the industry. However, management does have considerable freedom in determining the credit worthiness of customers and in collection policies to see that customers pay promptly. Whether an enterprise adopts a conservative or liberal policy regarding credit extension should be determined after consideration has been given to the anticipated additional profits which likely will result from a proposed policy.

Size and composition of inventories.   The determination of the optimum size and composition of inventories is of key importance in both manufacturing and marketing enterprises. For the manufacturing enterprise there are three types of inventories—raw materials, work in process, and finished goods. Beginning with the raw materials, value is added throughout the production process until the goods are completed and ready to be shipped to customers. Purchasing and production departments have primary responsibility for determining the specific levels of manufacturing inventories. However, the inventory policies which are followed influence the financial needs of the business enterprise. Hence, the finance department has a responsibility for anticipating requirements for funds which will arise from increasing inventories. Furthermore, the finance department should be concerned with the efficient use of inventories. For example, improvement of inventory

Employment outlook

Credit officials

Many daily activities of businesses and individuals depend upon receiving goods and services on credit or obtaining cash loans. In most forms of credit analysis a credit official makes the decision to accept or reject the application. These workers include credit managers, who authorize customer purchases when payment is promised at a later date, and loan officers, who approve cash loans by financial institutions. Employment of credit officials is expected to increase rapidly through the mid-1980s as the number of individual credit transactions continues to grow.

Although the increasing use of computers for storing and retrieving information will allow individual credit officials to serve more customers, this should not slow the growth of the occupation. As companies handle greater numbers of credit transactions, the credit official will spend more time supervising the credit management process in his firm. Moreover, many duties of credit officials, such as counseling customers and interviewing applicants, demand the tact and good judgment provided by personal contact.

In addition, attractive credit terms are a major tool for increasing the sales volume of almost any business. As firms strive to maximize their sales in the face of competition, there will be a greater demand for skilled credit officials.

turnover may result in lower inventories and a reduction in the amount of funds required to finance them.

Acquisition of fixed assets. The specific industry and the scale of business operations will generally determine the need for fixed assets. Fixed assets, sometimes called capital assets, include land, buildings, equipment, machinery, tools, furniture, and fixtures. The commitment of funds to fixed assets is of considerable importance to the finance department because fixed assets usually involve an investment of substantial size. Before making a major investment in fixed assets, there should be a careful appraisal of the need for the specific assets and the prospects for profits stemming from their acquisition. Funds committed to fixed assets may be tied up for many years. If borrowing is undertaken to acquire the funds the lender must be repaid regardless of how well the investment works out. If stockholders put up the money through the purchase of more stock they expect profitable use to be made of their funds. If the investment in fixed assets does not work out well it may be difficult, if not impossible, to dispose of the assets at anything near their book value. For these reasons the finance department should confer with other departments to assure that all reasonable steps have been taken to analyze the desirability of investment in a particular fixed asset.

Financing of assets

In addition to advising other departments on the acquisition of fixed assets, the finance department has the responsibility of determining the best means of providing the funds for these assets. Enterprise assets may be financed by debt, by the use of leases, or by owners.

The specific source of funds to finance a given project will depend on how long the funds are needed, the way in which funds have been acquired in the past, the attitude of management toward the risks of debt, and conditions at the time in the financial markets.

Financing by use of debt. Funds provided by outsiders through short-term, intermediate-term, and long-term debt are important sources of business enterprise financing. Although the classification of debt on the basis of length of time until maturity varies, short-term debt is that debt which falls due within a year. Intermediate debt usually represents funds obtained for periods of time running from over a year until about ten years. Long-term debt customarily has a maturity more than ten years in the future.

The length of time for which money is borrowed depends upon the purpose of the loan. Generally it is advisable to use the form of credit which has a maturity as long as the money will be needed. Thus, you should not finance a seasonal buildup in inventory to meet holiday merchandise demands with a long-term loan from a life insurance company. More importantly, you should not finance a factory building that is expected to last for at least 20 years with a six-month bank loan. In the latter case the possibility exists that the loan might not be renewed by the bank after six months. This could result in severe financial difficulties for the business enterprise if funds were not available to repay the loan. This problem can be avoided if money is borrowed for the length of time it will be needed.

Short-term sources of funds include bank loans and credit extended by suppliers. Short-term bank loans are an excellent way to finance inventory buildup to meet seasonal or unexpected needs for merchandise. After the merchandise has been sold, the bank loan is paid off with the proceeds from the sale. Suppliers frequently extend trade credit to their customers to finance merchandise or equipment purchases.

In this country formal notes recognizing liability for accounts payable to a supplier have not been widely used. Normally merchandise is shipped on open-trade account. However, when the enterprise is not known to the supplier or has been slow in paying its trade accounts, the supplier may ask that a note be signed to acknowledge the indebtedness.

Intermediate credit may be obtained through banks, insurance companies, or finance companies which specialize in equipment loans for a period of years. The *term loan,* as intermediate credit is customarily called, is characterized by a loan running for more than 1 year and less than 10. Periodic repayments are normally made to reduce the principal amount of the loan outstanding so that upon maturity only a small amount of the original loan will fall due. The conditions of the term loan are agreed upon by borrower and lender on an individual basis so there is room for considerable flexibility in the lending arrangements and provisions for repayment.

Long-term debt funds may be obtained through direct loans from insurance companies or through the sale of bonds to groups such as corporate pension funds, other business enterprises, or the general public. A *bond* is a debt contract whereby the borrower agrees to repay a certain sum of money at some specified time in the future in exchange for a given sum of money today. A wide variety of conditions may make up the *bond indenture* which is the legal contract giving the details of the arrangement between the issuing company (the borrower) and the bondholders (the lenders). If the borrower fails to live up to the conditions set forth in the bond indenture, there will be provision for some penalty which bondholders may invoke. The penalty might be restricting the dividends paid to stockholders, having the bondholders take certain of the enterprise's assets, or even taking over the management of the enterprise.

As you can see, borrowing long-term funds is a momentous occasion for the enterprise. Large amounts of money are involved, and the projects to be undertaken are substantial in their impact on future enterprise operations. Careful analysis of the desirability of projects requiring long-term funds and the means of their financing is necessary. It is the responsibility of the finance department to provide the leadership and technical knowledge for this analysis.

Financing by leasing. Leasing has increased in importance in recent years. The *lease* is a form of long-term renting contract which an enterprise may sign to obtain the use of assets without owning them. The lease arrangement is a formal obligation for the payment of money over a period of time in the future which creates a contingent liability upon future operations. Business has made extensive use of leases on both buildings and equipment.

One popular arrangement is the *sale-and-leaseback* agreement. An enterprise constructs a building to its specifications and then sells it to a financial institution such as an insurance company. Simultaneously it leases the building back for a long period of time. The result is that the enterprise has the use of the building without immediately tying up its funds. The enterprise then may use its funds for some other purpose, such as increasing inventories, improving product lines, or opening new marketing areas. The advantages of leasing are apparent. However, the lease arrangement should be investigated carefully before it is used. Possible problems include the long-term payments required and questions as to tax liabilities and final ownership of the property at the end of the lease.

Financing provided by owners. Besides funds provided by outsiders, funds are generated internally by business operations and from the sale of additional stock in the corporation (or of additional partnership or proprietorship funds if these legal forms of organization are used).

The amount of profits an enterprise retains to finance future needs depends upon the investment opportunities that are available and the amount of earnings that top management decides to pay to owners in dividends. The determination of the enterprise's dividend policy is one of the important responsibilities of top management and is discussed later in this chapter.

Because of the relative infrequency of the sale of stock by the corporation, when top management decides on this course of action the services of an investment banker are usually needed. You will recall the discussion of investment banking in Chapter 14. An investment banker aids the enterprise's finance department by setting the price of the stock, timing its sale, achieving wide distribution of the shares if the stock is not being sold to present stockholders, and handling the legal requirements of the Securities and Exchange Commission.

The dilemma of liquidity versus profitability

One way of summarizing the finance function in business is to say that the objective of financial management is to assure that funds are available to pay bills as they are due and to promote the long-run profit objectives of the enterprise. In a very real sense these two objectives are in conflict. In order to avoid being short of cash to meet financial obligations, huge cash balances could be kept on hand at all times. The major portion of the assets of the enterprise might be tied up in a bank checking account or invested in short-term government securities which could be turned instantly into cash. In this case, liquidity would be extremely high for the enterprise. All bills would be promptly paid and large cash balances would be available to meet any contingency, however remote. In achieving this objective of extreme liquidity, the finance department would ignore its other vital responsibility of promoting the profitability of the enterprise.

To maximize profitability the finance department might attempt to calculate the needs for cash so that cash inflow exactly matched cash outflow. No excess of cash would be on hand at any time. In this case all funds would be invested in working assets such as accounts receivable, inventories, or plant and equipment. These working assets would be the basis for operations which would result in large profit potential for the enterprise. There would be no idle cash in the bank account and no funds invested in low-interest government securities. This approach to financial management would promote profitability. However, it would subject the enterprise to the danger that liquidity would be impaired and bills could not be paid on time.

In the dilemma posed for the finance department by liquidity and profitability, neither extreme represents the best answer. Some funds must be invested in cash and near-cash assets to provide necessary liquidity. The credit rating of the enterprise must be maintained in good economic times so that when the need for credit is pressing, creditors will be willing to provide funds. At the same time, most of the enterprise's funds should be invested in assets which will be more profitable than cash and near-cash. The balance that financial managers strike between liquidity and profitability comes only after considerable calculating, deliberation, and discussion. Ultimately the decision will depend upon whether top management as a representative of the owners prefers to "eat well" with greater expected profitability or "sleep well" by having greater liquidity.

FINANCIAL RESPONSIBILITIES OF TOP MANAGEMENT

The top management of a business enterprise includes those who head the main divisions, such as the vice presidents of marketing, manufacturing, finance, and personnel; the chief executive officer who usually has the title of president; and the group of individuals representing the owners of the enterprise. In the corporation the board of directors is the group elected by the stockholders to represent their interests and to determine the overall policies for enterprise operation. The partners in the partnership fulfill the function of the board of directors, and in the proprietorship the sole owner determines overall policies.

The members of top management have responsibilities for financial decisions in the following areas:

1. Financial planning and organizing for profits.
2. Allocation of profits through dividend policy.
3. Determination of the capital structure of the enterprise.
4. Deciding special issues, such as consolidation and merger proposals.

Planning for profits

In the area of financial planning for profits, the top management has the overall responsibility for the effective utilization of enterprise funds. Investment proposals presented to top management should be scrutinized for anticipated profitability and the long-run benefits which are expected. The interests of the owners of the enterprise are important when top management is confronted by financial issues. If the financial affairs of the enterprise are not well managed, the owners stand to lose their investment. In the corporation it is the stockholders who possess the legal right to control the management and to change it if financial results are poor. This is true even though in the large corporation there are thousands of stockholders who do not exercise their right to vote on directors who will determine vital policies.

There are specific legal responsibilities which the board of directors has in a corporation. These include the restrictions imposed by the corporation's charter, the state laws of incorporation, and the general prohibition against *ultra vires* acts (those actions beyond the powers granted to directors). The board is required to act as a faithful steward of the enterprise's assets.

As an important part of profit planning the board of directors must select the enterprise's president and approve the selection of the financial officer from among the most competent candidates available. Top management has the further responsibility of seeing that the finance department is organized to deal effectively with the many financial issues which arise. One of the best tools for top management to evaluate and control financial operations is the budget. The use of budgets for planning, executing, and controlling the financial progress of the enterprise is very important, as is pointed out in Chapter 6.

Determination of dividend policy

The determination and execution of dividend policy is the second area of financial responsibility for top management. In the corporation the board of directors sets dividend policy. In the partnership the partners decide how much of the profits will be withdrawn. In the proprietorship the owner decides how much money will be taken from operations for his private use. The basic question of profits distribution is the same for all legal forms of organization—what policy will best allocate profits to satisfy the needs of the owners for income and at the same time meet the needs of the enterprise for funds for profitable growth and development. This discussion centers on the determinants of dividend policy for the corporation. However, the principles are generally applicable to the other legal forms of business organization.

The factors top management normally takes into account in determining a corporation's dividend policy are as follows:

Amount of earnings. Since dividends represent a distribution of the profits to the owners of the corporation, the amount of earnings is an important determinant of the level of dividends paid. Usually top management decides to distribute some proportion of earnings as cash dividends and retain the balance of profits for reinvestment in the enterprise. Although there is wide variation in dividend payout percentages, many corporations pay out between 40 and 60 percent of profits in dividends. Frequently, small or no cash dividends will be paid shareholders in the early stages of an enterprise's development when the need for funds is greatest. With the maturation of the enterprise dividend payments are usually initiated or increased.

Present level of dividends. In the established enterprise where a cash dividend policy is already in effect, the management is influenced by the level of cash dividends which was paid the last time directors considered the question. In general, managements are prone to maintain the dividend rate which was paid in a previous period. Most cash dividends are paid quarterly throughout the year. This means that directors are reluctant to increase the cash dividend rate per share from a previous quarter's payment unless they are fairly sure that the higher rate can be continued in the future. Likewise, directors are hesitant to reduce cash dividend rates even in the face of lower earnings if they anticipate that the drop in profits may be temporary. The logic behind this attitude is that directors are reluctant to incur the displeasure of stockholders stemming from the immediate reduction of cash dividends plus the decline in the market price for the corporation's stock which generally accompanies a reduction in cash dividends.

Profit prospects on new investments. In deciding upon the level of cash dividends paid to shareholders, top management also takes into account the opportunities which exist for investment of profits in new projects. If demands for investment in enterprise projects are great, with prospects for high rates of return, then management may be reluctant to pay out as large a cash dividend as it would if reinvestment prospects were not so bright.

Dividend practice in the industry. The type of dividend policy which prevails throughout an enterprise's industry is another consideration for directors. The fact that a competitor has a particular dividend policy is not a sufficient reason for management taking the same action. However, if management does deviate significantly from the dividend practice throughout the industry there should be a reason for this variance. Otherwise, stockholders may be penalized by a lower market price being offered for the corporation's stock merely because it is "out of step" with established industry practice.

Size of corporation's cash account. As directors consider dividend declarations, the ability of the corporation to have the cash on hand to meet this declaration is a mechanical factor which must be taken into account. This means that the finance department must manage the cash flows of the enterprise so as to have the money to meet the cash dividend payments which directors authorize.

Use of stock dividends. An alternative is the use of *stock dividends.* Instead of cash dividend payments or increases in cash dividend rates, the management issues more shares of stock to shareholders. The immediate effect of these stock dividends is an increase in the number of shares in the hands of owners. However, assuming management maintains or increases its present cash dividend rate, the long-run effect is to increase the amount of cash dividends because cash dividends are paid on an increased number of shares. Individual stockholders have given a generally favorable reception to the distribution of stock dividends, although they have shown a preference for cash dividends when given a choice between the two.

One approach to solve the dilemma faced by management in trying to meet the needs for reinvestment funds in the enterprise plus the legitimate request of stockholders for dividend income is to have a dividend policy which is clearly stated by top management to stockholders. Then at least stockholders will be aware of the guidelines under which management will operate in dividend matters. Stockholders may then tailor their individual investment portfolios to include the stock of those corporations which have a dividend policy that suits their needs.

Determining capital structure

One of the important responsibilities of the board of directors is the determination of the capital structure of the corporation. The *capital structure* is defined as all the long-term funds which are committed to the enterprise's operations. These long-term funds are supplied from two primary sources—owners' investment, both through the purchases of stock and the reinvestment of profits, and long-term debt. The determination of the balance between long-term debt and owners' funds to finance the assets of the corporation is a tedious issue for corporate managers. At one extreme, if there is no long-term debt there is no risk that the enterprise will ever be embarrassed by not being able to meet interest costs and principal repayments. This type of capital structure would provide a maximum of safety for the investment of the owners.

However, the sole use of ownership funds in the capital structure ignores the possibility of increasing the rate of return on the owners' investment when money is borrowed. This would occur if more is earned on the borrowed money than the cost of the interest paid. The use of debt with the expectation of increasing the rate of return on the owners' investment is called *trading on the equity.*

Does the advantage of trading on the equity mean that top management should continue to add more and more debt to the capital structure? By no means! The assumption of debt brings with it the obligation to pay interest on the borrowed money whether or not the enterprise operates profitably. Furthermore, at some time in the future the debt itself must be repaid. Thus, the advantage of an increased rate of profitability on owners' funds through borrowing must be tempered by the risks associated with undertaking the debt. Determining a proper balance between long-term debt and equity funds is one of the responsibilities of the board of directors. A final answer can be reached only after weighing the conflicting aspects of profitability and the risks associated with debt.

Consolidation and merger proposals

The last area for discussion of the financial responsibilities of the top management is that of special issues which arise from time to time during the operation of the business enterprise. These include consolidation and merger proposals. A *consolidation* is the joining of two or more independent business enterprises into a new enterprise under a single management. A *merger* occurs when a smaller enterprise is taken over by a larger business enterprise. Frequently in the case of a merger the acquired enterprise will become a division of the larger organization. In either of these situations, top management must determine the value of its enterprise in relation to the other enterprise which is a party to the merger or consolidation. The two basic techniques which management may use to determine the value of the enterprise are the valuation of enterprise assets or the valuation of the expected stream of profits of the enterprise.

In using the technique of valuation of enterprise assets, the assets may be valued on the basis of their *book value,* which is their worth based on original cost as shown in the accounting records; on *reproduction value,* which is what it would cost to replace the assets; or on *liquidation value,* which would be the value of the assets if they were sold. When the enterprise is valued on the basis of its *stream of profits,* the management must estimate future earnings and then determine the value of the business based on the yield resulting from those earnings.

No matter what valuation techniques are used the final determination of a satisfactory merger agreement will come about only as the result of bargaining by both sides after considering all factors, financial and others. Each board of directors has the responsibility to protect the interests of its own shareholders and to secure the best terms possible under the existing circumstances.

ORGANIZATION OF THE FINANCE DEPARTMENT

The broad financial policies determined by the board of directors set the boundaries for the finance department in the performance of its duties. Generally there is considerable latitude for further decision making in matters of financial management. In a particular corporation the degree of responsibility and authority exercised by the financial officer and the department will vary depending upon such factors as education and experience, personality, and how much confidence the president and the board of directors have in the financial officer.

In the large corporation there will usually be several executives who are concerned directly with financial management. Although there is a wide variation in the organization of finance departments and the titles used from one enterprise to another, a typical finance department (see Figure 15–1) includes the following positions. The top finance officer who may be titled *vice president for finance* directs the overall activities of the finance department. There is a good possibility that the financial officer will be a member of the corporation's board of directors. Considerable time is spent in long-range financial planning and preparation of long-term budgets as well as supervising the activities of subordinates. Besides the financial officer there will be a *treasurer* who is responsible for custody of cash funds, securities, insurance policies, and other valuable papers. Responsibilities include receiving incoming cash and approving cash disbursements as well as preparing financial data for directors, stockholders, and the public. The treasurer's office also deals with banks and other lenders.

The *controller* is responsible for the accounting function in the enterprise in both record keeping and in preparing financial statements and analysis based on these records. The controller, as the chief accounting officer, checks on budget preparation and follows up to see how well the budget is adhered to by the various departments of the enterprise. Although the treasurer will be responsible for all paychecks, the controller's office may prepare the payroll for the treasurer's approval. The *credit manager* may report to either the treasurer or the controller. As head of the credit department the credit manager is responsible for deciding which customers shall be granted credit and the extent of that credit. The credit manager presses collection of delinquent accounts and assists other financial executives in the determination of overall credit policies. The *auditor* and staff check on the functioning of the accounting and control systems in the business enterprise. Company auditors not only verify the reported performance of the

FIGURE 15–1

Partial organization chart of a finance department

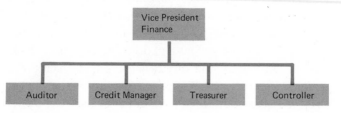

various divisions but also may act as staff advisors to make recommendations to management for the more effective operation of the enterprise.

Thus, financial executives perform a variety of functions. The assignment of these functions may vary with the particular enterprise and the person filling a particular position, but the functions exist in all enterprises. Generally in large corporations the higher the executive is in the organization structure of the finance department, the more time is spent in long-range planning, with outside sources of funds such as banks, insurance companies, and investment bankers, and with the president and the board of directors. The finance department has a responsibility to work with other departments to facilitate the production and sale of goods or services.

SUMMARY

The finance function is not only the disbursement of funds, granting of credit, and collection of receivables. In a more basic sense it includes responsibility for the profitable utilization of funds available to management and the securing of funds at their most economical cost. The finance department in each enterprise should develop guidelines:

To determine the optimum size of the enterprise.
To select the best balance among different types of assets.
To provide the funds necessary to finance these assets.
To deal with the dilemma of profitability versus liquidity.

The dilemma of liquidity and profitability refers to the need of the finance department to have sufficient cash on hand to pay bills as they fall due and yet to maximize profitability by investing funds in such assets as inventories or plant and equipment.

Members of top management have responsibilities for financial decisions in the following areas:

Financial planning and organizing for profits.
Allocation of profits through dividend policy.
Determination of the capital structure of the enterprise.
Deciding on special matters, such as consolidation and merger proposals.

Dividend policy determination should take into account the level of earnings now and anticipated for the future, the present level of dividend payments, the projected profits on new investments which might be made, the size of the corporation's cash account, and the prevailing dividend policy throughout the industry.

When determining the enterprise's capital structure, management must consider the desired balance between owners' investment and debt. Since creditors have a prior claim against assets, little or no long-term debt gives a maximum of safety for the owners but may result in a lower level of profitability on the equity funds. Borrowed funds which are profitably employed can increase the rate of return on owners' equity.

A consolidation occurs when two or more independent business enterprises are joined into a new enterprise under a single management. A merger occurs when a smaller enterprise is taken over by a larger company. In a merger or consolidation, the two basic techniques which may be used to determine the value of the enterprises are the valuation of the assets involved or the valuation of the expected stream of profits of the enterprises.

The top officer of the finance department is usually the vice president for finance who reports to the president of the enterprise. Subordinates of the financial officer include the treasurer, controller, credit manager, and auditor.

TERMS FOR REVIEW

finance function

term loan

bond indenture

lease

cash dividend

stock dividend

capital structure

trading on the equity

consolidation

merger

QUESTIONS

1. What are the major responsibilities of the finance department?
2. In what ways does an enterprise have control over extension of credit to its potential customers? How is the enterprise limited in its control over credit terms extended to customers?
3. List the sources of funds available to the large corporation. Discuss the different factors that management needs to consider in deciding on a specific source of funds for a particular project.
4. Explain the financial dilemma of liquidity versus profitability.
5. What factors should be taken into account in determining the amount of cash dividends to be paid to common stockholders?
6. *a.* How can the use of debt by the corporation increase the rate of return on the common stockholders' equity?
    b. How can the use of debt be detrimental to the common stockholders?
7. When a merger or consolidation is contemplated, what are the methods which may be used to determine the value of the enterprise under consideration?

Business briefs

The burden of debt

In the fall of 1974 Northwestern Bell Telephone, a subsidiary of AT&T, sold bonds at an interest rate of 10 percent annually. About the same time Boston Edison and Detroit Edison electric companies had to pay over 12 percent for long-term borrowing. Some business enterprises such as Avco, Pan American airlines, and Consolidated Edison experienced serious difficulties in obtaining debt funds at any price either to finance operations or to pay off debt that was falling due. Commercial banks experienced an increase in demand for short-term loans, and the prime rate reached 12 percent.

At the same time that many business enterprises were having difficulty obtaining loans, the stock market sank to a 12-year low making it difficult for corporations to sell common stock to provide cash.

The 1974–75 recession and the simultaneous inflation put pressure on profits in many enterprises. This reduced retained earnings as a source of funds for business. In summary, enterprises which had traditionally counted on selling bonds or stocks or retaining profits to finance expansion were in a real bind.

1. What alternatives could be considered by top management to the financial problems facing business in late 1974?
2. What can business managers learn from the 1974 economy and the financial market conditions at that time?
3. What dilemma faces the business manager who decides to limit expansion to retained profits instead of increasing the corporation's long-term debt?

Plow them back

Over 600 U.S. corporations are offering their stockholders dividend-reinvestment programs. These programs give stockholders an opportunity to reinvest cash dividends with low commission charges.

American Telephone & Telegraph, which has 3 million shareholders, reports more than 15 percent of its stockholders are signed up in its dividend-reinvestment program. More than 20 percent of Walt Disney's stockholders are enrolled in that corporation's plan, and General Motors indicates that between 5 and 10 percent of its stockholders participate. Other corporations with similar plans include American Electric Power, Firestone, Quaker Oats, and Travelers Insurance.

Most of the stockholders participating in dividend-reinvestment are individuals with relatively small blocks of stock. Therefore, the percentage of dividends retained by corporations is much lower than the proportion of stockholders participating in such plans might indicate.

1. What advantages are there for corporations in dividend-reinvestment plans?
2. What advantages are there for stockholders in such programs?

3. Would stockholders be in a better position if corporations simply did not pay any cash dividends and instead retained the cash which might otherwise be paid in dividends?

Public financing—private use

For many years municipalities have helped business enterprises finance factory buildings by issuing industrial revenue bonds. The practice started with Mississippi's BAWI (Balance Agriculture With Industry) program and rapidly spread through the South and across the country. Rentals or lease payments from the manufacturer are used to pay the bond interest and pay off the bonds when they fall due.

The interest paid investors on municipal bonds, including industrial revenue bonds, issued by communities and states is exempt from federal income taxes. Because of this the interest rates on such bonds are lower than on bonds issued by business corporations, the interest on which is taxable. The original intent of federal tax exemption was to assist governmental units in financing public projects at reasonable interest rates.

In 1969 the federal government limited individual industrial revenue bond issues to a maximum of $5 million to stem the tide of such bond issues which had reached almost $2 billion in 1968. In 1974 the volume of industrial revenue bond financing dropped to less than $350 million. Still, many small and medium size business enterprises were taking advantage of cities' offers to provide such financing to encourage relocation of factories or for the development of new plants. Interest rates on such industrial revenue bonds were 30 percent or more lower than the business corporations would have had to pay if they sold bonds themselves.

Chicago-based Allied Products Corporation has made extensive use of industrial revenue bond financing. Products making up Allied's $300 million yearly sales include agricultural implements, auto parts, and fasteners. About one third of its plants are located in the South. Between June 1973 and April 1974, Allied financed seven separate projects which totaled $17.5 million through industrial revenue bonds. Interest was less than 6½ percent. With a Ba rating by Moodys and a B plus by Standard & Poor's,[1] Allied would have had to pay at least 10 percent in the corporate bond market for long-term money.

---

[1] Moody's and Standard & Poor's are financial advisory services which rate bond issues. Higher bond ratings reflect a lower evaluation of risk. The lower the risk, the lower the interest rate is. Moody's highest bond rating is Aaa and ranges down to Caa in 9 steps.

1. If you were the financial officer of a manufacturing corporation would you seek out municipalities that would provide industrial bond financing if you located a plant in their area?
2. *a.* What advantages are there for the community in issuing industrial revenue bonds?
   b. What possible disadvantages are there for cities and states in issuing industrial revenue bonds?
3. From the point of view of public policy should the use of industrial revenue bonds by municipalities be continued?

Cases

Pine Tree Wood Products Company

The Pine Tree Wood Products Company, Inc., had been in Atlanta for several years. Its principal products were wooden and metal fences which had become quite popular with home owners. They were also used by industrial firms for security purposes. Other products included flooring and unfinished furniture. The company had a reputation for quality products and workmanship.

Jim Curtis, owner of Pine Tree Wood Products Company, was 58 years old. He had a son, 35, who was also engaged in the business. The company employed 8 or 9 persons on a full-time basis. Seasonal employment in the summer rose to about 40 as more sales personnel and laborers were required to meet the demand for fence installations.

Early in 1974, Jim Curtis approached Ned Ollis, loan officer of the First State Bank of Atlanta, for a loan of $80,000. The money would be used to acquire a small company which produced materials to treat and preserve wood posts and lumber. The First State Bank had done business with Jim Curtis since 1970, when he became acquainted with Mr. Ollis as the two worked on a United Way fund drive committee together. Shortly thereafter Mr. Curtis talked with Mr. Ollis about moving his banking business to the First State Bank from a smaller bank which had been reluctant to meet his increasing needs for loans as his business interests expanded.

Beginning in 1970 the First State Bank had provided the Pine Tree Wood Products Company with an unsecured line of credit of $50,000 to finance seasonal inventory increases and accounts receivable during the peak periods of business. Although the unsecured line of credit was to the Pine Tree Wood Products Company it was personally guaranteed by both Mr. and Mrs. Jim Curtis. Provisions of the loan agreement included a 30-day cleanup period during which the loan would be completely paid off. An added requirement was that funds for this cleanup were not to come from borrowings at other banks.

This line of credit was handled to the bank's satisfaction during 1970 and 1971. Borrowings were made in amounts of roughly $10,000 beginning in the early spring and reaching a peak in the late summer. Then the loan was reduced in amounts of $10,000 until it was off the books for about two months during the winter period. In 1972 Mr. Curtis requested that the credit line be increased to $60,000. This was approved by the bank's loan committee upon Mr. Ollis' recommendation. Summary financial information on the Pine Tree Wood Products Company and on Mr. Curtis' personal liabilities and net worth is provided in Exhibits 1 and 2.

In addition to the Pine Tree Wood Products Company, the Curtis family owned a 400-acre farm outside of Atlanta which was stocked with beef cattle. In early 1974 the bank had a loan of approximately $25,000 outstanding to Mr. and Mrs. Curtis to finance the herd of feeder cattle. This was in addition to the $60,000 line of credit for the company of which $20,000 was outstanding on December 31, 1973. Other personal liabilities, made up chiefly of real estate mortgages held by a savings and loan association, amounted to about $60,000 at the end of 1973.

It was in the autumn of 1973 that Mr. Curtis had first become aware of the possibility of purchasing a company located 150 miles from Atlanta. The company produced wood products, mainly fence posts, beams, and other lumber items treated with creosote and other wood preservatives. The company was owned by a man 67 years old who had expressed an interest in selling the business and retiring. Six or seven employees worked in the business. Timber products were purchased for cash directly from farmers and wood-lot operators in the area. Annual sales had varied between $75,000 and $125,000 per year with a few lumber dealers buying approximately 80 percent of the plant's output. Farmers and small business enterprises in the area constituted the remaining customers of the business and paid for their purchases in cash.

Mr. Curtis drove to the wood-treating plant and discussed the possible purchase of the business with its elderly owner. At the end of their discussions the owner verbally offered to sell the business for $80,000. Assets consisted mostly of machinery, used but apparently in good working order, and the inventory of wood products, some of which were treated, along with a supply of chemicals and petroleum products necessary for the treating process. Although formal records were scanty, on his initial visit Mr. Curtis estimated that profits had ranged between $8,000 and $20,000 in recent years. After the owner's offer to sell, Mr. Curtis left with the promise to return in the near future with his accountant to go over the company's records more closely.

Upon his return to Atlanta Mr. Curtis discussed the proposed purchase with the First State Bank loan officer. He sounded him out on the possibility of financing which might be available for adding this wood-treating operation to his Atlanta business. Mr. Curtis felt that the wood treating would be an ideal complement to his present business since the plant could supply many of the wood products which he currently was buying from outside sources. Also, he visualized markets for the wood-treated posts and lumber throughout the Atlanta area. Mr. Curtis pointed out to Mr. Ollis that he had space available behind his Atlanta shop for storage of a large inventory of wood-treated products so that expansion of his present facilities would not be necessary. Furthermore, he had an employee who had had experience in wood treating and could manage the new operation, which would be 150 miles away.

Approximately two weeks after his visit to the wood-treating plant, Mr. Curtis and his accountant returned. An examination of the records indicated that the best information about the business had to be taken from the owner's individual income tax returns. While detailed financial information on the company's operations was not complete it appeared that actual profits had been somewhat higher than Mr. Curtis had originally estimated and had varied between $12,000 and $25,000 per year.

Two days later Mr. Curtis offered $80,000 for the business, which was accepted by the owner. Since the offer was contingent upon satisfactory financing being arranged, Mr. Curtis immediately contacted the loan officer at the First State Bank to see if an $80,000 loan could be

EXHIBIT 1
Pine Tree Wood Products Company, Inc.

	Thousands of $			
	1973	*1972*	*1971*	*1970*
Sales....................................	$440	$410	$420	$395
Net income...........................	31	24	25	19
Net worth of corporation...............	120	100	76	80

EXHIBIT 2
Personal financial data, Mr. and Mrs. Curtis

	Thousands of $			
	1973	*1972*	*1971*	*1970*
Personal net worth (including owner-ship of Pine Tree Wood Products)	$220	$210	$180	$140
Personal liabilities (not including liabil-ities of Pine Tree Wood Products)	90	85	65	58

obtained and, if so, on what terms. He presented Mr. Ollis with pre-liminary statements on his 1973 sales and net income for the Pine Tree Wood Products Company along with the net worth of the corporation as of December 31, 1973.

1. What has been the extent of the bank's relationship up to this point with Mr. Curtis? How has this relationship worked out for both parties?
2. What consideration should be taken into account by the bank's loan officer in deciding whether or not to grant the $80,000 loan request?
3. From the information given, how would you decide this request if you were the loan officer? If you would make the loan, what con-ditions would you require? If you would not make the loan, what are your reasons? If you would not make it, what advice or assistance might you provide Mr. Curtis?

Zero Duplicator Corporation

Because of increasing demand for its products and good profit prospects, the Zero Duplicator Corporation's management decided to build a new factory located in the southwestern part of the United States where company manufacturing operations had not been previously located. The company's home office and manufacturing facilities were located on the outskirts of a large eastern city and would continue to serve the company's eastern customers.

Engineering estimates are that $5 million will be required for the new facility. Of this amount $1 million can be provided by reducing the corporation's cash and near-cash accounts, and $1 million will be generated within the coming year by retaining a large portion of expected profits in order to build this new plant. After consultation with investment bankers, management concluded the remaining $3 million might be raised in one of the following ways:

1. Sale of 30,000 shares of 8 percent preferred stock $100 par value.
2. Sale of $3 million of 10 percent bonds with a sinking fund to retire the issue over ten equal annual payments beginning the sixth year after the issue is sold.
3. Sale of 100,000 shares of common stock at $30 per share. The current market price of the corporation's stock is $35 per share. Investment bankers estimate that the new shares of stock could be sold at a price to net $30 per share to the corporation.

For the year just ended Zero Duplicator's balance sheet is summarized as follows:

Current assets (including		Current liabilities........	$ 8,000,000
cash and near-cash)...	$12,000,000	Common stock (2 million	
Net fixed assets.........	5,000,000	shares authorized, 1	
Other assets including		million shares out-	
patents...............	1,000,000	standing)..............	1,000,000
		Retained earnings and	
		other capital accounts.	9,000,000
		Total Liabilities and	
Total Assets.......	$18,000,000	Net Worth.......	$18,000,000

Earnings before interest and taxes were approximately $2.0 million in the year just ended, or $1.00 per share of common stock after taxes. Management expected earnings to increase by at least 20 percent in the current year without the new plant facility. For planning purposes it is expected that income taxes will continue at about 50 percent of taxable income. Management feels that prospects for future growth are excellent. Three years ago the company successfully defended itself against a patent infringement suit by a large competitor. Although the duplicating equipment field is highly competitive, Zero's management believes they hold some key technological patents. However, at the present time the company's share of the market is small.

No cash dividends have been paid to common stockholders since the corporation was organized a few years ago. The corporation's stock is rather closely held among members of management and a few wealthy investors but some shares are held by the public. The stock is inactively traded in the over-the-counter market. No one person holds controlling interest in the corporation's stock.

1. What key financial issues are involved in dealing with the immediate problem presented in this case?
2. Evaluate the pros and cons of each proposed method of financing.
3. What broad management policies should be considered in this case in addition to the financing of a new factory?

☆☆☆
☆☆

section six

Business in a
changing world

*Computer systems
greatly increase
management's capacity
to analyze business
operations.*

*E*lectronic computers have brought about a true revolution in the past 25 years! The computer has the ability to store and retrieve vast amounts of information, to make instant calculations, and to control many different operations. Major users of computers include governmental bodies, educational institutions, the legal and medical professions, and business enterprises. The production and distribution of computers has created an industry which was unknown prior to the early 1950s. In all likelihood the development of computers will be considered as important as the development of nuclear energy and automation when the history of the mid-20th century is written.

Your introduction to electronic computers for the business enterprise includes a discussion of the following questions:

How are computers used by management?
What are the essential components of the computer?
What is involved in programming?
Which factors need to be considered regarding the installation of a computer?

16

Computers

USES OF COMPUTERS IN BUSINESS

The electronic computer has three features which distinguish it from the mechanical desk calculator. These features are high speed, memory, and the ability to use programs. A *program* is a detailed set of instructions necessary to solve problems or to perform operations on data.

Speed is achieved through the use of electronic circuitry. Mechanical calculators are limited by the time required to start, move, and stop their mechanical devices. Electronic circuits operate at the speed of light, the speed at which electricity is transmitted. Also, computers can hold data and instructions in an internal memory unit which greatly speeds processing of data.

Computers can be helpful in the management of an enterprise in a variety of ways. A few of their uses include the speedup of routine record keeping; better control over purchasing and inventory management; and the design of more efficient production schedules and sales forecasts. Computers can assist management decisions in areas such as financial planning, plant expansion and location, and new product development.

Record keeping

Business record keeping has been readily computerized. The flood of paper work, reports, and records has made record keeping an important area for improved efficiency. It is estimated that more computer time is spent in record-keeping applications than in any other single function. The wide variety of records efficiently handled by computers include payrolls, inventories, purchases, customer records, and production scheduling.

Payrolls. When an enterprise has many employees the preparation of payroll records becomes a considerable clerical task. Each employee's record usually includes gross pay; deductions such as income taxes, social security payments, union dues, health insurance premiums, and perhaps United Way contributions; net pay; and totals for the year to date. Payroll checks with reports for the various deductions listed above have to be made frequently, in some cases on a weekly or twice-monthly basis. Also, reports are usually prepared which allocate a particular employee's pay to a specific department or cost center. When the business enterprise has hundreds of employees the use of electronic data processing for reducing payroll processing costs is important.

Inventories and purchasing. To account for changes in inventories a record is kept of each item showing the number of units on hand and the cost of these units. Each time an item goes into or out of the inventory it is necessary to update the record. Even inventories in small enterprises may include thousands of different items while large firms will have many more than this.

Department stores and supermarkets today can tie their inventory control systems to the check-out cash register. National Cash Register Company installs two different types of systems for this purpose. In the first system the cash register produces a magnetic type cassette of coded items which are sold. The cassette is then taken to the computer center to update inventory records. In the second system the cash register is electronically connected directly to the computer. Thus, when the check-out clerk enters the item on the cash register the computer immediately updates the inventory position.

Such inventory systems not only show changes in inventories but also are designed to provide calculations on optimal quantities to order, reorder points, detection of slow-moving items, and forecasts of future requirements. This information is a valuable aid to purchasing.

Customer records. Department stores, banks, insurance companies, manufacturers, and other business enterprises have lengthy lists of customer records which must be maintained on a current and accurate basis. These records include statements of amounts owed by customers and payments received from them. Department stores use computers to keep accurate records of charge accounts. Bank computers show current balances in individual accounts. Insurance companies use computers in the billing of customers. Also they feed information regarding a client's personal circumstances into a computer programmed to provide recommendations for possible changes in policy needs. Manufacturers use computers to keep sales accounts up to date. Computers have greatly aided the handling of individual customer records by increased speed and accuracy.

An account is maintained by the Internal Revenue Service for each individual and business taxpayer. A computer system reconciles individual tax returns with the wages reported by business enterprises, interest and dividend reports, and other sources of individual income. The comparison of these millions of reports is feasible only because of a computer system which is now nationwide.

Production scheduling. The complexity of coordinating personnel, raw materials, purchased parts, machine capacities, and orders for finished goods makes production scheduling a natural application for the computer. As was discussed in Chapter 12, a computer program can be designed to determine the schedule which minimizes cost and most efficiently utilizes production resources. Without computers, production scheduling is not only more time consuming but is likely to result in a less efficient use of resources in the production process.

Information retrieval

Because of the advances in technical knowledge in recent years, it is more and more difficult for an individual to keep informed of developments even within a relatively narrow field. Business, scientific, legal, and medical data are now being stored in computer systems and can be called upon by the analyst or researcher when needed. Codes are available for providing an abstract of the information desired along with references as to where detailed information may be obtained. Further advances are being made in the field of information retrieval. These will make research more productive and less time consuming, and will result in greater amounts of information quickly available for decision making.

Computer systems

Computers can do much more than process data for routine record keeping or retrieve information. Information systems are in use today which provide new dimensions of data handling. Such systems can completely handle information relating to a business transaction once the data are placed into the computer. This could include processing a customer's order; checking the customer's credit rating; fitting the order into the production schedule; withdrawing necessary items from inventory; calculating the cost of raw materials, labor, and overhead; providing shipping instructions; preparing the customer's statement; and notifying the customer of shipment!

Real-time systems. When the computer receives and processes data and affects the functioning of the environment *at that time* the computer system is called a *real-time system.*

There are different types of real-time computer systems. Continuous-process manufacturing industries, such as chemical producers and oil refiners, use real-time systems for measuring and regulating the production process. Computers are programmed to control production from start to finish with automatic feedback of corrections needed. The response time required for the system to make changes in the production process may be less than five minutes.

An airline reservation system is another type of real-time system. A central computer maintains a record of all scheduled flights for a period of time into the future. Each reservation agent is able to communicate with the computer through a terminal to determine if space is available

Employment outlook

Systems analyst

A systems analyst begins by determining the exact nature of a data processing problem. Then the analyst structures the problem logically, identifies all the data needed, and specifies how the data are to be processed.

Analysts usually recommend which data processing equipment is to be used, and prepare instructions for programmers. They also translate final results into terms that managers or customers can understand.

Employment of systems analysts is expected to grow very rapidly through the mid-1980s as data processing systems in business and government expand. Among the factors expected to contribute to a growing demand for systems analysts are the extension of computer technology to small businesses and the growth of computer centers to serve individual clients for a fee. Employment also will be stimulated by efforts to develop systems that will retrieve information more efficiently, and will monitor industrial processes.

on a customer-desired flight. When the customer makes a reservation the computer records this in a memory unit and automatically reduces the number of vacant seats available on the flight. The entire process requires a response time of only a few seconds.

Further advances are being made in the development of computerized systems. We can expect expanded use of real-time systems with greater sophistication in the future.

Time-sharing systems. An important development in computer systems is the concept of *time sharing*. Time sharing provides a number of users with access to a single computer at the same time from different locations for the simultaneous solution of different problems. This simultaneous, remote access to the computer is possible because the computer switches from one user to another in a matter of milliseconds, which appears to the individual to be instantaneous. Time sharing makes possible the use of one centralized, expensive computer installation by many persons at a reasonable charge to individual users. Thus the small business enterprise which cannot afford its own private computer may gain the use of a computer through time sharing.

Systems are now available for time sharing by over 100 simultaneous users. Each user has a terminal through which electronic communication is made with the computer. These terminals have keyboards much like typewriters which give individual users access to the computer from any part of the country. The computer keeps track of each user's time on the system, makes corrections, and is capable of providing helpful hints to unskilled users.

Complex computation and business simulation

Computers can perform complex calculations which would require years of time to do by hand or by mechanical calculators. The computer's ability to store programs for repetitive use reduces both the time and cost required for problem solutions. It is now possible to solve in minutes scientific and engineering problems which were not feasible to solve earlier because of the time or money required. It has been estimated that computers can do calculations for a cost of less than $50 that would take a trained operator with a desk calculator a year to do.

Computers handle the necessary calculations for mathematical models which simulate the real world. These data can be used for better managerial decision making. Through linear programming, mathematical models can be developed for a variety of business problems. These include achieving the optimum allocation of resources of a business enterprise, developing efficient shipping schedules, and determining the most profitable combination of products for a multiple-product company. Linear programming applications may require thousands of repetitive calculations. Without the computer these routine solutions would be impractical.

An example of a complex problem which could be solved by a computer is the scheduling of work in a large machine shop producing metal parts. Typically there are hundreds of machines in operation and thousands of orders in production or waiting to be put into production. A computer could be programmed to schedule these jobs so as to minimize idle machine time, reduce lead time on orders, and keep deliveries to customers on time.

An interesting application of computers is in the field of business systems simulation. A model of the enterprise and its environment is developed and programmed. Alternatives for management are fed into the computer. These include decisions for factors such as product prices, production levels, research and development spending, advertising budgets, and plant and equipment expenditures. The computer prints the results of these decisions in terms of profits, market share, inventories, and financial position. Such a program is only a model of the real world. However, it can provide valuable information on the possible consequences of decisions and can be a useful tool in business management.

COMPONENTS OF THE COMPUTER

Because of the variety of computer applications and the number of computer manufacturers, it is difficult to generalize about them. However, all digital computers[1] utilize the functions of data input, memory or storage, arithmetic processing, control, and output of information. The physical equipment which makes up a computer system is known as *hardware*. The program of instructions for the computer is

---

[1] The *digital* computer performs arithmetic operations on numbers. Because of its wide use in business data processing, the discussion in this chapter refers to the digital computer. Another kind of computer is the *analog* computer which functions by measuring continuous conditions in physical variables such as temperature, pressure, voltages, or liquid flows. Analog computers are widely used for scientific and engineering purposes, with business use generally limited to such applications as the control of certain manufacturing operations.

FIGURE 16–1
Components of a Digital Computer System

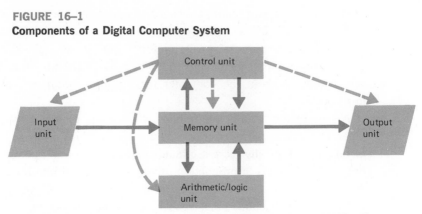

Note: Solid lines represent flow of data. Broken lines represent control functions.

called *software.* Figure 16–1 illustrates the components of a digital computer.

Input of data

The input unit of a computer system transmits data and instructions into the computer's memory unit. Operating instructions and the data to be processed are fed into the input unit through such means as:

1. Punched cards—such as school registration forms, utility bills, and time cards.
2. Magnetic-ink characters—such as those on the bottom of bank checks.
3. Handwritten numbers—which are fed in by optical-character scanners.
4. Magnetic tapes and disks—for use with large quantities of data which require updating such as payrolls.
5. Punched-paper tapes—such as may be prepared from cash register transactions.
6. Console typewriters—for such applications as individual use in time-sharing systems.

Whatever the means of transmitting data into the computer, the input unit translates it into a language the computer can electronically place in its data memory unit for processing.

Memory unit

The memory unit functions as the storage and file cabinet. This unit receives and holds not only the input data but also the program instructions for processing the data. The memory unit also receives and holds the results of the data processing from the arithmetic/logic unit before data are communicated to the user. When a very large mass of data must be stored, magnetic tapes or random access files such as disks, drums, or punched cards can be filed outside the computer. Their data can be fed into the computer when needed.

Control and arithmetic/logic units

The control and arithmetic/logic units are the heart of the computer system. The control unit issues directions based on the program of instructions to all other units of the computer to accomplish the mission for a particular problem. The control unit monitors the instructions to determine that they are in the correct form and that the system is functioning properly. The control unit controls the input and output units, the transfer of data to and from the memory unit, and the arithmetic/logic unit.

The arithmetic/logic unit receives instructions from the control unit and data from the memory unit. The arithmetic portion of the unit performs computations on data such as addition, subtraction, multiplication, and division. The logic portion of the unit makes comparisons, checks results, and does necessary adjustments in instructions and computations.

The sheer volume of calculations that can be done in a few seconds by computers is difficult to comprehend. One means of stating the speed of computer operations is in terms of MIPS (millions of instructions per second). Today large computers by Control Data Corporation have the capacity in raw speed to calculate addition instructions at a rate of up to 15 million instructions per second (15 MIPS). For example, it is said that all the telephone numbers in the New York City telephone directory could be added up and divided by any other number in two or three seconds. Such speeds enable business and scientific users to handle the flood of paperwork and calculations necessary to carry on operations today.

Output unit

The output unit communicates the results of the computer's work in a form that can be useful to management. One of the most widely used means of receiving information from the computer is on printed pages. High-speed printers are available that have the capacity of printing up to 3,000 lines a minute consisting of at least 132 characters per line. Computer output may also be in the form of punched cards or sheets for checks, invoices, or accounting statements. Output can be transmitted through visual display devices such as graph plotters, cathode ray tubes (like television tubes), or microfilm. Voice reply systems are also available to receive information from computers.

PROGRAMMING

Programming consists of providing the computer with a set of instructions necessary for solving a problem or carrying out a series of operations on data. Careful steps are necessary to assure a set of instructions which are usable by the computer. The programming process first includes an analysis of the data processing system itself. This means it is necessary to understand the capabilities of the system and whether the computer will be able to handle the assigned problem.

The second step in programming is to outline the necessary computer procedures in a logical fashion. At this step a program flowchart is constructed. Every specific instruction in the proper sequence is necessary since the computer will process the data exactly as the program directs. The third step in programming is to translate the program flowchart into a set of detailed coded instructions for the computer.

The final step is testing the program to eliminate errors. This debugging process is necessary to check the programmer's work. The output of information will be no better than the data put into the computer or the program used to process the data.

Flowcharting is a means of graphically presenting solutions to information handling problems. Flowcharting techniques have been adapted to computer applications of information handling. In 1970 the American National Standards Institute (ANSI) developed a revised list of flowcharting symbols. Some of these ANSI standard symbols are illustrated below.

Examples of ANSI flowcharting symbols:

Processing—a single operation such as an arithmetic manipulation or a defined set of operations.

Input or Output—a general symbol used to indicate the input or output of data.

Flowlines—with directional arrows indicate the continuity of operations in the data processing sequence.

Annotation—this outline provides a means of supplying explanatory or descriptive information. Dashed line indicates the outline to which this explanation applies.

Decision—a point from which one or more alternate pathways may be followed; a switching point.

Connector—when used with a number at the end of a flowline indicates that flowline is to be continued where the number appears elsewhere on the flowchart.

Terminal—this indicates the start, the end, or a delay in the flow.

Some of these symbols are used in the simple flowchart for processing an office employee's payroll record shown in Figure 16–2.

As this illustration indicates, computer programs must provide detailed, specific instructions for every step of the way through the data processing sequence. A program must tell the computer what to do under all possible conditions. When different circumstances may be en-

FIGURE 16–2
Flowchart of individual payroll

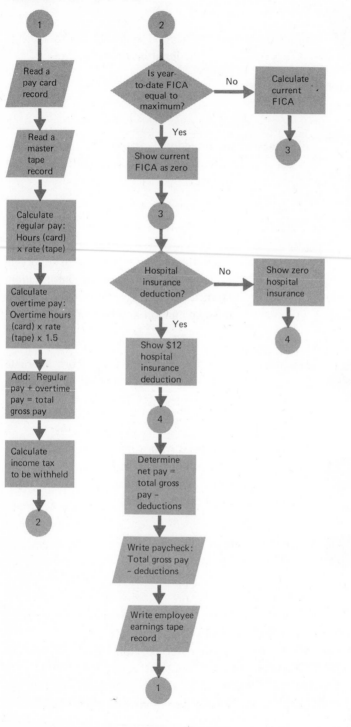

countered in dealing with data the program must specify exactly what is to be done.

With more applications for computer problem solving and wider use of these applications, a number of packaged programs have been developed which are now available to users. These standardized programs are useful for operations that are the same from one business enterprise to another. In some instances these programs can be modified to fit individual needs without having to write an entirely new program.

COMMUNICATING WITH COMPUTERS

The computer functions from directions given through electronic circuits which perform specific operations. It is necessary to translate the language understandable to a programmer into a language form which can be accepted by the computer. This operation is called compiling a program. Several compiler language systems have been developed to simplify the job of programming and to standardize computer operations.

There are two dominant compiler languages. FORTRAN (FORmula TRANslator) is an algebraic compiler particularly useful for research problems requiring the solution of mathematical or statistical formulations. COBOL (COmmon Business Oriented Language) is a commercial compiler useful for business problems involving file processing and record keeping. In all compiler languages certain words and symbols have specific meanings.

COBOL makes available a standard method of programming business data processing problems. Generally these applications have large files which require periodic or continuous updating. Such business transactions frequently involve large volumes of input and output data but may not require elaborate processing. FORTRAN provides a means of programming scientific data and business models which require relatively limited input and output but have extensive processing.

A number of other computer languages are used depending upon the purposes to be served and the particular manufacturer's computer which is available. Two of these are BASIC and PL/1. BASIC (*B*eginner's *A*ll-Purpose *S*ymbolic *I*nstruction *C*ode) is a language for solving numerical problems. It is sometimes used as a first step for students before they learn one of the more complex languages such as FORTRAN. BASIC is also useful in developing models to simulate business operations.

Employment outlook

Computer programmer

An electronic computer can process masses of information with great speed and accuracy, but the machine cannot think for itself. The programmer's job is to prepare step-by-step instructions for the computer to follow. The employment of programmers will grow rapidly over the next decade as the number of computer installations increases.

The number of programmers will increase as business continues to automate processes once done by hand. For example, many stores will computerize credit information and their ordering and inventory of merchandise. Employment growth also will be sharp in computer service bureaus which furnish computer services for a fee. Substantial growth will continue in firms that were among the first to use computers on a large scale, including banks, insurance companies, and factories.

The best opportunities will be for experienced persons qualified in both programming and systems analysis who have kept up with the latest equipment and techniques.

PL/1 (*Programming Language, Version 1*) is a language suitable for problems involving both business data processing and numerical scientific computations. It combines concepts from other computer languages and was developed because of weaknesses in some of the other languages. PL/1 was developed in the mid-1960s and has wide application in fields which had previously used FORTRAN or COBOL.

It is not necessary to have detailed knowledge of computers or programming to make valuable use of computers. Today individuals can be trained in a short time to use computers for problem solving. In these instances the computer will have already been programmed for the type of questions which will be asked. By placing a simple code into the computer through use of a terminal much like a typewriter the individual user can have the answer to a variety of questions. These could include airline schedules, inventory positions, a customer's account or bank balance, and solutions to problems in mathematics, statistics, or financial analysis. Additional training and knowledge are required before one becomes thoroughly acquainted with computer operations. However, a minimum amount of training is sufficient to enable the business manager or the student to make the computer a most useful tool.

CONSIDERATIONS WHEN INSTALLING A COMPUTER

Before a computer system is installed management must come to grips with a number of problems. There are two benefits which may come from the installation of electronic computer systems. First, information is available faster and in better form than is possible without the computer. Not only are former data processing chores accomplished more quickly, but a variety of additional information is available for management use. There will be applications which may come to light not originally envisioned when the computer was first installed. Volumes of data can be processed with computers which would be impossible in the time available without such assistance. The second benefit normally expected from a computer installation is a reduction in the number of employees required for data processing. However, the workers who will be required for computers normally will be higher paid and more skilled than the clerical employees whom the computer displaces. Different kinds of skills are required in computer centers than are typically required in many routine clerical positions.

The decision regarding computer installation should be made after a careful study by management as to the advantages and problems which likely will result from acquiring a computer. This decision will require time by management personnel. Therefore, sufficient staff should be made available to handle routine business operations for those executives who are involved in the investigation of the installation and use of a computer system.

Equipment choice

If a computer is to be acquired, the question arises as to what specific computer system is best for the business enterprise's needs. Cost estimates should be prepared for hardware from different manufacturers. Costs should be considered as well as the capabilities of the equipment to meet the enterprise's present and anticipated future needs.

The ability of the computer manufacturer to provide service and necessary software is also an important consideration in the selection of a computer system. The systems engineers, maintenance staff, and other highly trained personnel provided by the computer manufacturer can make a significant difference in determining how effectively a particular computer is utilized.

The management of the small business enterprise may consider acquiring one of the new smaller computer systems with packaged programs available. In deciding on an initial commitment to a computer, management should also analyze the possibility of acquiring the use of an older computer. This might meet the enterprise's needs effectively even though it is not the latest model.

Equipment leasing or time sharing

Management may decide to lease rather than purchase a computer. This is an important decision. Leasing may appear to be costly. However, the advantages of avoiding a large initial outlay for computer hardware and reducing the risk that new computer technology will render present systems obsolete makes leasing an alternative to consider.

Management may also consider time-sharing computer services discussed earlier rather than purchasing or leasing a computer. The availability of terminals connected to a large computer center which can be miles away may provide the economy and flexibility necessary for the small or medium-size business.

Employee attitudes

One of the most critical factors determining the success or failure of a computer system is the attitude of employees toward the new development. Employee morale will be affected beginning with the discussion of a computer installation. As indicated in Chapter 7 on human relations, a great deal can be done to reduce disruption of morale with proper communication. When the computer system is installed it is important that managerial employees as well as clerical and blue-collar workers be oriented to the purposes and advantages of the computer. If attitudes toward the use of a computer are not shaped properly, it may result in a reluctance by employees to provide accurate data for input into the computer. Also, managerial employees may drag their feet in using the new information provided by the computer. Positive employee attitudes are needed for the success of a computer operation.

A variety of other problems will be faced by those managements which have new computer systems. These range from the physical location of the computer to determining organizational relationships for computer personnel and the allocation of the cost of the computer system.

SUMMARY

The development of the computer has made it possible to store and retrieve vast amounts of information, to make instant calculations, and to control many different operations. Computers are used in business for functions such as record keeping, payrolls, inventories, purchasing, customer records, production scheduling, and information retrieval.

In a real-time system the computer receives and processes data so action is taken immediately to control the environment. Under a time-sharing system a number of users have access to a single computer at the same time from different locations for the simultaneous solution of different problems.

Computer applications are available for complex calculations and for simulation of the business enterprise's operations to test possible management decisions.

The components of a digital computer system include units for input of data, memory or storage, control of operations, arithmetic/logic functions, and output of data.

Computers use programs, which are a series of machine instructions to accomplish the mission for a particular problem-solving task or to carry out a series of operations on data. Standard symbols are used in programming, and special languages have been developed to simplify the job of programming. The two dominant computer languages are FORTRAN and COBOL.

In selecting a computer system management needs to consider not only cost but also the ability of a computer manufacturer to provide the needed service. Leasing, rather than the purchase of a computer, has the advantage of not requiring a large cash outlay for computer hardware and also minimizes the risk of equipment being outmoded in future years. Time sharing or leasing time on an existing computer installation can provide the small or medium-size enterprise a flexible and relatively economical way of obtaining the services of a computer.

When a computer is to be installed it is important to orient employees to the purposes and advantages of a computer since positive employee attitudes are needed for the success of a computer operation.

TERMS FOR REVIEW

electronic computer	*arithmetic/logic unit*
real-time system	*output unit*
time-sharing system	*programming*
digital computer	*program flowchart*
input unit	*FORTRAN*
memory unit	*COBOL*
control unit	

QUESTIONS

1. Discuss the different ways computers can be useful to business enterprises.
2. Make an appointment with a member of management at a supermarket, department store, bank, airline reservations center, or some other enterprise in your community that is using a computer.
   a. In what ways are they using the computer?
   b. What problems have they had?
   c. Do they plan additional uses for the computer in the future?
3. What are the advantages of a time-sharing computer system?
4. *a.* In what ways may data be fed into a computer?
   b. What means are available for the output of information from computers?

5. Why is attention to detail so important in computer programming?
6. If there is a computer center at your school, request a tour of the facilities. Determine the kinds of applications handled by the computer and the compiler language used.
7. Based on your study of this chapter and of current library materials, write a 300-word summary of the issues which should be considered by management in the process of installing a new computer system.

Business brief

Massed minicomputers

Even though some applications of huge computers have been made in controlling operations in continuous process industries such as oil refining and power generation, relatively little use of computers has been made in direct control of typical manufacturing operations. In the late 1960s a system was developed in which a large computer ran hundreds of different machine tools. However, this system created significant problems. When the large computer failed to function properly all the machine tools quit working. Also, the high cost of the large computer made it difficult to justify such an operation unless many machines could be operated continuously.

Today minicomputers are available for $2,000 or less which are more powerful and easier to use than were large computers costing $100,000 just ten years ago. Now a number of business enterprises are building new factories using dozens of minicomputers, each of which is programmed to control a single operation on one production machine. Production lines are being laid out to enable computers to control machine tools that measure, shape, and cut raw materials into component parts. Minicomputers do testing, inspection, and controlling of automated transportation and storage systems within the factory.

Phillip Morris is developing a huge cigarette factory in Richmond, Virginia, designed around a minicomputer system. Two hundred million dollars will have been invested in this plant by its completion in 1977. Significant savings in labor and materials are expected from this factory.

General Motors uses minicomputers in its carburetor testing and materials handling system. These provide more flexibility than did an older computer system which tied more than 100 test stands together. The new system allows individual control over each test stand. It is designed to test the more complex carburetors required by today's rigorous government auto emission standards.

1. What advantages do minicomputers provide for factory managements?
2. What potential problems may be raised by the extensive use of minicomputers in the production process?
3. Contrast the application of minicomputers to new factories as compared with old plants and production lines.

Cases

Middletown National Bank

The Middletown National Bank was located in a medium-sized city of approximately 150,000 in the Midwest. The bank was the largest in the community and had assets in excess of $200 million. In recent years its traditional territory had become more prosperous as additional light industry and service business enterprises moved into the area. At the same time additional banks were chartered in the community which competed with other long-established banks in addition to Middletown National.

Early in 1969, several members of the top management of Middletown National Bank were gathered to discuss the growth of the bank in recent years and the need for improved means of handling this growth. Conversation soon turned to a subject which had been discussed before, whether or not to install a computer.

As soon as the subject of computers was raised, Jim Jordon, personnel manager, voiced fears as to what changeover from traditional accounting and data processing methods might mean for the employees of the Middletown National Bank. "I have already heard discussion of computers among our employees," Jordon reported. "My secretary told me the other day that a number of our people are quite concerned that we may computerize our accounting operations. They don't know what this would mean for them. I don't think that most of our people could become computer technicians. How many of our employees would we have to let go with the installation of a computer?"

At this point Paul Bowlin, an officer who had come from a large bank in Los Angeles, entered the conversation. "Jim, I believe you are magnifying this personnel problem out of proportion. I don't think we will have a major personnel problem in making this changeover. As you know the bank's board of directors has already authorized studies for a new drive-in banking facility in an area of the city where we need to develop more business. If we can coordinate the development of this drive-in banking operation with the installation of a new computer, we can easily find jobs for any of our present clerical personnel whose jobs might be eliminated by a computer. I think that we should push right ahead and make a decision to install a computer. As soon as this decision is made we can test all employees for aptitude in dealing with the symbols and quantitative data required in a computer center. This ought to include testing of supervisory personnel as well since new jobs will be created and different types of skills required for these new positions."

"Hold on, Paul," interrupted the personnel manager. "Such a testing program might represent a threat to some of our employees. Some of our supervisory people who are giving quite satisfactory service to the bank may be very disturbed by this. We have supervisors with years of service to Middletown National. These men and women understand our problems as no computer will ever be able to do."

"I don't mean to say there won't be some problems," replied Bowlin. "We experienced this sort of thing in Los Angeles. However, it mainly involves teaching employees how to communicate with the computer. Don't sell our employees short. Once they learn the 'language' I'll bet many will be even more effective in fulfilling their jobs than they are now."

"Nobody's selling our employees short," said Jordon. "However, there is a lack of trained computer people. How would we ever get the necessary staff? Who would train them, and wouldn't an extensive training program be costly to the bank? Furthermore, if we put money into sending some of our employees through a training program, how do we know they'll stay with us? This is a tight labor market."

One of the junior officers of the bank suggested, "We could always raise their salaries to become more competitive with other firms requiring computer personnel."

The personnel manager's response was, "Yes, and that would drive up the cost of the computer center even more. Also, it would tend to disrupt our whole wage and salary schedule. How could we justify paying technicians more than long-term bank employees who really understand the whole banking process?"

At this point the executive vice president, Martin Jones, broke into the conversation. "Gentlemen, I think we are getting bogged down on some side issues which can be dealt with later. As I view the bank's operations and growth in recent years there are some very crucial reasons why we need to seriously consider installing a computer center in the near future. I have asked Tom Murray, our auditor, to outline some of these considerations for our discussion. Tom, why don't you tell us in general terms what your study indicates without going into all of the detailed figures at this time?"

"Thank you, Mr. Jones. First, we need to deal more efficiently with the growth in the number of accounts we have and the number of items we handle. We are at the point where further specialization in handling paper work isn't reducing our costs. Costs are rising in proportion to the rise in items handled. Part of this is because of the higher volume of transactions, which means more machinery and employees are needed for record keeping.

"Our figures indicate that there is more activity in each checking account when we measure it in terms of activity per thousand dollars in deposits. There is no question but that the increased cost of servicing our checking account customers is a matter of concern. We hope that the installation of a computer will stabilize these costs.

"Also there are space problems associated with our present accounting services. The machinery for bookkeeping, posting, and so on has put us into a serious cramp with respect to space. Frankly, I don't know where we can locate any more conventional equipment in our present facilities.

"In summary I think it is fair to say that we are facing higher costs accompanied by servicing more accounts. Don't forget that we are dealing with a number of commercial customers as well as individuals. Also, we must provide high-quality services for some 60 smaller banks throughout the area which depend upon us for correspondent services. As the bank's auditor I feel that a computer installation is the only answer to these problems."

"Thank you, Tom," said Mr. Jones. "Furthermore, we must realize that we face increased competition in the banking business. Computer installations are beginning to be installed in banks similar in size to ours in other parts of the country. Right now no other bank in Middletown has a computer. With our ever-increasing costs, more active relationships with correspondent banks, local competition, and the possibility that other banks in our own community will go to computer operations, we will ultimately have to look seriously at computers anyway. Since we are the biggest bank in the city I feel we should be first with a computer. If we are, this may give us a marketing advantage and some further prestige. If we don't have a computer and other local banks do, won't our customers wonder if we are the 'complete service banking institution' we claim to be in our advertising program?"

"Well, you men have some powerful ammunition," responded Jim Jordon, the personnel manager. "It may well be that we'll have to install a computer center, but if we do I think we should make some decisions in the near future to cut down on employee rumors. It's going to be hard enough to make this decision and perhaps a changeover without disrupting all the bank's operations."

1. Analyze the bank officers' discussion. Discuss the merits of the various points of view expressed.
2. What should be the bank management's next step?
3. If the decision is made to install a computer center what further issues will need to be considered?

A computer decision reviewed

"Hello, Bob," greeted Martin Jones, executive vice president of Middletown National Bank, as he shook hands with Robert Johnson, an officer of Castle County State Bank, which was located some 300 miles from Middletown. "We're glad to have you visit us to talk about our computer installation. We hope your trip will be worthwhile in helping your bank make the decision we went through a couple of years ago in installing a computer center here at Middletown."

After initial greetings, Mr. Johnson was taken to the bank conference room where the key bank officers of Middletown National Bank who had participated in the decision to install a computer center were gathered. (See Middletown National Bank case for preliminary discussion of this installation.) Besides the executive vice president and Mr. Johnson, there was Jim Jordon, Middletown's personnel manager; Paul Bowlin, who was in charge of the computer center; and Tom Murray, Middletown National's auditor.

After introductions were made, Mr. Jones explained, "As you will recall from my memo, Bob Johnson is here today to learn something about our experience in converting to a computer operation on our data processing system. After this conference he will visit the computer center and talk with people individually before his plane leaves this afternoon. I have asked each of you gentlemen to prepare something for this conference on how we dealt with a particular phase of our computer center conversion. Let's start with you first, Jim, on the personnel side of the issue."

The personnel manager replied, "As soon as the decision was made to install a computer at the bank, all employees were invited to a meeting which was held to announce the decision. The announcement included a statement that no jobs would be lost as a result of the changeover. However, we did point out that there would be some changing of job assignments and some upgrading of positions in the bank. This meeting was held to minimize employees' fears about their job future that might have stemmed from rumors if we had said nothing officially about our plans to begin taking the steps necessary to install a computer.

"We had hoped to tie in the installation of the computer with the opening of a new drive-in facility which would stabilize employment. In practice, it didn't work out because the computer changeover came after the drive-in was opened up. However, we found that more people were required in the computer center than we had originally anticipated. This factor coupled with normal resignations and moves meant that we were able to avoid any layoffs because of the computer installation.

"The programming staff of the computer center was made up essentially of the bank's own personnel. Whenever possible, existing bank employees were trained and given computer jobs. We utilized a testing program for all personnel to determine which employees had the best aptitude for computer work. This aptitude test was given by the computer manufacturer. Then our people were trained by the manufacturer's representatives, and some key personnel were sent to take special courses. A considerable amount of time and money was spent on training people for the programming and operation of the computer center. Also, it is important that bank personnel outside the computer center have the ability to talk with programmers on a more or less equal basis. Therefore, in our long-run training program more of our officers will get experience in dealing with the computer.

"With the advent of the computer some interesting things occurred within our work force. New people emerged on the computer jobs as leaders. Some people who had not been supervisors became very exceptional employees in the computer center and now have supervisory positions. On the other hand, some of the individuals who had been quite satisfactory in their old supervisory positions were not effective in working in the computer center. They couldn't cope with the new job either intellectually or emotionally. This illustrates the different kinds of skills required when you move into a computer operation. The work is much faster. Many more items are covered in a short period of time. There were symbols to be learned, a different kind of language, a different kind of system.

"A few of these supervisors who had been satisfactory in the past but were unable to adjust very well to the computer operation quit and found other jobs in the community.

"I think we can say in summary of the personnel phase of the computer that many new positions were created which required more ability and different kinds of skills. These jobs were generally more demanding and more sensitive than those they had replaced. Sometimes different people became leaders. We have faced some interesting human relations problems in making these adjustments over a period of time. On the whole, though, I am pleased with how our people have come through with this challenge."

"Thank you, Jim," the executive vice president said. "I think I should say that Jim was one of those who warned us about some of the personnel problems we might face with such a move. But his department has done a good job of minimizing the difficulties in this personnel area. Tom, why don't you discuss financial aspects of the computer decision next."

"Because of the rapid evolution of computer hardware it was decided that the bank would lease rather than buy the computer from the manufacturer," began the auditor. "We found that there are a number of different ways to lease a computer. For example, there are leasing companies which buy computers from manufacturers and lease them to business enterprises, such as the bank, at a rate of one half or one third of the manufacturer's lease rental charges. However, these lease firms require five-year leases in contrast to the manufacturer of our equipment which requires only a 30-day notice if we want the computer taken out. With the leasing firms we would have had to pay the lease amount for the entire five-year period even though new equipment which would be better for our needs might become available.

"We feel that for us the choice to lease directly from the manufacturer, even with the higher rental charge, proved to be a wise decision. Just two years after our original computer installation a new generation of computers came onto the market. This new computer system is compatible with our existing computer programs and we are now in the process of moving to the new, improved system.

"When we started the computer center we found that the cost of the computer hardware itself was relatively little in comparison with the other costs which are required in terms of personnel time. Our best estimates are that the cost of converting our conventional data processing equipment to an electronic computer system was about 4/7 for equipment and 3/7 for the other costs of transition, such as training programs and other essentially one-time costs. This means if the hardware cost $200,000, roughly $150,000 will be required for these other costs. I might add that the bank really had no expectation of breaking even over a five-year period while these conversion costs were being absorbed. So you see that we really had to look at this matter from the long-run point of view.

"We have pretty effectively converted the processing of our accounts along with some commercial jobs, such as payroll and inventory data handling for outside customers, to the computer operation. Also, we are effectively using the computer to handle our many correspondent bank items.

"I might add that we have been successful in selling computer services to some of our commercial customers on such items as handling their payrolls and inventory control. However, off the record, we may face the time in the future when competition from local banks with computers may force us to reduce these charges or perhaps provide some of these services free to particularly good customers."

The auditor concluded his remarks and the conference broke up for lunch. After lunch Mr. Johnson was taken on a tour of the computer center where he discussed technical aspects of the computer with center personnel. As he was flying back home later that afternoon, Mr. Johnson turned over in his mind his visit to Middletown National Bank and began to block out his report to the president of Castle County State Bank.

1. Appraise the apparent effectiveness of the Middletown National Bank management in dealing with the personnel problems associated with the transition to computer operations.
2. Based on information in these two cases, how did the expectations of the Middletown National Bank officers coincide with what actually happened in moving to a computer installation?
3. From your knowledge of computers gained through the Middletown National Bank case, this case, and Chapter 16, prepare a brief written report for the top management of Castle County State Bank on some of the problems to be anticipated in installing a computer.

Courtesy Heublein, Inc.

*American products are
sold around the world.*

*A*merican business managers view foreign industrialized nations with their rising wages and increasing standard of expectations as excellent marketing opportunities. At the same time United States markets are viewed aggressively by foreign manufacturers.

Business managers in Europe and the Far East have been effective in international trade because of their long experience in dealing in many markets. Some foreign governments give subsidies for international trade and permit business practices which would be violations of the antitrust laws in this country. The result has been increased competition for American manufacturers of automobiles, motorcycles, textiles, television sets, and cameras. To meet these challenges American business has improved production and marketing practices at home and also has established sales and manufacturing branches abroad.

The following issues in the field of international business are discussed:

What is the importance of international trade to the United States?

What issues are raised with the development of the multinational corporation?

How do international monetary and balance-of-payments problems affect world trade?

What other barriers affect international business?

How does the United States government promote world trade?

What are the differences between management in America and abroad?

17

International business

THE IMPORTANCE OF INTERNATIONAL TRADE TO THE UNITED STATES

Business enterprises participate in international business by the export and import of goods in world trade and by the manufacture and sale of products in foreign countries.

Reasons for the export of goods

In 1974 United States business exported $97 billion of goods to foreign countries. As illustrated by Table 17–1, American exports have increased over the years. Exports account for about 7 percent of our Gross National Product. The U.S. Department of Commerce estimates that international trade provides jobs for seven to eight million Americans. Domestic industries which rely heavily upon export business include agriculture, automobiles, chemicals, coal, and machinery.

The basic reason for the export of goods is that they can be sold profitably in other countries where there is a demand for them. The exporting country has raw materials, skilled labor, technology, or capital necessary to produce the desired goods. For example, because of its climate and technology the United States has been able to produce large quantities of basic food commodities such as wheat and soybeans for export. Our advanced technology and capital enable American computer manufacturers to build computers for sale around the world.

The management of an enterprise may find it desirable to export goods to increase sales and spread the fixed costs of doing business

TABLE 17–1

Merchandise exports and imports for the United States and Gross National Product, selected years 1940–1974 (billions of dollars)

Year	U.S. exports*	U.S. imports	U.S. GNP
1940	$ 3.9	$ 2.6	$ 100
1945	9.6	4.2	212
1950	10.2	9.1	285
1955	14.4	11.5	398
1960	19.7	14.7	504
1965	26.4	21.5	685
1970	42.0	39.9	974
1974	97.1	103.0	1,397

* Excludes military grants and aid beginning with 1950.
Source: U.S. Department of Commerce, *Business Statistics, 1971;* and *Survey of Current Business,* March 1975.

over more units of production. This lowers the unit cost of all goods produced.

In some countries manufacturers find less competition in selling their products than in this country. Some overseas markets are less saturated than those in the United States. As standards of living increase in foreign countries it is relatively easy for an enterprise to make large sales gains. For example, the Bureau of the Census estimates that about 90 percent of American households own refrigerators or freezers. Therefore, the growth of refrigerator sales in the United States is generally limited to replacements or to new family units. In foreign countries with rising incomes where only a small proportion of families own refrigerators there should be a larger market for these appliances.

Reasons for the import of goods

In 1974 imports of goods into the United States amounted to $103 billion. Traditionally merchandise exports have exceeded imports as

TABLE 17–2

Principal commodity exports and imports of the United States, 1974* (billions of dollars)

Exports	Amount	Imports	Amount
Agricultural products	$22.3	Coffee, cocoa, and sugar	$ 4.1
Automobiles and parts	8.2	Other food products	6.5
Chemicals	7.4	Automobiles and parts	12.4
Civilian aircraft and parts	5.6	Chemicals	2.4
Computers and office machines	3.1	Consumer durable goods	8.6
Construction machinery	4.0	Consumer nondurable goods	5.2
Other industrial machinery	7.3	Industrial and commercial machinery	8.9
Consumer goods, except autos	6.3	Iron and steel	5.8
Electrical machinery	5.0	Nonferrous metals	5.8
Fuels and lubricants	3.6	Nonmetal industrial supplies	2.5
Iron and steel	3.0	Paper	2.9
Nonferrous metals	2.9	Petroleum and products	24.2
Nonmetal industrial supplies	5.9	All other merchandise imports	13.7
Paper	2.6		
Scientific equipment	1.5		
Textile supplies	3.2		
All other merchandise exports	6.6		
Total exports	$98.5	Total imports	$103.0

* Exports include military grant shipments and re-exports.
Source: U.S. Department of Commerce, *Survey of Current Business*, March 1975.

shown in Table 17–1. However, beginning in the early 1970s American purchases of goods from foreign countries exceeded our exports.

The principal exports and imports for the United States for 1974 are shown in Table 17–2. There are certain commodities which the United States lacks and must import. These include bananas, coffee, cocoa, diamonds, natural rubber, tin, and nickel. Other goods such as oil are produced in this country but not in sufficient quantity to meet demand. Some imported items have special prestige appeal for consumers such as French fashions, perfumes, or wines.

Also, Americans have been heavy purchasers of foreign automobiles, steel, and other manufactured products. Some foreign manufactured goods such as portable typewriters, shoes, and textiles as well as some electronic products have been available at lower prices than if manufactured in this country. Reasons for the lower prices include lower wage rates paid foreign workers, more efficient production processes abroad, or lower costs for raw materials or parts. Figure 17–1 summarizes U.S. international trade by areas of the world.

DIRECT INVESTMENT ABROAD

In addition to the goods bought and sold abroad, American business enterprises have invested substantial amounts in foreign operations. American capital in private direct investments abroad reached an estimated total of $114 billion in 1974 compared with only $32 billion in 1960. Private direct investment in foreign countries is from funds sent from the United States or from profits generated in American-owned foreign operations.

The incentive for Americans to invest abroad rather than expand in the United States is the prospect for higher profits because of better market conditions, lower production costs, or lower taxes. Also, American business has invested abroad to avoid the external tariffs imposed by multinational groups such as the European Common Market.

Multinational business corporations

Because of the increased international investment by corporations, a new class of enterprises has developed in recent years called the multinational corporation. A *multinational corporation* is a business enterprise which has significant operations in several countries. Not only goods but also capital, technology, and management move across

FIGURE 17-1

United States exports and imports to areas of the world, 1974 (billions of dollars)

Source: U.S. Bureau of the Census, *Highlights of U.S. Export and Import Trade*, FT 990, December 1974.

national boundaries. The viewpoint of the management of the multinational corporation is worldwide rather than national.

Table 17–3 lists the 10 largest U.S. industrial corporations based on 1974 sales. Notice the proportion of total profits derived from operations outside the United States by these giant enterprises.

Business managers in the United States are able to make decisions without being unduly influenced by the political boundaries of the

TABLE 17–3

Ten largest U.S. industrial corporations, 1974 total sales (billions of dollars) and percentage of profits from international operations

Corporation	1974 sales	Percentage of total profits earned abroad
Exxon	$42.1	68%
General Motors	31.6	nil*
Ford Motor	23.6	20†
Texaco	23.3	71
Mobil	18.9	65
Standard Oil of California	17.2	66
Gulf Oil	16.5	62
General Electric	13.4	24
International Business Machines	12.7	50
International Telephone & Telegraph	11.2	49†

* GM reported no profits from international operations in 1974.
† From operations outside the United States and Canada.

50 states. In the same way decisions in multinational corporations generally are based on costs and prices regardless of national boundaries. Such independence raises fundamental questions regarding their economic power, effect on employment, and political allegiance and regulation.

Economic power. The size of many multinational corporations in assets, sales, and economic influence dwarfs the total national product of many of the countries in which they operate. When a corporation dominates an industry or the whole economy in a country both politicians and citizens become concerned. In a best-selling book, *The American Challenge,* the French politician and journalist Jean-Jacques Servan-Schreiber suggested that in the 1980s the world's third greatest industrial power behind the United States and Russia will not be Europe but American industry in Europe.

Effect on employment. Some union leaders and politicians claim that multinational corporations export jobs when they build new factories in countries having relatively low-cost labor markets. However, Commerce Department surveys have shown that employment in the United States by multinational corporations has increased at a faster rate than that by other American enterprises. There are employment problems in some industries as the nature of imports and exports changes. Even so, most economists believe that free trade and capital flows produce the greatest benefits to society.

Political allegiance and regulation. Other issues regarding the multinational corporations include these questions: What political allegiance should managements have to the countries where they operate? What happens when the national interests of the countries and the multinationals come into conflict? How will the multinational corporation be regulated with its operations extending beyond the power of any single country's control? These questions and the alternatives for their solution are being discussed now.

INTERNATIONAL MONETARY BALANCES

Balance of trade

A country's total imports of merchandise are subtracted from its exports to determine the *balance of trade.* When annual exports exceed imports the balance of trade is positive and is customarily called "favorable." When imports exceed exports the balance of trade is "unfavorable."

Traditionally the United States has had a favorable balance of trade. However, in 1971 the picture changed as the U.S. experienced a $2.7 billion deficit which jumped to about $7 billion in 1972. The trade deficit in 1972 resulted from a strong increase in demand by Americans for foreign goods as our economy expanded. Also, foreign demand for our nonagricultural exports was limited by the slower improvement in business abroad.

In 1973 there was marked improvement in our merchandise trade with exports exceeding imports by $500 million. The devaluation of the United States dollar made our goods less expensive abroad. Also, agricultural exports increased. However, in 1974 the United States again had a deficit balance of international trade of $6 billion, mainly because of the increased cost of imported oil.

Balance of payments

The balance of trade is part of a broader calculation called the international *balance of payments*. This includes all the funds flowing into and out of a country over a period of time. The components of the United States' balance of payments for 1974 are shown in Figure 17–2.

As Figure 17–2 shows, in 1974 the United States had a deficit in its international balance of payments of $8 billion. When the United States has a deficit balance of payments this results in an increase in American dollars held by foreign banks, governments, business enter-

FIGURE 17–2
United States balance of payments, 1974 (billions of dollars)

Funds inflows		Funds outflows	
Merchandise exports............	$ 97.0	Merchandise imports...........	$103.0
		Military transactions, net........	2.0
		Travel and transportation, net...	2.5
Income on U.S. investments abroad.......................	26.0	Income on foreign investments in the U.S.....................	16.0
		Remittances, pensions, and other transfers................	2.0
Other service exports...........	4.0		
Total inflows..............	$127.0	U.S. government grants.........	5.5
		Net capital outflows.............	4.0
Official transactions balance....	−8.0	Total outflows.............	$135.0

Deficit of $8.0 billion financed by increase in liabilities to foreign official agencies.
Source: U.S. Department of Commerce, *Survey of Current Business,* March 1975.

prises, and individuals. The dollar deposits in European commercial banks including foreign branches of American banks are called *Eurodollars*.

In the past foreigners considered it desirable to hold dollars since the U.S. dollar was considered the key currency for use in international trade. However, by 1970 the dollar became less attractive to foreigners. The reasons included our country's deficit balance of payments, inflation causing higher prices for American products abroad, and the U.S. government's budget deficits which tended to cause further inflation.

Despite these problems and those discussed in the remainder of this chapter, the U.S. dollar is still an important international currency. Many nations still relate the value of their currency to the dollar and hold dollars as monetary reserves. This country's GNP is the largest in the world, and our exports and imports are greater than those of any other nation.

National currencies in international business

Business transactions in international trade are complicated by the problem of different monetary systems and restrictions on the flow of funds among countries. Virtually every sovereign nation has its own monetary system. The U.S. currency is based on the dollar. There is the British pound, the Swiss franc, the West German mark, the Indian rupee, and so on for other nations. Something of the complexity of the problem may be visualized if each of the 50 states in this country had its own monetary system with restrictions on the flow of funds into and out of the state.

When a business enterprise wishes to buy goods from another country, the manager must obtain sufficient foreign currency to pay the exporter. The exchange of U.S. dollars by the American importer for the foreign currency is usually done through the importer's bank in the foreign exchange market. The units which one U.S. dollar will purchase in a foreign currency are expressed by the *foreign exchange rate,* which is the price of one currency in terms of the other. In dealing with foreign currencies the American business manager is advised to consult a bank's foreign exchange department to minimize the risk of loss through fluctuating currency prices.

From time to time a country's central banking authority may find itself short of another country's currency. This may result not only in changes in foreign exchange rates but also in exchange control. *Exchange control* is exercised by most governments over access to foreign currencies by their private citizens and business enterprises. Usually exchange control is carried out by holding foreign currencies in central government banks or under the control of government monetary authorities. Foreign currencies are then made available to private interests to settle international financial transactions. When a nation has a persistent outflow of its currency, it may be necessary for the government to restrict private transactions during the period of shortage of foreign exchange currencies.

In 1946 the International Monetary Fund (IMF) was established by 39 countries including the United States to foster international monetary cooperation and stability. The purposes of the IMF were to provide short-term international credit for nations, to facilitate consultation among nations on monetary policies and problems, and to achieve orderly changes in individual nations' currency exchange rates. Virtually all non-Communist countries now belong to the IMF.

The role of gold

In the past the ultimate means for settling international balance of payments deficits between nations has been the payment of gold by the deficit nation to the creditor nation. In the United States from 1933 through 1974 the government strictly controlled the possession of gold by Americans. During this period it was illegal for United States citizens to own gold for monetary purposes. It could be owned only for manufacturing items such as jewelry or for dental or medical uses. The United States government set an official price of $35 an ounce on its gold supply, which it used internationally for settling balance-of-payments transactions. Also, gold was used domestically as a 25 percent backing of the U.S. Federal Reserve notes which formed the basis of the nation's money supply.

Following World War II the United States had a large monetary gold stock which reached a peak of $24.6 billion in 1949. However, in later years this gold supply decreased because of persistent balance-of-payments deficits. These outflows resulted from a variety of factors including military spending overseas, government grants, American business investment in foreign countries, American tourists traveling abroad, and the lack of enough merchandise exports to overcome the total deficit. By 1968 our gold supply had dropped to $10.4 billion.

Gold tie to dollar cut. In 1968 following a $3 billion drop in the U.S. gold supply, Congress eliminated the 25 percent gold backing required for the Federal Reserve's money reserves. Thus the partial gold reserve on the country's domestic money supply was removed. However, pressure on our stock of gold continued from foreigners. The dollar claims of foreigners built up because inflation in the United States made the prices of our goods relatively less attractive abroad and we were importing more. Also, during this period America was spending huge sums overseas on military activities especially in Southeast Asia. Finally, in August 1971, President Nixon announced that the United States government would no longer permit the dollars held by foreign governments, banks, and private interests to be freely exchanged into gold. Thus the international tie of the dollar to gold convertibility was cut. The United States is no longer tied to gold either domestically or internationally.

The international value of the dollar for business and individual transactions is a relationship to other nations' currencies rather than to gold. This condition is known as a "floating" exchange rate because it is free to move up or down rather than being fixed by the government at a particular level. An international system of currency exchange is being worked out in cooperation among government central banking authorities, the IMF, and other international bodies.

Gold markets. Two markets exist today for gold. The first market is the value placed on gold for international currency standards by the IMF. As the result of two devaluations of the U.S. dollar since 1971, the dollar is now worth $42.22 an ounce of gold officially (although the U.S. government will not permit conversion of its gold stock into dollars at this rate). Other nations also state the value of their currencies in gold with the International Monetary Fund. The rules of the International Monetary Fund prohibit government central banks from buying gold or accepting it as an official international monetary settlement at more than the official price. Since the price of gold in the second or "free" market is substantially higher than the IMF price, virtually no international monetary settlements were being made for gold in 1975.

In the second gold market, that which operates outside the official monetary rates, the price of gold is determined by private buyers and sellers. In this free market for gold the metal is traded as a commodity with its price responding to supply and demand at a given time. In December 1974, it became lawful after more than 30 years for American citizens to own gold bullion. The price of gold on the free market reached $190 an ounce early in 1975. Thus for private business enterprises and individuals a market for gold exists just as for many other commodities such as silver, copper, wheat, or pork bellies. Active gold markets exist in London, Switzerland, and other locations around the world. Many commercial banks and investment brokers in the United States buy and sell gold bullion and coins for their customers.

TARIFFS AND OTHER TRADE BARRIERS

Tariffs

A variety of trade barriers may be used by governments to restrict the movement of products from one country to another. *Tariffs* are taxes placed on imported goods and are frequently used to limit the flow of goods between nations. Tariffs are based on a percentage of the product's value or on a set amount per item. Tariffs are used to protect domestic industry from foreign competition or to produce revenues for the importing country. Protective tariffs attempt to save domestic jobs and production from lower priced imports. They may be used to build up industry for a nation's military self-sufficiency or to improve a country's international balance of payments.

Quotas

*Quota*s are designed to place an absolute limit on the quantity of foreign goods imported into a country. A tariff allows consumers to buy as much of an imported good as they choose but increases the price of the import. A quota restricts the quantity of foreign goods available at any price. Quotas are used primarily for protection of domestic industries. Quotas have been used in the United States for products such as textiles to protect American producers of cotton and man-made textiles. Sometimes quotas are "voluntary" as the result of international agreements, made so that an importing country will not have to resort to mandatory quotas.

Embargoes

An *embargo* is a prohibition against the movement of goods. An embargo may be placed on products or nations. Embargoes have been used by the United States for health and political reasons. Embargoes on goods for health purposes include restrictions on the import of a variety of drugs. Also, there are embargoes on some agricultural products that may be infested with insects harmful to domestic crops. Political embargoes have been used against countries such as Cuba and the People's Republic of China.

Aid to domestic enterprises

A government may provide assistance to domestic enterprises to give them a competitive advantage over foreign producers. Direct export subsidies are sometimes used to encourage exports. Export subsidies are generally contrary to international trade agreements except for agricultural commodities. However, hidden subsidies exist through tax credits for certain exports. In 1972 the U.S. Congress created a new corporate category for tax purposes called the Domestic International Sales Corporation (DISC). DISCs are entitled to defer taxes on 50 percent of their export income until this income is distributed to stockholders.

Restrictions can be placed on imported goods which tend to aid domestic producers. These include health and safety standards, packaging, labeling, and marking regulations. Usually requirements that foreign goods be prominently labeled with the country of origin are meant to discourage consumers from their purchase. Also, requiring foreign products such as automobiles to conform to American anti-pollution laws places additional costs on foreign manufacturers. On the other hand, not to require this would place U.S. manufacturers at a competitive disadvantage.

The U.S. Department of Commerce maintains district offices across the nation to assist business in international and domestic trade. Government trade centers exist abroad to encourage the sale of American goods in foreign countries. Governments may provide financial support for research and development which aids domestic industry. Government agencies may also give preference in their purchasing policies to domestic products. For example, United States regulations under the *Buy American Act of 1933* require that domestic products be purchased by government agencies unless their cost exceeds by a specified percentage that of the same product from foreign sources.

Customs administration and technical regulations

Although a country's tariffs may be low on imported goods, using complicated procedures to administer customs laws can restrict imports. Delays in the customs clearance process may arise in classifying and valuing goods to determine tariff charges.

Most countries have antidumping regulations. *Dumping* occurs when an exporter sells a product in a foreign market at a lower price than in his home market. Most nations levy duties on dumped products to protect domestic industry.

Private barriers to trade

A variety of practices by private business enterprises can restrict competition in international trade. Licensing agreements, patents, and trademark laws can be used to divide markets. Cartels are encouraged by some foreign governments. A *cartel* is a group of business enterprises which agree to cooperate in the production and marketing of a product to fix prices and divide markets. The result of a cartel agreement is to reduce competition. You will recall from Chapter 2, that the general policy of the United States government is to foster competition. Hence, cartels are illegal in this country.

INTERNATIONAL TRADE COOPERATION

The general policy of the United States has been to improve trade among nations through legislation and international agreements. Significant U.S. participation has come through the General Agreement on Tariffs and Trade, the Trade Expansion Act, the creation of foreign trade zones, and a variety of federal and international agencies.

The General Agreement on Tariffs and Trade (GATT)

Following World War II in 1947, the United States and 22 other nations met in Geneva, Switzerland for the purpose of discussing international trade. Out of this conference came the General Agreement on Tariffs and Trade (GATT) which provided a means for reducing tariffs and other trade barriers among nations. Now there are more than 70 governments participating in GATT with continuing discussions on problems of international trade and reduction of tariffs.

The Trade Expansion Act of 1962 (TEA)

In 1962 President Kennedy signed the Trade Expansion Act. This empowered the president over a period of five years to negotiate lower tariffs with other nations and to enter into international marketing agreements with foreign governments. The legislation was designed to stimulate demand for United States goods abroad and to reduce barriers to international trade in general. The TEA led to what was called the Kennedy Round of tariff negotiations by the member nations of GATT from 1964 to 1967. The Kennedy Round resulted in an average tariff reduction of 35 percent on a wide range of industrial products.

Foreign trade zones

As the result of 1934 legislation certain areas of the United States may be designated as *foreign trade zones* where foreign goods or raw materials may be imported without being subject to tariffs or quotas provided the goods are to be exported from the United States at a later time. This means that a United States manufacturer operating in a foreign trade zone can import raw materials or component parts, complete the product, and re-export the goods without having to pay the usual U.S. tariffs. The purpose of these foreign trade zones is to stimulate international trade by American enterprises. They make American manufactured goods more competitive by taking advantage of lower-cost foreign raw materials or parts. There are now 12 approved foreign trade zones in the United States located in New York, San Francisco, Seattle, New Orleans, Kansas City, Toledo, Honolulu, Little Rock, Bay City and Sault Ste. Marie (Michigan), McAllen (Texas), and Mayaguez (Puerto Rico). There are facilities in these zones for storage, inspection, manufacture, and repacking of goods. Over 1,200 business enterprises make use of these foreign trade zones.

Free ports and free trade zones exist in approximately 40 countries, usually at seaports. Many manufacturers use these ports to repack goods for shipment in smaller quantities to customers in nearby areas.

Federal and international financing agencies

A variety of federal and international agencies have been created to help finance international business projects.

The *Export-Import Bank (Eximbank)*, established in 1934, is the oldest international finance agency of the United States government. Eximbank has financed loans totaling several billion dollars for American export of goods such as production equipment, agricultural machinery, basic raw materials, and commodities. Eximbank provides financing for feasible export projects where business has difficulty obtaining financing from private sources such as commercial banks. This agency also participates with commercial banks in loans and provides insurance for political and business risks.

The *Agency for International Development (AID)* is a U.S. government body which has jurisdiction over most government foreign economic aid programs. The agency encourages private American participation in foreign economic development. It provides guarantees against political and economic risks for private investments in more than 70 less developed countries. AID also has joint ventures and loan programs to foster the economic development of less developed countries by private and public organizations.

International agencies organized for the purpose of facilitating trade and international development include the global organizations of the *International Bank for Reconstruction and Development (World Bank)*, the *International Development Association,* and the *International Finance Corporation.*

Regional international agencies for economic development include the *Inter-American Development Bank,* the *Asian Development Bank,* the *European Investment Bank,* and the *African Development Bank.*

DIFFERENCES BETWEEN MANAGEMENT IN AMERICA AND ABROAD

Along with the monetary problems, tariffs, and other barriers to trade already discussed there are additional factors to be considered in the management of foreign operations. These factors can be grouped into five categories: government relations, financing commercial transactions, language and cultural barriers, relations with the home office, and the training of managers who go abroad.

Government relations

Business enterprises operating in the United States are subject, of course, to all the laws and regulations of municipal, state, and federal governments. The business manager is normally well acquainted with these domestic regulations including laws on taxes, labor relations, patents and trademarks, licenses, and health and safety. When an enterprise operates abroad the manager must conform to U.S. laws and also to the regulations of foreign governments.

Areas of government regulation for international business include export and import restrictions, tariff regulations, health and sanitation laws, packaging and labeling requirements, and national security policies. As already discussed, international monetary differences and currency exchange restrictions are important considerations in most countries.

Besides laws on imports and exports, foreign governments affect American enterprises through regulations on manufacturing and marketing operations. When Americans move into other countries to establish factories and sales branches it is *they* who are considered foreigners, not the governments or people of the locality. Foreign governments generally are interested in having their economies developed without being dominated by American business. Increasingly there are government restrictions on removing profits from the country where they are generated. Economic nationalism is important not only in such areas as Africa, Latin America, and the Middle East but also in such long-industrialized nations as Great Britain, France, and the United States.

In addition to the business risks described in Chapter 4, American capital when invested abroad is also exposed to the risk of expropriation by foreign governments. In some instances when American business assets are taken over by a foreign government the owners are compensated for their losses. In other cases no compensation is given. In 1960 Fidel Castro's revolutionary Cuban government expropriated without compensation all Cuban properties owned by American companies. In 1971 properties of some American corporations were expropriated by the government of Chile. Recently some of the international oil companies' production facilities in Africa and the Middle East were taken over by the host governments. In 1975 Venezuela moved to take over American oil companies' property.

There are now some means to compensate private investors who lose funds in international trade and investment. For example, the Foreign Credit Insurance Association made up of private insurance companies cooperates with the Export-Import Bank to provide insurance coverage for the political and commercial risks of doing business abroad. This insurance covers losses due to expropriation by a government, inability of the buyer to pay for merchandise, civil war, or cancellation of an import license prior to the arrival of goods.

Financing international commercial transactions

The means of financing international commercial transactions include cash payment, open account, bills of exchange, and letters of credit.

Cash payment in the form of bank checks or international money orders may be used. Cash as a means of payment upon shipment of merchandise is generally unattractive to an importer. When cash is paid with the order or before merchandise is shipped the buyer is highly dependent on the promptness and financial integrity of the exporter. Relatively little international trade is on a cash basis, although sometimes a deposit will be required by an exporter for special orders.

The *open account,* which is widely used in the United States as a means of providing financial arrangements for business transactions, is used relatively infrequently in international trade. The open account has no accompanying document calling for payment and no written acknowledgment by the purchaser of the liability. Because of legal differences among countries, fluctuating exchange rates, and differing customs, the shipment of exports under open account is rarely done except from a manufacturer to its own branches overseas.

Bills of exchange, or *drafts* as they are sometimes called, are the most common method of payment in international commerce. A bill of exchange is drawn by the exporter of goods and calls upon the importer to accept the obligation for payment of a sum of money at a specified time. The bill of exchange becomes a *trade acceptance* when an acknowledgment of the obligation is written across the face of the document by the importer.

The three parties to a draft transaction are:

1. The *drawer* who is the person executing the draft (the exporter or seller).
2. The *drawee* upon whom the draft is drawn and who is required to meet the terms of the document (the importer or buyer).
3. The *payee* who is the party to receive payment (the exporter or his bank).

There are various ways in which drafts can be used in business transactions. A *sight draft* calls for the drawee to pay the draft upon its presentation (on sight). A *time draft* calls for payment on a specified date in the future. The acceptance of a time draft obligates the drawee to pay the draft when it falls due. When drafts are drawn upon a bank and are accepted by the bank instead of an importer they become *bank acceptances* instead of trade acceptances. Although there are variations in the use of bank acceptances, their effect is to substitute the credit of the bank for the credit of the importer.

A *commercial letter of credit* is a document issued by a bank for an importer of merchandise. The terms and requirements by which payment will be made to the exporter are set forth in the letter of credit. The exporter is authorized to draw drafts on the bank. The bank agrees to honor the drafts if all requirements are met. The business enterprise which is importing the merchandise arranges to pay the bank for the drafts which the bank accepts. For this service the bank receives a commission for the letter of credit and handling charges for the drafts. These are paid by the importer. If the drafts are time drafts the importer may pay an interest charge.

A variety of documents are required for international transactions. The most important of these include the negotiable bill of lading, insurance certificate or policy, and the commercial invoice. The *negotiable bill of lading* when endorsed constitutes a receipt for the goods, a contract of transportation, and evidence of title to the property. The holder of the bill of lading is the lawful owner of the shipment. Other papers such as customs documents, export licenses, inspection certificates, and packing lists normally will be required.

When the merchandise is shipped, the bill of lading, draft, and other shipping papers are normally sent to the exporter's bank. The exporter's bank forwards the draft and shipping documents to the importer's bank which notifies the importer that the documents have arrived. The draft is presented to the importer for acceptance. Upon acceptance by the importer, the trade acceptance (draft) is then returned to the bank for transmission through banking channels to the exporter or the exporter's bank. When the maturity date on the trade acceptance approaches it is sent to the importer's bank, which presents it to the importer for payment.

When the draft is accepted, the importer is given the bill of lading by the bank. The bill of lading is presented to the freight agent as evidence of ownership of the goods upon their arrival. Sometimes an inspection of the goods is required upon their arrival before the importer will accept the draft which obligates the importer for payment.

If the importer had used a commercial letter of credit from the bank, the process would be essentially the same except that the bank would have accepted the draft under terms which had been agreed upon among the parties.

Figure 17–3 illustrates the financial transactions which would normally follow the application for and issuance of a commercial letter of credit. The numbered steps in Figure 17–3 are discussed briefly below:

1. General Textiles Company desiring to import woolen goods from Wool Company of Great Britain works out arrangements for the purchase with the British firm and then prepares an application for a letter of credit after consultation with its banker, Commerce Trust Company of Kansas City.

2. General Textiles forwards the application for the $10,000 letter of credit to Commerce Trust Company.

FIGURE 17–3
Illustration of a U.S. sight letter of credit transaction covering an import

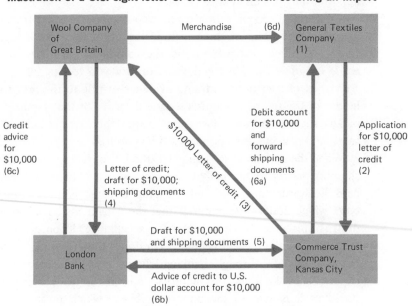

3. The Commerce Trust, having determined that the financial arrangements are in order, issues a $10,000 letter of credit and transmits it to Wool Company of Great Britain.

4. Wool Company sends the letter of credit, a draft drawn on Commerce Trust for $10,000, and the shipping documents to its bank, London Bank, which is also a correspondent bank of Commerce Trust Company. At the same time the merchandise is prepared for shipment and begins its transit voyage.

5. London Bank, acting for its customer, files the letter of credit and forwards the draft for $10,000 and shipping documents to Commerce Trust.

6. Commerce Trust, upon receipt of the documents, accepts the draft for $10,000 thereby making it a bank acceptance. Commerce Trust then (6a) debits General Textiles' bank account in payment for the merchandise and financial charges and sends the shipping documents to the importer so General Textiles may claim the merchandise from the freight agent (6d). At the same time Commerce Trust (6b) credits its correspondent, London Bank, with $10,000; and in turn (6c) London Bank credits the account of its customer, Wool Company of Great

Britain, for $10,000 in terms of British pounds sterling for payment for the merchandise, thereby completing the transaction.

Language and cultural barriers

Language differences. The English language is widely used throughout the world. However, the ability to communicate with nationals, local authorities, and customers in their own language is essential. With concentrated effort, learning to speak and read another language fluently is not overly difficult. An otherwise well-qualified candidate can probably master a second language for foreign assignment. The resident manager must be able to think in the language so as to be able to communicate effectively and to understand others. Indeed, the attitude of the manager who is unwilling to speak any language other than English may limit that person's effectiveness in a foreign assignment.

Cultural barriers. Cultural differences are an obvious but important consideration in the management of foreign operations. In many instances today the physical office and plant facilities will be similar to those in the United States. However, the cultural values relating to business, the individual, work, and social customs may be very different. Generally in the United States the role of the business manager is viewed with respect. Industry leaders are given recognition in business circles and in other sectors of society. In other countries the role of business is becoming more socially acceptable and receiving higher status. However, in the Orient this runs counter to a cultural background which for centuries has given the highest status in society to scholars, politicians, and warriors. In the past the merchant had no high social standing. This role has changed especially in the past quarter century. The international view of business is coming to be more that which prevails in the United States.

The ethical concepts which prevail in this country are not necessarily followed abroad. Bribery, illegal division of markets, rigged bids, and payoffs are not totally absent from our business scene, but they are not advocated by business leaders here and are considered scandalous when discovered. The manager dealing in foreign business operations may find a different system of values and practices prevailing. This does not mean that such deviations from American standards must be accepted. Indeed, confidence in the word of Americans abroad is an advantage over the long run. However, managers should be aware of general business practices in their locale and know how to face competition they may encounter. An understanding of what is considered honorable practice will enable Americans to learn when and with whom their confidence may be placed.

Social customs in every country abroad are different. Time will be required before an understanding of their subtleties is gained. The formalities of Oriental politeness; the different value placed on time in the Middle East and on the preliminaries to business discussion; the hours of work and dining; and a more reserved attitude toward strangers —these are examples of differences from American customs. The newcomer to international business is well advised to set about learning local customs in a friendly but not overly aggressive way.

Relations with the home office

The problems arising out of the relationship between the home office and foreign operations are the same type as those which exist between home offices and decentralized operations in the United States. However, there are complications caused by the greater distances between home offices and foreign operations, relations with foreign governments, and variations in the business and cultural environment abroad. The American manager of a foreign operation must be able to deal with the home office where there may be a lack of understanding of problems faced in the field. At the same time the manager must deal with foreign nationals and governments who have little understanding or interest in home office policies and problems.

Because of these complications, the manager abroad should have as much autonomy as possible to meet unusual circumstances. Management in the foreign office should be provided with guidelines or limits on its freedom of action. Management in the home office should make every attempt to avoid interference as long as operations are under these guidelines and according to overall forecasts. At least one key person in the home office should have had sufficient foreign experience to appreciate the circumstances faced abroad.

Laws abroad and dealings with foreign governments will differ from those prevailing in this country. Managers on the scene should be permitted to cope with these problems with a minimum of interference from the home office. Often there are sound reasons for dealing with governments overseas differently than with government in this country because of customs and political systems abroad. Especially in overseas operations, in today's complex world it is virtually impossible to separate economics and politics.

Even though a substantial amount of local autonomy is desirable for foreign operations, overseas offices can benefit from the systems and procedures developed in this country. Some modification may be required before they are placed in effect abroad. Usually a written policy statement is desirable outlining the decisions which can be made by managers abroad, especially regarding financial commitments. In some countries a written definition of the authority of corporate managers is required by law. An overseas manager must usually get permission from the board of directors before changing product lines, making large capital expenditures, or borrowing money in excess of a certain amount.

The foreign manager has a responsibility to keep the home office informed of important developments 'abroad and to explain the meaning of events which may not be understood at home. The importance of good communications stressed in Chapter 7 should be emphasized in international business. Despite improved communications and jet airlines systems which make London, New York, and Tokyo only hours apart, these areas are still great distances apart in many business practices and cultural mores. Furthermore, foreign business operations are not always located in big cities which are international centers of language and culture. Business may also be done in relatively isolated areas where communications and transportation may be inadequate when compared with metropolitan areas.

Communications between the home office and foreign branches are further complicated because of the difference in time zones around the world. As the manager is closing the office in London at 4 P.M., the members of the home office staff in San Francisco are just finishing their morning coffee and rushing off to their offices at 8 A.M. that day, while in Tokyo the time is 1 A.M. the next day.

Importance of good management

Despite the emphasis on the differences between managing in this country and abroad, many of the same concepts and functions of management still apply. The basic managerial function of directing the work efforts of employees to achieve effective results is necessary throughout the world. The same importance is placed upon good planning, organization, staffing, and control. It is the changed economic, political, and social environment which adds a new dimension to the manager's job. The manager who has demonstrated effectiveness with assignments in this country will find that many of these skills apply to the foreign assignment.

TRAINING FOR OVERSEAS ASSIGNMENT

Before a domestic manager accepts a foreign assignment, the executive and spouse will want to know the duration and compensation of the assignment, something about the living conditions in the part of the country where they are to be placed, and the nature of the educational system if they have children. The manager who accepts a foreign assignment should have some special training before going abroad. For the manager this means preparation for responsibilities in a new and different business climate. For the family it means preparation to accept new customs of living and orientation into the conditions which will be encountered in the new location.

In the area of job preparation the manager may be given special training in marketing, production, or finance to relate this knowledge to the conditions anticipated abroad. Before the executive's departure a thorough briefing should be given in the relationships which will exist with home office officials and other foreign-based personnel, and the degree of decision-making latitude.

Special foreign language training should be provided in the United States if English is not the native tongue in the foreign location. A desirable policy is to include the executive's spouse in language training for good adjustment to the new location.

Representatives of American business should have an understanding of the important social, political, and economic issues in the United States. Foreigners will be interested in the views of the new American manager. Therefore, the ability to discuss intelligently such subjects as American foreign policy, economic conditions, and the private enterprise system is vital. In many respects the Americans living abroad *are* the United States to those foreign nationals with whom they come in contact.

BUILDING THE WORK TEAM ABROAD

Upon arrival in the new location the manager will be faced with the responsibility of selecting, training, and directing the efforts of the management team. When the enterprise already has an established base of operations this job is made easier since an organization already exists. However, even so the new manager will have to review the situation carefully and may wish to make changes after understanding local circumstances. This is particularly true if the manager has been sent to correct a condition which the home office believes could be improved.

In many instances, however, it will be necessary for the executive to select and train personnel and to put together an organization to begin business operations. While there may be some American specialists from headquarters to assist, the proper selection, training, and treatment of local nationals is the key to successful future operations.

In building a new organization the manager's first step likely will be the selection of a national who thoroughly understands how to get things done in the country. This person can accomplish much that the new manager cannot and can act as a valuable advisor.

Despite the importance of language ability, this does not mean any foreign national who is bilingual will be an effective key employee in the overseas operation. Foreign nationals will probably require training about the enterprise and its products before they are valuable in decision making.

Other key appointments will be persons to handle buying and marketing functions in the enterprise. These assignments should go to people who have experience in these fields in the country and who are fluent in the language and aware of local customs. A good legal advisor can make the regulations in the foreign country understandable and can offer advice on how to avoid legal problems.

If the enterprise is engaged in manufacturing, the selection of production executives will be important. Frequently, home office engineers and some production managers will assist in start-up operations. However, control of production should be transferred to local employees as soon as possible.

In the recruitment of local persons the American manager should become acquainted with local wage rates and working conditions. The enterprise may pay somewhat higher wages than those prevailing in the community. But it is generally not desirable to be too far out of line —both to control costs and to avoid alienating local business against the enterprise.

A long-range plan should be developed to replace the enterprise's American managers with local personnel. This does not mean that some Americans may not be permanently stationed abroad. However, over the long run all key executive personnel positions should not be staffed with Americans. The new manager should establish employee training programs to improve the skills of workers and to develop technical and managerial persons. Morale of employees will be higher if the nationals have an opportunity to reach management positions. In summary, the success of U.S.-based enterprises abroad largely depends on the success of American executives in putting together an effective organization of foreign nationals who understand the objectives and methods of good management.

Organization for foreign operations

The organization structure of enterprises involved in international business is similar in many instances to that of enterprises operating only in the United States. When an enterprise has a functional departmental organization the factory manager abroad may report directly to the vice president for production in the home office. Similarly, the sales manager for foreign products may report to the vice president for marketing or to the general sales manager. However, there may be a vice president for foreign operations in the organization to whom foreign managers report. This gives recognition to the increasing importance of international business in many enterprises today.

Some firms which have been successful in international business have created separate organizations with their own presidents and operational autonomy. This arrangement is especially beneficial when foreign operations have passed the initial stages of development. Then the necessary staff personnel and organization required for independent operation can be economically justified. This separate arrangement has advantages of flexibility and operational mobility as well as some tax advantages. When an enterprise separate from its parent company is formed, control by the parent enterprise is maintained through stock ownership. The use of patent and trademark license agreements also provides a means of control by U.S. enterprises over their relatively independent foreign operations.

When business takes on a multinational character it may be desirable to decentralize these operations on a geographic basis. Lines of authority and responsibility should be well defined for businesses operating solely in the United States. The same is true for the enterprise with extensive foreign operations. Multinational management is faced with even greater challenges because of the political, economic, and cultural differences in international operations.

SUMMARY

While many American business managers have viewed foreign countries as potential markets for their products, many foreign manufacturers also aggressively view the United States as a great market for their products.

Although exports of merchandise make up only about 7 percent of our gross national product, these transactions provide job opportunities for seven to eight million Americans.

The incentive for American private direct investment abroad includes:

The prospect for profits stemming from better market conditions.

Lower production costs.

Lower taxes than exist in the United States.

Avoidance of external tariffs imposed by such multinational groups as the European Common Market.

The development of multinational corporations, with significant operations in several countries, raises a number of key issues.

A country's balance of trade is determined by subtracting its imports of merchandise from its exports. The balance of trade is part of a broader calculation called a nation's international balance of payments. This includes all funds that flow into and out of a country over a period of time.

The United States dollar is no longer tied to gold convertibility either domestically or internationally. The U.S. government will not permit conversion of its gold stock at the official rate of $42.22 an ounce.

Barriers used by countries to restrict trade include tariffs, quotas, embargoes, and delays in customs clearances.

The United States has acted to improve trade among nations by participating in the General Agreement on Tariffs and Trade, the Trade Expansion Act, the creation of foreign trade zones, and a variety of federal and international agencies to help finance world trade.

Imports may be financed by cash payment, open account, bills of exchange, and letters of credit. Bills of exchange which may become either trade acceptances or bank acceptances are the most common method of payment in world trade.

American managers sent abroad need a knowledge of the regulations, language, and customs of the country of their location. Also, the American manager overseas must deal with the home office which may lack an understanding of the problems faced in the field. When building a work team abroad it is desirable to train local nationals for management responsibilities as soon as possible.

TERMS FOR REVIEW

exports   *quota*

imports   *embargo*

multinational corporation   *expropriation*

balance of trade   *trade acceptance*

balance of payments   *bank acceptance*

foreign exchange rate   *commercial letter of credit*

tariff   *negotiable bill of lading*

QUESTIONS

1. Referring to Table 17–2, what American industries directly benefit most from foreign trade?

2. *a.* Using the most recent *Survey of Current Business,* determine the amount of exports and imports in the following industries:
   1. automobiles and parts
   2. iron and steel
   3. chemicals
   4. agricultural products

   b. By examining current periodicals establish what positions these domestic industrial groups have taken toward international trade questions such as U.S. import quotas and customs duties.

3. Why do U.S. business enterprises establish manufacturing or sales branches overseas?

4. What issues are raised with the development of the multinational corporation?

5. What are some of the barriers to world trade?

6. What possible problems may be encountered by the business enterprise engaged in foreign trade or manufacturing operations overseas that would not normally be encountered in the United States?

7. Trace an international trade transaction as illustrated in part by Figure 17–3.

8. In 1971 U.S. imports exceeded exports. It was the first time since 1893 that this country had a trade deficit. List some of the different actions that the United States could take to correct this imbalance of trade.

9. Based on your study of library materials and this chapter, prepare a 300-word summary analyzing the following statement: "More import controls and tariffs are needed to protect such American industries as textiles, steel, and automobiles against foreign competition."

10. What are the advantages to the U.S. economy and to consumers of reducing trade restrictions throughout the world? What disadvantages may result for some industries in the United States from freer world trade?

Business briefs

Computers to Russia

In June 1975, the Sperry Univac division of Sperry Rand Corporation announced the sale of a $10 million computer-based reservations system to the Soviet Union's airline, Aeroflot. The computer system is the largest to be sold to Russia by any U.S. computer manufacturer.

Discussions between Aeroflot and Sperry Univac took place for about two years. After a contract was signed for the sale Sperry applied to the U.S. Commerce Department for a permit to make the sale. Commerce Department approval is necessary for sales to the Soviet Union to prevent the delivery of strategic defense equipment. After 11 months of consideration the Commerce Department issued the necessary license authorizing the sale.

The computer system for the Russian airline, one of the world's largest air carriers, includes the Univac 1106-II which is a powerful computer but isn't the fastest or largest made by Sperry.

Sperry Rand officials indicated the hope of selling an additional $40 million of computer systems for Aeroflot if the initial $10 million sale was successfully completed. IBM reportedly is arranging to sell its System 370-Model 158 computers to the Soviet Union for an industrial complex and for handling reservations for In-Tourist, the Russian tourism organization.

1. What possible positive and negative consequences could result from Sperry Rand's computer sale to the Soviet Union's airline?

2. What criteria should be used by the U.S. Commerce Department in deciding whether to approve such sales by American manufacturers?

3. Even if sales of computers and other high-technology products are approved by the Commerce Department, would you make such sales to the Soviet Union and other Communist countries if you were a member of top management of an American corporation? Why or why not?

Foreign investment in the United States

How would you like to work in a steel mill owned by Japanese investors? Or have your money deposited in a bank controlled by Arabian oil interests?

For years United States business managers have built factories and sales branches abroad and for a longer period of time have controlled raw materials sources in foreign countries. Now the public is becoming more aware of foreign investment in the United States. In 1973 the value of foreign direct investment in this country amounted to almost $18 billion according to the Commerce Department, an increase of 24 percent over 1972. These investments are continuing to increase. Direct investment includes not only ownership of real estate and of production or distribution facilities but investments in securities which involve control by the foreign holder. The Commerce Department defines control as direct ownership of facilities or ownership of 10 percent or more of voting stock.

In 1975 a $28 million steel mill controlled by Japanese investors was to begin operations in upstate New York. Strong community support has been shown for this new industry which will purchase services and supplies and add to the town's payrolls.

Primarily because of higher oil prices, the surplus revenues from the Organization of Petroleum Exporting Countries amounted to between $50 and $60 billion in 1974. Some of these funds are being invested in the United States and other industrialized nations. However, these investments are not universally welcomed. An attempt on the part of an Arabian businessman to purchase a substantial block of stock in a national bank in California fell through after protests from some bank customers.

1. What limitations, if any, should be placed on foreign investment in the United States?
2. What possible positive consequences could result from direct foreign investment in this country?
3. What possible negative consequences could result from such investments?

Dial the Shah

Throughout the Middle East a construction boom is in progress as the result of billions of dollars obtained from sharply higher oil prices beginning in 1973. One of the many American corporations seeking to cash in on this spending spree is General Telephone and Electronics (GTE). GTE's 10 million telephones in the United States and 1 million overseas make the company second only to AT&T among telephone utilities.

GTE has a contract for more than $500 million to triple telephone services in Iran. The company's international division is handling the Iranian contract which calls for installation of electronic switching equipment for 950,000 lines in 500 central offices throughout Iran. Time pressure is on GTE since the equipment is to be installed by the end of 1356 in the Moslem calendar, which is March 20, 1978.

GTE won this contract in 1975 over competition from telephone suppliers in Germany, France, Holland, Sweden, and Japan including overseas subsidiaries of International Telephone and Telegraph. Much of the computer-controlled switching equipment will be provided by the company's Illinois-based plant at Northlake. A company spokesman indicated that the volume of switching equipment going from Chicago to Iran will approximate a giant 747 planeload each month. Some GTE equipment will also be produced in the firm's factories in Belgium and Italy. Prior to the telephone contract GTE had been involved in a group of firms which established a microwave system in Iran.

Persons and equipment from GTE's operating companies as well as manufacturing subsidiaries will be involved in the project. In addition to supplying telephone and switching equipment, GTE is responsible for establishing a training program and a joint venture manufacturing facility in Iran. This plant will be run in cooperation with the government Telecommunications Company of Iran.

1. What short-term and long-term benefits could result from this GTE contract with Iran for:
   a. GTE?
   b. The United States in general?
   c. Iran?
2. What factors likely contributed to the awarding of this contract to GTE by the Iranian government?

The "Six Pack" solar collector is an example of current research to harness the sun's energy.

18

Pollution and energy

*M*any Americans are expressing concern about the quality of our environment now and for the future. With increasing population and affluence the problems of pollution are more acute than ever before. Some scientists predict we have less than 40 years before disaster results from misuse of resources and overpopulation unless massive efforts are made to turn back the tide of pollution.

Also, beginning in 1973 Americans became dramatically aware of the increasing cost of energy and shortages in gasoline, electricity, fuel oil, and natural gas. The national concern over energy has produced additional changes for this country which will continue into future decades.

Business is affected by both of these challenges and is in a position to make positive contributions to their solution.

The following issues are discussed regarding environmental pollution and our energy situation:

> What elements of the environment are being polluted?
> What actions are being taken to control pollution?
> What problems does business face in reducing environmental pollution?
> How did the recent energy crisis develop?
> What factors are involved in improving the energy situation?
> Who will pay for pollution control and sufficient energy?

DEFINITION OF POLLUTION

The National Academy of Science has suggested the following definition which is relevant for our consideration:

> Pollution is the undesirable change in the physical, chemical, or biological characteristics of our air, land, and water that may or will harmfully affect human life or that of other desirable species, our industrial process, living conditions, cultural assets; or that may or will waste or deteriorate our raw material resources.

A definition by the Congressional Subcommittee on Science, Research, and Development seems appropriate when considering business in relation to pollution: "Pollution is regarded as waste management gone wrong."

INCREASING PUBLIC AWARENESS OF POLLUTION

One of the earliest outbursts of public concern over pollution came in the 1940s. Citizens' indignation over the smoke blanketing communities such as St. Louis and Pittsburgh led to the adoption of antismoke ordinances. By burning coal with lower sulfur content, more use of natural gas for heating, and the change from coal-burning to diesel locomotives, the smoke nuisance was substantially reduced in many urban areas.

In the 1950s the public learned of a new type of air pollution. This was radioactive fallout from the atmospheric testing of nuclear devices. The fallout was absorbed by plants which were eaten by cows and showed by as strontium 90 in the teeth of children who drank the cows' milk. Such evidence contributed to the signing of the 1963 nuclear test-ban treaty on atmospheric detonations.

In the 1960s the public became aware that water pollution resulted not only from sewage and industrial waste dumpings, but also from detergents and runoff containing fertilizers and chemical pesticides. In addition to pollution of water caused by such wastes, the ecological balance in bodies of water was affected by changes in water temperature. Such thermal pollution stems from industries which use water for cooling.

The third type of environmental pollution is caused by the disposal of solid wastes. As the population increased and concentrated in cities, the problems of trash collection and disposal mounted. With the increasing number of automobiles after World War II, Americans became more conscious of the trash which litters streets and highways.

The disposal of old and wrecked automobiles became a major problem as some seven million cars were junked every year.

American public awareness of the air, water, and solid waste pollution of our environment reached a peak in the early 1970s. With the recognition that these hazards to the environment were a real threat, the federal government began programs to deal with them. Antipollution standards were established. The action phase to combat pollution was underway.

SYSTEMS APPROACH TO FLOW OF MATTER

In dealing with the problems of pollution and energy we must recognize that when goods and services are consumed waste products are inevitable. Nothing is really destroyed but is merely changed in form. We talk about the consumption of goods by individuals and industrial users. Actually utilities are extracted from goods in the consumption process and waste materials are given off. In industry large amounts of pollutants result from extracting and manufacturing processes. As individual consumers we extract utilities from goods and discard the remainder such as an empty beer can, an old pair of shoes, or exhaust emissions from our automobile.

The systems approach to the production and utilization of material goods along with the wastes given off is shown in Figure 18–1. This flow of goods illustrates how the inputs of fossil fuels, agricultural products, and minerals are processed before becoming outputs to final consumption. As goods are utilized at different stages there are outputs of pollutants which lack usefulness in their present form. However, except for items such as art objects and precious gems, all goods are finally cycled back into the production process or into the environment as wastes.

This flow chart suggests that we cannot eliminate pollution problems. However, pollution can be controlled better. Pollution can be reduced by (1) recycling more wastes, (2) changing the form of wastes or being more creative in their disposal, (3) producing fewer goods or different goods, and (4) using less energy.

TYPES OF POLLUTION

Air pollution

The U.S. Council on Environmental Quality, created by the National Environmental Policy Act in 1969, has estimated that over 215 million

FIGURE 18–1
Systems approach to flow of matter

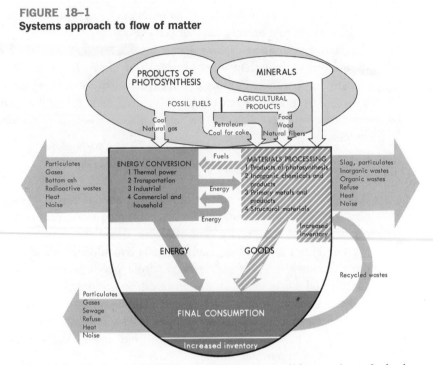

You can't get rid of matter, according to a well-known law of physics. All you can do is transform it. Modern economies, like that of the U.S., are good at taking the concentrated and transforming it into diffuse; they are not so good at doing the opposite. It is easy to turn coal into pollutants such as fly ash, gases, and soot, but difficult—economically, if not technologically—to turn the fly ash back into, say, cinderblocks. But we have to find ways to slim down those thick pollution arrows and fatten up that skinny recycled-wastes arrow. This diagram of material flows in the economy is adapted from a concept worked out by economist Allen V. Kneese and physicist Robert U. Ayres. Intermediate goods that are neither discarded nor used go into material-processing inventory, distinct from final-consumption inventory. The "final consumption" category embraces all goods that do not require further processing or assembly, regardless of who does the consuming.

Source: Tom Cardamone Associates, Inc. for Fortune Magazine, *Fortune*, February 1970, p. 121.

tons of the five most noxious air pollutants are released into the atmosphere over the United States each year. These five pollutants are carbon monoxide, sulfur oxides, hydrocarbons, dust (particulates), and nitrogen oxides. Figure 18–2 shows the composition of the total air pollution problem and the source of the pollutants.

FIGURE 18–2
Air pollution in the United States

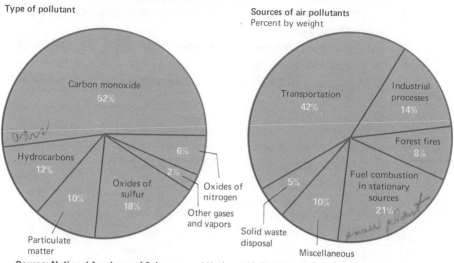

Type of pollutant

Sources of air pollutants
Percent by weight

Source: National Academy of Sciences and National Air Pollution Control Administration.

Automobiles, trucks, and buses powered by internal combustion engines are the major emitters of carbon monoxide, hydrocarbons, and nitrogen oxides. Most of the sulfur oxide is produced in the generation of electric power from burning coal and oil. Industrial operations cause the most dust and miscellaneous pollutants. You can see from Figure 18–2 that motor vehicles are the largest single source of air pollution. Industry and power generators together are the second largest source of air pollution. The major industries polluting the air are iron and steel, petroleum, nonferrous metals, chemicals, and pulp and paper.

Water pollution

Rivers and lakes have the natural ability to purify themselves. However, this is true only if they are not overloaded with wastes and if the oxygen level is high enough to support beneficial bacteria which consume some pollutants. Today the dumping of wastes by cities, industry, and governmental units such as the military has strained many waterways past the breaking point.

The composition of water pollution is very complex. At least six types of contaminants may be found in bodies of water today:

1. Phosphorus from detergents and fertilizers.
2. Pesticides and herbicides used by agriculture and home gardeners.
3. Bacteria and viruses contained in improperly treated sewage and other waste water.
4. Trace amounts of metals from industrial waste and other sources.
5. Acid from mine drainage.
6. Other organic and inorganic chemicals from a variety of sources.

The degree of pollution of some inland bodies of water was dramatically illustrated in the summer of 1969 when the Cuyahoga River near Cleveland burst into flames, threatening two bridges. It was reported that this river was so badly polluted with municipal and industrial wastes that little, if any, marine life could survive. This is not an isolated example of the fresh water pollution which existed in the late 1960s and early 1970s. Scientists, for example, spoke of the "death of Lake Erie," due in part to the phosphate-based detergents which had been discharged into the lake over a long period of time.

In addition to contamination of fresh water rivers and lakes the volume of pollutants being dumped into the oceans has raised questions about the ability of the oceans to absorb these wastes. Evidence indicates that already there are areas of the Pacific Ocean off California where marine life has been eliminated by human-caused pollution.

As mentioned earlier, industries using water for cooling have raised temperatures in some bodies of water to levels where life balance can be upset. In the United States electric power companies account for about 80 percent of this heat discharge. Nuclear power plants are becoming more common and do not pollute the air as fossil-fuel burning power plants do. However, nuclear power plants are a major potential thermal polluter since they use 50 percent more water for cooling than do conventional power plants.

Solid waste pollution

Overall about 4⅓ billion tons of solid wastes are disposed of in the United States annually. As Figure 18–3 indicates, almost four billion tons or over 91 percent of this volume comes from mining and agricultural operations. How these wastes are disposed of is important. Also important to the individual citizen is the disposal of the 250 million tons of trash from residences, commercial enterprises, and institutional sources each year along with 110 million tons of industrial wastes.

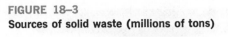

FIGURE 18–3
Sources of solid waste (millions of tons)

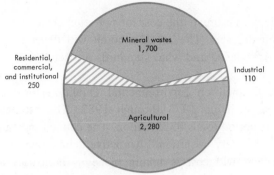

Source: Department of Health, Education and Welfare
and Department of Interior.

Only about half of this 360 million tons of trash currently is being recycled.

In some cities such as St. Louis solid waste is now being collected at central processing facilities. It is pulverized and the scrap metal is removed by magnets and sold. The remainder of the trash is used as fuel to generate electricity.

Noise pollution

Although it is difficult to measure, many of you are aware of noise pollution in our society. In 1970 the amendments to the Clean Air Act included an authorization for research into noise pollution. The noise created by jet aircraft and other forms of transportation as well as industrial noise is disturbing. There is evidence that noise can cause fatigue. Over a long period of time exposure to loud noise can damage the ability to hear.

Damages from pollution and costs of its control

It is almost impossible to determine with any degree of precision the costs of various types of pollution in the United States. However, the nature of damages to society can be categorized as:

1. Harmful effects of pollution on humans, animals, and plants.
2. Deterioration of materials in buildings and equipment.

3. Extra maintenance and cleaning of objects exposed to pollution.
4. Extra costs to ward off the effects of excessive pollution.

It is also difficult to estimate the cost for pollution cleanup and abatement in the United States. The actual amount will depend upon how much pollution is reduced and what standards are set to reduce future contaminants.

In 1974 the Council on Environmental Quality estimated pollution abatement costs from 1973 through 1982. The estimated cost over this ten-year period totals $325 billion. The council indicates these cost projections are "very uncertain." An active debate over how much pollution abatement will cost is taking place as industries are also making cost studies.

ACTIONS TO CONTROL POLLUTION

A number of trends in American society suggest that environmental pollution will continue to be a major problem for action. These trends include the increasing population, more concentration of the population in urban centers, increasing industrialization, and further technological developments. Also there will be increased demand for water and fossil fuels for heat and power sources. Actions are being taken by government, business, and the public to control those environmental problems.

Government actions

Pollution problems occur without respect to state or municipal boundaries. Therefore, federal legislation was necessary to improve environmental quality and to encourage regional cooperation. A summary of important federal laws regarding the environment follows.

Clean Air Act of 1963. The Clean Air Act of 1963 authorized federal grants to state and local air pollution control agencies to establish or improve their programs. It also gave the federal government power to take action in interstate air pollution cases. Research and technical activities were expanded in programs on motor vehicle and sulfur oxide pollution. The U.S. Public Health Service was directed to study the effect of pollution on human health and property.

In 1965 and 1966 amendments were passed to the Clean Air Act which authorized the Secretary of Health, Education and Welfare to establish emission standards on new automobiles and enlarged the grants-in-aid program to other governmental units.

Water Quality Act of 1965 and Clean Water Restoration Act of 1966. These laws provided for the establishment of water-quality standards and plans for their implementation. The federal government is working with state governments in programs such as improved treatment for municipal and industrial sewage.

Air Quality Act of 1967. This was a broad piece of legislation calling on the Department of Health, Education and Welfare to define geographic air-quality control regions and to develop air-quality standards for pollutants in these areas. State governments were to work with federal agencies in developing their own air-quality control standards. Air-quality monitoring programs were undertaken in cooperation with the states. In critical situations where health is immediately endangered the government can seek a court injunction to halt the practice causing the pollution. The act also increased the money being spent on air pollution research programs.

National Environmental Policy Act of 1969. This law has been characterized as a major statement of national environmental policy in the same way that the Employment Act of 1946 was a landmark statement of national economic policy. The legislation declares it to be the continuing policy of Congress "to use all practicable means . . . to create and maintain conditions under which man and nature can exist in productive harmony and fulfill the social, economic, and other requirements of present and future generations of Americans."

Federal agencies must consider the environmental effects of their programs and cooperate with the Council on Environmental Quality which was established by the act. The CEQ consists of three members reporting to the president. It is responsible for studies, policy recommendations, and preparation of an annual Environmental Quality Report.

To carry out the policies of the CEQ the Environmental Protection Agency was established. The Environmental Protection Agency's activities cover the programs dealing with air and water pollution, pesticide usage, radiation control, and ecological research.

Water Quality Improvement Act of 1970. Operators or owners of a vessel or facility can be held liable for the cleanup costs of an oil spill unless it can be proved that it is not their fault. If the owners are found guilty of willful negligence or misconduct there is no limit to the liability charges. Provisions of this act also cover nuclear power plants, mine acid drainage, and ships and pleasure craft.

Resource Recovery Act of 1970. A three-year authorization of several hundred million dollars was provided annually for research programs and grants to encourage the development of innovative solid waste disposal systems. Unlike earlier federal programs the legislation emphasized recycling and recovery of materials and energy from solid waste rather than merely disposal of the wastes.

Clean Air Amendments of 1970. These amendments had several key provisions which were quite specific in their intent to reduce air pollution.

Standards were set for auto emissions. Model year 1975 cars must have 90 percent less carbon monoxide and hydrocarbons emissions than the 1970 models had. Also, in 1976 models the level of nitrogen oxides were to be reduced by 90 percent compared with 1971 models. The legislation provided that one-year extensions might be granted to the auto industry by the Environmental Protection Agency if the standards could not be met on schedule. In 1975 the EPA extended the deadline on these emissions standards because of problems with catalytic converters used on many 1975 auto models.

This law also established controls on emissions by new stationary sources of pollution and provided new antipollution regulations for automobile fuels, aircraft engines, and aircraft fuels. The administrator of the Environmental Protection Agency was instructed to devise national air-quality standards relating to public health and welfare.

Water Pollution Control Act Amendments of 1972. These amendments to earlier federal water quality legislation are comprehensive. The law set the national goal of eliminating all pollution discharge into U.S. waters by 1985 with an interim goal of making waters safe for fish, wildlife, and people by 1983. Some $25 billion is authorized to improve water quality. About $18 billion is designated for construction grants for waste treatment plants. The pollution permit program authorized by the Rivers and Harbors Act of 1899 is to be phased out.

Actions by business

American business because of its technology and economic resources has the capacity to contribute significantly to the reduction of environmental pollution. Business is conducting research on pollution control at its source. Once pollutants have been released into the environment it is difficult, if not impossible, to correct the situation.

Auto industry technology. Automobile manufacturers are working with petroleum producers to develop better methods for reducing auto exhaust emissions. Automobiles produced beginning in the late 1960s were equipped to emit fewer pollutants than earlier models. Improvements have been made progressively through the 1976 models with further reductions in harmful exhausts planned. Some persons have suggested abandonment of the internal combustion engine in favor of electric or battery-powered cars. However, the present state of technology does not make this a likely alternative in the immediate future. Research continues for an internal combustion engine which will reduce auto-generated pollution and improve gas mileage.

Other antipollution technology. Technological improvements are being developed in other industries. Systems are in use in many plants for collection of particles from air and gas in industrial processing. The four main techniques for collecting industrial air pollution before it is thrust into the atmosphere are fabric cloth collectors, electrostatic precipitation systems, scrubbers, and mechanical systems.

Fabric cloth collection systems use natural or synthetic fibers such as cotton or glass fibers which are made into tubes that act as filtering devices for dust particles. This system works on the same general principle of pollution collection as the household vacuum cleaner.

Electrostatic precipitation systems operate on the principle that opposites attract. Particles in the stream of polluted air are charged negatively with electricity and are attracted to surfaces charged positively which hold the particulate matter.

Scrubbers or wet collectors spray liquid, frequently water, through gas streams containing particulates. The spray hits the particulate solids and washes them from the gas, cleansing the exhaust.

Mechanical systems employ various means including centrifugal force to separate dust particles from gas and air streams.

The recognized need for better handling of environmental pollution has provided the stimulus for a whole new industry. There is a multibillion dollar opportunity in pollution abatement which will provide jobs, investment, and profit potential. Enterprises engaged in the design and production of pollution control systems are expanding. Other companies are creating new divisions in this field, and new enterprises are being established to meet this need.

Industry begins to clean up. Many industries are involved in the battle against pollution. They have increased spending to reduce the contaminants from their production processes and products. The electric utilities, cement, chemical, metal processing, nonferrous metals, paper, petroleum, and steel industries all have major responsibilities in the cleanup of the environment.

An important question is whether the funds spent on antipollution systems will be too large a financial burden. Will such required expenditures drain capital funds away from expansion and modernization of production capacity which in turn can create more jobs? A study by Chase Econometrics Associates Incorporated reported that spending on pollution abatement facilities by American industries would average about three percent of total plant and equipment spending over a ten-year period.

However, an industry-by-industry analysis shows that the impact of antipollution spending varies widely. For example, the U.S. Department of Commerce reported in 1974 that the nonferrous metals industry spent 25 percent of its total plant and equipment funds for pollution control. In the iron and steel industry 22 percent went for pollution control equipment. The paper industry spent 20 percent; stone, clay and glass, 17 percent; petroleum, 13 percent; and chemicals, 12 percent.

In testimony before a congressional committee the president of Du Pont, the world's largest chemical producer, noted the firm's capital investment for pollution control takes about 13 percent of Du Pont's total capital budget. "That means we're getting 13 percent less capacity for our investment dollar," he said. Du Pont spent $175 million for pollution control facilities in 1975. The president pointed out this amount could build a new fiber plant employing 2,500 people. This new plant in turn could create "about 60,000 jobs in 'downstream' industries," the executive stated.

It is costly for industry to meet government antipollution standards. However, compliance also provides an opportunity for the modernization of plants to improve production efficiency as well as to achieve pollution control. In some instances older factories and processing plants are closed down because of the cost of meeting new standards. The financial impact of investment in control equipment is reduced in most enterprises by writing off the cost of this equipment as a tax-deductible expense over a period of years. Nevertheless, investments in antipollution equipment generally add to the costs of doing business.

Problems for business

There are a number of problems for business in dealing with pollution abatement. These include setting and enforcing standards, the limitations of present technology, and the problems of recycling waste products.

Problems in setting and enforcing standards. Some enterprises are reluctant to install expensive pollution control systems because government standards are not completely developed or are in conflict from one level of government to another. Clear regulations are needed.

However, there are problems in establishing environmental quality standards. Because of the difficulty of defining an absolute standard, many goals for pollution reduction are of the trend type. Thus, objectives are expressed in terms of percentage reductions from certain levels of pollution. For example, improvement in auto emissions for the 1975 models was stated as percentage reductions from the level of pollutants from 1970 models. Final standards of quality are hard to establish because of insufficient research on the effect specified amounts of pollutants have on the health of people.

There has also been a lack of uniformly applied pollution control standards both within industries and in various areas of the country. This places enterprises which have spent millions of dollars on pollution control at a cost disadvantage in competing with firms in the same industry which have not taken this socially responsible action. Enterprises which have spent money on pollution control must either increase prices or absorb these costs with lower profits.

This indicates the need for uniform federal standards, applied equitably. Then enterprises can act in a socially responsible manner and still maintain their competitive position in the marketplace. Without uniformity across the country, the temptation exists for business to relocate where regulations are more lenient or where they are not enforced by state or local governments.

Problems in developing antipollution systems. There is no easy or simple method to correct much of our present environmental pollution. In some instances a control mechanism will have wide applicability in easing the harmful effects of pollution. For example, in auto emissions control a technical development can be utilized widely. However, pollution abatement in most industrial situations requires each solution to be somewhat unique to correct specific problems. Variables such as topography, climate, size of industrial equipment, and population density make it necessary for solutions to be custom tailored. This makes pollution control expensive in money, time, and technical resources. Furthermore, although control equipment is being improved, it is still inadequate in some situations. Scientific knowledge of pollution reduction is generally more advanced than the engineering technology to prevent pollution or to deal with pollutants already in the environment.

Employment outlook

Environmental scientists

Environmental scientists such as geologists, geophysicists, meteorologists, and oceanographers help us live within our physical environment. They play an important role in solving environmetal pollution problems. These scientists, sometimes known as earth scientists, are concerned with the history, composition, and characteristics of the earth's surface, interior, and atmosphere. Since there are more environmental scientists specializing in geology than in the other fields, that occupation is discussed here.

More than half of the geologists work in private industry. Most industrial geologists work for petroleum producers, many for American companies exploring in foreign nations. Geologists also work for mining and quarry companies. Some are employed by construction firms to determine suitable construction sites.

The master's degree is required for beginning research and teaching and most exploration jobs. High-level administrative posts or research usually require the Ph.D. Employment opportunities for geologists with advanced degrees are expected to be favorable through the mid-1980s.

Geologists will help determine the feasibility of using geothermal energy (steam from the earth's interior) to generate electricity. Geologists also are needed to devise techniques for exploring deeper within the earth's crust and to develop more efficient methods of mining resources.

Geologists are needed to develop adequate water supplies, waste disposal methods, and building materials and site evaluation for construction activities. Increased emphasis on the environment by urban societies also should affect requirements for geologists. For example, pollution control, better land use and reclamation programs, and highway construction activities require the talents of geologists.

Problems in synthetics and recycling. Although technology can aid in abating pollution, sometimes it furthers it. Research by both government and business tends to contribute to the introduction of new materials. Many of these release contaminants into the environment which have unknown effects. Modern technology has spawned the development of thousands of synthetic substances and products. Some of these synthetics are resistent to the natural process of decay which recycles waste products into a form compatible with the environment. We have produced aluminum beverage cans that do not rust, radioactive wastes that continue to be toxic for centuries, and inorganic plastic products which will not decompose.

Even with increased emphasis on recycling, in many instances the original products are not in a form which can be readily or economically recycled. Thus, there are metal cans that contain alloys making them uneconomic to recycle. Nonreturnable glass bottles may have a metal ring around the top which was originally part of the cap. When these bottles are salvaged the cost of removing the metal from the glass makes recycling difficult to justify economically.

Who will pay for pollution control?

The cost to society of the environmental pollution caused in the manufacture and ultimate disposal of goods usually has not been considered in the pricing of products. Manufacturers and processors have generally considered bodies of water and open air to be free for disposing of pollutants. Thus, the polluters who do not have to pay for the costs of their pollution are able to sell their goods cheaper than if they were forced to bear the extra costs of manufacturing without polluting the environment. On the other hand, a plant down the river from a major polluter may face extra costs before using needed water. This tends to raise unfairly the costs of the second manufacturer's goods.

For example, a pulp and paper mill which is free to dump its wastes into a river may have its costs understated. Down river a chemical plant which incurs extra costs in purification of the polluted water tends to have the costs of its products overstated. The net result of this example would be that users of chemicals unknowingly subsidize the users of pulp and paper products.

Methods of encouraging pollution reduction. There are different ways to stimulate business to include the full costs of manufacturing products and disposing of wastes without damage to the environment. These methods range from public pressure by irate citizens to tough enforcement of antipollution laws which may even halt production until the production process is cleaned up.

One way to discourage pollution by industrial enterprises would be to make the penalty cost of pollution more than the cost of cleaning up production processes or installing better waste disposal systems. One plan to do this proposes a system of "effluent charges" which would require industry to pay by the pound for pollutants it discharges. If it were less expensive for industry to avoid pollution than to pay the effluent charges, industry would be stimulated to install antipollution systems.

To encourage the development and use of containers that would either be biologically degradable or economically recycled, a container tax could be imposed based on the difficulty of recycling.

A system of incentives could be worked out through which special tax credits would be given to encourage pollution reduction. This would tend to make the public as a whole bear the cost of pollution abatement rather than the manufacturers or consumers of a particular product.

An interesting proposal in Sweden would place a "junk tax" of up to $40 on all new automobiles. The tax would be returned to the final owner when the car was brought to a scrapping authority. This would discourage the abandonment of old cars, which is a problem in Sweden as it is in the United States.

Ultimate cost of pollution. Although business profits will be reduced in some instances, over the long run the cost of improving the environment will be borne in large measure by consumers and individual taxpayers.

Consumers will pay for reductions in industrial pollution through higher prices for goods and services. For example, because of a cost increase of two cents a gallon for unleaded gasoline, American drivers pay several hundred million dollars more each year for gasoline to reduce air pollution. To reduce the thermal pollution of Lake Michigan it has been estimated that consumers may have to pay up to 25 percent more in monthly electric bills.

Taxpayers pay the cost of government programs at all levels of government. Many believe that even though the cost of these improvements is high, the price tag for the individual consumer is low compared with the benefits both now and in the future.

THE ENERGY CRISIS

In addition to environmental pollution, by 1973 another problem demanded the public's attention. This was the shortage and increased cost of various energy sources, commonly called "the energy crisis." A number of symptoms indicated the widespread nature of this problem. Major cities suffered brownouts from overdemand for electrical power by industry and the public during hot summers. Some schools and factories had to close for a period of time in the winter because natural gas was not available for heating systems. Gasoline increased in price from 60 to 100 percent a gallon over the country with many motorists finding they had to wait in long lines to buy gas. Some scheduled airlines cancelled flights and combined routes because of the shortage and high cost of jet fuel.

CAUSES OF OUR ENERGY PROBLEMS

For several decades Americans had been encouraged to consume more energy. In the 1930s government policy was to keep energy costs as low as possible to stimulate its use. During that time of depression the development of low-cost power through such facilities as the Tennessee Valley Authority brought new factories and payrolls to many underdeveloped parts of the country. Thousands of homes were electrified for the first time as the result of government high dam projects providing low-cost electric power.

Increased use of energy

Following World War II and into the 1950s and 1960s America's love affair with the automobile resulted in more two- and three-car families with increased consumption of gasoline. Typically, American refiners were making about 50 percent of a barrel of crude oil into gasoline, while foreign refiners turned only about 15 to 20 percent of their crude into gasoline. America increasingly imported heavy fuel oil which was being refined abroad from cheap foreign crude.

The production of gasoline which American refiners emphasized resulted in a general oversupply. This encouraged price wars and kept the price of gasoline low. Americans could afford to indulge in their preferences for large cars and air travel, both of which use large amounts of petroleum products.

The price of natural gas, which the federal government regulates on interstate shipments, was also kept low. This encouraged the use of natural gas for factories and homes. The American lifestyle paid little attention to conservation and efficiency in the use of energy. Americans were comfortably indifferent to such uses as the thousands of ornamental natural gas lanterns which burned 24 hours a day in residential front yards. Also, the continuous pilot lights on kitchen stoves consume about one third of the gas used annually by gas ranges.

FIGURE 18–4
Consumption of fuel resources by major consumer groups in 1973

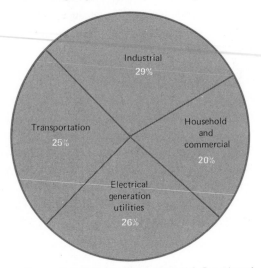

Source: *U.S. Industrial 1975 Outlook*, U.S. Department of Commerce.

Hundreds of thousands of Americans increased their consumption of energy by purchasing power boats, snowmobiles, motor homes, and travel trailers for use in their leisure time. There was a flood of new home appliances ranging from electric blenders and food choppers to electric toothbrushes, shoe polishers, and curling irons. As a result of this ever-increasing use of energy, the United States with only 6 percent of the world's population now consumes about 33 percent of the world's total energy output. Only about 4 percent of our GNP has been required in the past to pay for our extensive energy consumption. Figure 18–4 illustrates the proportion of fuel consumption by major consumer groups.

Energy costs increase

After experiencing a long period of ample and inexpensive energy, Americans had difficulty understanding why there should be a sudden shortage and increase in price. Both the domestic and international scene need to be examined to see why the "great energy joyride," as some have called it, came to an end.

After World War II the search for new oil reserves focused on foreign lands. Most of the oil that was in easy geographic and geologic access in the continental United States had already been discovered. Significant oil discoveries were made by the international oil companies in such areas as the Middle East, Venezuela, Africa, and the North Sea. Refinery capacity also shifted to other parts of the world.

On the domestic scene increased attention to environmental pollution caused substantial delays in developing new energy sources. Construction of the Alaskan pipeline to bring out newly discovered oil from the North Slope was delayed several years while the environmental impact of this project was determined. Environmental considerations over strip mining limited increased development of our huge coal reserves. The slowdown in building nuclear power generators has been caused in part by disputes over possible environmental pollution. Before these problems could be resolved, massive changes occurred on the international scene which created "the energy crisis."

Beginning in the early 1970s the cartel of the Organization of Petroleum Exporting Countries (OPEC) led by Saudi Arabia started raising oil prices. The price increased from less than one dollar a barrel to almost $3.50 a barrel in October 1973 at the start of the Arab-Israeli war. Then the "energy crisis" hit with a fury as the Arabs embargoed all oil shipments to the United States because of our support of Israel. OPEC also continued to raise oil prices. After the embargo was lifted in 1974 Americans were paying more than $10 a barrel for Arab oil. By 1974 it was increasingly apparent to many Americans that the era of cheap energy had ended.

APPROACHES TO THE ENERGY SITUATION

There are four courses of action to be considered in developing solutions to the energy situation:

1. Improve technology to utilize present energy sources more efficiently.

2. Reduce the growth rate of energy consumption.
3. Conduct research to develop new sources of energy which are economically feasible.
4. Attain both energy goals and environmental goals.

As America struggles to develop an energy policy, there is general agreement on two broad principles. First, we must do everything possible to avoid waste of our energy resources. Second, we must increase the efficiency of energy utilization.

However, agreement is not so universal on what constitutes a wasteful use of energy. What one person considers a waste may be a virtual necessity to another—so much has the extensive use of energy shaped our life style. For example, which of the following do you consider to be a waste of energy?

Electric toothbrushes.
Hair dryers.
Snowmobiles.
Nonreturnable soft-drink containers.
Lighted rooms with no one in them.
Enclosed shopping malls with year-round climate conditioning.
Climate-controlled airport facilities.
Enclosed air-conditioned sports stadiums.

Better technology needed

There has been a general acceptance in this country of a level of technological inefficiency which has wasted much of our low-cost energy. The following examples illustrate the need for improved technology so we can utilize our power sources more efficiently.

Present auto engines use less than 20 percent of the energy potential in gasoline. The rest is thrown off in heat and exhaust. A report from the Ford Foundation[1] suggests that government mandate improved auto fuel economy by gradually increasing the efficiency standards which auto engines must meet. This report suggests a goal be set so that by 1985 the average gasoline consumption rate for autos would be 20 miles per gallon compared with 12 to 13 in 1974. Taxes on less efficient cars or tax credits to encourage purchase of more efficient autos are other possibilities for stimulating technolgical improvement.

---

[1] *A Time to Choose: America's Energy Future,* Cambridge, Mass.: Ballinger, 1974.

Modern power generating plants are only about 40 percent efficient in energy utilization. Most of the energy loss occurs when heat energy is transformed into mechanical energy to turn steam turbines. At the Ninth World Energy Conference in Detroit in 1974 it was reported that the Soviet Union is using power plant energy which had been previously wasted to heat homes and buildings in the vicinity of the generating plants. Overall efficiency of these plants reportedly approaches 70 to 80 percent.

Problems have arisen in the technology of nuclear power systems. They are only about 30 percent efficient in generation of power. The rest is wasted in large amounts of heat. Furthermore, this heat raises the temperature in the bodies of water used for cooling to the point where environmental damage can occur to fish and plant life.

Conservation—slower growth of energy use

The present structure of utility rates tends to encourage excessive use of electricity since lower rates are usually charged when larger amounts of power are consumed. Eliminating the lower rate for larger amounts of electricity might reduce consumption. Also, demand for power by individual and industrial consumers tends to peak at certain times of the day. Electric utilities expand their facilities to meet the needs for electricity at times of maximum use. This results in substantial excess capacity at most other times. According to the Federal Energy Administration most of this capacity is wasted the majority of the time since utilities operate on average at 49 percent capacity.

In March 1975 the Federal Energy Administration announced it will fund four or five pilot projects by electric utilities which will charge less for electricity used in off hours and premium rates for peak-hour consumption. The FEA is proposing a rate structure in which prices will be based on *when* the electricity is used instead of simply on the amount consumed. Government officials hope that the pilot projects will lead to a new national policy for pricing electricity.

Heating and cooling of indoor space uses about 10 percent of our energy. Therefore, substantial conservation could result from designing homes and business buildings that would be heated, cooled, and lighted more efficiently. The practices of using great expanses of glass, which is a notoriously poor insulator; of installing minimum insulation; and of lighting halls in office buildings with candlepower sufficient for desk work all assume that cheap and ample energy is a basic fact of life.

Some experts have called for more stringent building codes to foster energy conservation.

Another suggestion is to encourage consumers to become energy-use conscious by requiring energy-efficiency labeling of small appliances and heating and cooling equipment. For example, some air conditioners cool just as well as others on much less energy.

Electric companies have already directed "Save a Watt" campaigns to customers to turn down heating thermostats and turn off unneeded lights. Improved home insulation and weather stripping of doors are other ways consumers can keep their spiraling gas and electric bills from going higher.

The general goal of such conservation measures is to cut the present growth rate of energy consumption from around 5 percent a year to about 2 percent.

Development of economical energy sources

The expansion of energy production has a number of facets. Though our fossil fuel sources are limited, they are certainly not exhausted. New reserves of coal, oil, and natural gas are being discovered, in part because of the higher price of energy. However, these reserves are often in scenic or remote locations. With our increased concern for the environment, the cost of new energy sources in scenic areas will include expensive land rehabilitation and pollution control measures. Remote areas add to the cost of development and delivery of energy.

Nevertheless, the energy resources are there. Large deposits of coal available by strip mining exist in the western United States. The cost of this coal will probably include the cost of restoring the land to preserve the environment. It has been estimated that 50 percent of our potential oil and gas reserves are in offshore deposits along the U.S. coasts. However, costs rise the further drilling rigs are sent into the oceans. Also, serious environmental opposition exists toward offshore drilling as the result of oil spills off the California coasts and elsewhere.

Nuclear power, with proper safeguards, will probably emerge as a major means of producing electricity. Coal will continue to be an important fuel for electricity-generating plants in the short run. However, it will require stack-gas scrubbers to remove sulfur dioxide pollution so as to conform to clean air standards.

New sources of energy are also being developed. For example, geothermal power is already being used in California's Sonoma County. Steam deep in the earth is used to drive turbogenerators that produce about one third of San Francisco's total requirements for electric power. Research in solar energy to convert sunlight into electricity is receiving increased attention. However, for technological and cost reasons, many authorities do not expect significant application of solar energy until toward the end of this century. Research continues on how to produce synthetic fuels in gas and liquid forms from the vast resources of coal we have in this country. Electric automobiles are still in the early stages of development.

Realizing both energy and environmental goals

Environmental and energy problems are closely linked. The head of the Environmental Protection Agency has stated that "Our energy ills and our environmental ills stem, essentially, from the same source: from patterns of growth and development that waste our energy resources just as shamefully as they lay waste our natural environment."[2]

Environmentalists and energy conservationists are in agreement that better land-use planning and the development of mass transit can achieve mutual benefits. Both approaches can lessen the need for automobiles.

Recycling, long an environmental objective, is also a useful means of saving energy. For example, far less energy is required to produce aluminum from scrap than from bauxite. Already progress is being made in recycling. About 20 percent of the aluminum, 25 percent of the steel, and 40 percent of the copper consists of reprocessed scrap.

WHAT CAN BE DONE

There is general agreement that a national energy policy should outline the objectives, standards, and roles of government, industry, and the public. All three of these groups need to have a positive role in dealing with our energy situation.

What government can do

Government can provide both for research into new energy sources and for improvement of energy technology. Energy consumption by governmental agencies is being reduced and can be reduced more. Tax and regulatory policies can be adopted that will encourage investment in energy-efficient facilities. Standards which are attainable can be set

---

[2] *The Wall Street Journal*, January 3, 1974, p. 1.

for business and consumers in many fields including transportation, construction, and public utilities.

In 1974 in an attempt to broaden the base for energy research the Congress created the Energy Research and Development Administration (ERDA) to replace the Atomic Energy Commission. While initial emphasis was on research in the nuclear field, the federal government states that ERDA will avoid preoccupation with nuclear research at the expense of other potential energy sources. For example, the agency's spending on coal research increased from 13 to 23 percent of its research budget from 1973 to 1974 while nuclear research dropped from 60 percent to 40 percent. Research spending in the fields of solar, geothermal, and oil shale energy is relatively small but increasing. The new government agency has six major programs covering fossil energy; nuclear energy; solar, geothermal and advanced energy systems; environment and safety; conservation; and defense.

What business can do

In addition to the suggestions already discussed, there are several basic actions business can take to improve our energy situation.

Each of the six major energy-consuming industries—steel, aluminum, paper, oil refining, chemicals, and cement—can reduce its use of energy and install more energy-efficient production processes. As long as energy was cheap there was little incentive to economize. In the past, when a manufacturer's costs for energy were only 5 percent of total expenses, plant managers frequently gave conservation programs a low priority. Now companies such as Union Carbide, Dow, Du Pont, Alcoa, and Greyhound have extensive programs underway to conserve energy, and these programs are paying off in cost savings.

There is a need for a new approach to product design which will emphasize reliability and longevity as well as appearance and function. Also, business can improve the design of products to reduce the energy required to operate them. For example, smaller automobiles with less weight require less gasoline to operate.

What consumers can do

Many of the actions consumers can take have already been suggested. In addition, the public can encourage and support government policies which reduce waste, further more efficient energy use, and protect the environment. Also, we can support business by purchasing those products that are energy efficient. Participating in recycling efforts and trying to change our own habits which waste energy will help.

The American public must recognize that the future price of energy will be higher than in the past. The added costs of expanding energy resources, like the cost of cleaning up our environment, will ultimately have to be borne by the consuming public.

The goals of a cleaner environment and more efficient use of energy reinforce each other, as we have seen. Many of the actions already proposed or taken can help to slow the growth rate of energy consumption. Over the long run the adjustment of the American economy to higher energy prices is part of the larger issue of world economic development and population growth.

There are important technical questions to be answered in the field of energy policy. The final decisions will be based on the values we consider most important. Responsible business men and women have an obligation to inform themselves on the alternatives and to work to influence public policy.

SUMMARY

Many responsible persons believe that environmental pollution has reached a critical point in the United States and requires the attention of all elements of society.

The systems approach to the flow of matter suggests that pollution cannot be eliminated from society but can be controlled better than is presently the case.

Emissions from motor vehicles, power-generating sources, and industrial processes account for more than three quarters of the air pollution in the United States.

Water pollution is caused by an overburdening of the waterways beyond their capacities of self-purification.

Although mining and agricultural operations account for most of the solid wastes produced annually, the disposition of the trash from residences, businesses, and institutions is a significant problem.

The damages caused by pollution and its costs are difficult to measure accurately. However, estimates indicate that improved control of pollution will require billions of dollars for years in the future.

Government legislation to control pollution includes the Clean Air Act, Water Quality Act, Air Quality Act, and the National Environmental Policy Act.

Because of its technology and economic resources, business actions to control pollution can be significant. Generally control of pollutants has to occur by reducing or eliminating contaminants before they are released into the air or water. Numerous companies are improving their products and production processes to reduce sources of pollution although there are many problems in accomplishing these objectives.

Pollution control will be costly in terms of total dollars required. Ultimately the consumer will pay for pollution control either in higher costs of goods and services or through higher taxes.

The shortage and increased cost of various energy sources is another problem of concern. For several decades Americans have been encouraged to consume more energy. Electricity, gasoline, and natural gas prices were kept low.

America relied increasingly on imports of oil. Development of new domestic sources of energy such as the Alaskan pipeline, offshore drilling, nuclear power plants, and increased strip mining was delayed by environmental considerations. The Arab oil embargo in 1973 brought the situation to the "crisis" stage.

In developing solutions to the energy situation there are four courses of action to be considered:

1. Improve technology to utilize present energy sources more efficiently.
2. Reduce the growth rate of energy consumption.
3. Conduct research to develop new energy sources which are economically feasible.
4. Attain both energy and environmental goals.

The future price of energy is not likely to revert to the low levels we enjoyed in the past. Over the long run the adjustment of the American economy to higher energy prices is part of the larger issue of world economic development and population growth.

TERMS FOR REVIEW

air pollution

water pollution

thermal pollution

solid waste pollution

Council on Environmental Quality

National Environmental Policy Act of 1969

Environmental Protection Agency

OPEC

geothermal power

solar energy

Energy Research and Development Administration

QUESTIONS

1. Why has environmental pollution become an important public issue?
2. What kinds of pollution are major problems today?
3. What solutions are there to combating environmental pollution in our society? What would be the result of the solutions you suggest?
4. By examining local publications, talking to local government officials and businessmen, and by personal observation try to determine the nature of environmental pollution in your area. What actions are being taken to reduce this pollution?
5. *a.* What responsibilities does government have in reducing pollution?
   b. What can business do to reduce environmental pollution?
6. What are the major provisions of recent legislation to improve the quality of the environment?
7. What difficulties are there for business in trying to reduce environmental pollution immediately?
8. What *negative* immediate results might occur for individuals and communities as the result of government actions to reduce environmental pollution?
9. Outline the major factors that contributed to our "energy crisis" in the 1970s.
10. How can our goals for sufficient energy come into conflict with our environmental goals?
11. Give five examples where achievement of our environmental goals will also help achieve energy goals.
12. *a.* Who will pay for pollution control and sufficient energy?
    b. Can society afford both? Explain your answer.

Business briefs

Attack the litter

The cost of picking up rubbish and litter has been estimated at $1 billion annually in the United States. Two states, Oregon and Washington, have led the way with laws aimed at reducing litter.

In 1971 Oregon's legislature passed a tough law banning no-deposit, no-return bottles and pop-top cans. In the past, empty beverage containers accounted for up to 75 percent of roadside litter. Citizens now pay deposits on containers ranging from 2¢ to 5¢. Since the returnable container law was passed the volume of bottles and cans in roadside litter has been reduced up to 90 percent.

Some container and beverage industry personnel are concerned about the impact of the Oregon legislation. Since 1959 the per capita consumption of soft drinks and beer has risen 33 percent. Flip-top cans were introduced in 1959 and have been a popular beverage container. Returnable bottles generally are more expensive than one-way containers as the returnable empties cost money to pick up and prepare for refilling or reprocessing by bottlers.

The Washington State law passed in 1972 is termed a "Model Litter Control Act." Citizen education and participation programs are stressed. Posters, bumper stickers, and signs encourage the elimination of litter.

The Washington law also provides for fines up to $250 for littering. Owners of cars and boats are subject to $10 fines if litterbags are not carried. In addition there is a tax of .015 percent on the gross sales of industries most subject to littering—newspapers, bottles, paper products, and supermarkets. Highway litter has been reached by 90 percent along some state highways following passage of the law.

In June 1975, Coca-Cola announced a new 32 ounce plastic bottle which the company claimed could revolutionize beverage packaging. The new lightweight bottle, manufactured by Monsanto, is made of plastic which is lighter, more shock resistant, and therefore less costly to transport. Monsanto is establishing recycling centers and reportedly paying 12.5¢ a pound for returned plastic bottles. The bottles have been attacked by environmental groups on the basis of their safety, but the Food and Drug Administration stated that the basic ingredient in the plastic bottle is safe for soft drinks and alcoholic beverages.

1. What are the likely results of anti-litter legisalation?
2. *a.* What costs will be avoided as the result of such legislation?
   b. What costs will be incurred as the result of these laws?
3. Is it reasonable to require each automobile to have a litterbag under penalty of fine for noncompliance?
4. What alternative solutions are there to America's litter problem?

Computer heat

The Hartford Insurance Group started construction in 1974 of a nine-story building in Hartford, Conn., that eventually will be heated by waste heat from the enterprise's computers.

Hartford Insurance, a subsidiary of International Telephone and Telegraph, began planning for the new building in the early 1970s with a view to saving on fuel costs. The many computers used by the insurance company generate a considerable amount of heat. This is true even of the latest solid state models. Company officials indicate that more than 80,000 gallons of fuel oil will be saved during the first full year of operation. Estimates are that 120,000 gallons of oil a year will be saved by 1980 when Hartford Insurance will be operating more computers.

The savings in fuel will pay for the extra cost of installation by the third or fourth year of operation. Initially an auxiliary gas-fired hot water system will be used to supplement the waste-heat recovery system. By 1980 the entire building will be heated by computer heat. At that time 1,800 employees will work in the building.

IBM 370/168 models will be used in the building. One of these computers generates 100,000 Btu an hour compared with 100,000 to 150,000 Btu in the average home heating system. Hot air from the computers and peripheral hardware will be sucked out and used to heat water. This hot water will pass through a system of pipes and coils throughout the building where fans will disperse the hot air from the coils. Waste heat from other machines and lights will also be recovered and recycled. The building has separate air conditioning equipment which will not be affected by the new heat recycling system.

The building is designed to reduce heat loss by having less glass area. Windows will be double glazed and tinted. Such features also reduce air conditioning costs.

1. What benefits other than cost savings can result from Hartford Insurance's recycling of computer heat?
2. What possible problems could be raised by this system?
3. Bring to class other examples of innovations business enterprises are using to save fuel.

Cases

Southwest Rendering Company, Inc.

The Southwest Rendering Company has a plant located just outside the city limits of a midwest community of 125,000. The plant has been in its present location for almost 40 years.

The rendering process basically consists of dehydrating and separating grease and protein elements in animal matter. Rendering companies convert waste products of the meat-packing and poultry-processing industries, dead animals, and restaurant greases into products which are used in both industrial and consumer markets. Tallow and grease extracted in the rendering process are used in many products, including soap, animal feeds, lubricants, cosmetics, and plastics. Protein products, including meat and bone meal and dried blood, are important nutritive additives in all types of livestock feed and pet food.

The raw materials from which grease and protein elements are extracted consist of waste fat, bones, and meat scraps from meat-packing plants, poultry-processing plants, restaurants, and food stores. These materials are picked up by the renderer's trucks on a regular route basis—generally once daily. In addition the rendering company picks up dead livestock on farms and cooperates with public officials in removing large animals which may be littering highways.

These waste products are dumped into two large hoppers (each of which has a capacity of 30,000 pounds), crushed, and ground to ⅛-inch particles. These particles are continuously fed from the grinder to cooker tanks, each having a capacity of 2,000 pounds of material per hour. Here the raw materials are cooked for at least 30 minutes under steam pressure at approximately 240° F.

During the cooking process the greases are constantly drained off into settling tanks. The protein materials are pressed through a system of expellers which reduces it to a mashlike substance that is then dried and transferred to bins for storage and blending into animal and poultry feed.

The Southwest Rendering Company had been relatively isolated from the city since it was located to the north of the city limits with little other economic or residential development in the immediate vicinity. When a new high school was located nearby and a subsequent residential area was developed, the management of the plant began to get complaints about odors coming from the plant.

The management of Southwest Rendering began to adopt various odor control devices similar to those used throughout the industry. A deep well was used to provide cold water to run jet condensors. A hot well was added along with an afterburner to take care of gases which could not have their odors reduced without heat. Despite these attempts to reduce odors, complaints from the neighbors continued. The management then adopted an in-plant spray system using chemicals to mask the odors created in the rendering process. Although this reduced the number of complaints, citizen criticism of the rendering plant's operations continued.

Following studies made by outside engineers, the management decided to incorporate a stack dilution process with a new type continuous dry rendering system. An equipment manufacturing company was requested to design equipment utilizing the latest known technology to make the plant as odor-free as possible. This new equipment was installed at a cost of $20,000.

However, the plant was located in a valley some 90 feet below the surrounding terrain. The gases from the rendering plant were of relatively low temperature. The plume of gases coming from the 150-foot stack did not have sufficient buoyancy to carry it high enough to dilute the odors adequately before they reached ground level.

The company continued to receive complaints about odors. Deciding that the stack was not sufficient, a chemical air-scrubbing system was added which treated the gases before they were blown up the stack into the open air.

By now, the company's total investment in air pollution control equipment had reached $68,000 with an annual operating cost of $32,000 or $5 additional cost per ton of produced material. Company records indicated that 18 percent of the original equipment cost was for air pollution control equipment and 15 percent of plant operating costs were for the control of odors.

Because of continued complaints, the county prosecuting attorney contacted the state health department requesting an investigation into the possibility that the plant was a health menace. A report was made by a health officer of the state division of health. In summary the report indicated that the overall sanitation in and around the plant appeared to be satisfactory. There was no offensive odor at the time of the inspection. In view of his inability to uncover any diagnosed illness as the result of the odors, the health officer was unable to certify that the plant constituted a public health hazard.

Upon receiving this report the county prosecutor went to the state capital to visit with the licensing and inspecting authority in the state veterinarian's office. Upon his return the prosecutor quoted the state veterinarian as saying that the plant was one of the most modern rendering plants in the United States; the firm was not a public nuisance; and that there would be a public nuisance if the plant was closed because there was no other firm in the area that disposed of dead animal carcasses. Based on his investigation the prosecutor concluded that he had no legal basis for court action unless new evidence was uncovered.

The Southwest Rendering Company was collecting over 30 million pounds of decay-prone waste annually for processing. Over $160,000 was paid to grocery stores, restaurants, meat packers, and poultry processing plants for the raw materials collected. Some 5,500 tons of high-energy protein and animal feed were being produced by the company and sold to area feed companies to mix into livestock, poultry, and pet food. The company's annual sales were approximately $2,000,-000, and 46 employees were paid over $250,000 in wages.

In a letter sent with a report to the state air conservation commission, the president of Southwest Rendering Company said:

. . . [ours] is a perfect case history of what can happen to a firm when it moves ahead too rapidly in the almost nonexistent methods of controlling air pollution. We moved entirely too fast in acquiring suggested, but unproved, equipment, the expense of which placed us in a position of having costs in excess of our competition, resulting in a net operating loss. . . . [now] there is no question that we have a unique economic disadvantage in our industry. We cannot add the cost of air pollution control to the selling price of our finished product [because of competition]. We must compete on an open market governed by the economic law of efficiency, or by lowering our raw product costs. In any event, we must be prepared to control our odors within the limits of what it is economically possible to do.

1. What factors have increased the problem of pollution for the Southwest Rendering Company?
2. How responsive was the management of Southwest Rendering in dealing with these problems?
3. Discuss the dilemma faced by the management of the Southwest Rendering Company in operating this business in the public interest.

Union Electric Company

In 1974 the Union Electric Company which supplies electric power to the St. Louis area announced the development of a power generation facility which will use the area's trash as fuel.

The new $70 million plant will generate about 6 percent of its power from the solid waste products of metropolitan St. Louis. This facility is scheduled to be operational by the middle of 1977. It is the first in the country to handle all of an area's trash and garbage either as fuel or recyclable materials.

The operating costs of the solid-waste disposal system are estimated at $11 million annually, but Union Electric officials expect the plant to be economically self-supporting. Revenues for the plant will come from the heating value of the solid waste, sale of recyclable materials sorted from the trash before it is burned, and dumping fees.

This project is a follow-up to an experimental pilot plant started in 1972 by Union Electric and the City of St. Louis to burn garbage in coal-fired boilers to make steam for the production of electricity. This experiment was partially funded by the Environmental Protection Agency. It was so successful that Union Electric made the decision to go ahead with the new $70 million plant. When completed the new facility will have the capacity of handling 2.5 million to 3 million tons of waste annually, enough for the area's entire solid-waste trash.

Five to seven collection-transfer centers will be set up to process up to 8,000 tons per day. Based on the pilot plant the process is as follows. At the processing centers the trash is shredded into particles less than one inch in size. Metals and abrasive materials such as glass are removed through a series of magnets and air stream separators. Then the shredded, combustible refuse is moved to a compactor where it is loaded into packer trucks or rail cars for transport to the power plant.

At the power plant the shredded trash fuel is stored until needed. This trash fuel is burned along with pulverized coal. Engineering reports indicate best results were obtained at the pilot plant when 10 percent trash was combined with 90 percent coal by heat value.

The heat value of the trash is about half the Btu value of the coal fuel. This results in a saving of one ton of coal for every two tons of trash burned. The trash fuel has a relatively low sulfur content which reduces this type of air pollution. Experiments on the pilot project show that other types of fossil fuel-fired boilers could be adapted to burn this shredded trash. Several other cities are investigating the possibility of similar facilities to produce power.

The scrap ferrous metals separated from the trash are sold to nearby Granite City Steel, the largest steel producer in the area. This scrap, which accounts for about five percent of the refuse, is used by the steel producer to reduce its requirements for iron ore.

The area's volume of solid wastes going to the sanitary landfills has already been reduced and the city's incinerator use has been reduced. When the facility is fully operational the recycling of noncombustible materials and the fuel use of other material will practically eliminate the need for land fills to dispose of the area's wastes.

1. What benefits are there in Union Electric's new solid-waste fuel system for the following groups:
   a. Union Electric Company and its stockholders?
   b. St. Louis and surrounding counties?
   c. Other business enterprises?
   d. Citizens living in the area?
2. What possible problems might arise in implementing this new system for handling solid wastes?
3. What benefits could come from this project which would extend beyond the St. Louis metropolitan area?
4. If Union Electric Company had decided it was not economically feasible to invest $70 million in this project, what possible actions might have been taken to achieve some of its benefits?

glossary

Glossary

Accelerated depreciation allowance A provision of federal tax law which permits a greater than proportionate depreciation charge in the early years of a capital investment's life (such as a machine). The purpose is to reduce taxable income for the enterprise in the early years of the investment and to stimulate increased productivity.

Accounting The recording, measuring, analyzing, and reporting of enterprise transactions in monetary terms.

Accounts payable Amounts owed to suppliers for purchases.

Accounts receivable Amounts owed the enterprise by customers who have purchased goods on credit.

Accumulated depreciation The total amount of the cost of fixed assets which has been charged as an expense of using those assets over the years.

Achieved status Status that comes when an individual works to fulfill the requirements for a particular position and attains it.

Acid test ratio A test of an enterprise's short-term liquidity; it is the relationship of an enterprise's quick assets (cash, short-term investments, and accounts or notes receivable) to current liabilities.

Actuarial studies Statistical analysis of accident and death rates for insurance purposes of calculating risks, premiums, and benefit payments.

Advertising The visual or oral communication of a message to a group regarding a good, service, or idea.

Advertising media The various means by which an advertising message can be transmitted to a potential consumer, including newspapers, television, direct mail, magazines, radio, or outdoor ads.

Affirmative Action Plan A program to provide equal opportunity for employment and promotion.

Agents Wholesale middlemen who customarily do not take title to goods, but negotiate the purchase or sale of merchandise for which they are paid on a fee or commission basis.

Air pollution The presence of one or more contaminants in the air in quantities great enough to be injurious to life or property.

Air Quality Act of 1967 This act extended federal authority in the field of air-quality control and provided for federal cooperation with state governments in developing air-quality control standards.

American National Standards Institute (ANSI) The national body which has worked out standard symbols for flowcharting for computer applications.

American Stock Exchange A major organized trading market for corporate stocks and bonds; located in New York City.

Analog computer A computer which functions by measuring continuous conditions in physical variables such as temperature, pressure, voltages, or liquid flows.

Antimerger Act A federal law, passed in 1950, that strengthened the Clayton Act. It provided that not only is the purchase of stock of a competing corporation a violation of the antitrust laws, but it is also illegal to acquire the assets of a competing firm.

Antitrust laws Legislative acts designed to promote competition and to prevent large business enterprises from practices such as illegal price setting and division of markets.

Application blank A form that a job candidate fills out, giving general information about himself or herself plus answers to questions the business enterprise has found to correlate with job success.

Applied research The practical application of scientific knowledge to definite problems or needs.

Appraised value The value of an asset determined by someone with expert knowledge for taxation, insurance, or other reasons.

Apprenticeship training The employee works under supervision of trained employees and is required to meet rigid performance standards. Used in jobs that require long periods of training and a high degree of skill.

Arbitration A judicial process in which an impartial third party assumes the role of a judge and makes a binding decision in a dispute.

Arithmetic/logic unit The part of the computer which performs computations on data and checks results.

Ascribed status Status assigned to a person on the basis of some inherited characteristic, such as sex, race, or family.

Ask price The price at which a stock market specialist is willing to sell securities.

Assessed value The value placed on property for purposes of taxation.

Auditor The financial officer who examines the accounting and control systems, including verifying assets and liabilities and making suggestions for overall management improvements.

Authoritarian leadership Leadership based on centralized authority and autocratic decision making. Subordinates are given little or no discretion in carrying out work assignments.

Authority The delegated power to make decisions.

Automation In manufacturing, the process by which goods are produced, moved, or inspected by self-operating machinery or electronic controls.

Average collection period A calculation that may be used to evaluate the quality of the enterprise's accounts receivable. It is the ratio of accounts receivable to average daily credit sales.

Balance of payments The difference between the total funds that flow into and out of a country over a period of time.

Balance of trade The difference between a country's total imports and exports of merchandise.

Balance sheet A statement of the financial position of an enterprise at a given point in time, usually the end of a fiscal period, which shows the assets the enterprise owns and the claims against those assets.

Bank acceptance A draft drawn on a bank and accepted by the bank instead of an importer or some other private party.

Bargaining unit The definition in the union contract of the empolyees and the employers covered by the agreement.

BASIC *B*eginner's *A*ll-Purpose *S*ymbolic *I*nstruction *C*ode is a computer language for use in solving numerical problems.

Best-efforts offering An agreement whereby an investment banker will sell securities for a corporation without underwriting the issue.

Bid price The price at which a stock market specialist is willing to buy securities.

Bill of exchange A document drawn by the exporter of goods which calls on the importer to accept the obligation for payment of a sum of money at a specified time. Drafts used in international business.

Blacklist A list circulated by an employer of former employees who have been discharged for union activities. This has been determined by the National Labor Relations Board to be an unfair labor practice.

Board of directors A body elected by the stockholders of a corporation to exercise control of the corporation in the best long-run interests of the stockholders.

Bond indenture The legal contract which details the arrangement between the issuing company (the borrower) and the bondholders (the lenders).

Bonds Interest-bearing certificates of indebtedness issued by a governmental body or private enterprise which promise to pay the holder a specified sum on a given date in the future in exchange for a specific amount of money today.

Book value The worth of enterprise assets based on original cost as shown on the accounting records of the firm.

Break-even chart A projection of an enterprise's operations, assuming a pattern of variable and fixed costs to analyze the profit or loss resulting from different levels of sales volume or selling prices.

Break-even point The point where revenues equal costs. At the break-even point, the equailty of sales and costs means there is neither a profit nor a loss.

Broker An agent who receives a commission for acting as an intermediary between a buyer and seller.

Budget A financial plan that serves as an estimate of and a control over the operations of the enterprise for a specified period of time.

Budgeting process The gathering of data to translate the goals of the enterprise into quantitative terms and to set a basis for control.

Business cycles The recurring expansion and contraction in the level of economic activity.

Business enterprise A privately owned and operated organization that brings together the factors of production to provide goods and services sold with the expectation of earning a profit.

Business profit The calculation of profit by subtracting the appropriate portion of fixed and variable costs from the total receipts for a product's sale.

Business systems simulation Development of a model of the enterprise and its environment, which is programmed into a computer so that business decisions can be tested to evaluate their consequences.

Capital In an economic sense, capital is wealth used to produce goods and services. In accounting terminology, capital is either the amount invested by owners in an enterprise or the total long-term funds committed to management's use.

Capital budget   A budget that details the investment plans for assets that will last longer than a year and the means for their financing.

Capital equipment   Machinery and facilities which have a length of life over one year, are used to manufacture other goods, and do not become part of the product being manufactured.

Capital market   The coming together of lenders and borrowers of long-term funds.

Capital structure   The composition of the long-term funds committed to management's use, including equity funds and long-term debt (if any).

Capitalism   An economic system in which the capital used in the production process is privately owned and invested with the expectation of earning a profit.

Cartel   A group of enterprises which agree to fix prices and divide markets. Illegal in the United States.

Cash   A legal medium of exchange. The most liquid of current assets.

Cash budget   An estimate of cash receipts and cash disbursements over a specified period of time and of cash on hand.

Cash disbursements   Any payment of cash by a business enterprise.

Cash dividends   The dollars paid to shareholders from earnings, usually stated on a per share basis.

Cash flow   The receipts and disbursements of an enterprise over a particular period of time.

Cash receipts   The cash received by a business enterprise over a specified period of time.

Chain of command   A detailing of authority-responsibility relationships, so that all employees know who their immediate superior is and for what they are accountable.

Channels of distribution   The series of enterprises through which goods flow in moving from the producer to the ultimate consumer.

Charter   A document issued by a government which authorizes the formation of a corporation and grants it certain powers.

Check   A written order that directs a bank to pay a specified amount of money on demand.

Checkoff clause   A clause in the union contract that authorizes management to deduct union dues from the employee's pay and to turn this sum directly over to the union treasury.

Child Protection and Toy Safety Act   Legislation providing increased protection for children from toys which might have mechanical or electrical hazards.

Cigarette Labeling and Advertising Act   Legislation which requires warnings on cigarette packages regarding the health hazards of cigarette smoking. Also regulates cigarette advertising.

Civil Rights Act of 1964   Federal legislation outlawing discrimination in voting, public accommodations, schools, federal assistance programs, and employment.

Clayton Act   A federal law, passed in 1914, directed against unfair competition. It outlawed price discrimination, exclusive and tying contracts, intercorporate stockholdings, and interlocking directorates.

Clean Air Act of 1963   Legislation with later amendments which authorized the federal government to take action in interstate air pollution matters and to establish exhaust standards for new autos.

Clean Air Amendments of 1970   Federal legislation which set specific standards for auto emissions beginning with 1975 models along with other pollution controls, such as on new stationary sources of pollution.

Closed-end investment company   An investment company with a fixed amount of capital stock outstanding which buys and sells securities for income and capital gains.

Closed shop   An employment situation in which workers must be members of the union before they may be hired by an employer. The closed shop was made illegal by the Taft-Hartley Act.

COBOL   COmmon Business Oriented Language. A compiler language for computers, useful in solving business problems such as file processing and record keeping.

Collateral   Property pledged as security on a debt.

Commercial banks   Financial institutions that accept demand deposits from the public and have the power to create money through a fractional reserve system.

Commercial letter of credit   A document issued by a bank on application of an importer of merchandise. The bank authorizes drafts to be drawn on the bank by the beneficiary and agrees to honor the drafts if all requirements are met.

Commercial paper   Short-term promissory notes sold by large business corporations to raise funds.

Common stock   Certificates which represent shares of ownership of a corporation.

Common stock account   A balance sheet account that contains a stated amount of the proceeds stemming from the sale of the corporation's common stock.

Communication   The transmission of understanding.

Comprehensive employment interview   An interview to complete or correct the file of the applicant provided by the screening interview, application blank, testing program, and job references.

Computer terminal   A device with a keyboard that allows an individual to make use of a computer which may be located a great distance away.

Conceptual skill   The ability to diagnose a problem in relation to its total environment and to develop creative solutions.

Conciliation   Action of a third party to bring together management and labor when a dispute exists between them.

Conglomerate merger   The joining together of enterprises that produce or distribute unrelated product lines.

Consolidation   The joining of two or more independent business enterprises into a new enterprise under a single management.

Constant dollars   Dollar amounts which have been adjusted for changes in the purchasing power of the currency to permit dollar comparisons between one time period and another in real terms.

Consumer durable goods   Products used by individuals and households that typically last over a period of years, including automobiles, television sets, refrigerators, and other appliances.

Consumer goods   Goods that satisfy individual needs directly rather than being used in the production process or for resale.

Consumer Product Safety Commission   Federal agency to improve the level of safety in product design and generally to protect the public from unsafe products.

Consumerism   The movement by consumers to exert pressure on business and government to improve the quality of products sold and to protect the interests of ultimate consumers.

Continuous process assembly line   The movement of goods from one stage of the production process to another by use of automatic conveyors.

Contract   An agreement between two or more parties which can be enforced by law.

Control   A systematic measuring of the progress the business enterprise is making toward its objectives, including the process of correcting deviations in performance.

Control unit   The part of the computer which issues directions based on the program to other units of the computer.

Controller   The financial officer who is responsible for the accounting system and for developing the necessary financial controls to assure the security and efficient use of funds.

Convenience goods   Products which are usually low priced and are purchased by consumers with a minimum of effort at the nearest available location.

Copyright   An exclusive right granted by law to the control of an artistic, literary, or musical work or a merchandising label for a period of 28 years with the option of one renewal for another 28 years.

Corporation   A legal entity, separate and distinct from its owners, who are called stockholders. A business corporation receives a charter from the state which outlines its powers to engage in business activity. It may have perpetual life, and the stockholders have limited liability.

Cost accounting   The branch of accounting that classifies, records, allocates, summarizes, and reports current and prospective costs.

Cost of goods sold   The value of merchandise sold, determined by adding together the cost of material, labor, overhead, and other expenses involved in the production of the goods, but not including selling costs or the general costs of management.

Council of Economic Advisers   Three professional economists appointed by the president to analyze and interpret economic developments and recommend national economic policy. The council was created by the Employment Act of 1946.

Council on Environmental Quality   The federal government agency which reports to the president and is responsible for studies and policy recommendations on the quality of the national environment.

Craft union A union that organizes workers who perform a particular skilled type of work. Entrance into full status in the craft is usually preceded by an extensive training and apprenticeship program.

Credit manager The financial officer who administers trade credit including determination of which customers will receive credit.

Credit rating The estimate of an individual's or enterprise's ability and willingness to meet payments when they are due.

Credit unions Cooperatives that promote saving by their members and also make loans to members at relatively low interest rates.

Creeping methods change A reduction in the time required to do a job as the employee through experience improves on the original method developed for a job through motion and time analysis.

Currency Token coin and paper money in circulation.

Current assets Assets that are cash, realizable in cash, or expected to be sold or consumed during the year.

Current liabilities Obligations that will fall due within a short period of time, customarily within one year.

Current ratio A test of an enterprise's short-term liquidity; it is the relationship of current assets to current liabilities. The current ratio is one of the most widely used balance sheet ratios.

Customs duty A tax or tariff on goods imported from a foreign country.

Debt Money owed to another by an agreement that creates a legal obligation to pay.

Decentralization The dispersion of decision making throughout an organization. Also, the location of facilities over a wider geographic area.

Deficit spending The condition when expenditures exceed revenues; applied to government finances when spending exceeds tax collections.

Delegation of authority The authorization of a subordinate to make certain decisions, thereby creating a new responsibility relationship from the subordinate to the superior.

Demand deposit A deposit in a commercial bank that may be withdrawn on demand (without advance notice), commonly called a checking account.

Demographic changes Changes in the size and composition of the population.

Departmentalization The division of the business enterprise into units or subsystems to accomplish the objectives of the firm.

Depletion allowance A charge made to account for the reduction of a natural resource such as oil or minerals over a period of time. This has the effect of reducing the amount of income taxes paid by enterprises in these industries.

Depreciation The decline in value of an asset over a period of years.

Depression A pronounced and prolonged recession in the business cycle.

Devaluation Reduction in the value of one currency in terms of gold or another currency.

Digital computer A computer which performs arithmetic operations on numbers utilizing the functions of data input, memory or storage, arithmetic processing, control, and output.

Dilemma   A situation in which one must choose between two or more alternative courses of action, each of which will have undesirable consequences.

Direction   The process of aiding an enterprise's employees in carrying out their work activities.

Discipline   Rules affecting conduct or actions in the business enterprise.

Discretionary income   The income left after deducting the amount of income required for necessities.

Dividend   The amount of profits distributed to shareholders in proportion to their ownership of stock in a corporation.

Dividend payout percentage   The proportion of earnings an enterprise distributes to shareholders as cash dividends.

Dow-Jones average   An average price for a composite of 65 common stocks of some of America's largest industrial, transportation, and utility corporations.

Downgrading   Transfer of an employee to a job that requires less skill than the job previously performed.

Draft   An order directing the payment of money from one party to another.

Dumping   Selling a product in a foreign market at a lower price than in its domestic market.

Earnings   Profits generated by an enterprise. When applied to individual workers, usually stated in terms of dollars per hour or per week.

Earnings per share   The amount of a corporation's net income (profit) divided by the number of shares of common stock outstanding.

Economic indicator   A measurement of one part of the economy that can help in evaluating the entire economy and in forecasting its future course. Economic indicators are classified as leading, lagging, or coincident with the general level of economic activity.

Economic profit   The calculation of profit by subtracting opportunity costs from business profit; the difference is called economic profit.

Economic resources   All the scarce natural, man-made, and human factors that go into the production of goods and services.

Economics   The study of how scarce resources are allocated in a society of unlimited wants.

Effluent charges   Payments that would be made to the government by an industry based on the amount of pollutants it discharged. Such charges presumably would stimulate industry to install antipollution systems or would provide funds to combat pollution.

Elasticity of demand   The responsiveness of demand to changes in price. Elastic demand is the condition in which a change in the price of a good results in a greater than proportionate change in demand for the good.

Electronic computer   A data processing device which is capable of the storage, processing, and retrieval of data through the use of electronic circuitry, memory elements, and programmed instructions.

Embargo   A prohibition against the movement of goods.

Employee hiring   Hiring of nonmanagerial personnel.

Employee induction A program of providing new employees with useful and accurate information about the enterprise, the policies that will affect them, and the services that may be provided for their benefit.

Employee training Instruction for a new job such as apprenticeship training, vestibule training, on-the-job training, or vocational-school training.

Employee transfer The movement of an employee from one job to another at about the same wages and on the same level in the organization.

Employment Act of 1946 Federal legislation that stated as a matter of national policy the responsibility of the federal government in assisting the private sector of the American economy to promote maximum employment, production, and purchasing power.

Energy Research and Development Administration (ERDA) Government agency which replaced the Atomic Energy Commission in 1974 and broadened its activities to include other energy sources.

Entrepreneur Originally a French word meaning enterpriser. The entrepreneur is a person who provides the managerial ability to bring together land, capital, and labor to produce goods and services; one who assumes the risk of doing business.

Environmental Protection Agency The federal agency established to carry out the policies of the Council on Environmental Quality.

Equal Employment Opportunity Commission This commission, established as a result of the Civil Rights Act of 1964, is charged with combatting employment discrimination based on such factors as race and sex.

Equal Pay Act of 1963 Federal legislation which requires employers to pay men and women equally for the same work.

Equity funds Ownership financing provided through the sale of stock in a corporation or by the retention of earnings. Also applies to owners' funds in partnerships or proprietorships.

Esteem The recognition and regard resulting from how well a person performs the role associated with his or her status.

Ethics A code of conduct and values that is accepted by society as being right and proper.

Eurodollars U.S. dollar deposits in European commercial banks including foreign branches of American banks.

Exchange control Government control over access to foreign currencies by private citizens and business enterprises.

Excise tax A tax levied on goods or services inside a country at the time of their manufacture, sale, or use.

Executive Order 11246 A presidential directive prohibiting federal government contractors from discriminatory employment practices.

Export-Import Bank (Eximbank) Federal agency to assist in financing international trade. Established in 1934.

Exports Goods sent out of a country to be sold in a foreign nation.

Expropriation Action by a government of transferring ownership of private property to the state.

Facilitating enterprise A business enterprise that performs auxiliary functions in fields such as finance, insurance, transportation, construction, or services.

Factoring   The purchase of a business enterprise's accounts receivable by a finance company, which then assumes the responsibility for collecting the accounts.

Factors of production   The four ingredients necessary for the production of goods and services—natural resources, labor, capital, and management.

Factory layout   The arrangement of machines and production lines in a factory in order to move materials through the manufacturing process.

Fair Credit Reporting Act   Legislation designed to protect consumers in credit matters, including individual credit ratings and their use by merchants, insurance companies, or employers.

Fair employment practices (FEP)   A type of legislation passed in the majority of the states which outlaws discrimination in hiring, promotion, and discharge of individuals.

Family income   The total money income received by family units over a specified period of time before deductions for personal taxes.

Featherbedding   A union practice that requires an employer to pay for services not performed. Declared an unfair labor practice by the Taft-Hartley Act.

Federal Deposit Insurance Corporation (FDIC)   A governmental agency that insures depositors' accounts up to $40,000 each in commercial banks that are FDIC members.

Federal Energy Administration   Government agency which assists executive branch in carrying out national energy policy.

Federal income taxes   Taxes which enterprises and individuals must pay to the federal government on annual profits or earnings.

Federal Insurance Contributions Act (FICA) taxes   Employment taxes which provide for old-age, survivors', disability, and health insurance payments from the federal government.

Federal Reserve discount rate   The interest rate that member banks must pay to obtain funds from the Federal Reserve bank in their district.

Federal Reserve System   A system of 12 Federal Reserve banks, presided over by a seven-member Board of Governors in Washington, D.C. It is charged with the responsibility of providing for a flow of money and credit to foster orderly economic growth and stable prices.

Federal Savings and Loan Insurance Corporation (FSLIC)   The governmental agency that insures each saver's account up to $40,000 in savings and loan associations that are members of FSLIC.

Federal Trade Commission (FTC)   A quasi-judicial administrative agency of the federal government established to strengthen the observance and enforcement of the antitrust laws. The FTC also has responsibility for policing advertising and marketing practices for consumer protection.

Federal Trade Commission Act   A federal act passed in 1914 to deal with prevention as well as punishment for monopolistic business practices. The act also established the Federal Trade Commission to police the antitrust laws and to protect consumer interests.

Feedback of information   The inspection by a machine of its own output and the activation of controls to correct deviations from previously established standards.

Finance companies Financial institutions that make loans to business enterprises and individuals. Those that specialize in direct loans to individuals are called consumer finance or personal finance companies, and those that provide loans to business enterprises are called commercial finance companies.

Finance function The activity involving the provision of funds from various sources for an enterprise's operations and the profitable use of those funds.

Financial institutions Establishments that regulate the money supply and channel savers' funds to business enterprises, individuals, and governmental bodies which need them.

Finished goods Goods that have completed the manufacturing process and have been placed in storage to await distribution to consumers.

Fire and casualty insurance companies Companies that sell insurance service to their clients to cover destruction of property by fire or other hazards. Some of these companies also provide other types of insurance protection, such as personal liability insurance.

First-line supervisor The management person who is directly responsible for the work efforts of employees in producing goods or providing services.

Fiscal period A span of time over which financial transactions are reported.

Fixed assets Sometimes called capital assets. These are long-term tangible assets, such as buildings, land, and equipment, which will not normally be turned into cash but are necessary for the operation of the enterprise.

Fixed costs Costs not directly affected by the number of units produced, such as rent, property taxes, and interest on borrowed money.

Flammable Fabrics Act Legislation which required children's night clothes to be flame retardent.

Floating exchange rate The international value of a nation's currency stated in relation to other currencies. The floating exchange rate fluctuates depending on supply and demand, in contrast to a one-price government-imposed and guaranteed rate for international transactions.

Food and Drug Administration The federal agency which has responsibility in areas such as the safety and effectiveness of drugs, cosmetics, and food products marketed in the United States.

Foreign exchange rate The price of the currency of one country in terms of the currency of another.

Foreign exchange transaction The purchase or sale of the currency of one nation with the currency of another.

Foreign trade zones Areas where goods may be imported, reprocessed, and exported without being subject to tariffs or quotas.

Foreman A supervisor who is the first level of management and who is in direct contact with workers engaged in the production process.

Form utility Utility that stems from a good's possession of the physical characteristics necessary for its purpose.

Formal organization A detailing of the status positions and lines of authority and responsibility from the board of directors and the president throughout the enterprise.

Formal training programs Structured training such as lectures, courses, discussions, or provision for employees to attend an institution of higher learning for professional management training.

*FORTRAN FOR*mula *TRAN*slator. An algebraic compiler language for a computer that is particularly useful for research problems requiring the solution of mathematical or statistical formulations.

Fractional reserve banking system The system of financial reserves used by commercial banks, whereby each bank is required to keep only a portion of its deposits in reserve form and may lend out those funds in excess of the required deposit reserves.

Frame of reference The perspective from which a person views his or her environment. It is influenced by the person's past experiences and value system.

Franchise The right to market a good or service in a particular area, sometimes on an exclusive basis.

Fringe benefits Items provided to employees that, in effect, increase real income but are not included in the basic wage. Fringe benefits include health insurance, disability benefits, sick leave, life insurance, pensions, and paid vacations.

Fully automated process Manufacture of a good by a process that includes the automatic inspection of production which actuates controls to correct deviations from established standards.

Functional departmentalization Organization of an enterprise by grouping together the activities of a similar nature, such as production, marketing, or finance.

GATT (General Agreement on Tariffs and Trade) International agreement for continuing discussions on trade and tariff reductions.

General purpose machine A machine that can perform a variety of jobs requiring the same type of work, such as a drill press that can drill different numbers of holes, in different sizes, different depths, and for different materials.

General Services Administration The federal government agency responsible for the maintenance and upkeep of federal buildings. Also negotiates purchasing contracts for supplies and services.

Geographical departmentalization Organization of a business enterprise on a territorial basis.

Geothermal power Utilization of steam deep in the earth to produce electricity.

Gold convertibility The ability to exchange a nation's money into gold. The U.S. dollar is no longer tied to gold convertibility either domestically or internationally.

Good In economic terms, anything useful in satisfying a human want.

Grapevine Informal communications that stem from informal work groups.

Grievance procedure A specified succession of steps through which workers' complaints are to be processed from lower to higher levels of management and union officials.

Grievances　Complaints expressed to management by employees about the work situation.

Gross income　Net sales less the cost of goods sold.

Gross National Product　The total retail market value of all the goods and services produced in a nation, usually stated in annual terms.

Gross profit　Another term for gross income which is net sales less the cost of goods sold.

Guaranteed loan　A loan which will be paid back by the government or some other institution or individual in the event that it is not repaid by the borrowing enterprise.

Guide　A recommendation for action, not necessarily mandatory.

Hardware　When used regarding a computer system, the physical equipment which makes up the computer.

Horizontal merger　A joining together of two or more companies that manufacture or distribute the same product.

Housekeeping staff　Staff personnel who perform custodial and maintenance duties, record keeping, health services, and routine personnel functions.

Human relations　The interactions arising out of the association of two or more persons. Management's actions to provide a climate in the business enterprise that will satisfy the employee's needs and achieve the broad economic objectives of the enterprise.

Human skill　The ability to work with people and to build effective work teams.

Human subsystem　That element of the work system which consists of the values, motivations, and interactions of persons in an enterprise.

Imports　Goods brought into a country that have been purchased in a foreign nation.

Income statement　A summary of the revenues and expenses of an enterprise's operations over a specified period, such as a year. The income statement is also called the profit and loss statement.

Income tax　An annual tax on the income of persons or corporations.

Industrial union　A union such as the United Auto Workers, which draws members on an industry-wide basis, regardless of the jobs performed.

Industrial user　Enterprises which buy products for use in producing other goods or services.

Industry　Those business enterprises that engage in the same type of economic activity.

Industry-wide bargaining　A situation in which a single series of collective bargaining negotiations result in an agreement or agreements covering substantially all the firms in an industry.

Inelasticity of demand　The condition in which changes in the price of a product bring about little or no change in the demand for it.

Inflation　An increase in the price of goods or services which takes place when the supply of money or credit in the economy expands faster than the ability of the economy to produce more goods and services.

Informal organization　A self-grouping of employees in the work situation based on the personalities of individuals rather than on formal organizational relationships.

Injunction A court order that directs an individual or an organization to do or not to do some act. A violator of an injunction is subject to a contempt of court proceeding.

Input unit The system of feeding information into computers by such means as punched cards, punched paper tapes, magnetic-ink tapes, optical-character scanners, or console typewriters.

Installment credit A credit system in which a purchased article is paid for by a series of payments to be made over a specified period of time.

Institutional advertising An advertising message which seeks to develop good-will for a business enterprise or an industry rather than directly selling a specific product.

Insurance premium The amount paid periodically to an insurance company or its agent for coverage that will provide reimbursement in case of damage or loss.

Interest The amount paid for the use of borrowed funds. In an economic sense, the return for capital resources.

Interest income In economic terms, the return to capital resources.

Intermediate-term credit Debt instruments that have a maturity from over one year to approximately ten years.

International Monetary Fund (IMF) An international agency formed to foster monetary cooperation and stability among nations. Established in 1946.

Interstate Commerce Commission (ICC) A federal agency that regulates carriers engaged in interstate commerce.

Inventories The stock of goods available for sale to customers. As a balance sheet item, inventories include the cost of finished goods, work in process, and raw materials.

Inventory turnover A ratio which indicates the number of times merchandise moves through the enterprise during the period under study. It is computed by dividing the cost of goods sold by the average inventory on hand over the period.

Investment banker An institution or person who functions as a middleman between corporations and investors in the capital funds market by selling new securities in the primary securities market and acting as a broker for purchase and sale of securities in the secondary securities market.

Investment company A financial institution that sells its shares and uses the proceeds to purchase securities of other corporations.

Investment portfolio The list of stocks, bonds, and other investments owned by a financial institution or individual.

Investment tax credit A direct reduction of a business enterprise's federal income taxes because the enterprise purchases a specified type of capital equipment. Designed to stimulate investment and increase business activity.

Invoice An itemized statement of merchandise shipped by the vendor.

Job description A description of the essential elements of a specific job including such factors as physical effort, skill, responsibility, mental effort, and working conditions.

Job evaluation A measurement of the value of each job in the enterprise in relation to the other jobs in the enterprise.

Job references A list of previous positions held by a job applicant, used to check the applicant's past work record.

Job rotation A planned approach to management training which involves transfer of the trainee through a series of different positions.

Job specifications A list of the requirements of a specific position in an enterprise.

Jurisdictional strike A work stoppage which grows out of disagreements over which craft union has the right to perform particular jobs or which union should organize the workers in a particular industry. Jurisdictional strikes were outlawed by the Taft-Hartley Act.

Labor All physical and mental talents that individuals expend in producing goods and services, with the exception of entrepreneurial talent, classified separately.

Labor contract See union contract.

Labor Management Relations Act of 1947 (Taft-Hartley Act) A series of amendments to the National Labor Relations Act of 1935 which added certain unfair labor practices for unions, permitted the president of the U.S. to obtain an 80-day injunction to postpone a strike threatening national welfare, and allowed states to have right-to-work laws outlawing the union shop.

Labor-Management Reporting and Disclosure Act of 1959 (Landrum-Griffin Act) Federal legislation that imposed certain limitations on unions in organizing workers and in the internal management of union affairs.

Labor relations A situation in which management bargains over wages, hours, and working conditions with employees as a group through union representatives.

Laissez-faire capitalism Stemming from a French term meaning "let us alone," laissez-faire capitalism in its most extreme form limited government's participation in economic activity to providing essential services such as police and fire protection.

Land In economics, all natural resources used in the production process, including timber, oil and mineral deposits, and water, as well as land itself.

Layoff A reduction in the size of the work force frequently stemming from a drop in demand for the enterprise's products.

Lead time The time required in development of the production process before goods can be produced.

Leadership The element of direction that causes subordinates to follow a superior and results in accomplishment of the goals of the enterprise.

Lease A form of long-term renting contract through which an enterprise obtains the use of assets without owning them.

Liabilities Claims against the enterprise's assets by outsiders.

Life insurance companies Business enterprises which provide insurance coverage on the lives of policyholders and a source of capital through investment of the insurance premiums they receive.

Limited liability A legal concept which when applied to a corporation means that if the enterprise fails, the stockholders' losses are limited to the amount of their investment in the enterprise.

Line function Those activities that specifically and directly result in achievement of the goals of the business enterprise.

Linear programming Determining the best allocation of limited resources through the use of linear equations and relationships by analyzing a number of variables given certain constraints.

Liquidation value The value of the enterprise's assets if they were sold.

Liquidity The degree of readiness of conversion of an asset into cash. Liquidity measures the ability of an enterprise to meet its current financial obligations when they become due.

Lockout Management's refusal to permit union members to enter the enterprise's facilities because of a dispute.

Long-term debt Loans that mature in more than 10 years.

Long-term liabilities A balance-sheet category made up of financial obligations that fall due more than one year in the future.

McGuire Act A federal law, passed in 1952, that permitted states to include in their resale price maintenance laws the nonsigner clause. It provides that all retailers in a state are bound by resale price agreements as long as one retailer in the state signs such an agreement.

Macroeconomic analysis The study of the functioning of the economy as a whole.

Maintenance force Employees whose work is to keep production facilities in efficient operating order.

Management The achievement of results by directing the activities of other people. Also, the group of individuals in an enterprise responsible for the achievement of results.

Management succession The process of providing for a source of qualified management personnel either through training and promotion of employees or by hiring executives from outside the enterprise.

Manufacturer's sales branch An office operated by a manufacturer separate from the factories for use by sales and service personnel. It may or may not carry inventories from which orders are shipped directly.

Manufacturing enterprise A business enterprise that fabricates consumer and producer goods out of raw materials and/or component parts.

Market A group of consumers who are willing and able to buy the goods produced by a business enterprise.

Market penetration pricing A policy of setting a relatively low initial price for a product to achieve mass market acceptance quickly.

Market system The coming together of buyers and sellers with money as a medium of exchange for goods and services.

Marketing The business activities that move goods and services from producers to consumers to satisfy needs. Marketing imparts place, time, and possession utility to goods.

Marketing concept of business An approach to business that centers management thinking around the importance of the consumer by recognizing a need, developing a product to satisfy this need, and in the process earning a profit for the enterprise.

Marketing enterprise A business enterprise that distributes finished goods to consumers.

Marketing mix The market program of a business enterprise consisting of the variables of product, promotion, price, and place.

Maslow's hierarchy of needs A priority of human needs discussed by the psychologist A. H. Maslow, including psychological, safety, love, esteem, and self-actualization needs.

Mass media advertising The promotion of a product to many people at the same time through newspapers, television, radio, magazines, or outdoor signs.

Maturity The date on which a financial obligation comes due.

Mechanization The application of power-driven tools in factory production, which results in a saving of both human energy and time.

Median In a series of data, the midway point that divides the number of units in half.

Median family income The midway point in the distribution of family income with half the families having incomes above this amount and half having incomes below.

Mediation The process whereby a third party brings together the two sides involved in a dispute and actively participates in the discussions in order to bring about a compromise acceptable to both parties.

Memory unit The part of the computer which receives and holds the input data and the program instructions for processing data.

Merchant wholesaler A middleman who purchases merchandise from manufacturers, and thereby takes title to the goods and assumes the risks associated with their sale.

Merger The taking over of a smaller enterprise by a larger business enterprise.

MESBIC A *M*inority *E*nterprise *S*mall *B*usiness *I*nvestment *C*ompany which is formed to provide capital and management assistance to minority-owned business enterprises.

Microeconomic analysis The study of the functioning of a specific unit of the economy, such as a given business enterprise.

Middlemen Enterprises or individuals, such as wholesalers and retailers, who handle the goods as they move from the producer to the ultimate consumer.

Miller-Tydings Act A federal law passed in 1937 as an amendment to the Sherman Act. It sought to aid small business by exempting resale price maintenance contracts from antitrust laws provided they were permitted by state law.

Minority group Part of the population distinguished from the dominant society by some characteristic such as race, nationality, language, or religion.

Miscellaneous payables A catchall account for any outsiders' recognized financial claims against the enterprise not listed elsewhere in the balance sheet.

Money market The coming together of lenders and borrowers of short-term debt which matures in one year or less.

Monopoly Control over the supply of a good or service in a given market by a single producer.

Monopoly profit The additional profit of an enterprise resulting from higher prices because of the enterprise's sole control over the production or distribution of a product.

Mortgage The pledging of property by a borrower to a lender as security for payment of the debt.

Motion analysis A determination by industrial engineers of the most efficient method of accomplishing a particular job by reducing waste effort to a minimum.

Motion and time analysis Work done by industrial engineers to provide a basis for production standards on factory jobs.

Multinational corporation A business enterprise which has significant operations in several countries.

Mutual fund An open-end investment company that does not have a fixed number of shares outstanding. It issues more shares whenever an investor wants to purchase shares in the fund, and stands willing to repurchase its shares from investors.

Mutual savings banks The oldest class of savings institutions in the United States. A mutual savings bank has no shareholders, but all depositors have a mutual interest and receive dividends for their savings.

National Alliance of Businessmen A voluntary organization of businessmen formed in 1967 to expand employment opportunities, especially for persons who were considered unemployable because of a lack of job skills.

National Environmental Policy Act of 1969 Legislation which commits the federal government to a continuing policy of improving the environment for present and future generations. The act established the Council on Environmental Quality.

National income The total earnings of labor and property that result from the production of goods and services by the nation's economy. National income is the sum of compensation of employees, proprietors' income, rental income, net interest, and corporate profits.

National Labor Relations Act Federal legislation passed in 1935 which guarantees the right of workers to form and join labor unions and to bargain collectively with employers. It defined certain unfair labor practices and established the National Labor Relations Board to enforce the act.

National Labor Relations Board (NLRB) The five-member body that administers and enforces the National Labor Relations Act.

National Traffic and Motor Vehicle Safety Act of 1966 Legislation which provides for the setting of standards for auto and highway safety and which requires auto manufacturers to notify first purchasers of cars of safety defects discovered after their delivery.

Near-cash Any asset immediately transferable into money form without risk of loss of value in the process, such as 91-day U.S. Treasury bills.

Need A lack of something that is useful, required, or desirable to carry out a way of life.

Negotiable bill of lading A document that when endorsed constitutes a receipt for the goods, a contract for transportation, and evidence of title to the property, and makes the holder the lawful owner.

Net profit The amount that remains after all relevant costs, including income taxes, have been deducted from revenue; the final figure shown on the income or profit and loss statement.

Net sales Gross sales less cash discounts given for prompt payment for goods and credits for returned merchandise.

Net worth The amount of the owners' claims to the enterprise's assets; also called owners' equity.

New York Stock Exchange The largest organized trading market for corporate stocks and bonds; located in New York City.

Nonprice competition Factors other than the cost of a product that influence consumer demand, such as sales promotion efforts, quality and service competition, and fashion.

No-strike clause A clause in the union contract that prohibits work stoppages by employees.

Notes payable A balance sheet item showing debts for which written acknowledgments have been made.

Objectives Statements that embody the broad goals toward which the group activity of the business enterprise is directed.

Occupational distribution The proportion of persons in various job categories.

Occupational Safety and Health Act of 1970 Federal law requiring employers to provide safe and healthful working conditions.

Odd lot Generally defined as the purchase or sale of stock in units of less than 100 shares.

Office of Federal Contract Compliance The Department of Labor agency which coordinates the administration of executive orders to prevent discriminatory employment practices by government contractors.

Office of Minority Business Enterprise (OMBE) The Department of Commerce agency designed to assist minority persons in establishing and operating business enterprises.

Oligopoly Control over the supply of a good or service in a given market by a few producers.

On-the-job training The worker is placed in the shop at a machine or workplace to be trained by a supervisor, a special instructor, or an experienced employee.

OPEC (Organization of Petroleum Exporting Countries) The cartel dominated by Arab governments which controls the export of oil from most of the oil-exporting countries.

Open account Extension of credit to a customer without requiring specific collateral or a written acknowledgment of the financial obligation by the purchaser.

Open market operations The purchase or sale of federal government securities by the Federal Reserve System to affect the level of commercial bank reserves.

Operating income The profit generated from the operation of the enterprise before interest payments and income taxes are deducted.

Operations budget A budget that covers operating revenue and expenses. Consists of a forecast of expected sales, along with an estimate of the costs necessary to achieve the sales goal. Operations budgets can be subdivided into budgets for sales, sales promotion and advertising, production, purchases, maintenance, and overhead.

Opportunity cost An economic concept that represents the cost assumed when a person or business enterprise forgoes the alternative of making some other use of economic resources.

Organizational subsystem That element of the work system which consists of the way in which the technical and human subsystems are organized, directed, coordinated, and controlled by management to achieve the enterprise's objectives.

Other assets A catchall category on the balance sheet that includes all assets not listed either as current or fixed, such as patents or trademarks.

Output unit Any of the numerous means of showing the results of a computer's data processing, such as by printer systems or visual displays.

Over-the-counter market The purchase and sale of securities through informal dealings, usually by telephone rather than on an organized exchange.

Owners' equity (net worth) The value of the assets claimed by owners of the business enterprise.

Participative leadership Decentralization of authority among subordinates. Suggestions are encouraged, and an emphasis is placed on communication between the leader and all members of the group.

Partnership A form of legal organization of business enterprise made up of two or more individuals who share in the ownership according to a contractual agreement. At least one partner must have unlimited liability.

Patent Exclusive rights to a product or process for 17 years, conferred by government authority to the holder.

Peak The high point in economic activity during a business cycle.

Pension funds Funds accumulated from the contributions of employers and employees, and invested to provide retirement income for the individual beneficiaries and their families in their old age.

Performance rating A formal rating of an employee, used to make merit wage increases within job classifications and to guide management in making promotions.

Personal assistants Staff persons who provide executives with information or who handle details the manager may not have time for but does not want to delegate to a lower level in the organization.

Personal income The total money income received by individuals before personal taxes are deducted.

Personal selling A method of promotion that involves an individual presentation of a product to a customer.

Personnel management The function in the enterprise of recruitment, selection, induction, and training of employees to build a well-motivated and effective work force.

Philanthropy Services and gifts to help mankind.

Physical distribution The process of moving and handling goods as they flow through the channels of distribution.

Pilot plant A prototype of the production process, which usually consists of a scale model of the complete factory or the production line.

PL/1 Programming *Language*, Version *1*, is a computer language suitable for problems involving both business data processing and numerical scientific computations.

Place The dimension of the marketing mix which provides products with time and place utility to satisfy customers. Includes determination of the channels of distribution and the transportation and storage of goods.

Place utility Utility that stems from goods being where the consumer has access to them.

Planning The process of rational decision making done sufficiently in advance to promote the more effective operation of the enterprise.

Poison Prevention Packaging Act Legislation requiring manufacturers to distribute dangerous substances in containers with safety caps which are difficult for children to remove.

Policy A statement of principles or purposes that provides a framework for decision making consistent with the objectives of the enterprise.

Pollution An undesirable change in the environment which can harm the quality of life.

Portfolio A list of securities owned.

Possession utility Utility that stems from a person's being able to own or control a good.

Preferred stock The class of ownership shares in a corporation that has preference over common stock to a stated amount of cash dividends each year. Preferred stockholders have priority over common stockholders in claims to assets if the corporation is liquidated.

Prepaid expenses A balance sheet item that represents a portion of an outlay for a benefit that will extend over more than one accounting period, such as for insurance or royalties.

Prestige The recognition and regard that result from a person's status.

Price/earnings ratio A measure for analyzing common stock prices which is calculated by dividing the stock's current market price by the past 12 months earnings per share.

Primary boycott Employees' refusal to use the products of an employer with whom they have a dispute.

Primary securities market The market that channels funds directly to corporations or governmental bodies in exchange for their securities.

Prime rate of interest The borrowing rate that commercial banks charge their most credit-worthy business customers.

Private enterprise system The form that capitalism has taken in America. It is characterized by private property, the profit motive, competition in the market system, a particular relationship between business and government, and consumer freedom of choice.

Private placement The sale of an entire issue of securities to a single or small number of investors.

Private property Property owned by an individual and therefore the right to exercise substantial control over it.

Procedure A specific method or a series of steps carried out in a particular sequence to implement a given policy.

Process design The development of the means by which a good will be produced.

Process layout The location of different types of machines or functions together, regardless of where the process comes in the production of any one product—i.e., all grinding would be done in one location, all drilling in another, and so on.

Processing enterprise A business enterprise that transforms the natural resources from the mines, forests, farms, or oceans into the raw materials used to manufacture goods.

Producer goods Tools, machines, and equipment used to make consumer goods or other producer goods; thus, they indirectly satisfy individual needs.

Product A good or service which satisfies customer needs.

Product advertising An advertising message which provides information and attempts to sell a specific good or service.

Product design The development of a product that will perform properly, have consumer appeal, and be sold at a price that will be profitable.

Product layout The arrangement of machinery and assembly lines by chronological steps so that as the product moves through the factory there is a buildup from raw materials or parts to the finished product.

Product life cycle The pattern of a product's sales and profit margins. The profit margin reaches a peak first and begins to decline while the sales continue to rise for a period of time before peaking and declining.

Product line departmentalization Organization of a business enterprise according to the various types of products it manufactures and sells.

Production The provision of goods with form utility by turning raw materials and semifinished products into finished goods for either consumer or industrial use.

Production control The coordination and control of the production process to meet delivery schedules.

Production scheduling A detailing of the sequence and timing of orders from the time orders are received from the sales department until finished goods are shipped.

Production transfer Changing of an employee's work assignments from one department to another because of a change in a department's job requirements.

Profit The residual left after all appropriate costs have been deducted from business revenues; the return to enterprises or individuals for risk bearing, innovation, or some degree of market control.

Profit and loss statement See income statement.

Profit center A responsibility center in which revenues are generated, enabling management to measure profitability as well as costs.

Profit motive The desire to engage in economic activity in order to earn profit; a central controlling mechanism in a capitalistic economy.

Program A mixture of policies and procedures that have been developed to achieve the outlined objectives of management.

Program flowchart Instructions given in the proper sequence for the computer to process the input data. The flowchart is translated into a set of detailed coded instructions for the computer.

Programming Providing a computer with a set of instructions necessary for solving a problem or carrying out a series of operations on data.

Promotion In personnel management, the advancement of an employee to a better job with more responsibility, increased skill, or higher status and an increased salary. In marketing, the communication of information regarding a product to potential customers to persuade them to buy.

Property tax A tax levied on the assessed value of tangible property such as land; business buildings, equipment, and inventories; and individuals' houses, automobiles, and home furnishings. Sometimes a tax is assesed on intangible property such as stocks and bonds.

Proprietorship A legal form of business organization owned by a single individual. The most common form of business enterprise, it is generally small in size and its owner has unlimited liability.

Prototype A model or pattern used as the basis for subsequent production, such as a clay model of an automobile made up during the design process to give a three-dimensional view of styling and appearance.

Proxy The written authority given to a person or organization to act for the signer in some matter such as in voting at a corporation's meeting of stockholders.

Psychological needs Needs that pertain to the individual's own self-image, including the need for love, self-respect, and a feeling of accomplishment.

Public relations Those functions concerned with creating a favorable image of the business enterprise and with communicating its purposes and programs to the different groups who constitute the public.

Purchase contract A purchase order that has been accepted by a vendor.

Purchase order A document that authorizes a vendor to deliver described goods at a specified price.

Purchase requisition A formal request for the purchase of a particular item.

Purchasing The procurement of industrial materials and supplies for use or for further processing, not for immediate resale.

Pure research Research carried on to extend our frontiers of knowledge without regard to the immediate application of its findings.

Quality Possession of the necessary characteristics that fit a product to a given use.

Quality control A system of inspection to determine which goods should be accepted or rejected, and a means for preventing the continued production of unsatisfactory goods.

Quota   A limit placed on the quantity of foreign goods which may be imported.

Ratio of profits to owners' equity   The profitability of a business enterprise or an industry measured by profits as a percentage of owners' equity.

Ratio of profits to sales   The profitability of a business enterprise or an industry measured by profits as a percentage of sales.

Raw materials   Unprocessed commodities and component parts purchased by a manufacturer to be assembled into a finished product.

Real income   The actual purchasing power of a person's or family's income after adjustment for changes in the prices of goods and services.

Real-time system   A computer system which receives and processes data so as to affect an environment *at that time.*

Recession (or contraction)   A decline in economic activity in the business cycle.

Recognition clause   A union contract provision that defines the bargaining unit and recognizes a particular union as the bargaining agency for the employees.

Recovery (or expansion)   The upturn in the business cycle characterized by greater demand for goods and services, higher production, and improved profits.

Recruitment   The process of seeking and hiring new employees.

Remedial transfer   A transfer made because of some problem that has arisen with a particular employee on a job.

Rent   In an economic sense, the return that accrues to land.

Repatriation of funds   Returning of monies from business operations in another country to the home country of the business enterprise.

Reproduction value   The amount it would cost to replace the assets of an enterprise with others of like characteristics.

Reserve requirements   The amount of reserve funds held by commercial banks to back up deposits, usually stated as a percentage of deposits.

Resource Recovery Act of 1970   Federal legislation which provided for research programs to encourage the development of innovative solid waste disposal systems.

Responsibility   Accountability to others by those who have authority.

Responsibility centers   A designated unit of a subsystem in which the manager can be held responsible for the control of costs.

Retailer   A merchant who sells goods or services directly to individual consumers.

Retained earnings   The amount of profits earned by an enterprise over the years and kept in the business to strengthen and expand operations; less frequently called earned surplus.

Right-to-work laws   State laws that make illegal the provisions in labor contracts under which workers are required to join the union after a specified period of time.

Robinson-Patman Act   A federal law passed in 1936 as a revision of Section 2 of the Clayton Act. It sought to give increased protection to smaller retailers against unfair competition from large competitors.

Role The expected behavior pattern associated with a status.

Round lot Generally defined as a stock transaction unit of 100 shares.

Routing The detailed instructions on how a particular order will move from department to department, which machines will be used at each point along the line, and when inspections will be made.

Rule An established regulation that must be obeyed.

Rumor Incomplete, unconfirmed information, which may be incorrect or malicious in its intent.

Sale-and-leaseback agreement An arrangement in which an enterprise constructs a building to its specifications, then sells it to a financial institution such as an insurance company and simultaneously leases the building back for a long period of time.

Sales budget A subdivision of an operating budget that translates the goals of the enterprise into quantitative terms not only for anticipated sales revenues but also for the expenditures necessary to generate those revenues.

Sales finance companies Financial institutions that specialize in installment loans by purchasing installment receivables from retailers who sell durable goods, such as autos and appliances. Sales finance companies also loan money to retailers and wholesalers to finance their inventories.

Sales promotion An attempt to bridge the gap between personal selling and mass media advertising through use of displays and other sales aids, material for training salespersons and contests and premium programs for customers.

Sales tax A tax levied on goods or services at the time they are sold to consumers.

Savings deposit An account which draws interest in a commercial bank or other savings institution.

Savings and loan association A type of cooperative financial institution to promote thrift and home ownership. The savers who place their funds in the association become shareholders and receive dividends on their savings.

Scarce economic resources All the natural, manmade, and human factors that go into the production of goods and services.

Screening interview An interview to make a preliminary decision about an applicant's suitability for employment.

Seasonal changes Fluctuations in economic activity due to the changing seasons of the year, holidays, or the calendar.

Secondary boycott Action by workers against a company with whom they have a dispute by bringing pressure against a third party who is not directly involved in the dispute. The secondary boycott was declared illegal by the Taft-Hartley Act.

Secondary securities markets Security markets where stocks or bonds already outstanding are bought and sold among investors.

Securities and Exchange Commission (SEC) A federal government agency that regulates interstate corporation stock transactions. The SEC requires corporations to provide investors with information about new stock and bond issues, and to reveal dealings in their own stock by enterprise executives, and in general protects the interests of the public.

Security A general term that encompasses transferable certificates of stock or debt. The term is sometimes used to mean collateral for a loan.

Seniority Priority or status attained by an employee based on length of service in the enterprise.

Services Intangible products which provide consumer satisfactions.

Share One of the equal parts into which a corporation's ownership interest is divided.

Sherman Act A federal law, passed in 1890, which made restraint of trade and monopolization federal offenses.

Shift transfer Transfer of an employee from one time shift to another.

Shop stewards Workers elected or appointed by a union to represent employees in a department or area of a factory, particularly with regard to grievances.

Shopping goods Products which are compared with competing products for price, quality, style, or service by the customer before the good is purchased.

Short-term debt Debt which matures in one year or less.

Sight draft A document that calls for the drawee to pay the draft on its presentation (on sight).

Single project type departmentalization Organization of an enterprise to carry out by department one-time projects that will extend over a period of months or years, such as highway construction.

Skimming-the-cream pricing A policy of setting a relatively high price for a product, usually in the introduction stage of the product's life cycle or when nonprice competition is important.

Small Business Administration (SBA) A federal agency concerned with the problems of small business management.

Social needs All the needs that grow out of a person's relation to other individuals and groups, including the need for recognition, acceptance, and group activity.

Socialism An economic system in which the concept of private profit is lacking and the means of production and distribution of goods are owned by the state rather than by individuals.

Software The program of instructions for a computer.

Solar energy Utilization of the sun's rays to produce usable power such as electricity.

Solid waste pollution Pollution caused by the disposal of agricultural, mineral, industrial, and residential products or wastes.

Solvency The enterprise's ability to pay long-term financial obligations when they fall due, as well as to meet the interest payments on outstanding debt.

Span of control The number of subordinates a manager can supervise.

Special-purpose machine A machine specifically designed to produce a particular product or to do a given job.

Specialist A member of a stock exchange who makes a market in a particular stock by offering to buy or sell the security through a continuous two-way auction.

Specialty goods Products for which customers show strong brand preference or which have features that encourage a special buying effort by customers.

Spread The gross margin or profit between what an investment banker or specialist pays for the securities he buys and what he hopes to sell them for.

Staff function All activities that assist the line management in fulfilling the enterprise's objectives.

Staff personnel Personnel necessary to support the line activities. These include technical advisers, personal assistants, housekeeping staff, and other specialists. They can advise but normally do not issue orders to line organizational units.

Staffing The provision of qualified managerial personnel for the enterprise.

Standard A predetermined performance level. These include monetary standards, physical standards, and intangible standards.

Standard Metropolitan Statistical Areas Areas of the United States designated by the Bureau of the Census as urban areas with a population of 50,000 or more.

Statement of changes in financial position The accounting statement which summarizes the funds generated from operations and other sources and shows how these funds are used over a period of time.

Status A particular position in the formal organization of the enterprise.

Status symbols Visible evidence of a person's rank in the business enterprise or some other organization.

Stock dividend Additional shares of the distributing corporation's own stock issued to shareholders.

Storage function The holding of goods from the time they are produced until their final use, including warehousing, handling, and order processing.

Stream of profits An approach to determining the value of an enterprise based on the yield of its estimated future earnings.

Strike Action taken by workers to cease work. Picketing usually follows to prevent other personnel from entering the struck plant.

Subsidiary A business enterprise which is owned or controlled by another company.

Subsidy Government assistance to a private enterprise.

Subsystem The elements within a system.

Supplementary unemployment benefit plan A plan whereby employers make payments to a fund used to pay employees who have been laid off. This money supplements unemployment benefits paid under government programs.

Surtax An extra tax in addition to the tax already levied. Sometimes used to increase the tax rate that must be paid if income exceeds a specified level.

Syndicate A group of investment bankers organized for the purpose of marketing a particular security issue.

System A set of elements which have a relationship to each other.

Tariff A tax on imported goods.

Taxes payable The amount of tax liability owed to various governmental units.

Technical advisors Staff personnel, such as lawyers, public relations personnel, and engineers, who provide information of a highly specialized nature.

Technical skill A manager's ability in and knowledge of a particular process or technique.

Technical subsystem That element of the work system which consists of the equipment, layout, and technology required to produce and distribute a particular product.

Technology The accumulated fund of knowledge which promotes efficient organization for the production of goods and services.

Tennessee Valley Authority (TVA) The federal government agency which produces and distributes electricity and provides flood control, recreation areas, and other services in connection with the Tennessee River system.

Term loan Customary name for intermediate credit; a loan running for more than one year and less than ten years.

Thermal pollution The presence of excessive heat in a body of water as the result of some industrial process, such as the generation of electric power.

Time deposit A type of bank deposit that bears interest. Formal notice must be given before withdrawal of funds.

Time draft A draft that calls for payment on a specified date in the future.

Time-sharing system A computer system that provides a number of users with access to a single computer at the same time from different locations for the simultaneous solutions of different problems.

Time study analysis A determination by an industrial engineer of how much time is necessary to carry out a job under actual factory conditions.

Time utility Utility that stems from goods being available when they are wanted.

Tooling The attachments for machine tools, gauges, loading devices, and other fixtures to adapt machinery and assembly lines to the production of a particular product.

Trade acceptance A bill of exchange that has had an acknowledgment of the obligation written across its face by the importer that obligates him to pay the amount specified at the designated time.

Trade credit The credit extended to business enterprises by suppliers for merchandise or equipment purchases usually for stated periods of from 30 to 60 days.

Trade creditor An individual or enterprise supplying merchandise or services to a business customer and willing to ship merchandise without requiring cash payment on delivery.

Trade Expansion Act (TEA) Law passed in 1962 which permitted negotiations to reduce tariffs and to stimulate world trade.

Trade journal A periodical that specializes in a specific field, such as a particular industry or business function.

Trademarks Words or symbols that identify a particular brand of merchandise. Trademarks may be registered for 28 years and the registration renewed for another 28 years, which prevents their use by unauthorized persons or enterprises.

Trading on the equity An increase in the return on the owners' investment by using borrowed funds profitably in the business enterprise.

Transfer payment Income paid to a person from whom no service is currently received, such as a social security payment or veterans' benefit.

Treasurer The financial executive who is responsible for the company's valuable papers, management of cash receipts and disbursements, and the development of banking relationships.

Trend The underlying long-run tendency that persists despite short-term cyclical or seasonal fluctuations in economic activity.

Trough The low in cyclical economic activity during a recession before recovery takes place.

Trust A business combination created when the owners of the shares of stock in corporations transfer control of their shares to trustees in exchange for trust certificates that entitle them to a share in the profits of the combined corporations.

Trust company A financial institution that takes legal possession of personal assets and manages them for the benefit of the person who created the trust or for some other designated person. A trust department of a commercial bank also performs this service.

Truth-in-Lending Act of 1968 Legislation requiring creditors to furnish individual borrowers with a statement of the amount of financing charges and the annual percentage rate of interest on the loan.

Type-of-customer-served departmentalization Organization of an enterprise so that each particular department will be geared to meet the requirements of a particular class of consumer.

Ultimate consumers Individuals or households who use goods or services for the satisfaction of personal needs.

Ultra vires acts Actions beyond the powers granted to a board of directors.

Underwriting As applied to investment banking, the assumption of responsibility for the sale of a corporation's stock or bonds, guaranteeing the corporation a specified amount of money for these securities.

Undistributed profits The amount of earnings retained by a business corporation rather than being paid out to owners as dividends. Also called retained earnings.

Unemployment insurance tax Taxes paid by business enterprises to finance payments to workers who are out of work.

Union contract The agreement negotiated by management and union representatives which spells out the terms agreed on with regard to wages, hours, and working conditions.

Union shop A labor agreement provision that requires a worker to join the union after a specified period of employment, often within 30 days.

Utility In economics, the power to satisfy human wants.

Value A belief held by persons in a society as to the rightness or wrongness of an action, custom, or institution. In economic terms, the monetary worth of a good or service.

Variable costs Costs directly influenced by the number of units produced, such as materials used in production and the wages of production workers.

Vendor One who sells goods or services.

Vertical analysis of the income statement A percentage breakdown of the income statement to show what proportion of sales the various expenses are, and the profit margin.

Vertical merger The joining together of enterprises involved in the successive stages of production or distribution of a product.

Vested interest in pension plans A pension plan whereby after a specified period the employees are entitled as a matter of right to the amount contributed by the employer for the employees' pension, whether or not they are still employed by the enterprise at retirement age.

Vestibule training Off-the-job training in which workers are trained in an area of the plant physically separated from their work place, but with machinery and under conditions similar to the shop where they will work.

Vocational school training Special practical training taken by employees outside the enterprise—such as courses in welding or blueprint reading.

Wages The amount paid to labor.

Wages payable An account that reflects what is owed to employees for their services performed.

Wagner Act The name sometimes used to refer to the original National Labor Relations Act passed in 1935.

Want A recognized need.

Water pollution The presence of one or more contaminants in bodies of water in quantities great enough to be injurious to life or property.

Water Pollution Control Act Amendments of 1972 Legislation setting the goal of eliminating all pollution discharge into U.S. waters by 1985, with interim goal of making waters safe for fish, wildlife, and people by 1983.

Water Quality Act of 1965 Federal legislation providing for the establishment of water-quality standards and plans for their implementation.

Water Quality Improvement Act of 1970 Federal legislation which provided that cleanup costs of oil spills or other water pollution would be the liability of the persons or enterprises causing the pollution.

Wholesalers Middlemen who perform the economic functions of storing, financing, and distributing a manufacturer's output to retailers.

Wholesome Meat Act of 1967 Legislation which updated and strengthened inspection standards for red meat animals at slaughterhouses and packing plants.

Wholesome Poultry Products Act of 1968 Legislation which extended federal inspection standards to poultry sold within a state as well as that which crossed state lines.

Work in process Materials that have been placed into the production cycle and increase in value as they move through production.

Work system A model of the business enterprise which includes technical, organizational, and human subsystems. Inputs to the work system are material and human resources. The outputs are goods and services and other satisfactions of human needs.

Working capital The amount of current assets after the deduction of current liabilities.

Workmen's compensation tax Insurance payments required of business to finance payments to workers who may suffer loss of income because of job-related accidents or injury.

Yellow-dog contract An agreement signed by workers stating that as a condition of employment they will not join a union. Such an agreement is unenforceable under federal and state anti-injunction acts, and is an unfair labor practice under the National Labor Relations Act.

index

Index

*This book has been set in 10 and 9 point Times
Roman, leaded 3 and 2 points. Section numbers
are set in 24 point (large) Helvetica Medium.
Chapter numbers are set in 66 point Weiss
Series I figures. Section and chapter titles are
set in 24 point (small) Helvetica. The size of
the type page is 26 x 46½ picas (plus 3 picas in
left margin).*

American business activity, 1914–1975

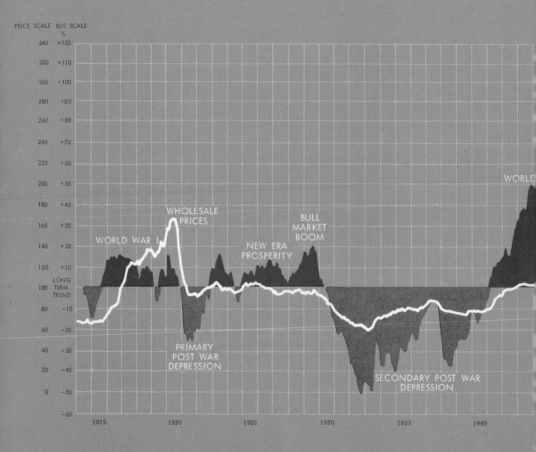

PRICE SCALE BUS SCALE
%

WORLD WAR I

WHOLESALE
PRICES

NEW ERA
PROSPERITY

BULL
MARKET
BOOM

WORLD

LONG
TERM
TREND

PRIMARY
POST WAR
DEPRESSION

SECONDARY POST WAR
DEPRESSION